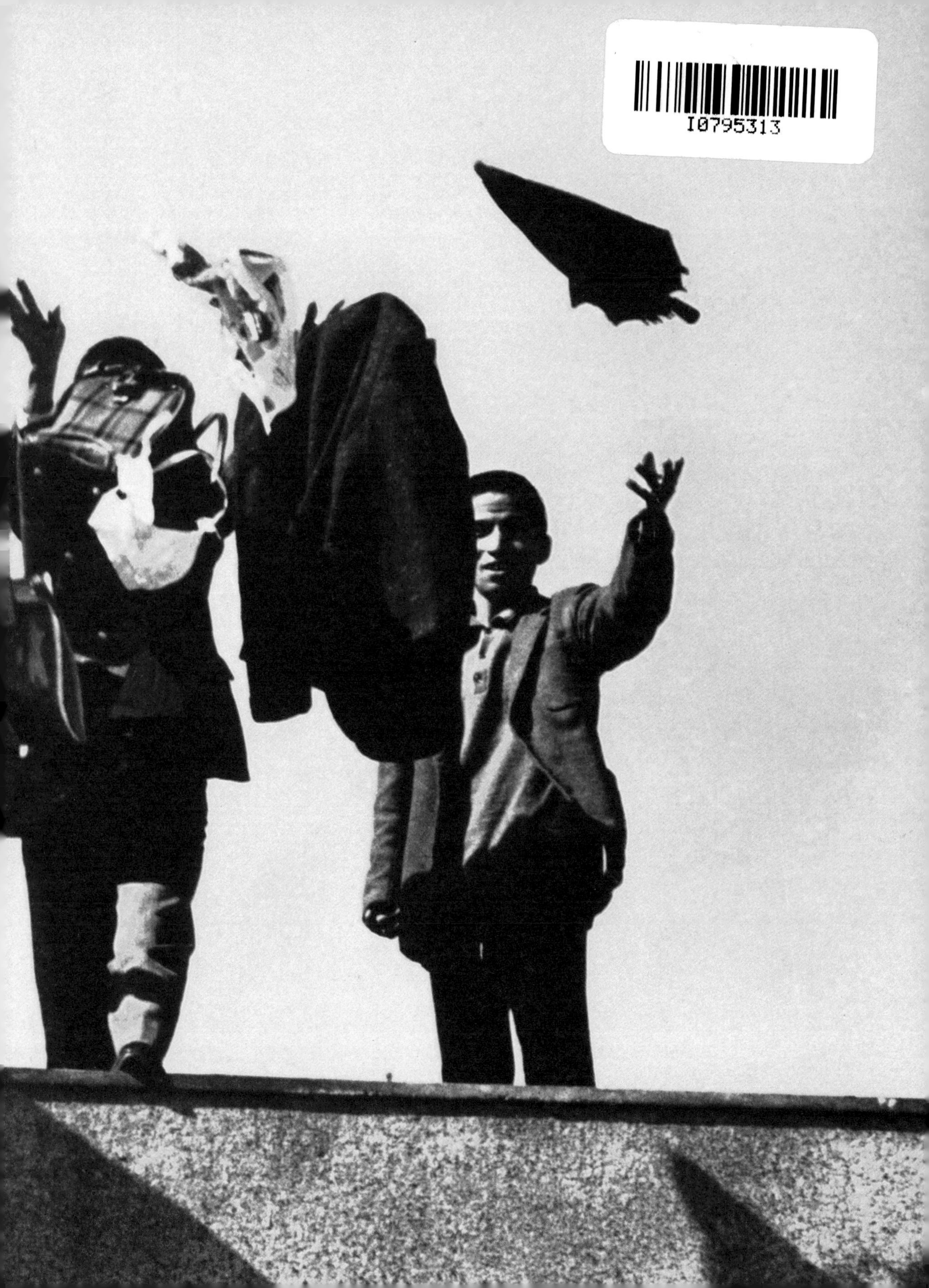

WORK ETHIC

HELEN MOLESWORTH

Essays by
Darsie Alexander
Chris Gilbert
Miwon Kwon
Helen Molesworth

Catalogue Entries by
Julia Bryan-Wilson
Janet Kraynak
Helen Molesworth
Judith Rodenbeck

THE BALTIMORE MUSEUM OF ART
BALTIMORE | MARYLAND

THE PENNSYLVANIA STATE UNIVERSITY PRESS
UNIVERSITY PARK | PENNSYLVANIA

work ethic

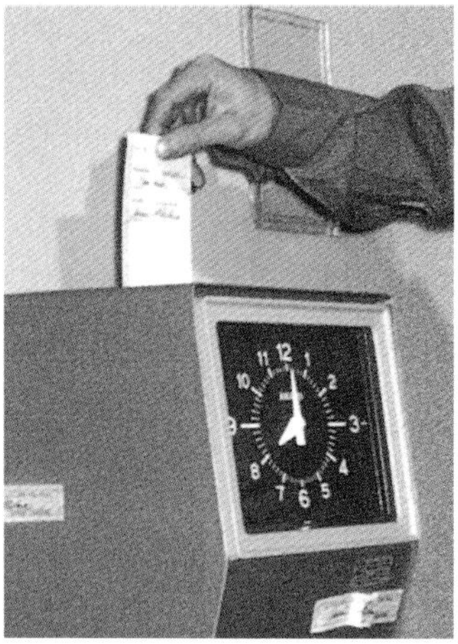

This volume has been published in conjunction with the exhibition *Work Ethic*, organized by The Baltimore Museum of Art, Baltimore, Maryland, and held at:

The Baltimore Museum of Art
12 October 2003–4 January 2004

Des Moines Art Center
15 May–1 August 2004

Wexner Center for the Arts
Columbus, Ohio
18 September 2004–2 January 2005.

This exhibition is made possible by an Emily Hall Tremaine Exhibition Award and a grant from The Andy Warhol Foundation for the Visual Arts.

Additional support is provided by Howard S. Brown, Suzanne F. Cohen, Nancy Dorman and Stanley Mazaroff, Fifth Floor Foundation, the Friends of Modern Art at The Baltimore Museum of Art, and Katherine Hardiman.

Published by The Pennsylvania State University Press,
University Park, PA 16802-1003

Library of Congress Cataloging-in-Publication Data

Work ethic / Helen Molesworth ; essays by Darsie Alexander ... [et al.] ; catalogue entries by Julia Bryan-Wilson [et al.].
p. cm.
Includes bibliographical references and index.
ISBN 0-271-02334-1 (alk. paper)
1. Avant-garde (Aesthetics)—United States—History—20th century—Exhibitions. 2. Art, American—20th century—Exhibitions.
I. Molesworth, Helen Anne. II. Alexander, M. Darsie. III. Bryan-Wilson, Julia. IV. Baltimore Museum of Art. V. Des Moines Art Center. VI. Wexner Center for the Arts

N6512.W65 2003
709'.73'0747526—dc21 2003010676

It is the policy of The Pennsylvania State University Press to use acid-free paper. Publications on uncoated stock satisfy the minimum requirements of American National Standard for Information Sciences—Permanence of Paper for Printed Library Materials, ANSI Z39.48–1992.

Designed by Lisa C. Tremaine

Printed in China

Endpaper illustration: Hi Red Center, *Ochanomizu Drop (Dropping Event)*, 1964. Photograph: Minoru Hirata.

Page 4 illustration: (detail) Tehching Hsieh, *One Year Performance 1980–1981 (Time Piece)*, 11 April 1980–11 April 1981. Photograph: Michael Shen.

CONTENTS

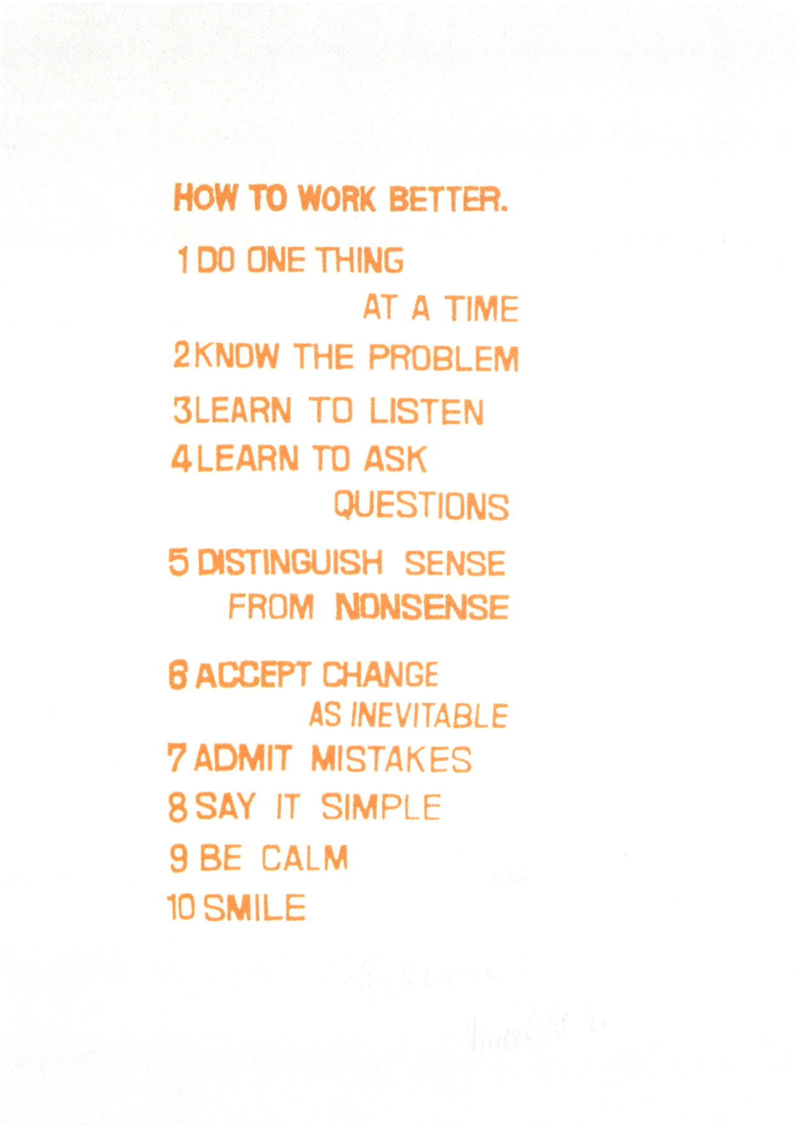

Fischli and Weiss, *How to Work Better,* 1991.

FOREWORD

THE ARTISTICALLY TURBULENT decades explored in *Work Ethic*—1960 to the present—have seen fundamental changes in the role of the artist and in the very nature of artwork. The artist is no longer predictably trained and skilled (although she or he may be more broadly educated), and the artist's hand is no longer the sole means of expression. What happens to art when traditional skills, typically the criteria of aesthetic judgment, are superseded?

Art is no longer always an object that can be bought or displayed in ways once expected by galleries, collectors, museums, and visitors. The artist's work lies in ideas and concepts, sometimes surviving only in the documentation of photography, video, or even a written set of instructions that allows others to re-create the experience the artist envisioned. The uniqueness and even the very endurance of artwork has been challenged.

In *Work Ethic*, the museum visitor will see the artist as worker, manager, and creator of experiences; the visitor acts as viewer, consumer, and participant. This exhibition will be an experience, and it demands the hard work of looking closely and thinking deeply.

If the roles of artist and viewer are different, what about the role of the museum as presenter? Museums have changed profoundly over the past four decades. Their purview, once focused only on collections and their artistic significance, has expanded to embrace audience, community, education, and marketing. These decades saw the introduction of the blockbuster, the rise of museum retail operations, and the globalization of art museums. Such changes have brought benefits but have also caused tensions—intellectual, financial, and practical.

As always, exhibitions begin with curatorial insights: in this case, the creative thinking of Helen Molesworth, from 2000 to 2002 BMA Curator of Contemporary Art and now Chief Curator of Exhibitions at the Wexner Center for the Arts. We are grateful to Helen for her imaginative presentation of the challenging art in *Work Ethic*. Exhibitions today—including *Work Ethic*—are so ambitious that a cross-disciplinary team of experts is required to realize their full potential. In this context, the role of the curator, while no less central, has changed. No longer a sole operator producing a predictable product, the curator has become partner, collaborator, and manager, one whose success relies heavily on colleagues to complete the work effectively. At the BMA, we are fortunate to have dedicated educators, advocates for the needs and interests of our audience; we also benefit from the talents of our exhibition staff, whose imaginative minds always find a new and completely effective way to present each exhibition. Added to these very visible results in the galleries are the unseen efforts of literally dozens of BMA staffers—those who raise the funds that support Museum programs, those who promote and market the exhibition, those who pack, ship, and preserve the art, and of course, those who protect the artworks every day.

The BMA's organization and presentation of *Work Ethic* reflects the Museum's long commitment to contemporary art. Since the nineteenth century, civic-minded Baltimoreans have collected contemporary art and enriched the Museum's collection with generous gifts. This generosity has resulted in the BMA's renowned collection of modern art—including the most comprehensive collection of works by Henri Matisse in the world—and an impressive grouping of nineteenth-century French art. In 1994 the BMA opened a wing for Contemporary Art; today, it houses contemporary work from 1945 forward. In 2003, the BMA reaffirmed its commitment to contemporary art in a strategic planning process that articulated the Museum's artistic focus as the modern era—the nineteenth century to the present day. *Work Ethic* thus comes at a critical moment, as we are poised to make contemporary art (and the responsive, fresh, and adventuresome spirit it inspires) an even more central part of the Museum's identity.

I would like to thank the artists, lenders, and donors whose generosity made this show a reality. We are grateful to our colleagues at the Des Moines Art Center and the Wexner Center for the Arts, who have worked with us in the public presentation of this exhibition. *Work Ethic* has drawn from many different collections to tell a rich story to the Museum's visitors. Finally, great and challenging ideas demand daring funders. The Emily Hall Tremaine Foundation, recognized as a leader in supporting the most avant-garde work proposed by contemporary artists and curators, endorsed this project almost from its inception with an Emily Hall Tremaine Exhibition Award. The Andy Warhol Foundation for the Visual Arts, perpetuating the artistic innovation of its namesake, enabled the BMA to enjoy more than its allotted fifteen minutes of fame. Howard S. Brown, BMA Board Chair Suzanne F. Cohen, Trustee Nancy Dorman and Stanley Mazaroff, Fifth Floor Foundation, the BMA's Friends of Modern Art, and Trustee Katherine Hardiman joined these national funders with generosity and commitment to contemporary art and its presentation in *Work Ethic.*

Now our work is done, but for you—it's time to clock in!

Doreen Bolger
DIRECTOR
The Baltimore Museum of Art

LENDERS TO THE EXHIBITION

Vito Acconci, New York
Francis Alÿs, Mexico City
Eleanor Antin, San Diego
The Art Institute of Chicago
The Baltimore Museum of Art
Benjamin H. D. Buchloh, New York
Chris Burden, Topanga, California
Collection of Rena Conti and Dr. Ivan Moskowitz, Brookline, Massachusetts
Generali Foundation, Vienna
Hope Ginsburg, New York
Solomon R. Guggenheim Museum, New York
David Hammons, New York
Tehching Hsieh, New York
Nancy Reddin Kienholz, Oregon
Alison Knowles, New York
The LeWitt Collection, Chester, Connecticut
Tom Marioni, San Francisco
Museum Jean Tinguely Basel, Switzerland
The Museum of Contemporary Art, Los Angeles
Nagoya City Art Museum, Japan
Yoko Ono, New York
Roxy Paine, New York
Robert Rauschenberg, New York
Seattle Art Museum
Richard Serra, New York
The Gilbert and Lila Silverman Fluxus Collection, Detroit
Elizabeth Sisco, Louis Hock, and David Avalos, San Diego
Mierle Laderman Ukeles, New York
Dean Valentine and Amy Adelson, Los Angeles
Dorothy and Herbert Vogel
Wadsworth Atheneum Museum of Art, Hartford, Connecticut
Private Collections

ACKNOWLEDGMENTS

EXHIBITIONS STAND AS a testament to the labors of many people, and *Work Ethic* is no exception. The entire staff of The Baltimore Museum of Art worked diligently to bring this project to fruition. I am deeply grateful to them. Acknowledgments are due first to Director Doreen Bolger and Deputy Director for Curatorial Affairs Jay Fisher for their support of challenging contemporary art. Senior Registrar Melanie Harwood negotiated the loans with her consummate good humor and attention to detail. Director of Exhibition Design and Installation Karen Nielsen and the entire staff of the Installation Department embraced the challenges of new media and audience-participatory works without blinking. Michelle Boardman, Manager of Creative Services, ably managed the exhibition catalogue. Deputy Director for Education and Interpretation Allison Perkins fashioned a lively education program. Former Administrative Assistant Randi Vega assiduously handled the details, aided by former Curatorial Assistant Valerie Paulewicz. Thanks are also due to two interns who donated their summers to the project: Linda Park of the Bard Center for Curatorial Studies and Sarah Hromack of the Maryland Institute College of Art. I owe a special debt of gratitude as well to all my colleagues at the Wexner Center for the Arts, particularly Director Sherri Geldin and Curatorial Assistant Steven Hunt, for their support, both tacit and material, of this project. *Work Ethic* was generously funded by an Emily Hall Tremaine Foundation Exhibition Award, with additional support from The Andy Warhol Foundation for the Visual Arts. Howard S. Brown, Suzanne F. Cohen, Nancy Dorman and Stan Mazaroff, Fifth Floor Foundation, the BMA's Friends of Modern Art, and Katherine Hardiman also graciously helped fund the exhibition. While a curator at the BMA, I enjoyed the generosity of spirit of many trustees, patrons, docents, and visitors committed to contemporary art. They have all lent their support to *Work Ethic*, and, more importantly, their goodwill to its curator. Both have meant a great deal to me.

Many people helped determine the whereabouts and secure loans of numerous objects: Marian Goodman and Leslie Nolan,

Marian Goodman Gallery; Elyse Goldberg, James Cohan Gallery; Peter Gould, L.A. Louver Inc.; Steve Henry, Paula Cooper Gallery; Margarete Roeder, Margarete Roeder Gallery; Jon Hendricks, Curator of the Gilbert and Lila Silverman Fluxus Collection; Antonio Homen, Sonnabend Gallery; Kitty Cleary, Museum of Modern Art; Anna Kustera, Jack Tilton/Anna Kustera Gallery; Trina McKeever, Richard Serra Studio; Zach Minor, Gagosian Gallery; Kelly Nipper, Assistant to Allan Kaprow; Jeanne Greenberg Rohatyn, Artemis Greenberg Van Doren Gallery; Lisa Rosendahl, Lisson Gallery; Andrea Rosen and Michelle Reyes, Estate of Felix Gonzalez-Torres; Susanna Singer, Sol LeWitt Studio; John Thomson, Electronic Arts Intermix; and David White, Rauschenberg Studio. On behalf of The Baltimore Museum of Art, I want to thank all of the lenders for entrusting us with their precious objects.

Early in the project, the BMA convened a panel of advisors: Alexander Alberro, Darsie Alexander, Cornelia Butler, Jane Farver, Janet Kraynak, Miwon Kwon, and Judith Rodenbeck. Their comments and criticisms helped shape the project for the better. Alexander, Kraynak, Kwon, and Rodenbeck are joined as catalogue authors by Chris Gilbert and Julia Bryan-Wilson. Their diverse contributions attest to the energy and debate this field has engendered. Gloria Kury, Art History and Humanities Editor at Penn State Press, was a wonderful advocate and interlocutor throughout the making of the catalogue. Lisa Tremaine designed the catalogue with intelligence and enthusiasm.

Both the catalogue and the exhibition have been the topic of numerous conversations with friends and colleagues. A warm thanks to David Avalos, George Baker, Stefano Basilico, Norton Batkin, Mel Bochner, Moyra Davey, Donna DeSalvo, Leah Dickerman, Andrea Fraser, Chris Gilbert, Hope Ginsburg, Ann Goldstein, Lynn Gumpert, Jon Hendricks, David Joselit, Ben Kinmont, Linda Norden, Cesare Pietrousti, Jason Simon, Frazer Ward, and Chris Whittey. Thanks as well to audiences at the University of California at Los Angeles; the Bard Center for Curatorial Studies; Mills College, Oakland; and the State University of New York at Purchase. Alex Alberro, Aruna D'Souza, and Tom McDonough each generously gave their time to read drafts of the lead catalogue essay, and their suggestions were indispensable. Susan Dackerman's critical and humorous mind guided this curator in every way. My last and most thorough thanks and appreciation go to the artists featured in the exhibition—for their continual challenge to the conventional categories of art and their restless refusal of business as usual.

Helen Molesworth

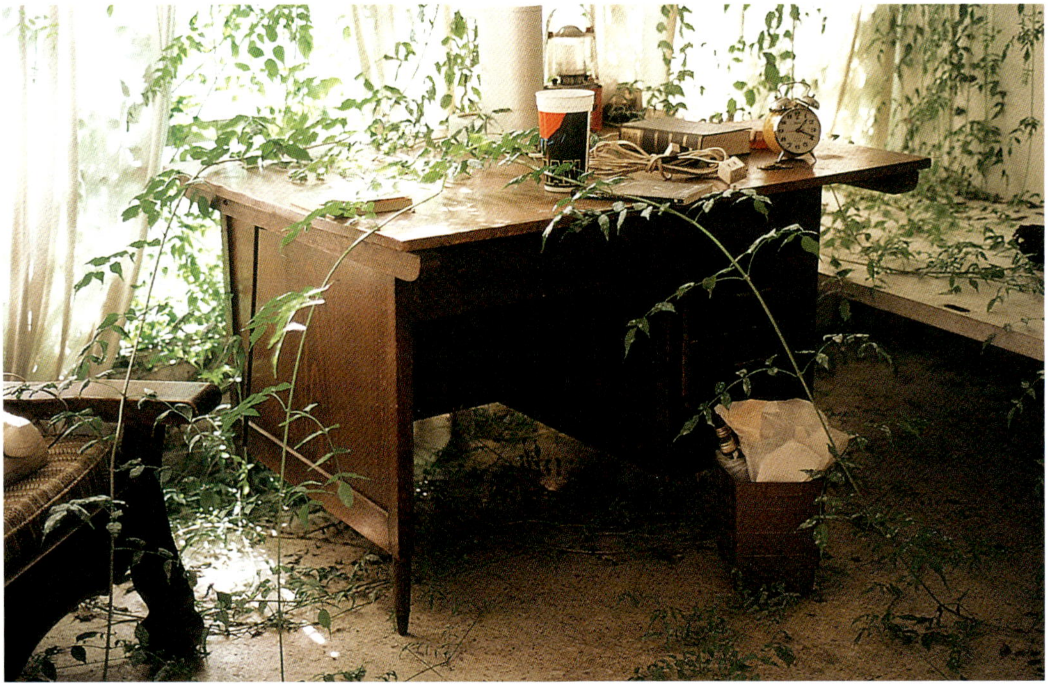

Gabriel Orozco, *La Oficina,* 1992.

INTRODUCTION

MUSEUMS WITH COLLECTIONS of modern and contemporary art are haunted by the often unanswered questions of their visitors. Confronted with works that deny the traditional visual pleasure and seduction of mimetic representation, visitors frequently ask: Why is this art? How long did it take to make this? They indignantly feel that modern and contemporary works appear to be made with neither skill nor labor—a sentiment best exemplified in the scandalous utterance, "My kid could do that." Often, this statement is true; many artworks made after the 1960s were produced without traditional artistic skills, and there certainly does not *appear* to be much work involved in them. Rather than simply ignore these questions, *Work Ethic* attempts to answer them by placing the art of our time within its larger sociocultural and economic context. The exhibition thus hopes to transform the tone of the audience's questioning from bewildered accusation to curiosity and engagement.

Traditionally, artists have drawn, painted, and sculpted, and they have done so after extensive training, either through an apprenticeship, instruction at an art academy, or, after World War II, attendance at an art school. An artist's ability to represent the world faithfully as it appears or to image the world in an idealized fashion has formed the basis of how artworks were judged. Toward the end of the nineteenth century, however, artists grew tired of slavishly representing the world mimetically and instead began to experiment with increasingly rigorous forms of abstraction. As they did so, the parameters of what was considered good art became increasingly plastic. By the second half of the twentieth century, artists consistently explored the limits of what could be conceived of as art—and, by extension, what could be considered legitimate artistic labor. They did so in large measure by turning away from traditional media such as painting and sculpture, finding them too static, too commodifiable, too predictable, and too emblematic of traditional elite culture.

Work Ethic highlights works from a wide variety of artistic movements that had their genesis in the 1960s, such as Fluxus, Conceptual art, Process art, Feminist art, and Performance—practices that shared a resistance to the very idea of ever being displayed or housed in a museum. Artists involved in these movements purposefully made art that was temporally and materially transient, art that was only tenuously an object. Hence, even a dedicated museum visitor might be unaware of an entire avenue of artistic inquiry that has taken place over the past forty years. Much of this art, in its rejection of the museum, also abandoned the idea that art was a rarified activity only available to highly trained professionals and their elite patrons. Instead, these diverse movements gave birth to an "anyone can do it" ethos in art making. While this democratizing gesture was meant as an act of generosity on the part of avant-garde artists, it has often been met with hostility from audiences who continued to expect conventional versions of art.

More than a mere introduction to avant-garde practices of the past forty years, *Work Ethic* poses the following thesis: After World War II, the basis of the United States economy shifted from manufacturing to service, transforming traditional definitions of labor. As the conditions of labor changed for the vast majority of the American populace, so too did it change for artists. Many artists (like their working and professional counterparts) no longer felt compelled to offer a discrete object produced by hand. Rather, they explored ways of producing art that were analogous to other forms of labor. Art could thus be made with unskilled manual labor, with highly regimented managerial labor, or with labor that resonated with ideas borrowed from the service economy. While art was being created by the same mechanisms that governed other forms of labor, it did not *look* like work (or art, even), much like sitting at a desk might not look like work to someone laboring on a factory assembly line.

In recent years, there has been a return to artistic strategies of the 1960s. This renewed interest in the avant-garde's challenges to traditional definitions of art during the 1960s has been the subject of numerous academic books and articles as well as museum and gallery exhibitions. *Work Ethic* contends that one reason for this revived interest is that the early twenty-first century has also been marked by radical transformations of the global labor force. As commodities are now almost exclusively produced in developing and non-Western nations, the labor of developed nations has increasingly become the management of information and the production of experience. Experiments in Conceptual and Performance art of the 1960s seem particularly germane in this context and may even offer strategies for understanding, coping with, and resisting these recent developments in our ever more globalized economy. To this end, *Work Ethic* contains works of art made from the 1960s to the present.

The exhibition is divided into four separate sections, each expanding on how artists have staged the problem of artistic labor. The first is "The Artist as Manager and Worker: The Artist Creates and Completes a Task." Here artists mime the traditional division of labor between mental and manual realms. Most of the artists in the exhibition, however, deploy a radically unskilled form of manual labor, one that rejects the traditional skills of academic art training. Additionally, most works in this section engage in labor that is utterly nonproductive, as artists set about to critique the increasingly commodified status of art. The second section, "The Artist as Manager: The Artist Sets a Task for Others to Complete," concerns itself largely with Conceptual art's understanding that the idea is more important than the object. Many artists mimicked their managerial counterparts by commissioning others to bring their ideas to fruition. The third section is replete with works in which the audience and/or the viewer is pressed into service. In "The Artist as Experience Maker: The Audience Completes the Work," artists are primarily engaged with creating situations, experiences, and/or objects designed to be used by the viewer. In each instance, the viewer has to participate in order for the event to become art. Finally, the exhibition ends with a meditation on *not* working. In "Quitting Time: The Artist Tries Not to Work," we encounter the increasingly blurred boundaries between work and leisure.

The catalogue is divided into two sections and is graced by the work of several authors. The first section of the catalogue contains four essays. Helen Molesworth's essay situates post–World War II advanced art practices within their sociological and historical contexts and argues that the challenge to the discrete art object is analogous to shifts in the structures and definitions of labor in a globalized economy. Given that so much of the art in *Work Ethic* has a temporal and non-object dimension, the role of photography in documenting performance activities expanded dramatically during this period. Darsie Alexander addresses how artists deployed the medium of photography, with its inherent fluidity, to navigate the distinctions between the photograph as documentary evidence and the photograph as an art object. Chris Gilbert suggests that the new theories of work and leisure being plumbed by avant-garde artists were visible in popular culture as well, and he wittily draws connections between the rarified realm of contemporary art and the wildly popular *Herbie the Love Bug* films of the 1970s. Finally, a ruminative essay by Miwon Kwon considers audience participation through the logic of the gift. Far from articulating these works as acts of beneficent generosity on the part of artists, Kwon takes the audience to task, suggesting that it has yet to meet the reciprocal obligations of such artistic gifts. The second half of the catalogue is more experimental in nature, as it loosely replicates the four-part structure of the exhibition. In it the reader will find catalogue entries on individual artists as well as entries on major ideas and movements. This section includes short texts by art historians Julia Bryan-Wilson, Janet Kraynak, and Judith Rodenbeck that offer general information on the artists as well as specific interpretations of selected works. The entries are clustered around certain ideas or practices; although they fall sequentially, there is no reason to read them as such.

Work Ethic is an experimental exhibition. Rather than mounting a "typical" museum exhibition about a specific artistic movement, or a monographic exhibition of an artist's oeuvre, or a theme show about a common trend, the exhibition has been inspired by the risk-taking and interdisciplinary quality of the art it champions. *Work Ethic* is an art-historical hypothesis writ large in the galleries of the museum. Can the art of our time be understood within a framework larger than art history and the museum? Can artworks designed to challenge the museum be exhibited within it without being stripped of their experiential and experimental qualities? If the most critical avant-garde art is made accessible to a broader public, can it inspire that public to question and challenge ideas as large and complex as the changing definitions of labor, the role of the museum, and the function of art? Hopefully, these questions stand as provocations to the debate the art of our time so yearns to spark.

Helen Molesworth

ESSAYS

Robert Rauschenberg, *Erased de Kooning Drawing,* 1953. San Francisco Museum of Modern Art, purchased though a gift of Phyllis Wattis.

Work Ethic

HELEN MOLESWORTH

Some people like to go out dancing; other people like us have to work.
—The Velvet Underground

ONE OF THE more curious attributes of avant-garde art after World War II was the increasing disregard for traditional artistic skills such as drawing, painting, and sculpting. Robert Rauschenberg's legendary *Erased de Kooning Drawing* (1953) consisted of just that—the artist erasing a drawing by Willem de Kooning. Frank Stella's *Club Onyx* (1959) is a painting of black stripes of house paint; their width is determined by the store-bought brush. And when Robert Morris made *Box with the Sound of Its Own Making* (1961), critic Leo Steinberg described it as

> A plain wooden box and a tape recording of the sawing and hammering that put it together. The work strips the adverb from the definition of art. A thing done—period.[1]

Steinberg had distilled the problem. Here was a work of art content to be described in the language of *work* as opposed to that of art. Sawing and hammering had replaced drawing and composition. And in replacing the skills of art with the activities of work, artists began to make art that eschewed artifice and illusion and instead presented itself to the world as it was: a box with the sound of its own making, an object insistent upon the labor of its maker.

This essay argues that one unifying principle of the extraordinarily heterogeneous field of post–World War II avant-garde art was a concern with the problematic of artistic labor. A historical convergence had occurred. Just as artists relinquished traditional artistic skills and the production of discrete art objects, the status of labor and the production of goods in the culture at large were also changing profoundly as the American industrial economy, based in manufacturing, shifted to a postindustrial economy rooted in managerial and service labor. The concern with artistic labor manifested itself in implicit and explicit ways as much of the advanced art of the period managed, staged, mimicked, ridiculed, and challenged the cultural and societal anxieties around the shifting terrain and definitions of work.

Frank Stella, *Club Onyx,* 1959.

One of Modernism's many promises was that art offered possible resistance to an increasingly regimented and segmented life under the auspices of industrialization. From the Arts and Crafts movement to the Bauhaus, the history of modern art is shot through with the dream of an integration of the realms of art and life, work and leisure, such that the alienation produced by the fragmented nature of modern labor would be ameliorated. This essay argues that in the period following World War II, artists came to see themselves not as artists producing (in) a dreamworld but as workers in capitalist America.[2] They navigated the avant-garde desire to merge art and life under dramatically different social structures than their Modernist predecessors. Artists during the 1960s made art in the midst of the corporatization of American culture, the professionalization of the category of "artist," and a burgeoning New York market for contemporary art. These sociohistorical forces placed extraordinary pressures on artists to redefine themselves and their work, and often they did so by thinking through and acting out the profound transformations of late-twentieth-century labor in their work.

It is a well-worn tale that the end of World War II ushered in an era of remarkable economic growth for the American economy. Just as the manufacturing base quickly reconfigured itself to meet the needs of a wartime economy, with similar ease it transformed into a manufacturing economy of commodities for an increasingly affluent and mobile middle class. This, in turn, was accompanied by the rise of the managerial class, whose labor was no longer defined by the production of objects. Rather, the work of management was to oversee the labor of others, and it often involved making representations of work, such as diagrams, graphs, and flowcharts.[3] Paul Osterman and the other authors of *Working in America* describe how "at least since the New Deal, a clear view of how work is organized has been embedded both in law and policy. On that view, there is a sharp and identifiable divide between the activities of managers and those of workers, the former being responsible for conception and planning and the latter for execution."[4] Joseph Pine and James Gilmore note in *The Experience Economy*, however, that "it was in the 1950s when services first employed more than 50 percent of the U.S. population, that the Service Economy overtook the Industrial (although this was not recognized until long after the fact)."[5] While the recognition of the change in labor demographics from a manufacturing to a service economy may have been slow in coming, management's cultural ascendancy aided this shift. Hence, Pine and Gilmore argue that with the codification and rise of management, the work executed by workers has also been transformed from goods ("tangible products that companies standardize and then inventory") into services ("intangible activities performed for a particular client").[6] While the manufacturing base of the United States was diminishing, the production of goods increasingly happened elsewhere—usually in "unseen" faraway places such as China, Korea, Japan, Malaysia, and India, and, as the decades wore on, in places such as Mexico—closer to home but still just as much out of sight. Ironically, the manufactured commodity's vanishing in America was accompanied by the disappearance of the traditional art object as well; the changing economy had a significant impact on how postwar art was made. This economic transformation was accompanied by an artistic one that further shaped artists' exploration of the problem of artistic labor: the increasing influence and importance of the work of Marcel Duchamp.

Conceivably, no twentieth-century artist was more ambivalent about artistic labor than Marcel Duchamp. In the teens, he purchased mass-produced commodities (most famously a urinal he titled *Fountain* [1917]) and dubbed them "readymades." The readymades defied two historical definitions of art: namely, that art should be unique and that it should be produced by a highly trained artist with a requisite set of learned skills. By challenging the necessity of traditional artistic labor and the value of unique objects and by establishing a potential continuum between the space and activities of everyday life and the rarified realm of art, Duchamp's readymades constituted the most serious attack on the category of Art since the Renaissance.

Far from destroying art, Duchamp's profound challenge ultimately served to create an enormous field of aesthetic possibility. It helped liberate artists from conventional modes of working, contributing to a climate that permitted and rewarded an increasingly porous idea of art's possibilities. Artists no longer needed to content themselves with the production of visually aesthetic objects. Art became a realm of ideas. This freedom did not come immediately; the most important reception of Duchamp in the United States occurred in the late 1950s through John Cage, Jasper Johns, and Robert Rauschenberg, all of whom rejected the supposed purity and emotionalism of Abstract Expressionism and enabled a fuller exploration of Duchamp's questioning of skill and labor.[7] Notoriously heterogeneous, the art of the 1960s and 1970s produced a wide range of movements, including Minimalism, Conceptual art, Fluxus, Performance, Process, Feminist art, and Happenings. The new art was described in various ways. It was dematerialized; it pursued the aesthetics of silence; it was anti-illusionistic; it was conceptual; it was anticommodity; it was democratized. The new art remained, however, extremely difficult for lay viewers to understand or interpret. Its difficulty lay, in large measure, in its double rejection: as artists stopped employing traditional artistic skills, they also stopped making works of art that imagined the museum or the collector's home as their final destination. Instead, artists attempted to make works of art that would actively resist easy assimilation into the realm of the art market, where art was seen to be one luxury commodity among many.[8]

The liberation of art from traditional artistic skills, the production of a unique object, and the primacy of the visual necessitated new aesthetic criteria less focused on appearance and more concerned with ideas. Morris's *Box with the Sound of Its Own Making* and Rauschenberg's oeuvre provided Leo Steinberg with a new hermeneutic, one he went so far as to call postmodern. In his deeply influential essay "Other Criteria" (1968), he stated plainly that new art presents itself not as "art" but as "work," and as such needs to be analyzed in sociocultural terms in addition to those taken from the discourse of art.

Much as the category of Art was in question, the role of the artist was being rearticulated. Two texts also important to the formation of postmodern ideas declared the newly problematized author/artist. One was a short speech delivered by Duchamp, "The Creative Act" (1957), and the other was an essay by French theorist Roland Barthes, "The Death of the Author" (1967). Both appeared in the eclectic avant-garde journal *Aspen* in 1967—Duchamp's spoken by the artist and distributed on a floppy record, and Barthes's in its first English translation. Both texts would become legendary. Duchamp's argument became a received idea in art schools across the United States, and Barthes's text would become standard college reading in the humanities.

Duchamp's lecture put forward the then radical idea that "the creative act is not performed by the artist alone." Denying both the autonomy of the artwork and the privileging of the artist's intention, Duchamp instead turned the focus of attention upon the viewer, stating that "the spectator brings the work in contact with the external world by deciphering and interpreting its inner qualifications and thus adds his contribution to the creative act."[9] Barthes similarly challenged the idea that "the explanation of a work is always sought in the man or woman who produced it, as if it were always in the end . . . the voice of a single person, the *author* 'confiding' in us." Citing the public and ideological character of language, he suggested that the author could no longer be seen as an omnipotent, singular, and codified dispenser of meaning. Instead, the reader is the privileged subject, for the "reader is the space on which all the quotations that make up a writing are inscribed . . . a text's unity lies not in its origin but its destination." Emphatically, Barthes's essay ends with the oft-quoted line, "the birth of the reader must be at the cost of the death of the Author."[10] By positioning the reader as the final destination of a text, Barthes's essay rhymes in spirit with Duchamp's. Both shift the value and emphasis away from the producer of the work of art or literature in favor of the viewer or reader.[11]

"The Death of the Author" crystallized a point of view by succinctly describing an increasingly prevalent form of anti-authorial artistic practice. Many artists and writers in the 1960s found the idea of the author's metaphoric death liberating, and they deployed a variety of means to undermine or downplay their own authorship. Some (e.g., John Cage) used chance operations, feeling that when the conscious choice of the artist was eliminated, so too was artistic intention. Others (e.g., Sol LeWitt) adopted serial systems, reasoning that a predetermined mathematical logic diminished the display of artistic subjectivity. Many artists (e.g., Donald Judd) felt increasingly comfortable turning over the production of their work to paid assistants and fabricators. Still others (e.g., John Baldessari) turned to the camera, hoping that a mechanical tool would lessen any trace of their hand. And then there were those (e.g., Yoko Ono) who turned the completion of the artwork over to the viewer in a literal way, creating participatory proposals that were only considered "art" once engaged by a viewer.

When artists challenged the role of the author, they also, wittingly or not, questioned the status and even value of their labor. In effect, to problematize the role of the author/artist is to place the producer of the text/art object in question. By diminishing traces of their intentionality and subjectivity, attributes of the work of art usually associated with its fabrication were removed: traces of the artist's hand, reliance upon a learned set of skills, a prolonged duration for the creation of a work, a studio complete with tools and equipment. Even though artists embraced these new anti-authorial modes of artistic production, they did so at some peril. Were artists still required, in any subjective or authorial specificity? (Anyone can follow through a serial system, click the shutter on a camera, throw a pair of dice.) If not, what exactly was their role? What was to constitute their labor? This was felt particularly keenly in the visual arts, where one effect of the ebbing of the authorial role was that the resultant art was often only tenuously an object.

Sol LeWitt, whose work was also included in *Aspen*, discussed the new artistic process in the following way:

> The aim of the artist would not be to instruct the viewer but to give him information. Whether the viewer understands this information is incidental to the artist; he cannot foresee the understanding of all his viewers. He would follow his predetermined premise to its conclusion avoiding subjectivity. . . . The serial artist does not attempt to produce a beautiful or mysterious object but functions merely as a clerk cataloguing the results of his premise.[12]

That LeWitt imagines himself a clerk is not surprising. The newly problematized relationship to artistic authorship and its attendant modes of artistic labor hardly happened in a vacuum. America's shift from an industrial to a postindustrial society was to have as profound an effect upon art as it had upon the daily lives of all workers. Far from being a timeless and unchanging entity, art of the 1960s reflected the rise of a highly professionalized managerial class and the simultaneous development of a service economy.

Some art historians have viewed the strategies of anti-authorship, such as LeWitt's imagining of himself as a clerk, as part of the "de-skilling" of the artist. Yet it is more accurate to treat this transformation as a re-skilling, for as artists weathered the change from a manufacturing to a service economy, it stands to reason that the declining value for one set of skills would be accompanied by a rising value for another. So what, then, were the new sets of skills needed to be an artist? What kinds of artistic labor would come to be seen as legitimate within this new socioeconomic context?

In the early 1940s, there were 60 candidates for graduate degrees in studio art enrolled in eleven American institutions. By 1950–51, there were 322 candidates at thirty-two institutions. The trend continued through the end of the century. Thirty-one new Master of Fine Arts (MFA) programs opened in the 1960s, and forty-four in the 1970s. From 1990 to 1995, ten thousand MFA degrees were awarded in the United States. These numbers are astounding. What do they mean for artists and the art they produce?

In *Art Subjects*, historian Howard Singerman persuasively argues that after World War II, artists were increasingly professionalized in academic art programs in the United States. With the G.I. Bill fueling the professionalization of degree-granting art departments, the way art was taught changed markedly. This shift is most evident in the diminishing importance accorded to the traditional skill of drawing—long the core of artistic training. The predominance of Abstract Expressionism, with its emphasis on unconscious processes and a highly rigorous version of abstraction, often meant that the technical skill of drawing was no longer encouraged. In this context, Rauschenberg's *Erased de Kooning Drawing* takes on a new (and renewed) significance. Of all of the Abstract Expressionists, de Kooning was renowned for his draftsmanship, something that Rauschenberg was doubtlessly aware of when he asked the artist for a drawing he would subsequently erase. That Rauschenberg should request to erase one of de Kooning's drawings can be seen less as an anti-oedipal urge and more as an acknowledgment that one form of artistic skill was being supplanted by another—draftsmanship erased in the face of conceptual art's nascent ascendancy. Despite the lack of technical skill required to erase the drawing, Rauschenberg claimed to have worked very hard to erase the drawing well. And the results of his hard labor are evident: not even the slightest trace of the drawing remains.

As art departments continued their professionalization and artists continued to undermine the significance of technical skill, contradictory ideas emerged about the teaching of art. On the one hand, the idea arose that art could not be systematically taught. On the other, there was a consensus that art could be learned and that it was acquired in large measure by being around artists and listening to them talk. This "talk" took place in the form of the "crit," the guest artist lecture, and the phenomenon of the studio visit, all of which signaled a significant break with traditional academic art training. In such training, the "assignment and product are given in the same language"—life drawing, for instance. In the postwar period, however, a split occurred, and the language of the "assignment" was quite different from the language of the finished product. For example, the assignment might be to "make a void," a kind of problem solving that can take any form.[13] If the separation of mental labor from manual labor is one of the hallmarks of managerial professionalization, then, Singerman argues, postwar artistic training was designed to train artists in a theoretical discourse separate and distinct from manual labor. The result was a generation of college-educated artists whose skills were no longer manual and visual but largely theoretical and verbal. The rise of the MFA artist—an artist trained in large measure to become a teacher in MFA programs and whose proficiencies are mental rather than manual—reflects the shift in labor experienced by the vast majority of American workers. And just as many Americans now earn their livings without ever making a sellable commodity, many artists have stopped making commodities such as painting and sculpture designed to be bought and sold on the market.

Yet there was (and remains) a curious resistance to the idea of the professional artist—a person for whom being an artist was a job, a way to make a livelihood (often through teaching) as much as an existential "calling." When Harold Rosenberg, an influential critic of the 1950s and a champion of Abstract Expressionism, wrote "Everyman a Professional" in 1959, he opined:

> Thus the essential mark of a profession is its evolution of a unique language. . . . The more incomprehensible the lingo is to outsiders, the more thoroughly it identifies the profession as such and elevates it out of the reach of mere amateurs and craftsmen.[14]

Even though Rosenberg criticized artists for this development, his commentary supports Singerman's contention that part of what it meant to become an artist in the late 1950s and 1960s was to learn how to talk about art with other art professionals. But the romantic myths of the artist as outcast, the artist as lone genius, the artist as inspired (not trained) or, conversely, the artist as one possessing a highly distinctive set of laboriously learned skills still held sway in the popular imagination. In these scenarios, the rise of the professional artist was viewed as a cynical degradation of art's magical or auratic status. The nostalgia for certain sets of skills was countered, however, by a generation of artists who acknowledged that art and artists are both in and of the world, helping produce it and being produced by it. In this light, the use of a non-object-based art made by an academically trained artist and described in an increasingly professionalized language echoes similar transformations in other forms of production (of both knowledge and objects) from the university to the corporate boardroom, as postwar culture at large came to be dominated by the logic of the management and service sectors of the economy.

The professionalization of the artist did not happen immediately or easily. As artists grappled with the emergent terms of a postindustrial world in which the conditions of labor were changing dramatically, one of their responses was to portray themselves as workers. The Abstract Expressionists maintained and helped to promulgate the largely European myth of the isolated artist in his studio, but, as art historian Caroline Jones argues, they also presented themselves as workers by participating in the creation of a documentary image-world of the artist at work in his studio. These images varied greatly: artists presented themselves as members of the working class, as typified by photographs of Jackson Pollock in his work shirts and blue jeans, and as members of the business class, as seen in Barnett Newman's professional images, complete with suit and bow tie.[15] Yet it was the emergence of Frank Stella and Andy Warhol that set into motion a new set of practices as well as images for the artist as worker-professional. Both Stella and Warhol made art where the interior life of the artist, as expressed through an individualized mark, was utterly absent from the final artistic process. To do so, both adopted a mechanistic production apparatus: Stella developed a highly regimented stripe of paint, equal to the width of the store-bought paintbrush, and Warhol borrowed mass-produced images that he subsequently silk-screened in an assembly-line fashion. And

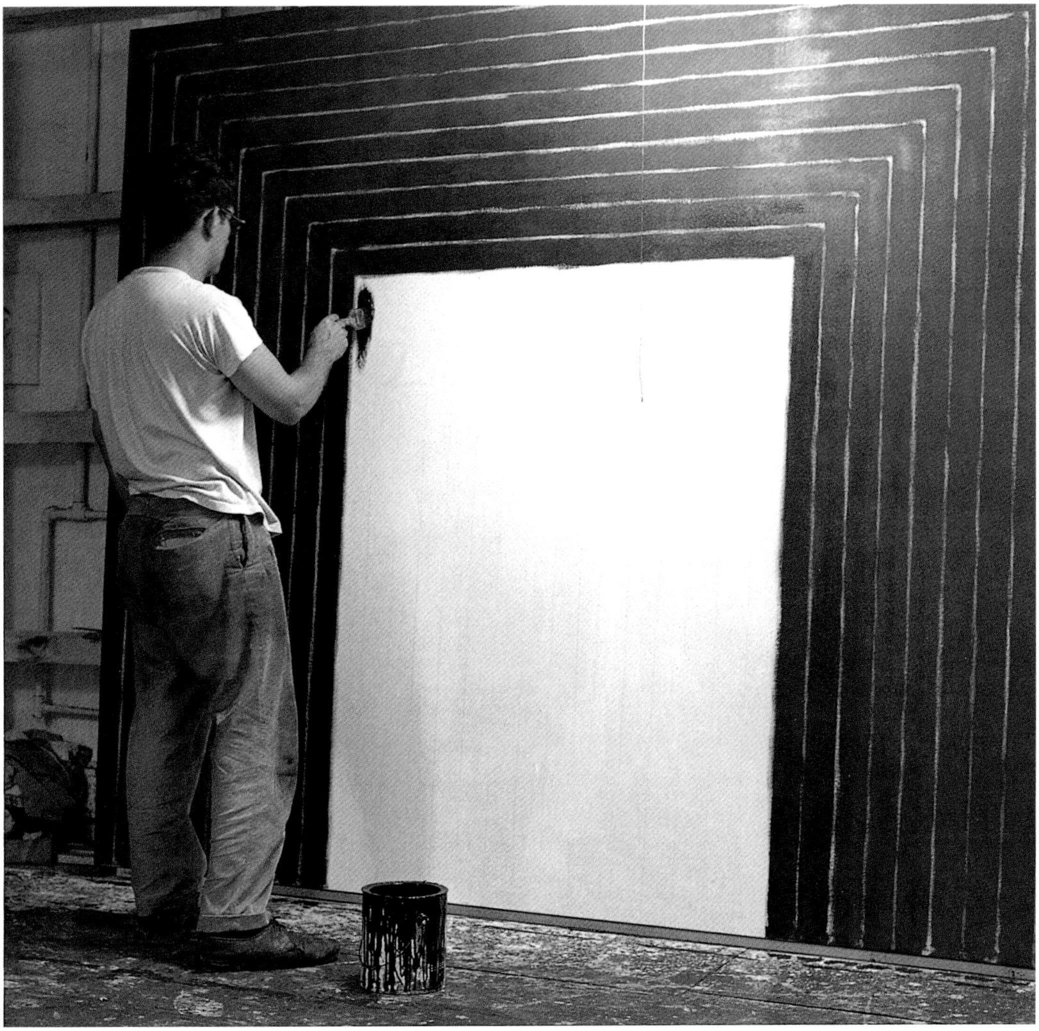

Hollis Frampton, Frank Stella in his studio working on *Getty Tomb (Second Version),* 1959.

while Stella shocked the art world with his idea of an "executive artist" who has others do his work for him, Warhol actualized this model when he established The Factory and famously quipped that if people wanted to know about his work they should ask his assistants. Despite their embrace of the executive model, both artists also flirted with other forms of identification, projecting an affinity with members of the working class. Stella's adoption of house painting's tools and techniques was accompanied by the following recollection: "it sounds a little dramatic, being an 'art worker.' I just wanted to do

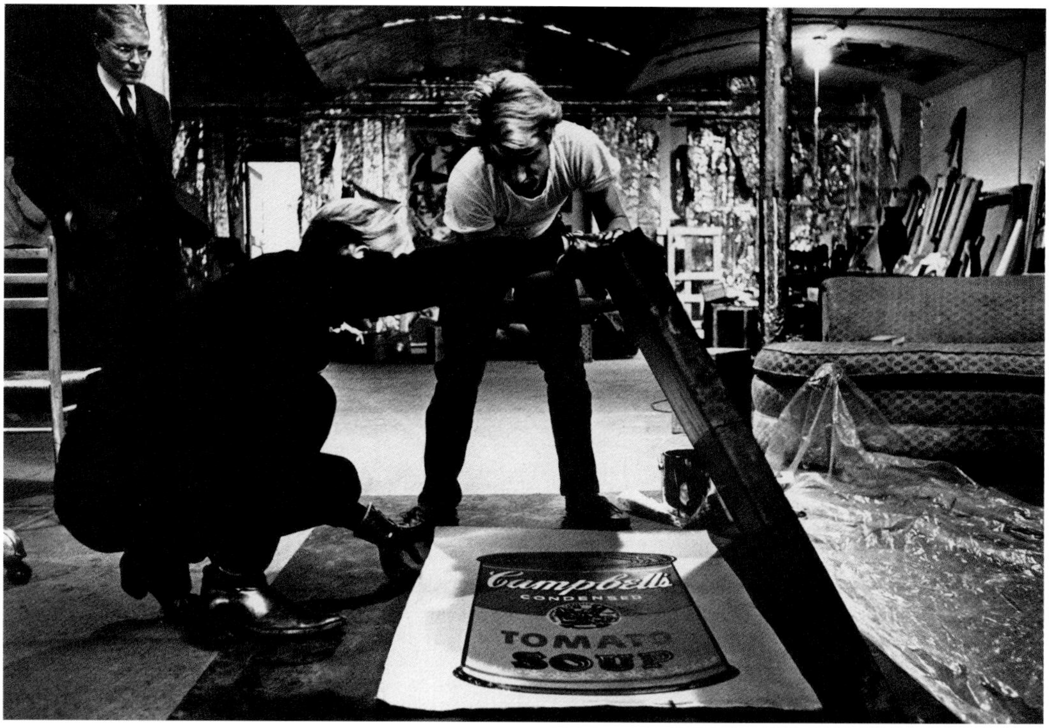

Andy Warhol and assistant Gerard Malanga screening Campbell's soup can canvases in The Factory, 1964. Photograph: Ugo Mulas.

it and get it over with so I could go home and watch TV."[16] Here, Stella mimed the stance of the hourly worker, not the corporate executive, and it is telling that Hollis Frampton's photographs of Stella painting in the studio are a strictly blue-jeans-and-white-tee-shirt affair. According to Jones, Warhol was also ambivalent about his role as either art worker or business executive, which may account for his vacillation between a blue-jeans aesthetic and his position as the head of The Factory.

For some, the idea of the artist as worker-professional was less ambivalently structured. Artist Allan Kaprow's description of the contemporary artist in "Should the Artist Become a Man of the World?" (1964) matter-of-factly states that artists "resemble the personnel in other specialized disciplines and industries in America," so much so that "on the street they are indistinguishable from the middle-class from which they come and towards whose mores—practicality, security, and self-advancement—they tend to gravitate." The problem for Kaprow was not professional status but that the artist must work within a "subtle social complex whose terms he is only beginning to understand."[17]

An important aspect of this new social complex was the post–World War II emergence of New York as the capital of the art world. In addition to the influx of European artists during the war and the rise of an increasingly lucrative art market, part of New York's becoming the mecca of the art world was the phenomenon of loft conversion. Wildly different in scale and effect than the garret apartments of prewar artists, loft spaces were typically abandoned light manufacturing buildings. In the illuminating study *Loft Living: Culture and Capital in Urban Change*, Sharon Zukin tracks the rise of SoHo and loft living, demonstrating how artists displaced light manufacturing only to be displaced themselves by members of the elite service industry.[18]

One unique quality of SoHo was that artists from disparate artistic movements lived and worked there simultaneously. Stella occupied a loft space on West Broadway in 1958, and Alison Knowles and George Maciunas, both Fluxus artists, were some of the first artists to buy buildings in SoHo. Allan Kaprow's Happenings took place in SoHo lofts; artists involved in the new sculpture (Donald Judd, Robert Morris, Richard Serra) lived and worked there, as did Conceptual artists (Sol LeWitt, Mel Bochner). This highly abbreviated list suggests that no matter how divergent the aesthetic concerns and practices, the infrastructure of SoHo was a common denominator in putting pressure on artists to perform or stage their work in new ways. For instance, the Artists' Tenants' Association was formed in 1960–61 in order to protect artists' right to live in lofts zoned for manufacturing. In their attempts to gain the attention of Robert Wagner, then mayor of New York, they threatened to boycott all art exhibitions in the city unless officials stopped their eviction policies. That artists could bond together as professionals and envision themselves as participants in a boycott already conveys a level of professional identity through affiliation. It also suggests that they understood their identities as not only the producers of culture but also its potentially primary consumers. Artists thus straddled the nascent economic transformation from production to consumption within their own professional identities.

The loft laws were resolved to ensure artists' ability to inhabit them. But residency came with a requirement that the spaces be studio-residences: the lofts could not be used only for living (as opposed to living and working).[19] Hence the edict *to work* was in place as a mandatory component of the legal solidity of SoHo as the artists' neighborhood. If one of the most enduring legacies of the early-twentieth-century avant-garde was the desire to blur the boundaries between art and life, then loft living may have furthered this initiative. The combination of the scale and historicity of such spaces, along with the new legalistic imperative to produce at a time when production was very much in question, was bound to have an enormous influence on contemporary art practices.

Artists stood at a crossroads in the 1960s. The influences exerted upon them and their conditions of possibility were extraordinary: the postwar reception of Duchamp, a profound alteration in the conception of the artist's role, the shift in the economic structure of the Western world, the rise of a new type of academic art training, and a dramatic change in the site of artistic production all came to bear on the production and reception of avant-garde culture. This essay has argued that shifts in artistic practice were bound up with a changing economic structure. The transformation from an industrial to a postindustrial society is perhaps best described by Ernest Mandel, who historicized this period as late capitalism. For Mandel, one of late capitalism's most distinctive characteristics is the spread of the logic of work into all areas of life, resulting in an increasingly bureaucratic and disciplinary society. He writes, "Mechanization, standardization, over-specialization and parcellization of labor, which in the past determined only the realm of commodity production in actual industry, now penetrate into all sectors of social life." Mandel continues with a particularly germane example: "The 'profitability' of universities, music academies and museums starts to be calculated in the same way as that of brick works or screw factories."[20] The visual and plastic arts were particularly well poised to negotiate this historic shift, as the value found in art has traditionally been positioned within a dialectical set of social practices.

Produced by both mental and manual labor, it is also a mixed site of leisure and work. Furthermore, throughout the twentieth century the avant-garde has set out to blur the distinctions between art and life. All these factors contribute to contemporary art's increasing porousness to the economic and social conditions of its production as well as its ability to represent and critique these transformations.

At this crossroads, much of the most important and challenging art of the period staged the problem of labor's transformation, its new divisions, and the increasingly blurred boundaries between work and leisure. Generally speaking, artists responded in one of four ways. Some played the part of both manager and worker, restaging the late-nineteenth- and early-twentieth-century division of labor. Others, emboldened by the professionalization of the category of artist and liberated by an economic shift away from manufacturing, simplified things by adopting a purely managerial position. Still others had a prescient understanding that the burgeoning service economy would ultimately give way to a leisure economy based on experience.[21] These artists turned to participatory strategies, directly involving the audience in the art. And finally (although this mapping is by no means chronological), there were those artists who experimented with not working at all, or at least trying to figure out how to work as little as possible.

Many artists staged the tension of the changing definitions of labor by mimicking the logic of labor's division into mental and manual realms. By establishing a task and then performing it, these artists acted out the roles of both manager and worker. It follows that in the absence of traditional artistic skills and concrete objects, the artist's studio, the space of artistic production, became a highly charged arena. What exactly was an artist supposed to do there? Bruce Nauman laconically presented the problem as follows: "If you see yourself as an artist and you function in a studio . . . you sit in a chair or pace around. And then the question goes back to what is art? And art is what an artist does, just sitting around the studio."[22] Yet Nauman never simply sat. He dictated for himself a set of task-like activities—playing a note on the violin, bouncing balls arrhythmically, walking around the studio in an exaggerated manner—all of which were filmed, transforming the studio into a performative arena.

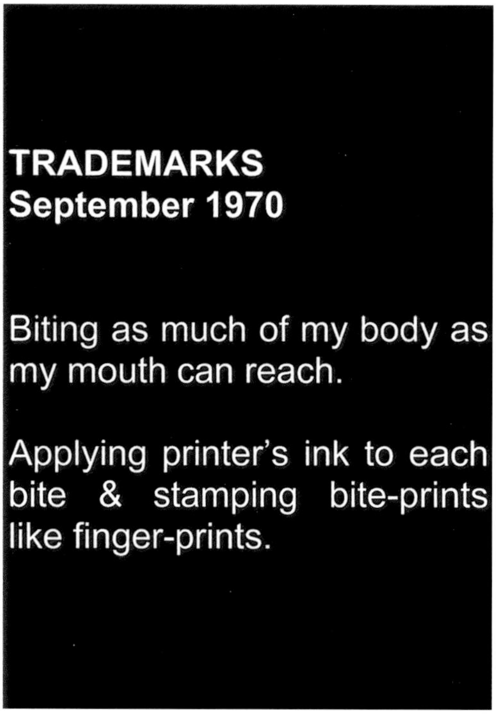

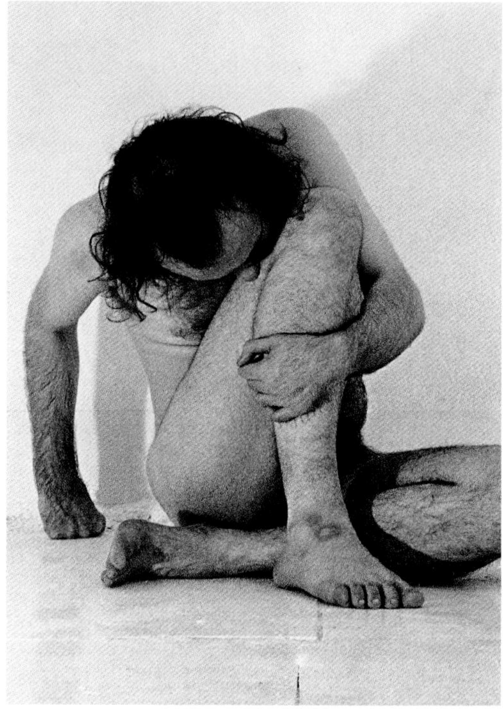

If Nauman's activities betray a literal, futile, and restless quality, then Vito Acconci's *Trademarks* (1970) can be seen as a humorous send-up of some of the anxiety provoked by the studio. In *Trademarks,* Acconci bit himself repeatedly on the arm and leg, trying to make a perfect dental impression on his skin. The impression was inked and "prints" were made, which were subsequently given away as gifts. In a parodic gesture of artistic mark making, Acconci deploys his body as the exclusive agent of artistic production, yet he does so in a way that empties out any particular subjective dimension. Not quite as efficient (or as iconographic) as a thumbprint, *Trademarks* offers an unskilled but physically arduous art activity, suggesting that even though the artwork was just barely an object, it still required a lot of effort to make.

Artists who assigned themselves tasks and then performed them rejected traditional artistic media and their attendant skills and turned instead to a presentation of the work of art in the language of "a thing done," a task performed. In doing so, many developed an obsessive reliance upon documentation.[23] Often the films

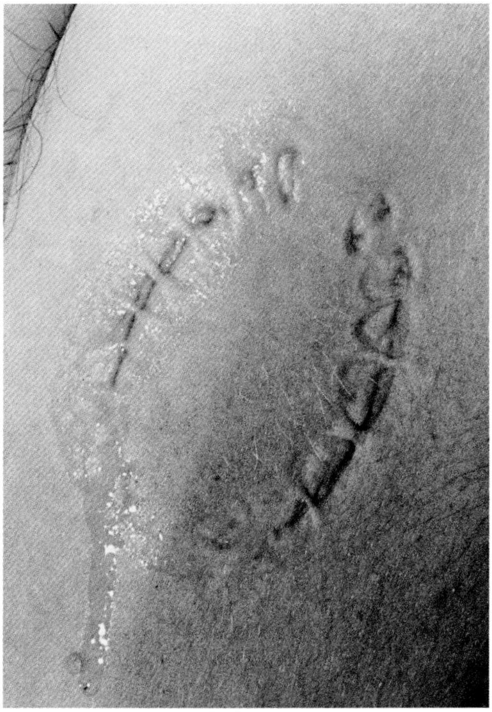

Vito Acconci, *Trademarks,* 1970/2001.

and photographs produced in this manner are fairly banal, produced with a deadpan lack of affect that is usually quite humorous. Yet the humor masks a certain level of anxiety surrounding the making of the art. When is the work finished? Is it "enough" work? It repeatedly appears that mimicking the strategies of efficient and productive labor in a parodic and deliberately unproductive way both enacts the artist's desire to embody a stereotypical American work ethic while simultaneously critiquing it. Consider Chris Burden's *Honest Labor* (1979), in which the artist himself dug a ditch over a period of three days while acting as a visiting artist at an art school. Typical of much task-based work and Process art, the end "product" or result of *Honest Labor* is "useless": a ditch without a purpose. What is valued is the *process* and/or the performance of the artist. Elevating the process was seen as a way to deemphasize the traditional values—both aesthetic and financial—attributed to the final product or artwork. Here, the artist does an "honest day's work" yet refuses to produce a luxury commodity object.

Artists emphatically suggested in the 1960s that the importance of a work of art lay more in how it was made rather than in the final product. Often referred to as Process art, this shift in emphasis was offered as a critique of the commodity status of art and was bound up with artists' desire to retain a degree of autonomy for the artistic act—a last-stand protection of sorts against an increasingly commodified world. Another way to conceptualize "process" is to read it as "artistic labor," for the process through which a thing is made is where its labor resides. So although we have seen that during the 1960s the art object underwent an internal split between mental and manual labor, with the privilege continually afforded to the realm of thinking, the emphasis on process provided a way for artists to maintain and even give value to the manual labor still inherent in the production of an object. Hence Burden's highly physical activity of ditch digging is ultimately presented as a photograph and a typed description of the activity—manual labor presented in the aesthetic of conceptual art.

Process art and task-based works were not the only places in which the language and logic of work were mimed by artists. Conceptual artists (perhaps more than any other group) disavowed the final object or product status of art, opting instead to emphasize cognitive processes. In doing so they often relegated the production of their work to others, replicating the logic of managerial labor. LeWitt seemed to have no trouble in taking a classic white-collar stand in regard to work's production. In his widely read "Paragraphs on Conceptual Art," he states, "When an artist uses a conceptual form of art, it means that all of the planning and decisions are made beforehand and the execution is a perfunctory affair. The idea becomes a machine that makes the art."[24]

But machines do not make LeWitt's wall drawings; assistants do, further completing the professionalized separation of mental and manual forms of artistic labor. As many Conceptual artists relied heavily upon the language and logic of the instruction, they functioned like managers, producing graphs, charts, and diagrams with directions for others on how to perform the labor required to make the object. Art historian Benjamin Buchloh described this aspect of Conceptual art as the "aesthetic of administration," arguing, "this aesthetic identity is structured much the way this class's social identity is, namely, as one of merely administering labor and production (rather than producing) and of the distribution of commodities."[25] In this context, John Baldessari's presentation of himself as a "nine-to-five artist," reflecting his daily routine of going to the studio, takes on a new resonance—even if, when he arrived at the studio one day in 1972, he taped himself singing Sol LeWitt's "Sentences on Conceptual Art" to the tune of *Camptown Races*.[26] Baldessari's *Commissioned Paintings* (1969–70) consist of a series of works painted by Sunday painters chosen and approached by Baldessari, who asked each of them to represent faithfully banal snapshots of a friend pointing at objects in a domestic and/or studio space. Each painting was subsequently taken to a sign painter, who "captioned" the paintings with the phrase "This is a painting by Pat Nelson" (or whoever the Sunday painter was). Finally, Baldessari placed his signature on the back of the canvas. *The Commissioned Paintings* are a witty jab at the problem of the artist as genius. They also restage the division of labor inherent in the production of all commodities. Baldessari's critical gesture thus becomes that of drawing attention to the problem of the differentiation in value between the named producer of the painting on the front (in this instance, the "manual laborer") and Baldessari's (managerial/authorial) signature on the back.

The question of the differentiation of value mandated by a division of labor was most problematic, perhaps, for artists influenced by feminism. As shifting definitions of labor came to structure both art and everyday life, the traditionally unpaid labor of housework and child rearing became material for artists interested in problems of work. That many artists who were women tried to combine their housework and their artwork indicates that the traditional division of labor between manager and worker does not apply to domestic tasks. So, too, it is difficult for the necessary tasks of housework to be rendered parodically as useless or noncommodifiable labor. While Minimalist artists farmed out instructions for sculptures to factories, Martha Rosler turned her video camera on her household tasks. In *Backyard Economy* (1974) we watch the artist mow the lawn and hang out the laundry. Daily, necessary, unpaid chores do double duty: they "get done" while art is being made.[27] To this end, Feminist art issued a multilayered critique: one was clearly sociological, drawing attention to the status of women's unpaid labor in the marketplace;

another was directed at contemporary "critical" art, inasmuch as the miming of industrial and managerial forms of labor in much Minimal and Conceptual art did not enact the same forms of humor and critique when applied to the women's work that is never done.

All of the above artworks engage the problem of labor through the figure of the artist, either as a combined worker/manager or simply as a manager. But our discussion opened with "the death of the author" and the newly central place of the viewer. The viewer is hardly universal, however, and the type of viewer imagined and interpolated by works of art varies greatly. Some artworks are not complete, though, without viewer participation, and as the viewer is pressed into service, it remains unclear whether the activity is work or play. In each instance, the role of the artist as someone who fabricates something designed to promote contemplation is radically altered: the artist now is someone who provides an experience for an audience.

For instance, Allan Kaprow staged an event in 1967 called *Fluids*. Urged on by simple posters that consisted of a schematic drawing and typed instructions, the work consisted of voluntary participants building a wall of large ice bricks in Southern California and—upon its completion—watching the fruits of their labor melt. Kaprow's work, later called "Happenings," always involved an intense interpenetration of art and life, and his events often were guided by a string of refusals. He provided no discrete or permanent object, no comfortable or passive spectatorship. Instead, *Fluids* offers a highly staged version of "useless" labor. This strategy of refusal continues today: Kaprow disallows the documentation of the Happenings in museums, insisting that they are deeply experiential and cannot be understood adequately through documentation.[28] So while we can surmise that the work of fashioning the ice wall was both physically arduous and pleasurable, distinctly blurring the boundaries between work and leisure, the artist rejects spectatorship that is nonparticipatory.

Fluids negated the logic of art as a commodity object by virtue of the artwork's disappearance and it questioned the labor of the artist and the leisure of the spectator by virtue of its method of fabrication. Fluxus, a loose grouping of international artists, also explored ideas of uselessness, play, and the blurring of art and life, work and leisure. George Maciunas, the "ringleader" of the group, gathered the ideas of

Fluxus artists (which often took the form of instructions for nonsensical and nonproductive behavior) and fashioned them into game boards, little puzzles, and an entire array of Cracker Jack–like trinkets designed to be sold cheaply and actively handled. Creating a veritable cottage industry of game production, Maciunas and his Fluxus counterparts did not reject the commodity form but humorously embraced it, subverting its logic. They also skewered the logic of managerial instruction. Fluxus instructions, or "scores" (a term they borrowed from musical composition), were often of a bodily nature and silly, such as Mieko Shiomi's "Smile" piece, in which the participant was asked to smile as slowly as possible. Even though they were created by a disparate group of artists, Maciunas's games and products had a visual and tactile similarity, relying strongly on the modest means of envelopes, letter printing, small plastic boxes, and colored cardboard. The graphics evoke nineteenth-century American carnivals and circuses, drawing a strong corollary between the role of art and the traditional spaces of play and leisure. Ernest Mandel argues that late capitalism is determined to infiltrate every aspect of our lives with the logic of the commodity. In response to this interpenetration, Fluxus insisted on recreation without a profit motive. This is the spirit that drives one of Maciunas's most endearing works: a series of modified Ping-Pong paddles, one with a gaping hole, one with a tin can, one with a soft doughy substance, and so on. Made to be played with, Maciunas's altered rackets imply that above all, the strategy of Fluxus was to be utterly nonserious (or seriously playful), for the world was serious enough.[29]

Unlike artists who imagined the audience as joyful participants, Yoko Ono and Valie Export presented the completion of the work of art on the part of the audience as a kind of dilemma. In Ono's *Cut Piece* (1964), audience members were invited to cut off pieces of her clothing, and in Export's *Tapp und Tastkino* (*Touch Cinema* [1968]), viewers were allowed to grope her breasts in public. In both instances, spectators were confronted with desire—their own and that of others—in a negotiation of the (problematic) social boundaries of the human body, especially the female body. In each instance, viewership was presented as an activity bound up with the enacting and solving of ethical situations: Should audience members dissuade other audience members from taking too much of Ono's clothing? Should audience members censure the activities meted out on Export's available body? In other words, the audience is placed in a fraught situation in which its potential passivity is made manifest.[30] By emphasizing the role of the viewer/participant and the struggle it entails, these performances pressure the category of leisure, questioning whether audience-participatory works are a space of deregulatory release or whether they, too, come with responsibilities. As popular as the ideas of sexual and creative liberation—largely put forth by the German intellectual Herbert Marcuse—were in the 1960s, both performances imply that the refuge from work in leisure activities structured around voyeurism have always had as part of their sexual liberation a hidden "price": the potential subjugation of women.[31]

The artists involved with participatory works imagined or interpolated varied audiences, but they shared a common goal of reinvigorating and enlivening the bureaucratic subject of postindustrial labor. Could the repressive structures of an administered society be loosened without risking an (unwitting?) repression elsewhere? As we have seen, the solution for some artists has been to establish a realm of participatory ludic play. The Duchampian legacy, replete with its ambivalence toward work and art, presented many artists with a humorous conundrum: If what artists make is art, then is *anything* an artist does art? Numerous artists attempted to blur the distinctions between art and life, work and play, by bestowing the name and value of art upon their everyday "non-art" activities. Often this has looked like nice work if you could get it. For instance, *Smashed* (1972) is a deadpan parody of task-based work, as Gilbert and George offer black-and-white photographs of their drunken antics. Similarly, Tom Marioni held a weekly "performance," *The Act of Drinking Beer with Friends Is the Highest Form of Art* (1970), in which friends and artists came together to drink beer, stacking up their empty bottles as an indexical sculpture, clear evidence of process being more important than product. In these works, the artists suggested that rather than blurring art and life for its own sake (a kind of avant-garde formalism) or parodying the structure of a highly administered workplace (a repetition of business as usual), the encroachment of work into the space of leisure could be effectively countered by creating a situation where leisure overtakes work.

Many, if not all, of the works included in *Work Ethic* possess a utopian dimension. This utopianism was made possible, in part, through the widespread social upheavals of the 1960s—rebellions that, in the words of Michael Hardt and Antonio Negri in *Empire*, created a "massive transvaluation of the values of social production and production of new subjectivities [that] opened the way for a powerful transformation of labor power."[32] Yet the 1960s may have been the end of one historical phase and the slow beginning of another. *Empire* contends that late capitalism is on the wane, as nation-based economies are being supplanted by a globalized economy and the postindustrial service economy is becoming an information economy. Hardt and Negri propose that in the midst of this massive transformation—one that threatens to leave many behind in its churning wake—a sophisticated and articulate account of labor's changing roles and face is imperative for any kind of social change. They offer a map of labor's metamorphosis from what they term "productive labor" (the production of goods and services during late capitalism) to "immaterial labor" (the production and management of information under our current conditions). Further, they contend that immaterial labor is divisible into three basic types. The first is industrial production rendered as information, where "manufacturing itself is considered a service." The second is the "creative and intelligent manipulations [of information] on the one hand and routine symbolic acts on the other." And the third is labor in the bodily mode, meaning the production and manipulation of affect.[33]

There is an almost uncanny homology between Hardt and Negri's assessment of our current economic transformations and the strategies deployed by artists negotiating the ramifications of labor's prior transformation. Artists who play out the roles of both manager and worker in task-based and Process works render the logic of industrial production into aesthetic information. Artists who mime the structure of management both creatively and routinely manipulate information. (What better way to describe a serial logic?) And artists who turn to the viewer to complete the work consistently do so in a bodily and affective mode. Given these sympathies, it is perhaps no mistake that Hardt and Negri argue that we need "to recognize *the profound economic power of cultural movements*, or really the increasing indistinguishability of economic and cultural phenomena."[34] All of the artists in this exhibition in some way stage, manage, and/or resolve the cultural and societal anxieties that surround changing definitions and divisions of labor. Some seem to have understood these transformations in an almost prescient manner. This is crucial, as work and professional life constitute an increasingly powerful site of our identity (as much, if not more so, than family, religion, and ethnicity). As we try to cope with the increasing regimentation and administration of our daily lives—both at work and at leisure—artists offer tentative, temporary solutions, stopgap measures, or blockades in the road.

Perhaps we can learn a lesson from the current tendency of contemporary artists to repeat various 1960s practices. While some critics might see Gabriel Orozco's *Mesa de ping-pong con estanque* (*Ping Pond Table* [1998]) as a mere repetition of Maciunas's altered Ping-Pong paddles, I would like to suggest that artists borrowing 1960s strategies do so precisely because they were so instrumental in thinking though the changing dynamics of labor.[35] *Mesa de ping-pong con estanque (Ping Pond Table)* is a particularly powerful contemporary instance of this. Two Ping-Pong tables are spliced together to form the shape of a crucifix. In the center is a square "pond" containing water lilies. The table comes equipped with four paddles and several balls. Viewers are invited to play. Because there are no preestablished rules, the terms of engagement depend upon the participants. The museum's imagining of viewers as solitary is disallowed; instead, a contested (and competitive) public space is offered where participants come together as equals to negotiate a situation. In many regards, Orozco's work offers a utopian microcosm of the traditional public sphere in which disinterested citizens are encouraged to come together to debate the function of their society. Citizens thus bear responsibility for the work of public life. Today, however, such a public sphere has largely ceased to exist, as corporate interests almost entirely shape public debate, and here, debate (or its potential) is substituted with play. Deploying the Fluxus strategies of the nonserious, the game, and the radically altered commodity, Orozco is able to revisit the site of the museum as the primary arbiter of art's role and meaning in society.

Recently, the museum has been discussed in both the popular press and the art media as an institution in crisis. Structured by

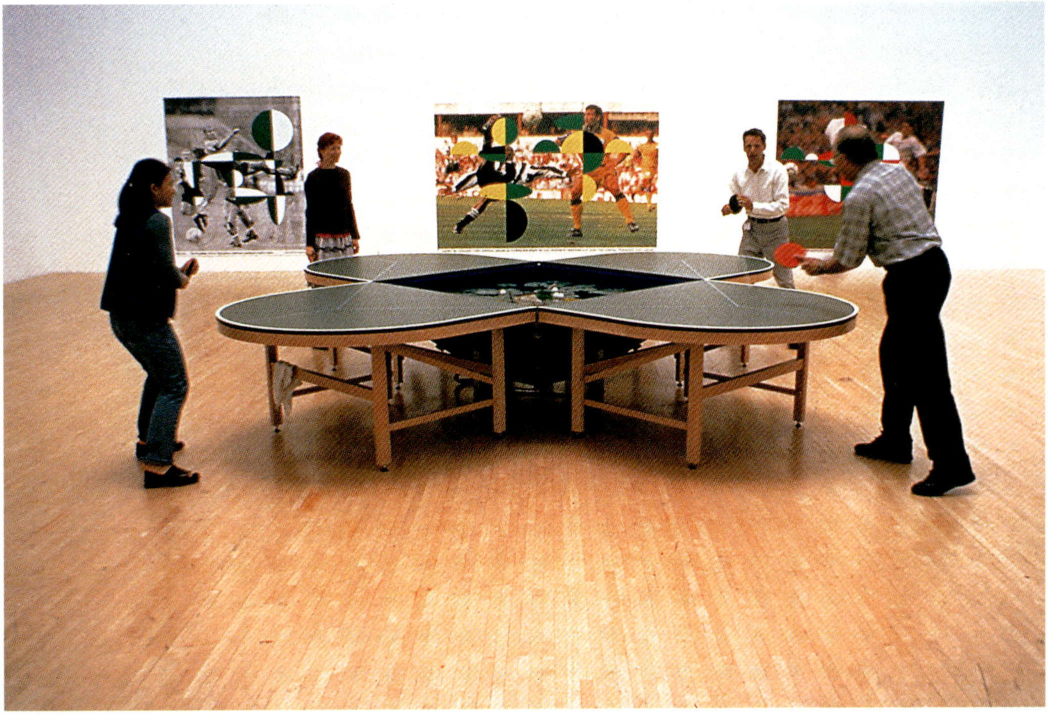

Gabriel Orozco, *Mesa de ping-pong con estanque (Ping Pond Table),* 1998.

contradictions, it is a place of work (scholarship and conservation) and leisure (a tourist destination), as well as a site of public service (education) and a place dependent upon private funds (growing corporate support of the arts). Increasingly, the pressures exerted on museums mean that they have become sites of experience as opposed to spaces of interpretation.[36] *Ping Pond Table*, as an object, is both a sculpture and a game, and its dual identity intimates that the space of the museum is a fraught one. As a sculpture it needs to be interpreted and conserved; as a game, it offers an experience (tellingly, though, the experience it offers is impossible without the active and critical participation of the viewer). In *Ping Pond Table* viewers complete the work, but they are asked to do so in a fashion that is more communal than solitary. *Ping Pond Table* thus suggests that in the face of diminishing spaces for critique and debate within a hypercommercialized experiential art world, perhaps the space of play can be reclaimed as having a potentially critical dimension. Far from a mere repetition, such a reinvention (provisionally) resists the contemporary forces of global capital—forces that have transformed art into a mere commodity and museums into mandatory tourist destinations—and articulates the potential politics and pleasure in both resisting and shaping new forms of labor and leisure. Contemporary art may hold a key, then, to new identities and to how the conditions of social possibility can be reshaped in the new millennium.

1. Leo Steinberg, *Other Criteria: Confrontations with Twentieth-Century Art* (London: Oxford University Press, 1972), 60.

2. This essay argues that art practices and labor practices are inextricably linked. Although the transformation of the American economy has had global ramifications, this essay deals primarily with the ways in which American artists negotiated the changing definitions of labor. The intricate relations of labor practices, ideologies, and their impact on art making in other parts of the world are beyond the scope of this essay.

3. See Mark Seltzer's *Bodies and Machines* (New York: Routledge, 1992). Writing about the phenomenon of Taylorization and the rise of scientific management, Seltzer observes: "The real innovation of Taylorization becomes visible in the incorporation of the *representation* of the work process into the work process itself—or, better, the incorporation of the representation of the work process *as* the work process itself" (159).

4. Paul Osterman et al., *Working in America: A Blueprint for the New Labor Market* (Cambridge: The MIT Press, 2001), 33.

5. Joseph Pine and James Gilmore, *The Experience Economy* (Boston: Harvard Business School Press, 1999), 8.

6. For the shift from a goods-based to a service-based economy and the definitions of each, see ibid., 8–9. This work also claims that we are currently in the midst of a shift from a service-based economy to an experience-based economy, with experiences described as "events that engage individuals in a personal way" (12).

7. On the importance of Duchamp's reception in America, particularly its deferred nature, see Hal Foster's "What's Neo About the Neo-Avant-Garde?" *October* 70 (Fall 1994): 5–32.

8. The rejection of the museum means that while much advanced art from the 1960s and 1970s now forms the canon of art history within the academy, its entrance into the narrative of art history offered by the museum has been infinitely slower. This has changed in recent years with the advent of important exhibitions. See, for instance, Ann Goldstein and Anne Rorimer, *Reconsidering the Object of Art: 1965–1975* (Los Angeles: The Museum of Contemporary Art, Los Angeles; Cambridge: The MIT Press, 1995); Luis Camnitzer et al., *Global Conceptualism: Points of Origin, 1950s–1980s*, exh. cat. (New York: Queens Museum of Art, 1999); Paul Schimmel, *Out of Actions*, exh. cat. (Los Angeles: The Museum of Contemporary Art, Los Angeles, 2000).

9. *The Writings of Marcel Duchamp*, ed. Michel Sanouillet and Elmer Peterson (New York: Da Capo Press, 1973), 140.

10. Roland Barthes, "The Death of the Author," in *Image Music Text*, trans. Stephen Heath (New York: Hill and Wang, 1977), 143, 148.

11. For more on the relations between these two texts, see Benjamin H. D. Buchloh, "Readymade, Objet Trouvé, Idée Reçue," in *Dissent: The Issue of Modern Art in Boston* (Boston: I.C.A., 1985), 106–22.

12. Sol LeWitt, "Serial Project #1, 1966," *Aspen* 5/6 (Fall/Winter 1967): unpaginated.

13. Howard Singerman, *Art Subjects: Making Artists in the American University* (Berkeley and Los Angeles: University of California Press, 1999), 144. When Rauschenberg was a student at the Art Students' League in New York, he rebelliously turned his back on the live nude model and made a white painting with numbers instead.

14. Harold Rosenberg, "Everyman a Professional," in *The Tradition of the New* (New York: Horizon Press, 1959), 63.

15. Caroline Jones's *Machine in the Studio: Constructing the Postwar American Artist* (Chicago: University of Chicago Press, 1996) argues that a

veritable industry of documenting artists at work in their studios accompanies the rise of Abstract Expressionism. I would like to suggest that a certain anxiety may have been at work regarding whether abstraction was legitimate artistic labor; the inordinate amount of documentation might seem to make it so. For a discussion of Pollock's and Newman's self-presentation, see chapter 3 in particular.

16. As quoted in ibid., 121.

17. Allan Kaprow, "Should the Artist Become a Man of the World?" (1964); reprinted in his *Essays on the Blurring of Art and Life* (Berkeley and Los Angeles: University of California Press, 1996), 35.

18. Sharon Zukin, *Loft Living: Culture and Capital in Urban Change* (Baltimore: The Johns Hopkins University Press, 1982), 5. Zukin argues that in a concerted effort to create high-end office space and equally luxurious residential spaces, city and bank investments consistently foreclosed manufacturing options in Manhattan. She contends that "the residential conversion of a manufacturing space provides a substantial part of the infrastructure for a supposedly post-industrial economy," adding that "this infrastructure fulfills the physical needs of the service-sector and white collar employees" (19).

19. Ibid., 50.

20. Ernest Mandel, *Late Capitalism*, trans. Joris De Bres (London: Verso, 1978), 387.

21. According to Harvard School of Business professors Pine and Gilmore, authors of *The Experience Economy*, the service industry is in the process of being eclipsed by the "experience economy." Here, services are tailored to clients in ways that increase their experiential quotient. A cup of coffee is no longer served to you by a counterperson but by a "barista," and the event takes place in an environment dedicated to the experience of coffee as opposed to a "mixed-use" environment (like a lunch counter or deli). This shift is what enables a $3.00 cup of coffee. Such micro-managed and highly orchestrated services become "experiences" whose driving motive is the creation of profit.

22. As quoted in Tony Godfrey, *Conceptual Art* (London: Phaidon Press, 1998), 127.

23. See Darsie Alexander's "Reluctant Witness: Photography and the Documentation of 1960s and 1970s Art" in this volume.

24. Sol LeWitt, "Paragraphs on Conceptual Art" (1967); reprinted in *Conceptual Art: A Critical Anthology*, ed. Alexander Alberro and Blake Stimson (Cambridge: The MIT Press, 1999), 12.

25. Benjamin H. D. Buchloh, "Conceptual Art, 1962–1969: From the Aesthetic of Administration to the Critique of Institutions," *October* 55 (Winter 1990): 128.

26. As quoted in *John Baldessari*, exh. cat., texts by Marcia Tucker and Robert Pincus-Witten (New York: The New Museum, 1981), 15.

27. See Helen Molesworth, "Housework and Artwork," *October* 92 (Winter 2000): 71–97.

28. Allan Kaprow, telephone conversation with the author, November 2002. Kaprow's work was never designed to be exhibited in museums, and he continues to resist the kind of historicization that such exhibiting entails.

29. Fellow traveler Henry Flynt would organize, along with Maciunas, a 1963 demonstration against "serious culture" (directed at the Metropolitan Museum of Art, Lincoln Center, and The Museum of Modern Art), suggesting that high art had already fallen prey to the logic of late capitalism, a logic that could potentially be fought with the weapon of nonseriousness.

30. For the ethical problematic of much 1960s and 1970s performance, see Frazer David Ward, "False Intimacies, Open Secrets: Public and Private in the Performance Art of Vito Acconci and Chris Burden" (Ph.D. diss., Cornell University, 2000). See also Miwon Kwon's "Exchange Rate: On Obligation and Reciprocity in Some Art of the 1960s and After" in this volume.

31. Herbert Marcuse was the most influential thinker of the postwar period regarding issues of work, leisure, and creativity. In *Eros and Civilization* (1955), he argued that "the play impulse is the vehicle of liberation." Linking libidinal urges and play urges, he advocated a desublimation of work's repressive tendencies. See *Eros and Civilization: A Philosophical Inquiry into Freud* (Boston: Beacon Press, 1966), 171. Also see, in this volume, Chris Gilbert's essay on Marcuse's theories of leisure, "Herbie Goes Bananas: Fantasies of Leisure and Labor from the New Left to the New Economy."

32. Michael Hardt and Antonio Negri, *Empire* (Cambridge: Harvard University Press, 2000), 275.

33. Ibid., 293.

34. Ibid., 275; emphasis in the original.

35. On the repetition of Dada strategies throughout the postwar period, see Helen Molesworth, "From Dada to Neo-Dada and Back Again," *October* 105 (Summer 2003): 177–81.

36. For an expansion on this dichotomy in museological practice, see Sir Nicholas Serota, *Experience or Interpretation: The Dilemma of Museums of Modern Art* (New York: Thames and Hudson, 1997).

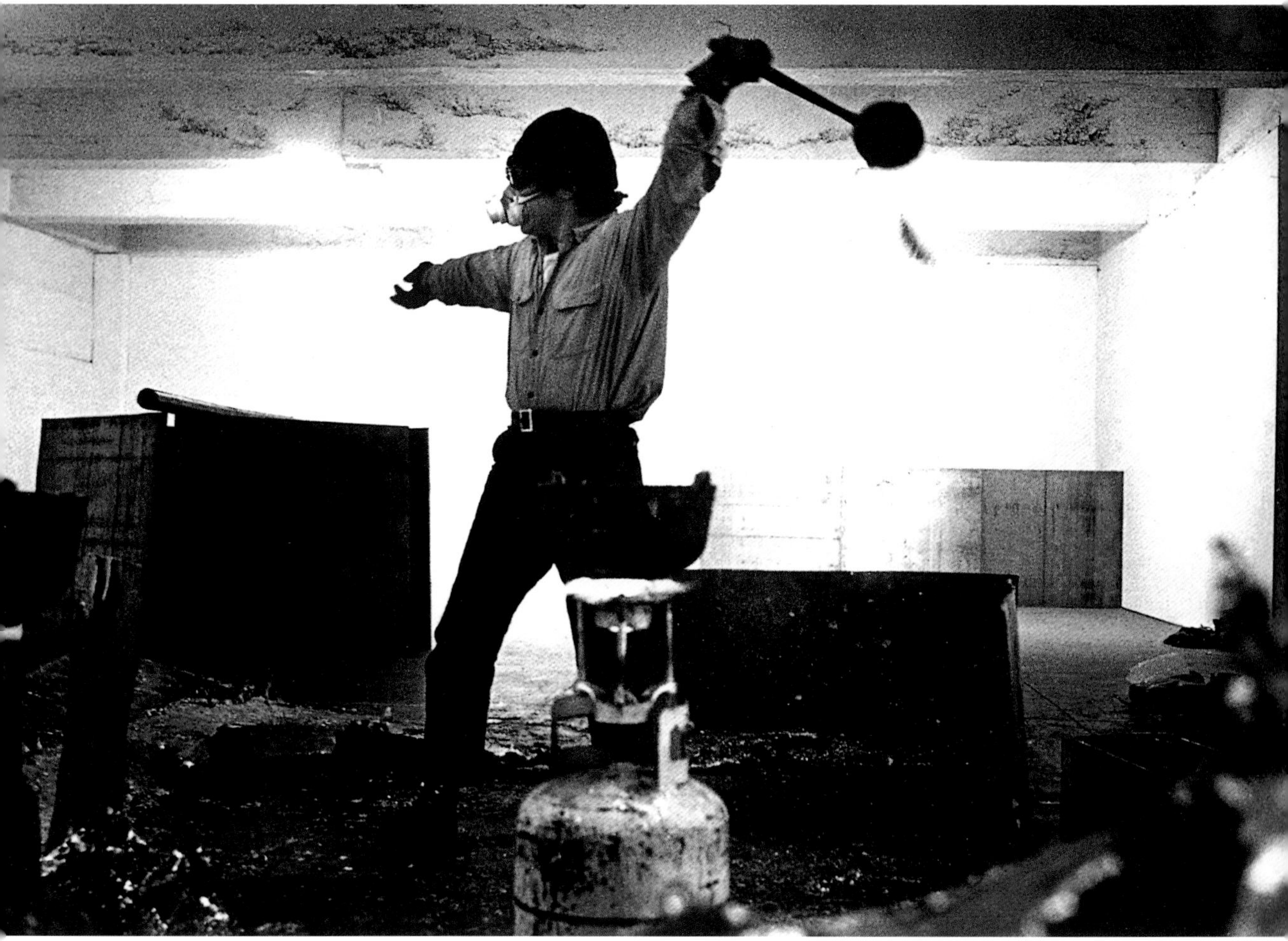

Gianfranco Gorgoni, Richard Serra throwing molten lead for *Castings* at the Castelli warehouse, New York, 1969.

Reluctant Witness: Photography and the Documentation of 1960s and 1970s Art

DARSIE ALEXANDER

You can't locate the work in terms of its record. It's like a series of snapshots or something.
—Robert Morris

I sort of allow photographs because they . . . prove the point that there was nothing to photograph.
—Robert Barry

One day the photograph is going to become even more important than it is now. . . . But I am not particularly an advocate of the photograph.
—Robert Smithson

WHEN PERFORMANCE AND conceptual artists of the 1960s picked up the camera and used it as a pragmatic tool to document their works for posterity, they highlighted aspects of the medium that simultaneously reasserted its complexity and altered its history. For more than a century, the camera had been used to record and archive works by sculptors, painters, and architects. But in the late 1960s, a range of artistic investigations into the concepts of art, phenomenon, site, performative presence, and process radically changed the terms of art and the role of photography within its newly formed boundaries. For the first time, artists with no particular interest or investment in photography were forced to consider its significance as a powerful vehicle of validation and communication. The new art that they produced—including earthworks, streetworks, installations, and performances—was virtually unknowable to the general public without some kind of visual representation, and photography was called upon to provide it. As a medium, it offered a supreme form of evidence for these spatial, temporal, and often completely inaccessible forms of art. As Conceptual artist Dan Graham pointed out, "a work had only to be exhibited in a gallery and then written about and *reproduced as a photograph* in an art magazine. Then this record of the no longer extant installation, along with more accretions of information after the fact, became the basis for its fame, and to a large extent its economic value."[1] While photography served the purpose of documentation, then, it also occupied a crucial place in a broader network of dissemination.

The initial draw of photography for artists whose work took the form of actions, installations, and/or process pieces was its apparent artlessness and low status as a visual medium. Cheap, easy to use, infinitely reproducible, and ultimately disposable, the photograph represented, according to artist and writer Jeff Wall, the perfect readymade, the "quintessential anti-object."[2] In this respect, the camera as a simplistic record-keeping device was ideally suited to the aims of artists who deliberately sought to challenge the skills required to make the kind of art that adorned the walls of galleries and collectors' homes. Rather than the masterful manipulation of paint, artists relied on other talents—physical endurance and concentration among them—as the basis of their artistic labor. Mierle Laderman Ukeles, who undertook four projects at the Wadsworth Atheneum (Hartford, Connecticut) in 1973, for example, transformed the art of painting into a form of janitorial service by washing the floors inside and outside of the museum, at once cleaning them and creating a mark with her utilitarian brush. The photographs that exist of these works, many of them by her husband, offer an account of her actions in the most descriptive terms possible, ignoring the conventions of framing and focus needed to produce a "good" (i.e., aesthetically pleasing) picture. As such images make clear, the objective of the photographer was neither to replace Ukeles's art nor the experience of watching her perform it *in situ* but rather to make it consultable for those not present. As a form of "channel art," a phrase coined by Lawrence Alloway in 1970,[3] the photograph was employed as a means of transmitting information, one that validated through its supposedly transparent devices the fact that an artist's work resided in the act of conceptualizing and producing art but *not* in recording it through the rudimentary act of taking a picture. For many, photography was thought to be inherently laborless, requiring no skill beyond seeing, pointing, and shooting.

Artists newly acquainted with the medium nevertheless recognized photography's power to depict the creative act in memorable form—particularly in Hans Namuth's famous images of Jackson Pollock. Dramatizing his "trancelike state, his rhythmic movements, and the seemingly random quality of his compositions,"[4] these widely reproduced photographs deeply influenced a younger generation. Gianfranco Gorgoni's 1969 image of Richard Serra slinging lead

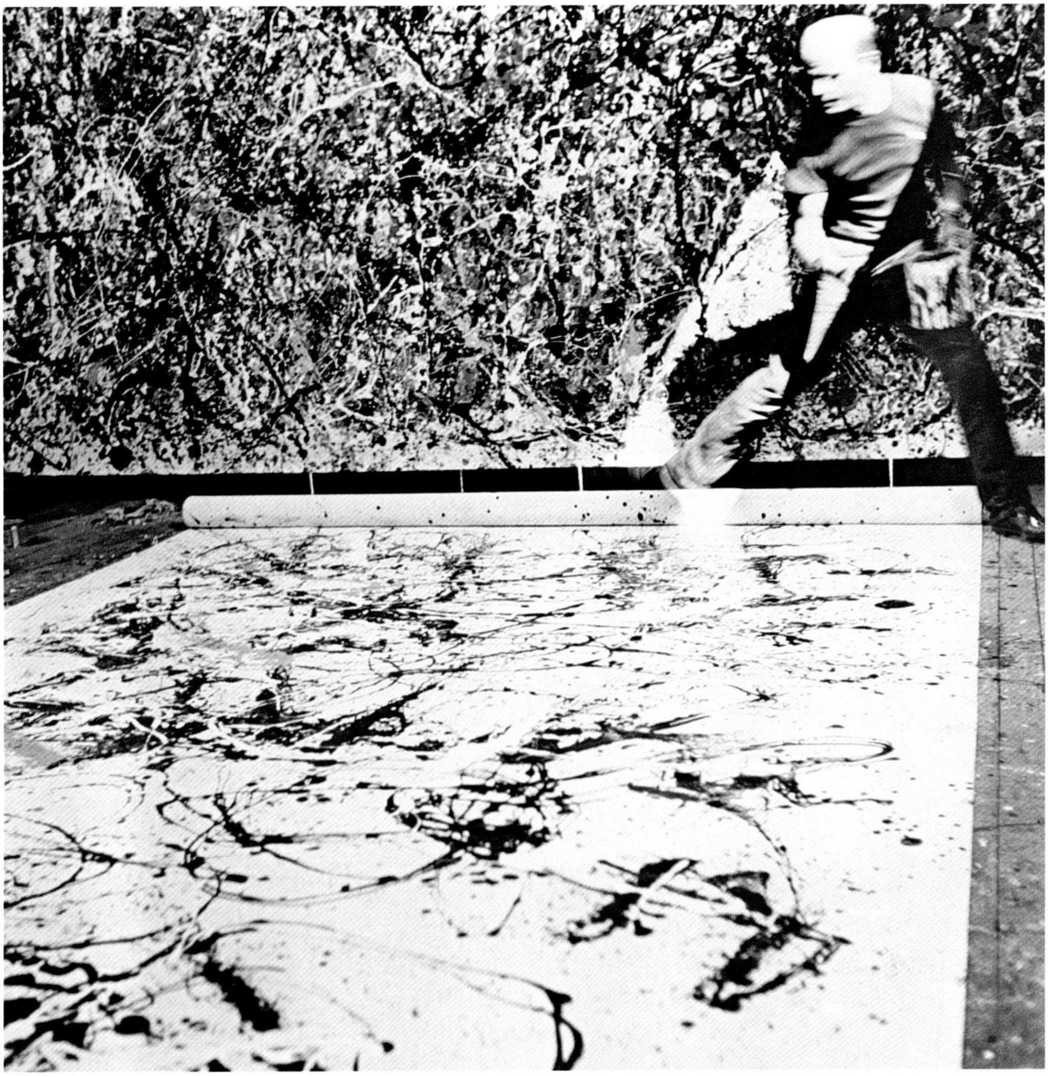

Hans Namuth, Jackson Pollock painting *Autumn Rhythm,* 1950.

in Leo Castelli's warehouse registers the lasting effects of the Pollock pictures by representing the intense physical labor of the artist's work. Serra, wearing a mask and heavy work gloves, is captured bending his left arm as he prepares to hurl a ball of molten lead against an interior wall. Neither the face of the artist nor the products of his manufacture are clearly visible in the image,[5] which reveals a debris-filled space occupied by steel slabs and shards of metal. Far from the secure personal environment of the artist's stu-

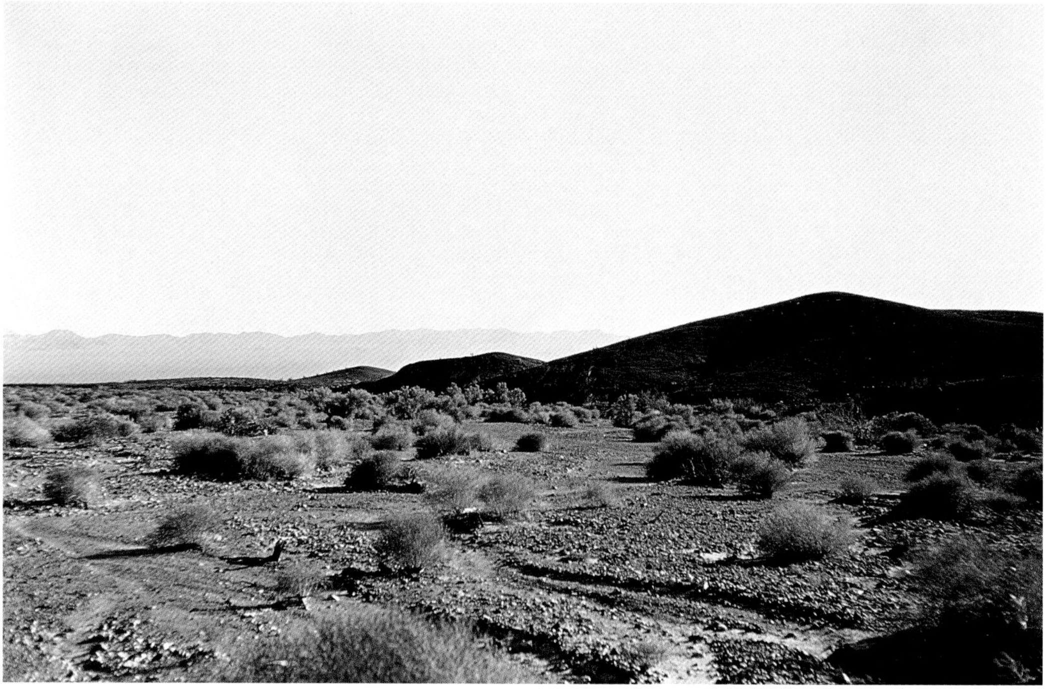

Robert Barry, *Inert Gas Series: Helium,* 1969. "On the morning of March 6, 1969, somewhere in the Mojave Desert in California, 2 cubic feet of helium were returned to the atmosphere."

dio, Serra presents himself in the attire and surroundings of a construction worker, refusing to let his facial or artistic identity dominate the representational focus of the image. Gorgoni positions his camera to suggest obliquely the merger of the artist's body with common warehouse equipment; a large propane tank, situated by the lens as if extending from Serra's left hip, occupies a position of visual dominance and anchors the artist's anatomy to the work site. Serra's self-directed gesture and the compositional strategies of the photographer collude to form an impression of the artist as foreman of his own labors, fully engaged in all of the arduous and sometimes dangerous tasks such a job would require. As with the Pollock photographs, the Serra image derived its meaning from granting viewers privileged access to the otherwise private moments of his artistic production.

Just as photography made visible the creative work of a renowned Abstract Expressionist like Pollock, it also affirmed artists' conceptual authority over works that could not be seen so easily.

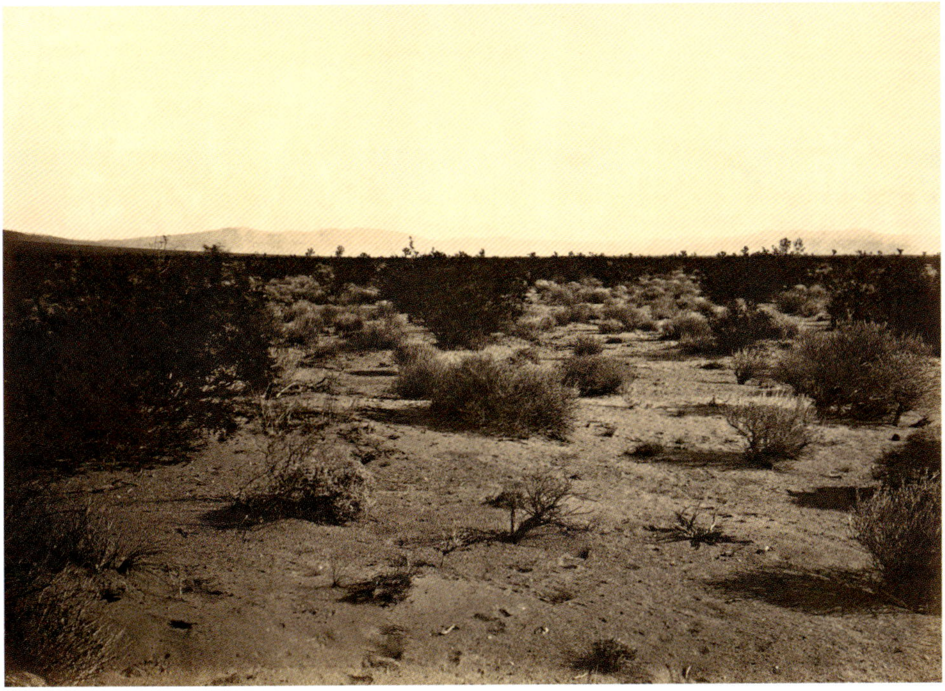

Alexander Gardner, *The Mojave Desert, in the Great Basin, California, Sierra Nevada in the Distance, 1,650 Miles from the Missouri River,* 1867–68.

Artists such as Marcel Broodthaers, Dennis Oppenheim, and Robert Barry denied permanence by using highly ephemeral materials in their work, including snow, sand, and air. Photography allowed these fugitive pieces a type of presence and solidity, even when the artists themselves resisted the materiality of the medium as a representational form. Robert Barry, who produced telepathic and environmental works, among other kinds, deployed the camera as a means of taking ownership of art that was utterly intangible, making it "real" and perceptible to a viewing audience. Though Barry maintained that his images actually proved the immaterial nature of his work by showing that there was nothing to photograph, he nevertheless exploited the evidentiary properties of the medium to illustrate and verify his efforts. In a picture of a particularly remote work, for example, Barry showed the site where "on the morning of March 6, 1969, somewhere in the Mojave Desert in California, 2 cubic feet of helium were returned to the atmosphere." It is an austere landscape of barren hills and tumbleweeds, where the only sign of human life can be found in barely visible tire tracks in the foreground. Yet for a few moments on that particular day in 1969, this piece of the Mojave Desert was Barry's territory. In registering this site photographically, the artist accomplished several goals: he identified the location of his work and endowed an otherwise bleak terrain with artistic significance. The photograph's caption plays a particularly significant role in this regard, explaining to viewers that the art they are meant to see is in the site itself and not its transcription as a photograph. In its descriptive titling and visual characteristics, the picture bears a striking resemblance to one made nearly a century earlier in the same region by Alexander Gardner. Gardner, employed as part of a railroad survey campaign in the 1860s, pictured a wilderness full of potential—a place to be inhabited, cultivated, and enjoyed for its untarnished beauty. For Gardner, the photograph conveyed beauty and opportunity, a means of archiving a distant land and making it available as a thing to be physically and visually claimed. Barry used the camera to mark the place where his art occurred and to define its existence in subtly proprietary terms. In doing so, he also made a landscape picture, linking up unexpectedly (and perhaps unintentionally) with established genres in photographic history.

Artists like Robert Barry understood that when they created photographic documents of their work, they simultaneously made images that could eventually be bought, sold, and taken out of context. This reality presented artists with a philosophical challenge. To produce a photograph derived from phenomenological, performative, or temporary art seemed contradictory, if not highly problematic, in light of the antimaterialist stance such works upheld. For artists like Joseph Kosuth, taking a photograph or bringing fragments of site-specific works into the gallery was a nearly blasphemous act that muddled the original premise and idea "into invisibility."[6] Any concrete form of documentation, whether a photograph or an instructional outline, was susceptible to a price tag. While insisting on the secondary role of artifacts ("the interest was in doing it, seeing it go through those stages—engaging in the process—and not the documentation"[7]), artists knew that objects were critical to the process of disseminating their work and paying the bills. Vito Acconci recognized the problems associated with producing sellable goods out of his performances, but he also felt that photography was necessary to "prove myself as an artist . . . make my place in the art-world: in order to do this, I had to make a picture, since a picture was what a gallery or museum was meant to hold (all the while, of course, I was claiming that I was denying that standard, rejecting it . . . claiming that my work was meant to subvert the closure of museum and gallery)."[8]

Deeply conflicted about the long-term ramifications of photography for the legacy of their works, artists were forced to face serious questions about the medium. How were they to decide the most appropriate means by which to photograph their work, and how were such images meant to function in relation to the entire process of a work's evolution? To what extent could one designate an order of significance to works accompanied by more than one picture? What were the potential liabilities of photographic documents that too forcefully asserted an aesthetic?

The last thing artists using photography wanted to do was to make images that in any way evoked the tradition of art photography embodied in the work of such lauded Modernists as Walker Evans, Edward Weston, and Henri Cartier-Bresson. On the one hand, photography itself was widely disdained as secondary to the fine arts of painting and sculpture. Though photography was taught in art schools in the 1960s, most famously at the Institute of Design in Chicago, it was nevertheless perceived as a form of professional training, not as a serious means of making art. At the same time, artists had to contend with the rising status of photography as a commercially and aesthetically viable medium that was gaining prominence in museums and galleries. They did so by insisting on the separateness of photography, by demarcating their own use of the medium as guided by practical and not visual interests. Their art, they regularly asserted, was about ideas. Thus they veered strongly from the production of pictures that retained any appearance of artistry. Such images could potentially be tied to a history they derided; moreover, objects of any kind stemming from conceptual or performative practices were ultimately decontextualized artifacts that could not do justice to the original.[9]

Objections to photography took many forms. As a time-stopping agent, it was openly criticized as static and residual. Robert Morris, whose reception of photography changed over time (an early performance was documented by the celebrated Pollock photographer, Hans Namuth, for example), nevertheless grew to resent the medium deeply. Morris argued that "there is probably no defense against the malevolent powers of the photograph to convert every visible aspect of the world into a static, consumable image." In his article "The Present Tense of Space," he reasoned that the photograph disrupts and ultimately destroys the immediacy of spatial art by turning the (live) subject into an (inert) object that exists as something remembered rather than known. He openly condemned the still qualities of the medium as antithetical to the "filmic real-time experience"[10] required by much 1970s art, stating that works created in and defined by a situational context (on the street, in the gallery, amid nature) demanded a "present tense" encounter between the viewer and the work of art. Morris's stated views reflected the widely circulated opinions of Susan Sontag (who is cited in a footnote to his article). Sontag's *On Photography* had recently been published, and in it she analyzed and enumerated photography's vices, articulating its capacity to legitimize voyeurism, distort information, and distance viewers from firsthand experience by "limiting experience to a search for the photogenic, by converting experience into an image, a souvenir."[11] Photography's death-grip on its subjects, as described by Sontag, was a particularly unsettling attribute for the makers of live-action art.

Underlying the ample criticisms of photography as a means of documentation was the growing recognition that the photograph was not merely a window onto the world but also a complicated object with no particular claims on truth; photography did not record innocently. Simply by means of releasing the shutter, the camera's operator isolated, fragmented, and froze the content he or she sought to capture, giving it a particularized form of representation that often looked very different from the reality experienced in person. As Dennis Oppenheim—who produced earthworks and performances—stated, "the photograph gives constant reference to the rectangle. This forces any idea into the confines of pictorial illusionism."[12] Ideas were not the only subjects truncated by photography's limitations. The physical and psychological spaces of contemporary art were necessarily constricted by the camera's lens, subjected not only to a form of monocular vision but also to the whims of personal

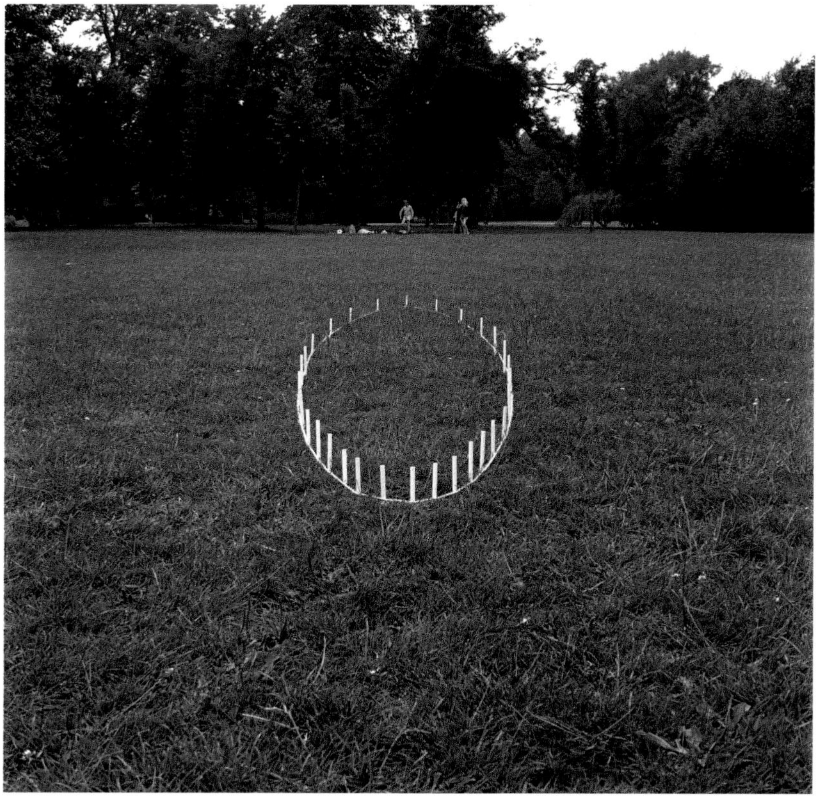

Jan Dibbets, *Perspective Correction,* 1969.

timing enacted by the person taking the picture. The fact that the camera possessed its own way of seeing, especially when guided by an untrained hand, could not be ignored.

How were artists to contend with photography as a method of execution unlike any other? Out of such a rudimentary question came a range of responses, played out in photographic experiments by many of the same people who had denigrated photography as an artistic dead end. The realization that photography merited a thorough form of investigation, particularly in light of its necessity as a documentary tool, brought about a new phase in its reception by artists. As newcomers to the medium, many were frustrated by its complexities. But some addressed these problems as formal and conceptual challenges, engendering a new level of critical self-awareness. The Dutch artist Jan Dibbets, for example, found that the fundamental properties of photography that made the accurate documentation of his three-dimensional works so difficult were in fact a rich subject in their own right. Originally a painter, Dibbets redirected his focus to photography, deconstructing the medium by exploiting its mechanisms of distortion. In a systematic progression, the artist asked pertinent questions about both the visual and conceptual effects of the camera's lens, shutter speed, and transcription of light. His interests were not strictly technical; they were based in a profound curiosity about the medium and its innate representational characteristics.

Exploring the tricks and biases of photography increasingly inspired the work of young artists who approached the medium from outside its aesthetic conventions. Though some artists continued to see photography merely as a means of illustrating their three-dimensional work, others recognized that the process of taking pictures permanently transformed and complicated their art. Indeed, for Eleanor Antin, Hannah Wilke, and Vito Acconci, photography became the engine of much of their performative work. In a group of images from 1969–70, for example, Acconci created a series of actions for the sole purpose of having them photographed. Each work involved a physical and photographic gesture, with the artist moving through space and taking pictures simultaneously. Acconci then transferred the images to black panels and annotated them, often with words that described the camera's internal mechanics. Though he was careful to distinguish these works as "photo-pieces" and not documents, they were in fact both. Acconci demonstrated that the act of creating a visual record with the camera could be rendered thoroughly commensurate with the task-oriented objectives of performance, forging a merger of artistic and documentary properties that artists had long considered mutually exclusive.

Through the actual use of photography to record transient or immaterial art, artists were forced to come to terms with their own biases, skepticism, and even naiveté about the medium. Some never moved beyond the assessment of photography proposed at the beginning of this essay: that it required no talent beyond seeing, pointing, and shooting. Others discovered, somewhat by accident, that photography offered a means of reinventing and transforming their work. Regardless of these artists' divergent attitudes toward photography in the 1960s and 1970s, their investigations had lasting

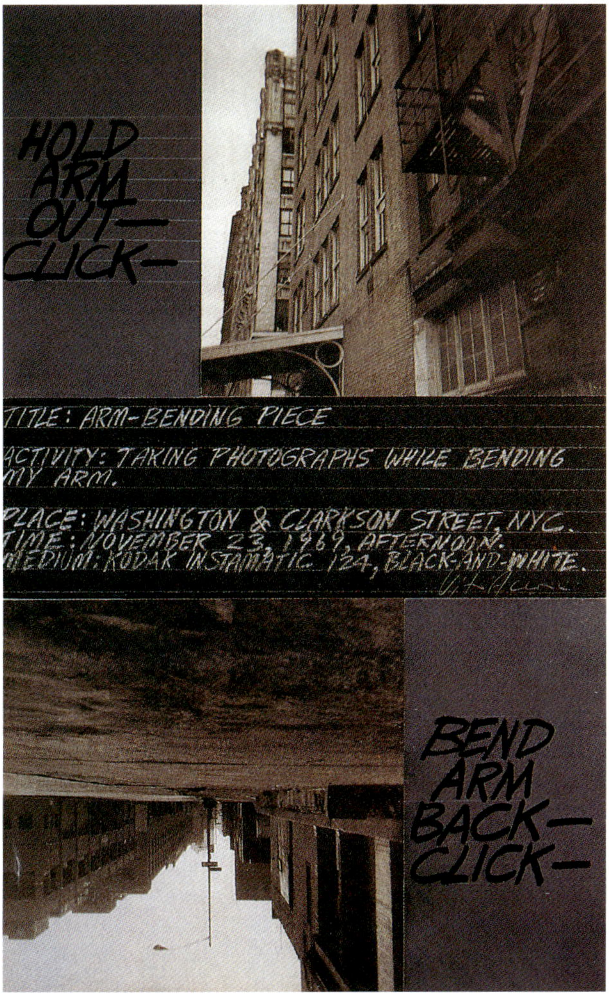

Vito Acconci, *Arm-bending Piece,* 1969.

effects, creating a new framework for understanding the deceits and complexities of the medium. The idea, for example, that one may anticipate the photographic act in planning a performance provided a conceptual basis for what became known as staged photography, emblematized by artists such as Cindy Sherman. And like Sherman, many of the people discussed in this essay adopted a variety of styles in their use of photography, producing highly conceived images one moment and grainy on-the-spot depictions the next. The versatility of photography was perhaps its greatest attribute. Artists discovered that a document could acquire many "looks" while providing the same basic service: rendering visible and permanent the most fleeting forms of art.

The photographs that survive from this period have indeed come to shape our understanding of it, for better or worse. It is clear that the many artists who relied on photography to document their work were thinking in terms of their own historical legacies, and they were wise to do so. Though artists may have scoffed at the photograph as but a meaningless fragment, most wanted their works to be known and remembered. No means was better suited to sealing an artist's fate than photography. As the art of the 1960s and 1970s is resurrected in catalogues and history books, the reproduced photographic image is ubiquitous. One cannot imagine a history of this period without the photograph—not only as evidence of what happened but also as a nostalgic return to a moment that can never be recuperated.

1. Quoted in David Campany, "Conceptual Art History or a Home for *Homes for America*," in *Rewriting Conceptual Art*, ed. Michael Newman and Jon Bird (London: Reaktion Books, 1999), 133; my emphasis.

2. Jeff Wall, "'Marks of Indifference': Aspects of Photography in, or as, Conceptual Art," in *Reconsidering the Object of Art: 1965–1975*, exh. cat., by Ann Goldstein and Anne Rorimer (Los Angeles: The Museum of Contemporary Art, Los Angeles; Cambridge: The MIT Press, 1995), 252. In this essay, Wall addresses the use of photography as an anti-aesthetic for artists during the 1960s. Focusing on the appeal of photographic amateurism for Conceptualists, Wall investigates the notion of skill (and its absence) for artists using the medium.

3. Lawrence Alloway, "Artists and Photographs," *Studio International* (April 1970): 163. Alloway distinguishes between photographs as documentation and as source art—that is, art in its own right.

4. The historical legacy of Namuth's photographs is outlined in Pepe Karmel's "Pollock at Work: The Films and Photographs of Hans Namuth," in *Jackson Pollock*, by Kirk Varnedoe (New York: The Museum of Modern Art, 1999), 97.

5. For an assessment of this photograph as a "portrait of the artist at work," see Rosalind Krauss, "Richard Serra Sculpture," in *Richard Serra: Sculpture*, exh. cat., ed. Laura Rosenstock (New York: The Museum of Modern Art, 1986).

6. See John Roberts, "Photography, Iconophobia, and the Ruins of Conceptual Art," in *The Impossible Document: Photography and Conceptual Art in Britain, 1966–1976*, ed. John Roberts (London: Camerawork, 1997), 14. The statement was originally published in Kosuth's introductory note to *Art-Language* 1, no. 2 (1970).

7. Robert Morris, interview by Patricia Norvell, May 16, 1969; reprinted in *Recording Conceptual Art*, ed. Alexander Alberro and Patricia Norvell (Berkeley and Los Angeles: University of California Press, 2001), 59.

8. Vito Acconci, "Notes on My Photographs, 1969–1970," in *Vito Acconci*, ed. Kate Linker (New York: Brooke Alexander, 1988), unpaginated.

9. In her essay "The Photographic Idea: Reconsidering Conceptual Photography," *Afterimage* 25, no. 6 (1999), Lucy Soutter compares the use of photography by those considered "artists" and those considered "photographers," illustrating their shared interest in subverting the conventions of photographic vision. She reveals the biases against photography by writing, "taking artists at their word, writers have also been able to divorce conceptual photography from this history of photography more broadly, maintaining a rigid distinction between conceptual and fine art photography of the same moment" (8).

10. Robert Morris, "The Present Tense of Space," originally published in *Art in America* (January/February 1978); reprinted in *Continuous Project Altered Daily: The Writings of Robert Morris* (Cambridge: The MIT Press, 1993), 201–2, 178.

11. Susan Sontag, *On Photography* (New York: Farrar, Straus and Giroux, 1977), 9.

12. Alloway, "Artists and Photographs," 163.

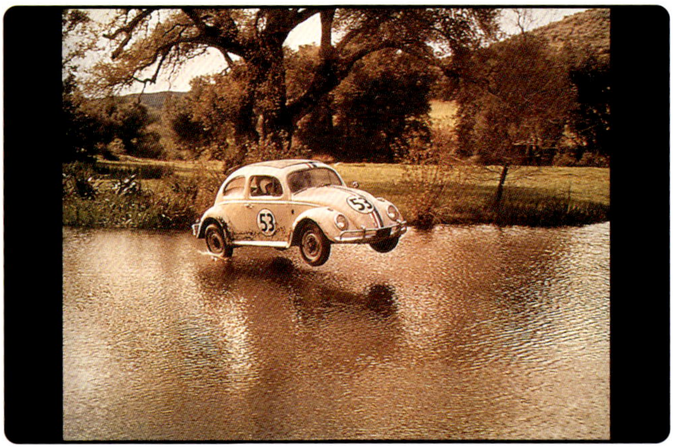

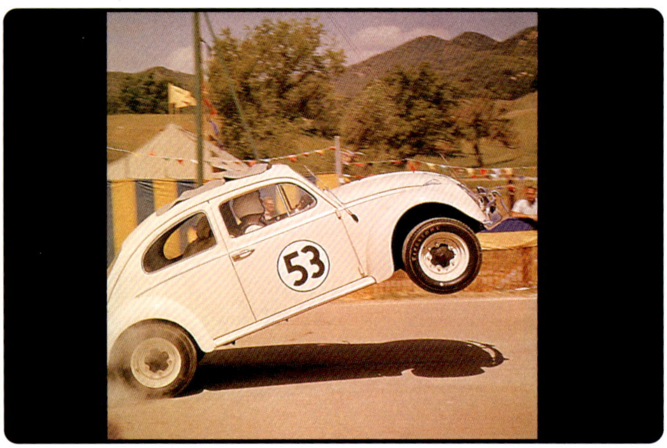

Herbie the Love Bug.

Herbie Goes Bananas: Fantasies of Leisure and Labor from the New Left to the New Economy

CHRIS GILBERT

I can relate myself humanly to a thing, only if the thing relates itself to the human being humanly. —Karl Marx

IN THE 1969 Disney movie *The Love Bug*, a self-propelled Volkswagen Beetle called Herbie is the motive principle of the plot. A mechanized id, the "bug" follows a law of its own that is in sharp contrast to the stuffy, workaday world around it. *The Love Bug* was in many ways Disney's nod to the alternative, "hippy" lifestyle that permeated the culture and much of cultural production that year. Although the VW Beetle was a self-chosen icon of that counterculture, the film's portrayal is not always generous: a pair of idiotic "longhairs" at a drive-in and a dumbfounded policeman accused of spending too much time with the Haight-Ashbury crowd are typical of its backhandedness. As Herbie, however, the vehicle becomes a pleasure-seeking, subversive, yet mainstream hero—to the extent that when asked what the little car's secret is, Buddy Hackett, playing the Buddhist mechanic who is Herbie's best friend, can give a flower child's response: "Heart."

The Love Bug was extremely popular, ultimately ranking as Disney's top-grossing film of all time after *Mary Poppins* (1964). The original film spawned three sequels: *Herbie Rides Again* (1974), *Herbie Goes to Monte Carlo* (1977), and *Herbie Goes Bananas* (1980). What may have accounted for the enormous success of the Herbie movies (apart from Disney's savvy marketing) was how the films, while remaining mainstream, skillfully negotiated key concerns from the 1960s through the 1970s about leisure, work, pleasure, and play. In the course of almost seven hours of running time, the Herbie films touched upon such issues as the alienation of people in their work and the possibility of a society in which labor is integrated with leisure. This concern with the laborer's lifeworld provides a surprising connection to the contemporary theorists of the New Left—among these, the car's namesake, critical theorist Herbert Marcuse (1898–1979)—as well as vanguard artists of the period. All, to vary-

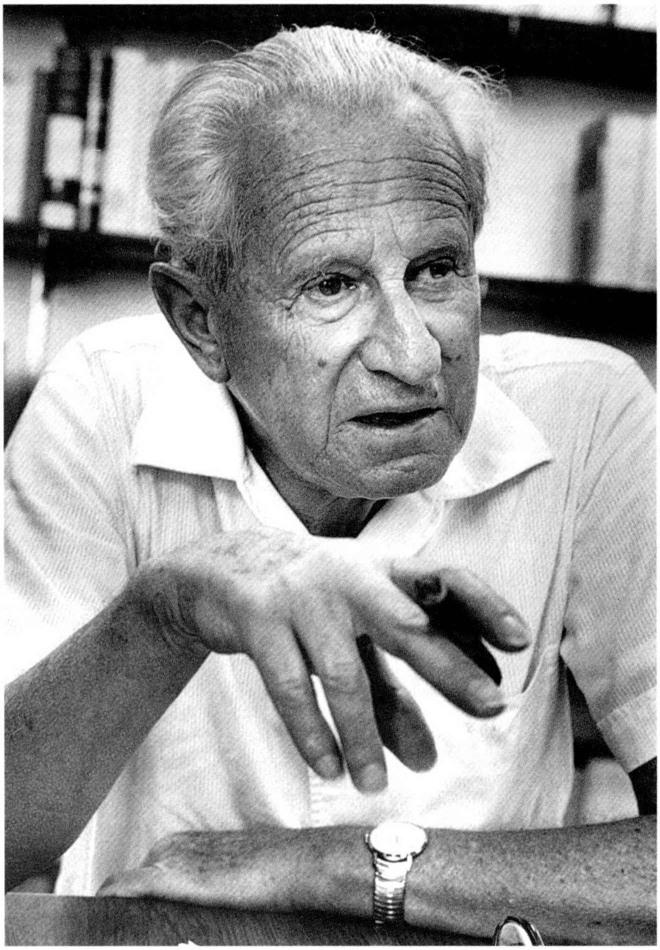

Herbert Marcuse. AP/Wide World Photos.

ing degrees, were engaged with the social issues couched in Hollywood myth that were at the core of these films and their crazed plots hinging on the leisure-mixed-with-work enterprise of automobile racing.

Cinematic fictions of the 1960s and 1970s are extremely important. Far from being mere cultural oddities, imagined fusions of leisure and labor in the films of these decades were central to a countercultural push to redefine work, relocate it nearer the domain of pleasure, and free it from strictly instrumental or "productivist" determinations. These fantasies would, of course, be differently inflected in other parts of film production—in, for example, the counter-idyllic visions of Jean-Luc Godard's *Weekend* (1967)—but the Herbie films are useful because they were widely distributed and span more than a decade. Hence, they serve to frame a comprehensive discussion of an era's shifting fantasies of the life free from industrial labor. That discussion will touch on key points of the American social *imaginaire*, ranging from the domestic utopias of the New Left to the obfuscation of labor that underpins the globalized post-1980 economy. It is primarily a story about work, play, and leisure, but it is also about the relations between human beings and objects in a world where the pleasure principle, rather than the reality principle, reigns supreme.

> *Without a real car, I'm only half a man.*
>
> —Jim Douglas

The first Herbie movie, *The Love Bug*, is a story of reconciliation with mass-produced objects in which the fantasies of the life without toil and the "friendly" commodity play a pivotal role. Adapting the formula of screwball comedies such as *My Man Godfrey* (1936) and *Bringing Up Baby* (1938), *The Love Bug* follows a down-on-his-luck racer, Jim Douglas, pitting his genial VW Beetle repeatedly against the high-tech cars of the villainous British driver, Peter Thorndyke. After a series of perils that include Herbie's losing two wheels and several unnervingly literal cliffhangers, Douglas lands the girl and the prize money. By the film's conclusion, he has secured the real object of his affection—the car—from Thorndyke's greedy clutches and underhanded schemes.

To connect this Hollywood plot (which, on a basic level, is a story about objects and how objects mediate human relations) to New Left ideas about work requires backing up in history and charting the emergence of these ideologies. Although the utopian thought of Marcuse, who is sometimes considered the father of the New Left, became well known in the 1960s, this body of ideas had its origins in the 1920s and 1930s, within the horizon of a rediscovery of the work of the young Karl Marx.[1] A key text in the newly recovered material was *The German Ideology*, written in 1844, when Marx was just twenty-seven. In this text (which Marx and Engels abandoned in manuscript form), Marx looks forward to the day when it will be possible "to do one thing today and another tomorrow, to hunt in the morning, fish in the afternoon, rear cattle in the evening, criticise after dinner, just as I have a mind."[2] This idyllic passage is not anomalous. Marx's writing up until about 1848—key texts of which were published for the first time during Marcuse's student years—frequently references a future world in which labor is no longer constrained and imposed and in which man will enjoy a liberated existence founded on self-fulfilling activities. In this free condition, human existence will be "naturalized," and nature and the object humanized. Marx's notion of the humanized object, far from being a mere supplement or footnote, is central to his vision of future human-object relations: the *humanized* object in the life of unconstrained labor will ultimately replace the cruelly impersonal and alien objects produced under the conditions of industrial labor. Although a full discussion of Marx's concept of estrangement *(Entfremdung)* is beyond the scope of this essay, it suffices to say that under capitalism, labor is seen as drawing off man's vitality and forming it into expropriable objects that are for that reason strange to him.

Marx's utopian speculations (later elaborated by Marcuse) may have had little political currency from their "discovery" in the 1930s through the 1950s—a time when the antirevolutionary stance of Stalinism dominated communist parties in Europe. By the late 1960s, however, such ideals were ready to "ride again" under the aegis of a "new" Left. At the forefront of this revival was, unsurprisingly, Marcuse: by this time, Marcuse had relocated to the United States, first to Brandeis University and then in 1965 to UC San Diego. Marcuse's ideas, formed two decades earlier in Germany, hinged on a return to the fantasies of the leisure life in communist society that Marx himself had suppressed in his later work, believing that they jeopardized the scientific character of socialism. In a series of very popular publications, including *Eros and Civilization* (1955) and *One Dimensional Man* (1964), Marcuse told the story of how proposed utopias of leisure, instead of being unscientific and insubstantial imaginings (as orthodox Marxists had come to believe), were now actually feasible, given modern technological advances. Utopian possibilities were "inherent in the technical forces of advanced capitalism and socialism," though suppressed.[3] They needed only a new configuration of government, the end of an unnecessary social system based on repression and exploitation, and a new sensibility to bring them into being.

In the generally utopian mood of the 1960s, such ideals resonated deeply. They hooked up with the period's fine art (especially its more positivist moments, offering such ideals as the dematerialization of art and the transcendence of traditional genres) and, as we have indicated, its popular cultural production. Given cinema's position as *the* popular medium, it is hardly a stretch to say that Marcuse's technologically driven utopias are embodied in the Herbie movies' vision of technology. Recall that this vision posited a technological entity liberated to the point of anthropomorphism and the spectacularly optimistic vision of a car that drives itself, even supplying gratuitous wheelies. The parallels run deeper, however. The visualization of this technologically driven liberation—the car's numerous antics and driving stunts—results in "trippy" imagery that loosely parallels the "surrealistic forms of protest" of the 1960s, such as burning draft cards and giving flowers to the police, that Marcuse saw as hallmarks of the antirationalist "new sensibility."[4] Further, Herbie himself is a consummate "humanized object," replete with personable qualities and cute responsiveness. If the car's winks and honks seem to foreshadow the cozy eroticism of our present-day user-friendly technology, they also parallel the humanizing of technology's instrumental and mechanical qualities that Marcuse at the time was calling for as an "aesthetic reduction."[5]

> *After the revolution, who's going to pick up the garbage on Monday morning?* —Mierle Laderman Ukeles

Mierle Laderman Ukeles's question, though uttered in 1969, seems to sum up proleptically the disillusionment, on all levels, of the decade that was to come. Amid the block-long gas lines of the early 1970s, one was hard-pressed to construe a car as anything other than an economic proposition—certainly not an object that "relates itself to the human being humanly." It was also a time in which socially transformative ideologies—not least a vision of leisure and labor synthesized—seemed untenable. Fittingly, the two Herbie movies made during this decade, *Herbie Rides Again* and *Herbie Goes to Monte Carlo*, show the strains on the Herbie myth as the popular utopian ideals of the 1960s (and those of the New Left in particular) went into retreat. The first sequel, made a year after the Watergate scandal erupted, takes us into a bleak and distinctly anti-utopian story in which both Herbie and his owner's house are threatened by a real estate developer's ambition to create an eponymous "Hawk Plaza." The film ends with a *deus ex machina* rescue of the house reminiscent of the Western genre cliché of a cavalry rescue. The blatant escapism of that ending, which is typical of *Herbie Rides Again*, is also symptomatic of 1970s and 1980s popular culture, in which the myths of the past, of Westerns, and of comic books would brace up a social fabric that had endured defeat in Vietnam and a serious recession.

The widespread difficulties and concerns of the time over the way work could function registered in a less escapist, more openly problematic manner in contemporary fine art production. Vanguard artists of the late 1960s through the 1970s, from Art & Language to Ian Wilson, were, as a rule, obsessed with the idea of work. In their discussions, which were informed by readings in both the Old and New Left (Marcuse included), the word "work" itself was bandied about and stretched as artists complained, paradoxically, of being both "out of work" and overworked. Some even thought that they formed a "new proletariat." Others peppered their talk with neologisms such as "artworkers" and "workeritus."[6] If the period's fascination with labor was told in snapshots, key images would have to include artists dressed in overalls, work boots, and Levi's or engrossed in the labor histories of Eric Hobsbawm and E. P. Thompson. In one telling instance, Seth Siegelaub's "Office Show" (1969) featured a group of Conceptual artists emulating the capacities of office workers.

In part, the extensive play given at this time to the term "work" and its cognates results simply from a generalization of the term's meaning. This semantic shift is traceable to developments in late Modernism that led to art's losing its medium specificity—or so Joseph Kosuth argued, convincing many, in 1969[7]—to become a generic art function that is no longer essentially connected to any material base. Instead of "painting" and "sculpture," then, "work" expands in common usage to cover both, and in so doing slips neatly between referring to *work as object* and *work as action*. In the latter sense, the term begins to denote a wide range of activities

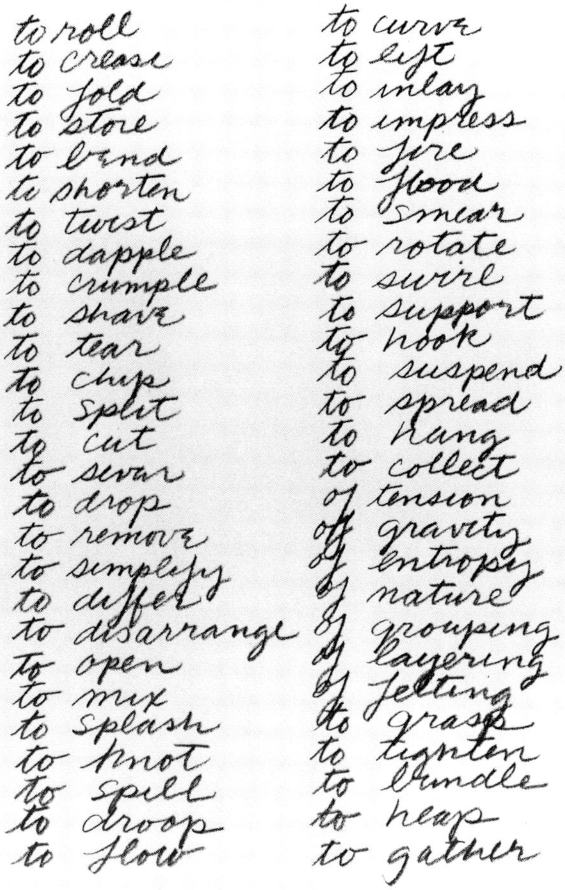

to roll
to crease
to fold
to store
to bend
to shorten
to twist
to dapple
to crumple
to shave
to tear
to chip
to split
to cut
to sever
to drop
to remove
to simplify
to differ
to disarrange
to open
to mix
to splash
to knot
to spill
to droop
to flow
to curve
to lift
to inlay
to impress
to fire
to flood
to smear
to rotate
to swirl
to support
to hook
to suspend
to spread
to hang
to collect
of tension
of gravity
of entropy
of nature
of grouping
of layering
of felting
to grasp
to tighten
to bundle
to heap
to gather

Richard Serra, *Verb List,* 1967–68.

(cf. Richard Serra's 1967–68 list of process verbs including "to crease," "to tear," "to spill") that are by no means specific to art. But while the *work of art* may, as a result of its widening reference in the 1960s, have increasingly come to seem one thing—like labor itself under capitalism—there was no consensus about the value of this work and its redeeming qualities from the late 1960s to the mid-1970s. Indeed, the lack of consensus may be indexed to an ideological divisiveness in the broader culture.

The extremes of this array in fine art are worth noting. At one pole, a number of artists actually ceased production. These artists' (usually temporary) abandonment of art making can be linked to Marcuse's notion of the "Great Refusal," the rejection of liberal

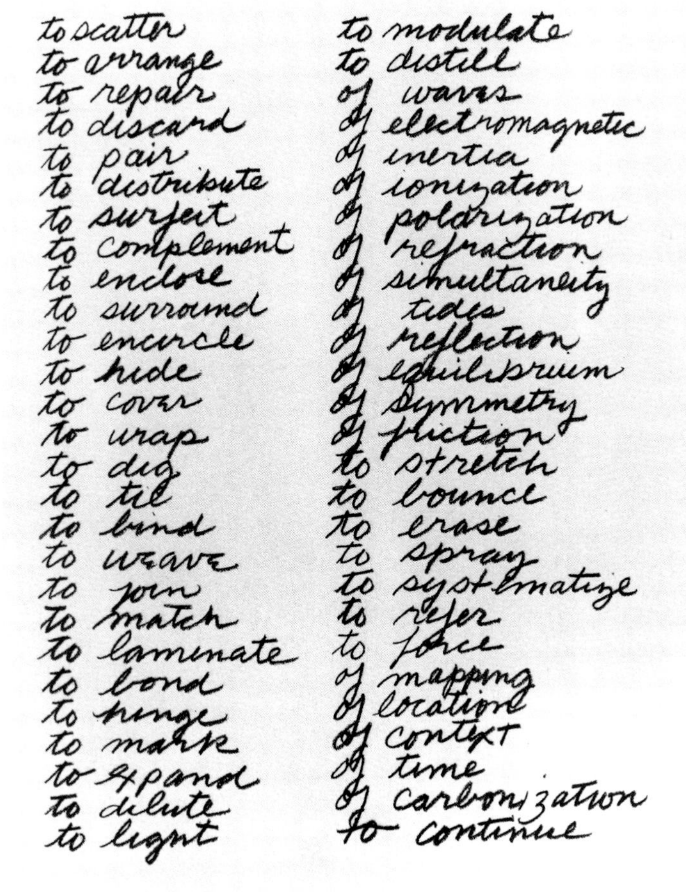

Richard Serra, *Verb List,* 1967–68.

"affirmative" culture the philosopher first outlined in *Eros and Civilization.* (An exemplary decision of this kind, to come back to the world of Herbie, might be one that leads to becoming a Buddhist mechanic instead of a real estate developer.)[8] Usually this rejection is taken to focus on mainstream society, but for Marcuse it could just as well target most forms of art making, which he found inadequate because they were overly reactive and negational.[9] The list of artists who either stopped working or shifted their work considerably in this period is remarkably long. Among those who had a hiatus in their activity are Jannis Kounellis (1965 to 1967), Adrian Piper (who gave up making objects in 1970 and reprised it only later in the decade), and Marcel Duchamp (in some ways the grandfather of so many 1960s artists, he had officially given up painting since 1923 and was devoting himself to chess as well as secretly working on *Etants Donné*).

Not exactly giving up but altering their practices considerably, Lygia Clark and Hélio Oiticica went from painting to more bizarre and interactive practices that held out liberating agendas, while Ed Ruscha stopped painting from 1969 to 1971 to create his funkiest work ever—a series of "drawings" with unusual materials such as gunpowder and fruit juice. At the other extreme are artists who embraced work and the fantasies of work. Here we find a rift between those who adopted blue-collar personae (Carl Andre, Richard Serra, and Frank Stella) and others who developed the pose of "suits" (Gilbert and George, Mario Merz, and Frank Stella again). Some among those who embraced leisure may have celebrated mere hedonism, like Tom Marioni with his beer-drinking performances *(The Act of Drinking Beer with Friends Is the Highest Form of Art).* The majority, however, pursued socially transformative versions of leisure, paralleling Marcuse's notion that the impulse to Great Refusal under the guidance of reason could have critical potential. Key among these artists were Hélio Oiticica, with his concept of *Crelazer,* or creative leisure, as well as Lee Lozano, who wielded the idea of systematic withdrawal from the art world as a "total personal and public revolution" and actually carried out her program according to a rigorous schedule.[10]

The remarkable convergence of the ideals of artists and the New Left may lead us to think that this was a time of consensus. But ideologically, it was a moment of crisis for art—"Modernism's nervous breakdown," as Mel Ramsden of the Art & Language group called the period. The large rifts and multiple fissures among artists of the time are mirrored in the post-1969 near debacle of Leftist ideology that, especially in Marcuse's case, foundered in popularity in the wake of the routed student movement. During the course of the 1970s, a shared sense emerged among artists and political radicals of the unlikelihood of a world without commodities and the unworkability of any real synthesis of leisure and labor. To posit garbage collection as the stumbling block of the revolution, as Ukeles did in 1969, aptly summarized the "realistic" spirit of the time. By the end of the

1970s, the culture seemed primed for a depoliticized postmodernism, prefigured in the nostalgic rather than utopian Herbie films of the decade, and the new global economy's settlements with labor.

> *[As] the highly rational societies of the Renaissance felt the need to create Utopias, we of our times must create fables.* —Francis Alÿs

The effects of the global economy deeply inform *Herbie Goes Bananas* (1980), the last of the sequels, which quite literally takes a new direction—one that leads far from the homegrown utopianism of the New Left into a new world both of oppression and of new possibilities for resistance. Instead of a "First World" (U.S. and European) drama, the movie is framed by a trip to the south, as the protagonists cruise on board the *Sun Princess* from Mexico's Puerto Vallarta though Panama (avoiding Nicaragua, where just the year before the Sandinista revolution had erupted). They are diverted from their final destination (the "Grand Premio of Brazil" in Rio de Janeiro) into a madcap race through what appears, despite the presence of Inca ruins, to be an Amazonian jungle. The plot's shift toward the tropics might be taken to reflect both a general migration of North American fantasies of leisure in a southerly direction (in global tourism) and its insidious obverse—the grim reality that these touristic fantasies screen—in the real displacement of labor in that direction that began to intensify in the late 1970s. An apt summary of the formula that underpins both the 1980s Herbie and the new leisure life in the era of globalization is the metaphor of the cruise ship's southern passage, in which the lower latitudes come to be the mythical locus of both labor and pleasure fantasies. In this complex trope, which reconciles leisure and labor by dividing them along class and geographic lines, the tropics become the site of mute toil (heavily mythologized as banana production) as well as tourists' leisure and play (a place for *going bananas*). The relatively static class divisions of the new global economy—which, interestingly, include a real-life shift of VW production at this time in a southerly direction—are reflected in *Herbie Goes Bananas*'s plotline. In true *Love Boat* fashion, the story proposes no fusion of labor and leisure in the middlebrow activity of car racing and is instead framed as a mere pleasure cruise.

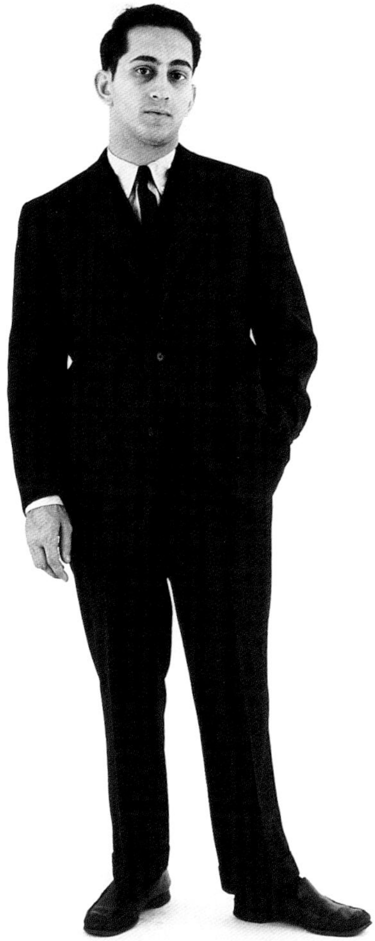

Hollis Frampton, *Frank Stella,* 1959. Collection Walker Art Center, Minneapolis, gift of Marion Faller.

The effects of the new global order inform not only the film's plot but also its characters. Hence, the plot's dynamism comes not from a technological entity—marking a difference from the Herbie car that stood at the nexus of technological and utopian aspirations—but a human character, a Mexican child called "Paco." Paco is Herbie's sidekick throughout the movie and frequently usurps the limelight.[11] An incurable trickster like Herbie, he is also a plausible

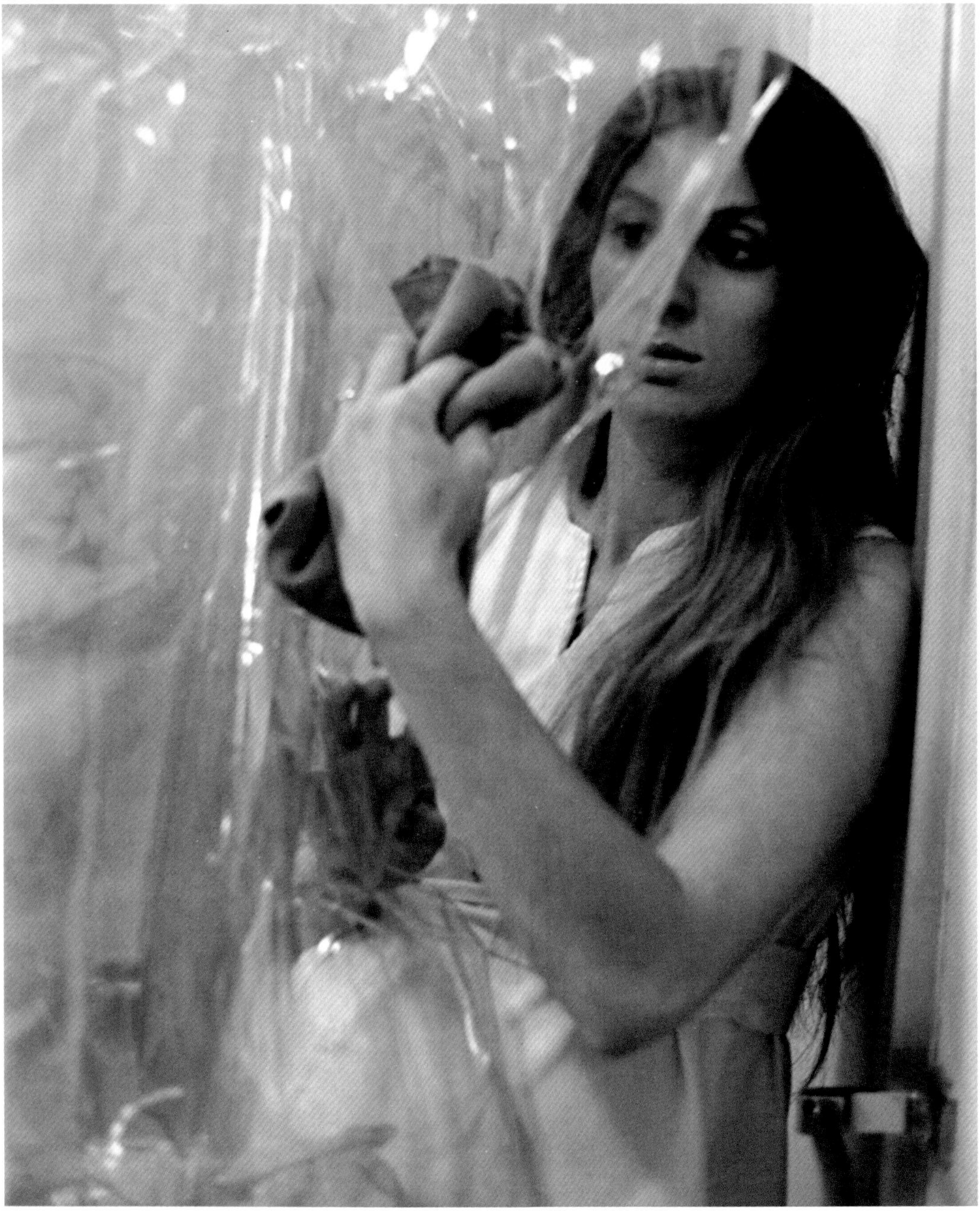

Mierle Laderman Ukeles, *Private Performances of Personal Maintenance as Art,* 1970–73. Photograph: Jack Ukeles.

living street kid, inhabiting a world dominated by Western powers, one in which no viable utopias exist. In this "realist" spirit, the linchpin of the *Bananas* story is no longer a sweeping utopian *Love Bug* fusion of work and leisure that follows from a carefully orchestrated, almost Hegelian reconciliation between subject and object, but it is decidedly post-utopian and post-Marxist. It turns on Paco's incessantly creative actions throughout the film, which, while they serve mostly for comic relief, are also reminiscent of the tactics of *making do* of the weak in the world of the strong that cultural theorist Michel de Certeau deploys to contest both the global utopianism of Marxism and the antitransformational stance of postmodern theorists such as Michel Foucault. These everyday tactics include diverting work time in *la perruque* and other nonproductive activities that resist, as Paco does in the film, the rationalization of behavior that serves an oppressor.[12]

Such tactics could be called an "art of operating," and indeed interesting connections exist among Paco's actions in this mainstream film and comparable forms of subversion by a group of nonutopian and nonrevolutionary contemporary artists. These artists' practices unravel the workaday world, not in its entirety nor with the hope of fully tossing it off, but instead inflecting and altering that world in its moments—in its capillaries, as it were, rather than in its arteries or veins. We have noted the impasse that seemed to mark 1970s art and politics with regard to labor—how proposed general resolutions of leisure and labor lost credibility. For more than a decade, artists were unable to formulate lasting solutions to the conflict of leisure and labor. There remain, then, only less ambitious subversive actions that may be "artful" but are not exactly artistic. In this spirit, Paco in the last Herbie film takes on smaller forms of resistance than the car protagonist he replaces. His work (of "making do") consists of a variety of sometimes absurd activities, such as picking the pockets of his North American friends, bullfighting with the car, fishing in muddy canals, and living for a while in Herbie's trunk.

One of the contemporary artists whose work falls under this general rubric of subversive artistry is Francis Alÿs. Alÿs's "tactics" include promoting tourism as a profession, as he did in *Turista*, and drugged ambles *(Paseos)* through urban environments. Another comparison is to be found in the work of Austrian artist Erwin Wurm,

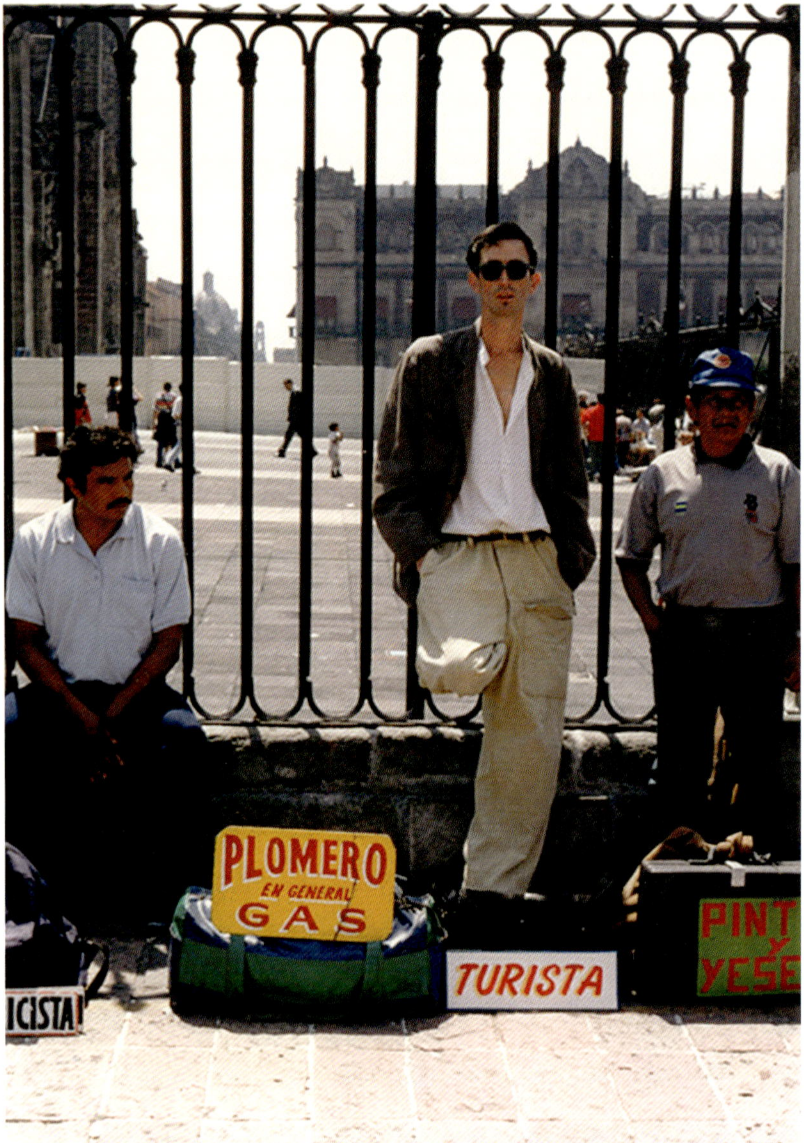

Francis Alÿs, *Turista*, 1997.

whose understated participatory events with ordinary objects include pointlessly having viewers sit on a bed of oranges, position toilet paper rolls on their rear ends, or press beach balls and buckets to the wall with their heads—works that are brought together in the series of *One Minute Sculptures* made from 1988 to 1998. Alÿs's absurd inactivities and Wurm's unproductive actions with consumer objects are surely not labor and certainly not obviously leisure, nor are they the synthesis of the two in any lasting sense. But the actions of both can be seen as limiting cases of Marx's idea of labor as self-chosen activity and latter-day versions of Marcuse's dream of the creative, not always rational actions of the "new sensibility." In any case, their oeuvres provide us with a primer in the micro-strategies of resistance that have come in our time to seem the most viable radical alternative to the utopias of the New Left—or, for that matter, of Disney.

1. Richard Wolin, *Heidegger's Children: Hannah Arendt, Karl Löwith, Hans Jonas, and Herbert Marcuse* (Princeton: Princeton University Press, 2001), 139–42.

2. Karl Marx, "The German Ideology," trans. S. Ryazanskaya, in *The Marx-Engels Reader*, ed. Robert C. Tucker (New York: W. W. Norton, 1978), 124.

3. Herbert Marcuse, *An Essay on Liberation* (Boston: Beacon Press, 1969), 4.

4. Ibid., 30. The phrase "surrealistic forms of protest" and the examples of burning draft cards and giving flowers to the police are Marcuse's own.

5. Herbert Marcuse, *One Dimensional Man: Studies in the Ideology of Advanced Industrial Society* (Boston: Beacon Press, 1964), 239–40.

6. The proletarianization of classes other than blue-collar workers was an idea promoted by members of Art & Language: see "The Lumpen Headache," in *Fox 3* (New York: Art & Language Foundation, 1976), 6–8.

7. See the "Function of Art" section of Kosuth's "Art After Philosophy" in Joseph Kosuth, *Art After Philosophy and After: Collected Writings* (Cambridge: The MIT Press, 1991), 15–24.

8. For a discussion of Marcuse's ambivalent use of this phrase, see Paul Breines, "Revisiting Marcuse with Foucault: *An Essay on Liberation* Meets *The History of Sexuality*," in *Marcuse: From the New Left to the Next Left*, ed. John Bokina and Timothy J. Lukes (Lawrence: University Press of Kansas, 1994), 47–48.

9. Marcuse, *Essay on Liberation*, 47–48.

10. Simon Osthoff, "Lygia Clark and Hélio Oiticica: A Legacy of Interactivity and Participation for a Telematic Future," in *Corpus Delecti: Performance Art of the Americas*, ed. Coco Fusco (London: Routledge, 2000), 165–66; Lee Lozano, *General Strike Piece, Feb. 8, 1969*.

11. This plot device of the Mexican child as Herbie's sidekick is telling—perhaps more telling than had been intended. Volkswagen production had increasingly begun to shift toward manufacturing plants in Mexico; in the late 1970s, an expansion of facilities in Puebla allowed Volkswagen de Mexico to move into manufacture for both U.S. and German markets. (Until then, most North American Volkswagens had been made in a plant in Westmoreland, Pennsylvania, which would close in 1987.) See Roberto Garcia, "Volkswagen de Mexico: Toward Conversion to World-Class Performance," posted online at <http://www.umich.edu/~cibe/Casestudyabstracts.html>. Some of the results of Mexican production, models such as the 1200 Beetle made only in Mexico, are shown in the film. I owe this insight to Phil Matthews's in-depth discussions of the vehicles used in the making of the Herbie movies at <http://www.clubvw.org.au>.

12. Michel de Certeau, *The Practice of Everyday Life* (Berkeley and Los Angeles: University of California Press, 1984). *La perruque* (literally, "wig") refers to the practice of performing one's own work on the job. De Certeau's examples include a secretary writing a love letter on company time and a cabinetmaker "borrowing" a lathe to make a piece of furniture for his living room (25).

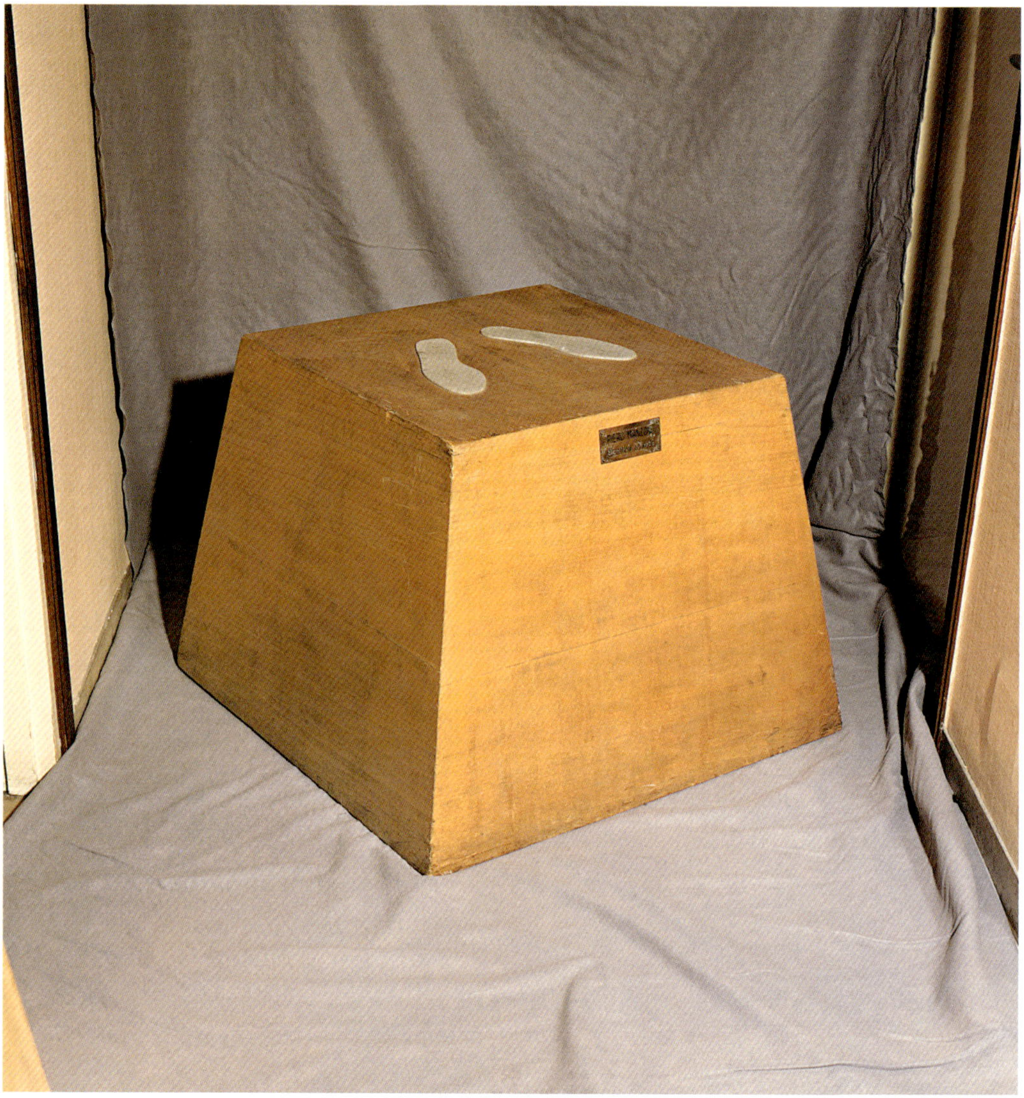

Piero Manzoni, *Base Magica,* 1961.

Exchange Rate: On Obligation and Reciprocity in Some Art of the 1960s and After

MIWON KWON

IN THE FACE of a plethora of visual art experiments of the late 1960s—all tamed by now into discrete categories, such as Conceptual art, Land art, Happenings, Performance, Process art, activist art—the influential art historian and critic Lucy Lippard proposed the overarching concept of "dematerialization" as a means to understand their collective motivation. She predicted in her 1968 essay "The Dematerialization of Art":

> As more and more work is designed in the studio but executed elsewhere by professional craftsmen, as the object becomes merely the end product, a number of artists are losing interest in the physical evolution of the work of art. The studio is again becoming a study. Such a trend appears to be provoking a profound dematerialization of art, especially art as object, and if it continues to prevail, it may result in the object's becoming wholly obsolete.[1]

Listing an eclectic array of what she called "post-aesthetic" works from this period—including Robert Rauschenberg's erasure of a Willem de Kooning drawing, Yves Klein's "empty gallery" show in Paris, On Kawara's daily date paintings, Joseph Kosuth's photostat *Art as Idea as Idea*, Christine Kozlov's open film canister with a reel of transparent film inside, Hans Haacke's condensation and frost sculptures, Robert Smithson's maps and earthworks, Ed Ruscha's books, George Brecht's "events," and Ray Johnson's mailings, among many others—Lippard acknowledged the moment as indicating a major art-historical shift.[2] Away from art as product to art as idea or art as action, she declared.

Reflecting back on this moment in the introduction to the 1997 reissue of her book *Six Years: The Dematerialization of the Art Object from 1966 to 1972*, in which a wider range and a longer list of art projects and publications are inventoried, Lippard elaborated further on the dematerialization principle, emphasizing its political significance.[3] Partly quoting herself from 1969, she wrote:

> Anti-establishment fervor in the 1960s focused on the demythologization and de-commodification of art, on the need for an independent (or "alternative") art that could not be bought and sold by the greedy sector that owned everything that was exploiting the world and promoting the Vietnam War. "The artists who are trying to do non-object art are introducing a drastic solution to the problems of artists being bought and sold so easily, along with their art."[4]

Which is to say, dematerialized art, in which the "idea is paramount and the material form is secondary, lightweight, ephemeral, cheap, unpretentious,"[5] is viewed as a strategic subversion of the commercialization of art and the commodification of the art object. In 1968, Lippard had reasoned that "since dealers cannot sell art-as-idea, economic materialism is denied along with physical materialism."[6]

Such a claim, energizing and generation-defining at the time, seems poignantly utopian now. Clearly, dealers *have* figured out how to sell art-as-idea or art-as-action. The reconstitution of art that seemed dematerialized in the late 1960s via what Lippard called its "epilogue," the residual materials that physically evidence the idea or action in the form of a proposal, instruction, "score," relic, souvenir, or documentation, is a commonplace in today's art market.[7] The very nature of the market economy has also shifted since the late 1960s, and immaterial, invisible aspects, such as services, information, and "experience," are now quantifiable units of measure to gauge economic productivity, growth, and profit.[8] Ideas and actions do not debilitate or escape the market system because they are dematerialized; they drive it precisely because so. Despite these profoundly changed realities, however, which inevitably recast the wisdom of certain political ambitions of 1960s and 1970s art, the presumption that dematerialization = anticommodity still persists in structuring contemporary art discourse. This is not to cast the past investment in dematerialization as a historical mistake on the grounds that it failed to escape the commodity system or did not understand it well enough. Rather, given the conceptual impasse of the equation (denial of physical materialism = denial of economic materialism) and the changed historical circumstances, we might approach again the art of the 1960s and 1970s with a different set of questions or frames of reference.

In concert with *Work Ethic*'s ambition to present a major reconsideration of the art of this period, specifically through the lens of the changing status of work and artistic labor, this essay sketches some issues pertaining to a related problematic, the nature of exchange. My working hypothesis is as follows. Much of so-called dematerialized art may have complicated the conventional methods of buying and selling art by not conforming to an agreeable and readily exchangeable commodity form. But the radicality, or the intelligence, of such art does not merely lie in its non-object status; the negation of the object form is not an automatic challenge to the abstraction of commodity exchange. I would argue that of greater significance is the fact that many works from the 1960s and 1970s and later—art as idea, art as action, Conceptual art, Performance art, Happenings, and so on—attempt to install alternative models of exchange that counter, complicate, or parody the dominant market- and profit-based system of exchange.[9] In fact, many of them engage the logic of the gift economy as one such alternative. By this I mean that the artwork in such cases functions as a mechanism to instigate social exchanges or interactions that specifically put into motion a circuit of obligation and reciprocity, typically involved in giving, receiving or accepting, and giving in return. Furthermore, in addition to reorganizing the position and relationship of the art maker and art audience in a general sense, such artwork, through the process of exchange, tests each person's sense of honor and dishonor, shame, power, risk, fear, status, humiliation, and prestige.

> *[The] giver's undeclared calculation has to reckon with the receiver's undeclared calculation, and hence satisfy his expectations without appearing to know what they are.* —Pierre Bourdieu

Let's consider the following works drawn from the *Work Ethic* exhibition. On a typewritten piece of paper, Alison Knowles humbly suggests (or sternly demands, depending on how one interprets the statement), "Make a salad." Piero Manzoni builds a pedestal for view-

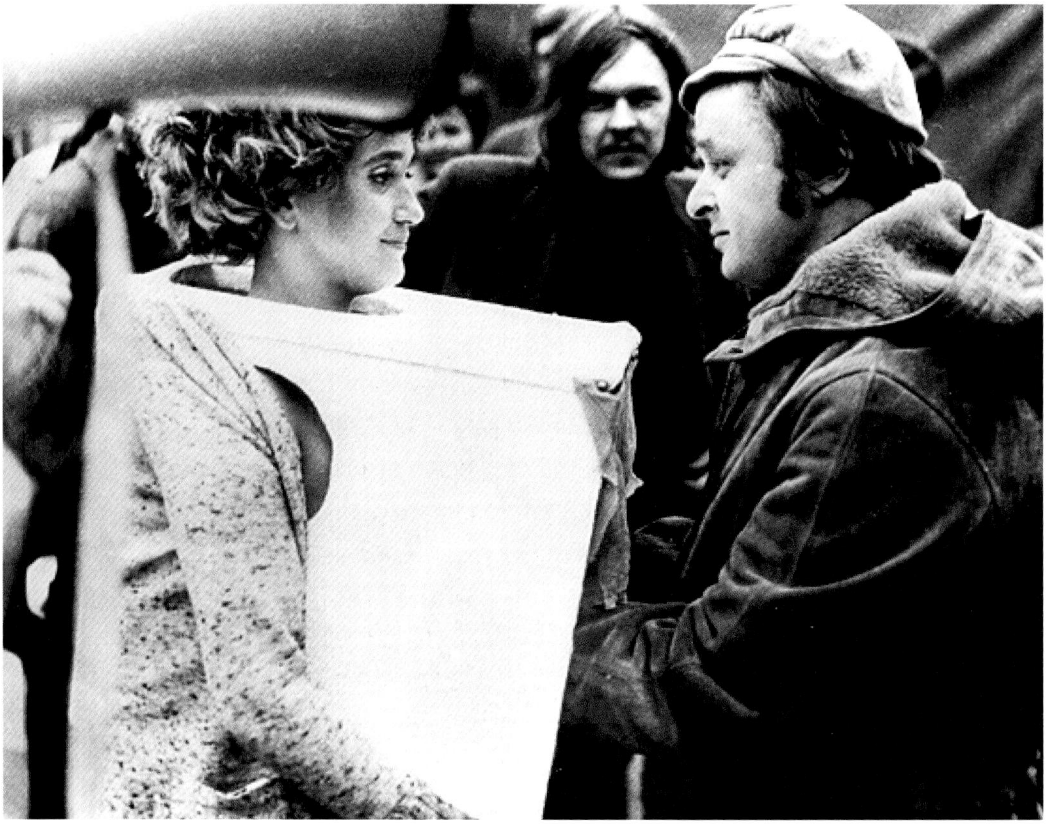

Valie Export (with Peter Weibel), *Tapp und Tastkino (Touch Cinema)*, 1968. Photograph: Werner Schulz.

ers to stand on so that they can be transformed into works of art. Yoko Ono instructs her audience members to cut off pieces of her dress and take the scraps away with them. Eleanor Antin notarizes her plan to leave a group meeting immediately if she fails to address certain persons from behind them. Valie Export bares her breasts inside a modified cardboard box, to be touched, though not seen, by random people on the street. Edward Kienholz proposes in writing several different versions of a "concept tableau" to suit a potential patron's preference and/or pocketbook. Lee Lozano demands of herself that she not participate in any art-related events or activities starting February 8, 1969.

Claiming that artworks such as these engage the logic of the gift is not to say that they are literally gifts. Few of them, indeed, appear to satisfy the conventional definition of the gift as a voluntary act of generosity, even a sacrificial offering, that harbors no expectation of a return in kind or of personal gain on the part of the giver (i.e., Export, Ono).[10] But by invoking the gift economy here, I mean to call attention to the more complex ways in which artworks such as those mentioned above *operate like gifts*, presenting explicit and implicit demands, challenges, invitations, and dares that create an obligation to reciprocate with a suitable response. As we know from the work of Marcel Mauss, the French sociologist and author of the hugely influential *Essai sur le don* (*The Gift* [1924]) as well as subsequent theories of the gift, there is no such thing as a free gift or entirely disinterested, uncalculated giving.[11] And, as recently summarized by anthropologist Maurice Godelier, Mauss teaches us that "the interest of giving-while-appearing-disinterested resides ultimately in one fundamental characteristic of gift-giving, which is that . . . what *creates the obligation to give is that giving creates obligations.*"[12] So the question remains: What kind of obligation do artworks of this kind impose upon their audience? That is, how are we to "reciprocate"?

Sometimes, as in the examples of Antin, Lozano, and Kienholz, the artist gives instructions that obligate him- or herself to fulfill his or her own challenge. These cases present a self-enclosed circuit of obligation and reciprocity that will be beyond the scope of this essay. In other instances, as in the cases of Manzoni, Knowles, Ono, and Export, the viewer/audience is put in an "indebted" position, obligated to respond to the artistic instruction or offering via the avenues prescribed by the works themselves—i.e., engagement, interaction, participation. This kind of situation, in which the audience is given the opportunity to "complete" the work, is usually described as resulting from an artist's self-abnegation. The artist ostensibly gives up to the audience, as if it were a gift, his or her authority of creative authorship. This displacement, often loosely associated with Roland Barthes's well-known notion of the "death of the author" (and the "birth of the reader"), is commonly viewed as a critique of exclusive and elitist cultural values upheld by the art market and mainstream art institutions. Moreover, to borrow Lippard's words, it is generally considered an "attack on the notion of originality, . . . an attack on the genius theory, the hitherto most cherished aspect of patriarchal, ruling-class art."[13] But if we accept this act of relinquishing the privileged right or ownership of artistic author-

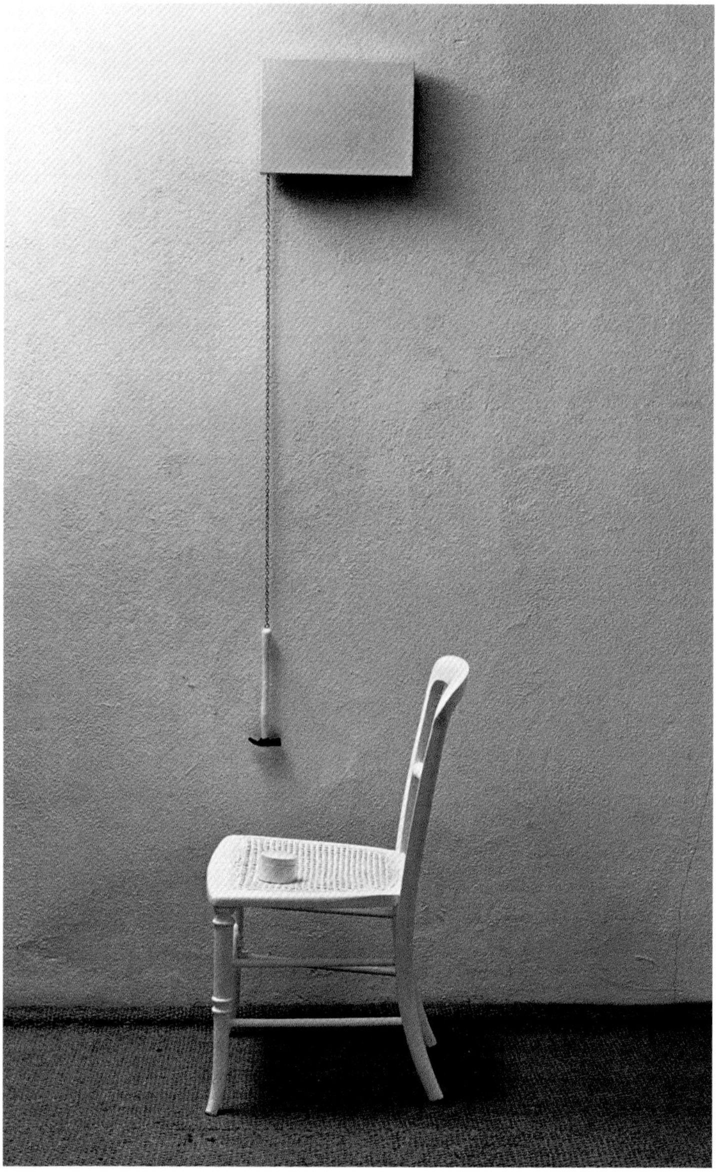

Yoko Ono, *Painting to Hammer a Nail,* 1966.

ship as indeed an act of critical generosity—even as an effort to democratize art, as some have argued[14]—then we must also attend to the full extent of the paradoxical condition that this act actualizes.

Consider the following passage from Godelier's *Enigma of the Gift*, substituting the author's use of the terms "giver," "receiver," and "gift" with "artist," "audience," and "artwork," respectively.

> The act of giving seems to create simultaneously a twofold relationship between the giver and receiver. A relationship of *solidarity* because the giver shares what he has, or what he is, with the receiver; and a relationship of *superiority* because the one who receives the gift and accepts it places himself in the debt of the one who has given it, thereby becoming indebted to the giver and to a certain extent becoming his "dependant" at least for as long as he has not "given back" what he was given.
>
> Giving thus seems to establish a difference and an inequality of status between donor and recipient, which can in certain instances become a hierarchy: if this hierarchy already exists, then the gift expresses and legitimizes it. Two opposite movements are thus contained in a single act. The gift decreases the distance between the protagonists because it is a form of sharing, and it increases the social distance between them because one is now indebted to the other.[15]

Following this insight, we can confirm that the gift of sharing the authorial role of the artist, rendering the audience into active participants or partners to complete the work, registers the artist's desire for solidarity or equality with his or her audience while at the same time reaffirming the artist's superior position.

The work of Brazilian artist Lygia Clark from the 1960s and 1970s is a paradigmatic example of this power dynamic. Like many artists of her generation, she rejected ego-centered art production. Her work—from simple objects and contraptions to more elaborate group events—elicited direct physical participation from audiences usually more accustomed to a passive, distanced, and exclusively visual appreciation of art. But if Clark was "content to simply propose to others to be themselves," as critic Guy Brett claims, then it is equally true that she imagined her audience as unable, lacking the means and knowledge, to "be themselves" without her particular artistic intervention.[16] Clark presupposed that people generally suffer from fragmentation of body and mind, from alienation from self and others, and that basic multisensory engagement with objects and/or other people would stimulate repressed aspects of their perceptual capacities, encouraging them to regain a holistic and renewed sense of self. It is no coincidence that Clark eventually came to think of her audience as "patients" and her art as a form of unorthodox psychotherapy—that is, as a form of healing. In her case, the sharing of creative or authorial power between artist and audience constitutes nothing short of a gift of life, the reinstatement of a full subjecthood.

While Clark's practice represents an extreme case of art as gift and artist as gift giver, more recent works mobilize, if less explicitly, a similar economy of exchange in which the artwork functions as an invitation or a challenge provoking the audience into active participatory roles. Erwin Wurm's *One Minute Sculptures*, for instance, provide instructions that allow potentially anyone to become a work of art, however briefly. A seemingly lighthearted and simple project that belies a complex engagement with distinctions of media and the function of time in the constitution of a work of art, *One Minute Sculptures* are initiated in the form of drawings and written propositions that diagram variously humorous, provocative, and nonsensical actions.[17] Wurm suggests holding one's breath while thinking of Spinoza, balancing a roll of toilet paper on one's back while forwardly bent over, propping up a line of balls and buckets against a wall with one's head, lying on tennis balls without letting one's body touch the floor, putting on a pair of pants over one's head as if it were a sweater. Although *One Minute Sculptures* are usually exhibited as already accomplished deeds—as already reciprocated "gifts"—through photographic and video documentation, any future viewer's attempt to fulfill Wurm's challenging propositions (with built-in failure) will result, in principle, in another unique "sculpture." Thus, the work sustains itself as an open-ended invitation that has the potential to obligate respondents continuously, converting artistic reception into artistic production anytime and anywhere.

Gabriel Orozco's *Mesa de ping-pong con estanque* (*Ping Pond Table* [1998]) likewise offers its audience an opportunity to "complete" or become a work of art. In Orozco's case, the "gift" is an unexpected group interaction based in play. His eccentrically reconfigured Ping-Pong table, now extended and four-sided with a square, lily-filled "pond" in the middle, recalls Arte Povera's prevalent use of natural elements as sculptural material on the one hand and Claude Monet's famous Impressionist lilies on the other. More important than such art-historical references, however, is how the work brings into the

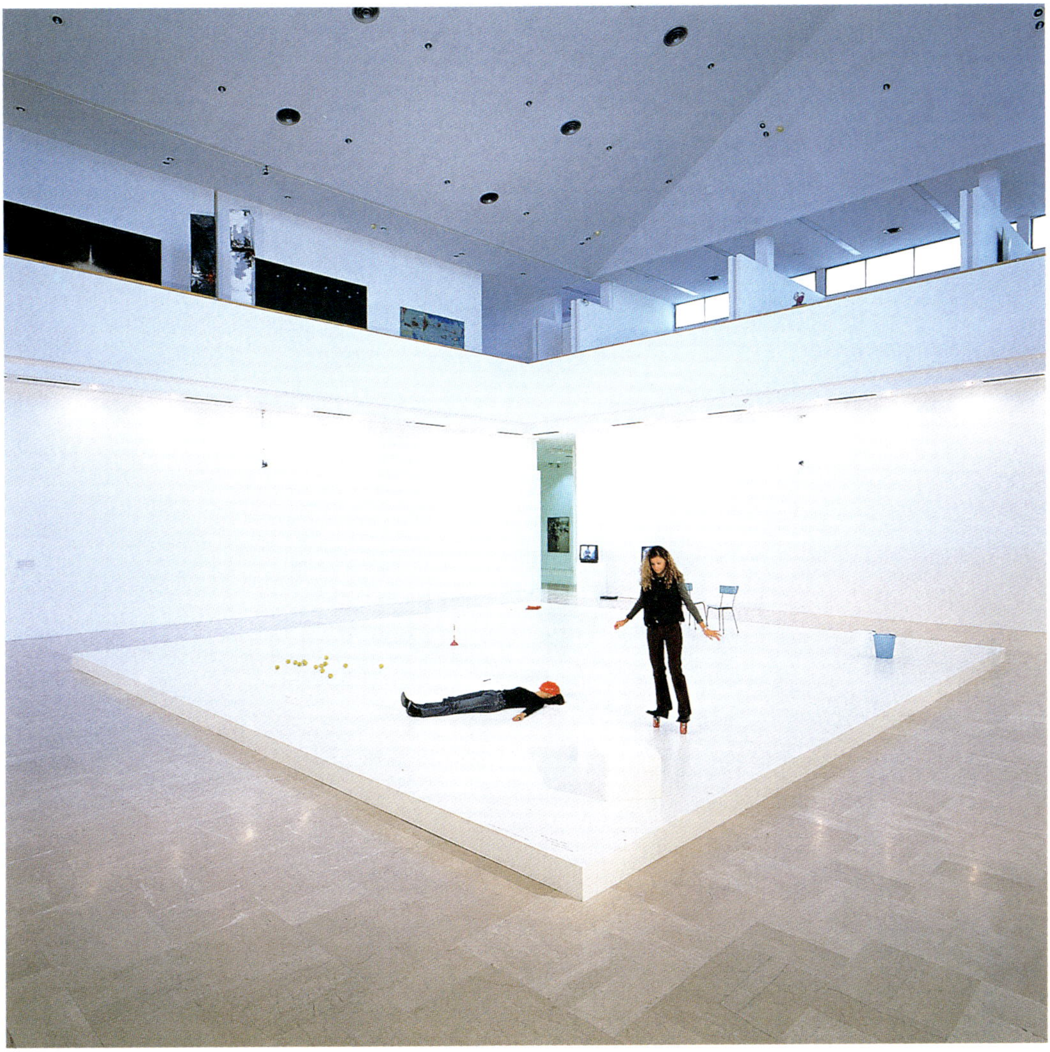

Erwin Wurm, *One Minute Sculpture,* 1997. Installation at Galleria d'Arte Moderna, Bologna.

museum space, which traditionally demands quiet secular reverence, a "low" recreational sport that can transform it into a spirited site of social exchange. Whether seen as a critique of institutional conventions, exposing what is normally repressed by them, or as a capitulation to the rising tendency toward entertainment-oriented programming among museums, *Ping Pond Table* leaves up to its audience the rules of engagement and potential competition. The work's status as a sculptural object or a performance prop also depends entirely on the reaction of the people gathered around the work at any one time, on their inclination or aversion toward interacting with others, possibly strangers. Orozco's distorted game of Ping-Pong, in other words, offers its audience the capacity to determine its meaning and purpose.

This kind of authorial generosity, however, also maintains a distance between artist and audience, securing the "superior" position of the former, as noted earlier. The hierarchy of relations between the artist as creative thinker/maker and viewer as disciplined consumer/receiver is not ultimately negated or refuted, as is often claimed. It is rather expressed and legitimized in the very gesture of giving away the ownership of the creative act.[18] Giving things away is tied up with ego-consolidation; abdication of one's authority asserts one's superiority. This is a point that many critics (especially those who champion "interactive" and participatory art generally, such as museum educators, public art sponsors, and Internet enthusiasts) continue to miss.

But what of the gift that is refused or otherwise unacknowledged? A dinner party to which no one comes? An instruction that goes ignored? As much as the accepting of a gift puts one in debt, in an inferior position to the giver until the debt is cleared through reciprocation, the refusal of a gift functions as a rejection of both the giver's superiority and his or her invitation to solidarity. Consequently, there is always the risk of personal humiliation and of a breach in social relations involved with gift giving. The dreadfulness of this breach was brought home to me during a visit to the 1995 Guggenheim Museum retrospective of works by Felix Gonzalez-Torres, an artist noted for translating so many lessons from the art of the 1960s and 1970s.[19] Of great popularity in the exhibition were his well-known paper stacks and candy piles, which invite viewers not only to touch the art but also to take pieces of it with them. The large number of museum visitors cheerfully collecting sheets of paper and grabbing handfuls of candy as they moved through the spiraling exhibition seemed to bear out the observation of many critics and curators that these works are acts of unusual generosity. And the thought of Gonzalez-Torres's work being distributed around the world through the movement of his audience (rather than through the standard art market as a precious and expensive commodity) heartened me, as I considered how modestly yet effectively art can enter the spaces of people's daily lives.

Even before leaving the museum, however, I was shocked by the sight of overstuffed garbage cans in the lobby, jammed with rolled and scrunched sheets of paper from Gonzalez-Torres's stacks. Outside the museum, too, Fifth Avenue waste bins were filled to capacity with what were, only a few yards away inside the museum, "works of art." Granted, one can argue that the brilliance of Gonzalez-Torres's work lies in making evident precisely this kind of categorical slippage. But the ungracious scene of the audience's hoarding and then trashing Gonzalez-Torres's "gift" threw into harsh relief another fact: the thinness of the line separating honor and humiliation and the tenuousness of the very notion of the gift. The "repudiation of artistic control" in Gonzalez-Torres's giveaway works, as in other works of the past and present that offer authorship privileges to the audience (many included in *Work Ethic*), may continue to bring high esteem to the artist as a generous gift giver. But this esteem is predicated on the belief that anonymous recipients for whom the work is intended accept the "gift of the artist" unconditionally and properly.

If we take stock of the gift's rejection, however—or, in Gonzalez-Torres's case, its apparent acceptance at the outset followed by its quick disposal as trash—the artist's standing seems to diminish dramatically and become vulnerable, as though he or she were a victim of a brutally hurtful personal rebuff. (How sad and truly exposed would Yoko Ono have appeared if her instruction to her audience in *Cut Piece* had been met with no response—utter silence, inaction, and indifference?) The throwing away of the gift/work may be an unpremeditated or uneducated act, thus of little consequence to the meaning of the work, but that would render the taking of the gift/work all the more significant as potentially an act of thoughtlessness instead of interaction. The trashing of the gift is akin to the rejection of the solidarity that the artist/artwork proposes. Through the repudiation of a work's (and by extension, an institution's) generosity, the audience/receiver can assert its "superior" position.[20]

▪▪▪ ▪▪▪

As French sociologist Pierre Bourdieu has noted, an "inaugural act that institutes communication (by addressing words, offering a gift,

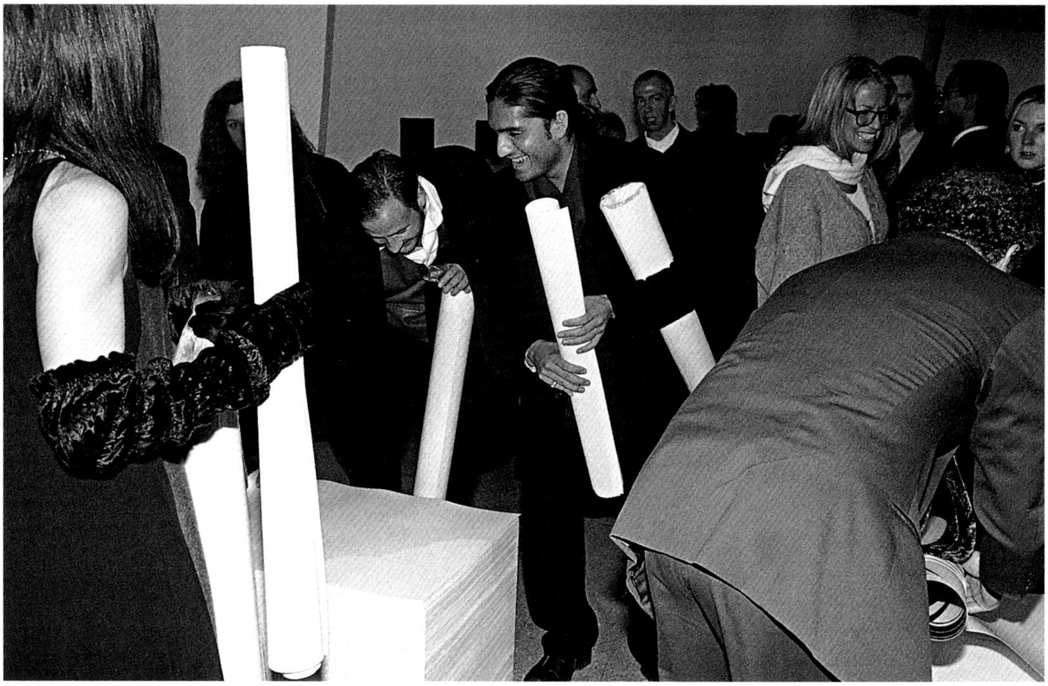

(this page and opposite) Reception for Ross Bleckner and Felix Gonzalez-Torres, March 2, 1995, Solomon R. Guggenheim Museum, New York.

issuing an invitation or a challenge, etc.)," like so many of the dematerialized artworks under consideration here that propose an action or expect a response, "always entails a kind of intrusion or even a calling into question . . . [that] inevitably contains the potentiality of a bond, an obligation."[21] This possibility of a bond, an ongoing relationship of mutuality and exchange—between artist and audience, between persons—is at the heart of the anticommodification efforts. For if the economy and moral code of commodity exchange is based on alienable objects and alienated subjects, whose ties of dependence to one another are cancelled at the moment of exchange, the economy and moral code of gift giving asserts the impossibility of that cancellation. Just as the acceptance of a gift immediately puts one in debt to the gift giver, a debt that must be repaid in an appropriate and timely manner following certain cultural rules in order that one not lose face or insult the gift giver, these artworks place upon their addressees—upon us, even many years hence—a burden to answer their call for solidarity and communality.

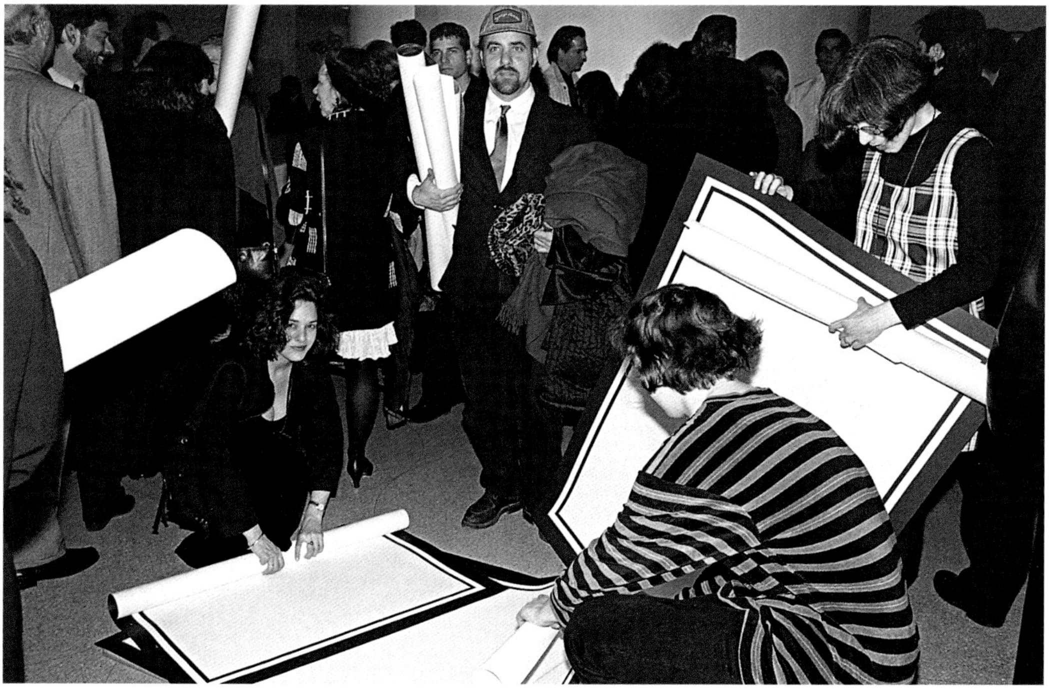

But such art, as I have tried to show, also hazards the possibility of legitimizing and reinforcing existing hierarchical power relations (the giver/artist maintains superiority). It can also reveal the impotence of generosity, especially when the gift is rejected, when there is no counter-gift or riposte, when the call goes unheeded. Again, Bourdieu: "It is true that . . . one can always choose not to reply to the interpellation, invitation, or challenge or not to reply immediately, to defer and to leave the other party in expectation. But non-response is still a response, and it is not so easy to shrug off the initial calling into question, which acts as a kind of *fatum*, a destiny."[22] This resonates with the particular temporality of the artworks I have considered in this essay. Like the temporality of the gift, each work anticipates a social process and a future. The articulation of as-yet-unrealized possibilities of social interaction and relations *is* the work. This is why when these works are exhibited only through object residues, they seem so inadequate: the immediacy of "presence" is missing, of course, but in addition, the *promise* of potential actions and relations—of mutual dependence, reciprocity, and solidarity—is denied.

A final thought. On certain occasions, when one receives or accepts a gift, the obligation is not to reciprocate with a comparable counter-gift but to hold on to the original one. Continuity of social relations is secured not always in the moment of taking or receiving a gift but in keeping it over time.[23] As implied in the Gonzalez-Torres incident, it takes a certain commitment and vigilance to abide by the obligation to *keep* a gift, to withhold it from dominant modes of circulation and exchange, to protect it from becoming alienable. The weight of *this* obligation seems more ambiguous and heavier than the obligation to reciprocate. For once this kind of gift is accepted, we are continually beholden to imagine different destinies for art than what they have been.

1. Lucy Lippard and John Chandler, "The Dematerialization of Art," *Artforum International* 6, no. 6 (1968): 31–36; reprinted in *Changing: Essays in Art Criticism* (New York: E. P. Dutton, 1971), 255.

2. Lippard heeds Joseph Schillinger's evolutionary mapping of artistic development in his 1948 book *The Mathematical Basis of the Arts*, which posits the eventual "disintegration of art" and the "abstraction and liberation of the idea." While she argues for this moment as almost a historical inevitability, Lippard claims Dada and Surrealism as precedents for the "post-aesthetic" dematerialization of art that she sees around her. Marcel Duchamp is championed above all as the forerunner, the model of the artist as thinker rather than the artist as maker ("Dematerialization of Art," 258, 268–270).

3. Lucy Lippard, "Escape Attempts," introduction to *Six Years: The Dematerialization of the Art Object from 1966 to 1972*, ed. Lucy Lippard (New York: Praeger, 1973; Berkeley and Los Angeles: University of California Press, 1997), vii–xxii.

4. Ibid., xiv. The quotation from 1969 concludes, "The people who buy a work of art they can't hang up or have in their garden are less interested in possession. They are patrons rather than collectors."

5. Ibid., xiii.

6. Lippard, "Dematerialization of Art," 270.

7. See, for instance, Paul Schimmel, *Out of Actions*, exh. cat. (Los Angeles: The Museum of Contemporary Art, Los Angeles, 2000).

8. See my *One Place After Another: Site-Specific Art and Locational Identity* (Cambridge: The MIT Press, 2002).

9. Random examples include Edward Kienholz's watercolors that depict the object or monetary sum to be bartered with the painting; David Hammons's Dada-esque sale of different sizes of snowballs on a New York City street corner; and Elizabeth Sisco, Louis Hock, and David Avalos's distribution of an NEA grant to undocumented workers in the San Diego/Tijuana area as a tax "rebate."

10. For a reading of Yoko Ono's *Cut Piece* in relation to the gift, see Julia Bryan-Wilson, "Remembering Yoko Ono's *Cut Piece*," *Oxford Art Journal* 26 (Spring 2003): 99–123.

11. Marcel Mauss, *The Gift: The Form and Reason for Exchange in Archaic Societies*, trans. W. D. Hall (New York: W. W. Norton, 1990). Recent publications on the gift include Alan D. Schrift, ed., *The Logic of the Gift: Toward an Ethic of Generosity* (New York: Routledge, 1997); Maurice Godelier, *The Enigma of the Gift* (Chicago: University of Chicago Press, 1999); and Jacques Derrida, *The Gift of Death*, trans. David Wills (Chicago: University of Chicago Press, 1995).

12. Godelier, *The Enigma of the Gift*, 15; emphasis in the original.

13. Lippard, "Escape Attempts," xv.

14. See, for instance, the rhetoric around "new genre public art" described in Suzanne Lacy, ed., *Mapping the Terrain* (Seattle: Bay Press, 1995).

15. Godelier, *The Enigma of the Gift*, 12.

16. As noted by critic Guy Brett, Clark's eccentric goggles, gloves, bags, masks, suits, restraints, elastic netting, and "biological architecture," all emphasizing tactility and bodily engagement over opticality, allowed those "who had been art's spectator . . . [to] rediscover his or her own poetics (expressivity, creativity) in themselves and come to be the subject of their own experience." See Guy Brett, "Lygia Clark: Six Cells," in *Lygia Clark*, exh. cat. (Barcelona: Fundació Antoni Tàpies, 1998), 18.

17. For an insightful analysis of the various manifestations of Erwin Wurm's *One Minute Sculptures* (i.e., drawing, performance, photography, video), see Michael Newman, "Photography and Video as Sculpture in the Work of Erwin Wurm," in *Erwin Wurm*, exh. cat. (London: The Photographer's Gallery, 2000), 4–8.

18. In Lygia Clark's case, her generosity secures the "superior" position of the artist as the healer/therapist in relation to a pathologized audience's state of debilitation and lack. Interestingly, it seems that Clark was quite aware of the paradoxical nature of this kind of generosity: "my self-centeredness which being so great made me give everything to the other, even the authorship of the work" (Brett, "Lygia Clark: Six Cells," 18).

19. See Nancy Spector, *Felix Gonzalez-Torres*, exh. cat. (New York: Solomon R. Guggenheim Museum, 1995).

20. Felix Gonzalez-Torres was contrarily very specific about the responsibilities and "rights" of those who would come to own the paper stack and candy pile pieces as "works," be they individual collectors or museums. He made a distinction between ownership and participation. On the complexities of Gonzalez-Torres's certificates of authenticity and the issues that they raise for authorship, ownership, and the question of what constitutes a "work," see David Deitcher, "Contradictions and Containment," in *Felix Gonzalez-Torres* (Ostfildern-Ruit, Germany: Cantz Verlag, 1997), 104–9.

21. Pierre Bourdieu, "Marginalia: Some Additional Notes on the Gift," in *The Logic of the Gift*, ed. Schrift, 238.

22. Ibid.

23. See Annett Weiner, *Inalienable Possessions: The Paradox of Keeping-While-Giving* (Berkeley and Los Angeles: University of California Press, 1992).

CATALOGUE

Julia Bryan-Wilson JBW
Janet Kraynak JK
Helen Molesworth HM
Judith Rodenbeck JR

DURING THE 1960S, MANY artists began to explore new ways to make art. No longer content with the historically sanctioned divisions among drawing, painting, and sculpture, and equally dismissive of art's traditional skills of mimetic representation, artists instead confronted a fundamental question: What is art? They increasingly came to define art as anything an artist did. Bruce Nauman asserted: "If you see yourself as an artist and you function in a studio . . . you sit in a chair or pace around. And then the question goes back to what is art? And art is what an artist does, just sitting around the studio."[1] Yet throughout the 1960s, artists rarely just sat around in their studios. Many responded to this newly liberated idea of art by assigning themselves a task—often delineated by time or by the physical limitation of a material—and then subsequently performing that task.

THE ARTIST AS MANAGER AND WORKER

The Artist Creates and Completes a Task

Frank Stella
Vito Acconci
William Anastasi
Robert Morris
Chris Burden
Tom Friedman
Hugh Pocock
Performance
Bruce Nauman
Richard Serra
Feminism
Eleanor Antin
Mierle Laderman Ukeles
Martha Rosler
Wage Labor
Edward Kienholz
Tehching Hsieh
David Hammons
Hope Ginsburg
Francis Alÿs

In creating and then performing these assignments, artists were replicating the roles of both manager and worker in the production of art: managers assign tasks that workers perform.

These artistic experiments are notable for their almost total lack of interest in the finished product. For the most part, as artists shifted emphasis and interest away from the art object as a finished product, they grew increasingly interested in the activity of making art. This work came to be known as Process art. The emphasis on process was, in essence, a foregrounding of acts of artistic labor. Video, film, and photography were often used to document these activities, transforming artists' labor into a form of performance. This is certainly the case in Bruce Nauman's and Richard Serra's studio films. For instance, in *Hand Catching Lead*, Richard Serra filmed himself catching (and failing to catch) strips of falling lead. Bruce Nauman's video *Bouncing Two Balls Between the Floor and Ceiling with Changing Rhythms* documents the artist trying to create a rhythmic system of bouncing balls in his studio. In an early and defining exhibition, *Anti-Illusion: Procedures/Materials*, Marcia Tucker wrote: "Since the emphasis is on the activity, the piece must be analyzed in terms of the kind of work that has gone into its making."[2]

In examining this "kind of work," one finds that although these tasks or processes may have mimicked the logic of managerial and manual labor, they also refuted it. The primary motivation for the twentieth-century division of labor into managerial and manual realms was the symbiotic logic of efficiency and profit. Introduced by Frederick Winslow

Hi Red Center, *Cleaning Event,* 1964. Photograph: Minoru Hirata.

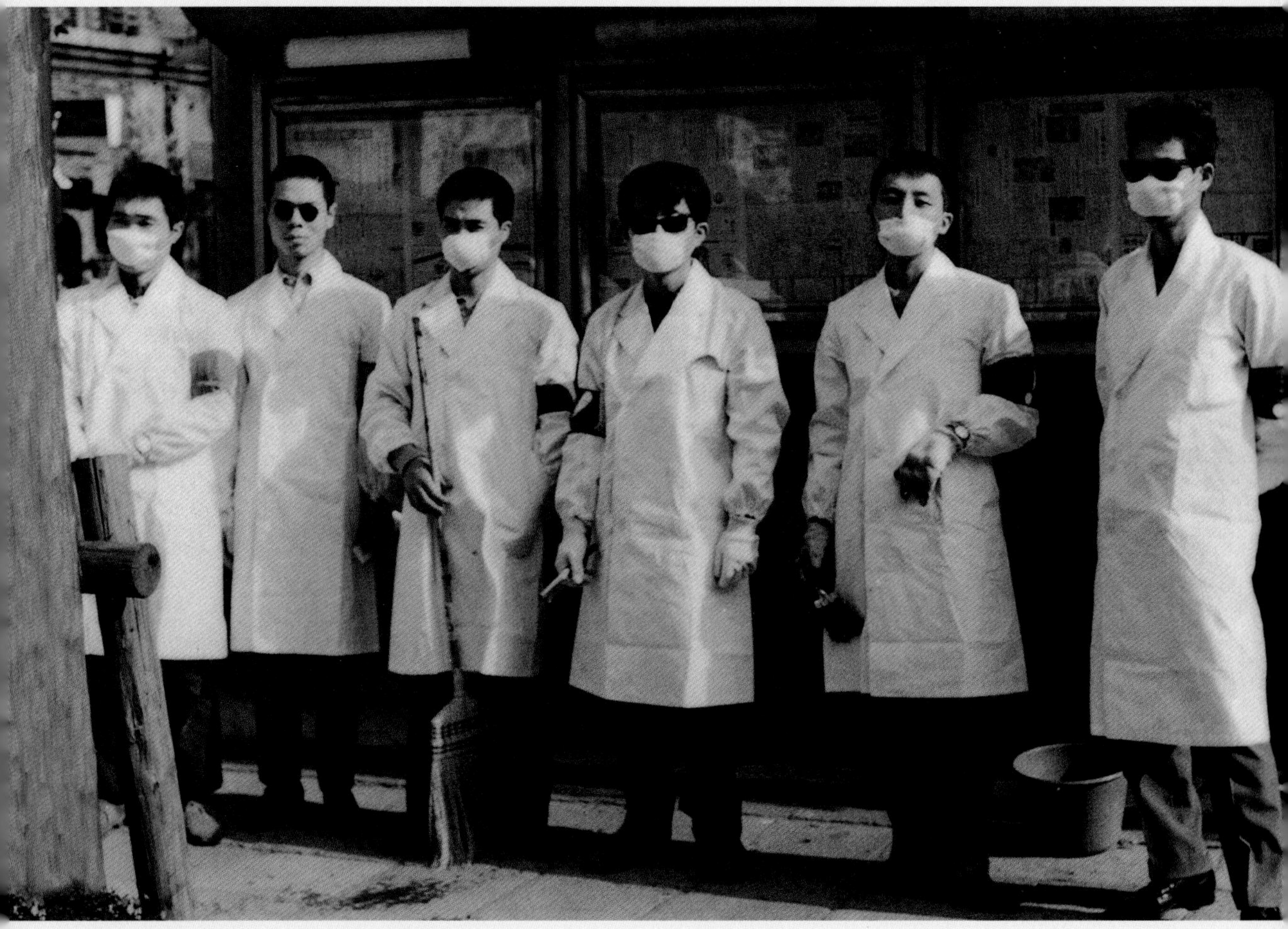

Taylor and perfected by Henry Ford, the logic of the assembly line, complete with managers who represented labor through charts and graphs and workers who did the labor through highly repetitive physical motions, transformed the production of mass-produced commodities. Artists of the 1960s, however, continually emphasized process over product in an attempt to alter the framework of value placed on art objects. Instead of valuing art objects as commodities to be bought and sold on the market, they advocated an art practice that valued artistic labor as such. Robert Morris described the critique of Process art by writing: "In a broad sense art has always been an object . . . what is being attacked, however, is something more than art as icon. Under attack is the rationalist notion that art is a form of work that results in a finished product."[3] Art was being reconceived as a form of work to be valued in and of itself.

The critique of rationalized work would be taken one step further. Artists may have mimed the division between management and workers, but they also playfully manipulated each form of labor as well. Rather than employing a system of charts and graphs, they often represented work through deliberately flat, grainy black-and-white photographs or film with consummately low production values. Just as artists resisted the polish and professionalism of typical managers, so too they obviated the efficiency and rationality of assembly-line labor. Indeed, most Process artists were interested in what Morris would call "change, contingency, indeterminacy—in short, the entire area of process,"[4] meaning that the critique of rationality was not only directed against an end product but also addressed equally sharply to the logic of efficiency and planning. In this regard, Process art often entails an obsessive, even ludicrous, form of labor, which is routinely marked by a pervasive sense of "failure," as witnessed in Serra's difficulty catching the lead.

HM

1. As quoted in Tony Godfrey, *Conceptual Art* (London: Phaidon Press, 1998), 127.

2. *Anti-Illusion: Procedures/Materials*, exh. cat., organized by Marcia Tucker and James Monte (New York: Whitney Museum of American Art, 1969), 35.

3. Robert Morris, "Notes on Sculpture Part 4: Beyond Objects," *Artforum International* 7 (April 1969): 54.

4. Ibid.

Frank Stella

American, b. 1936

Frank Stella, *Club Onyx,* 1959.

Frank Stella's series of *Black Paintings* (1958–59), first exhibited in 1959 when the artist was twenty-three, are often regarded as one foundation of Minimalist art. The paintings manifest a workmanlike attitude toward art making; rather than waiting for inspiration to strike, Stella set a job for himself and then did it. As Caroline Jones has noted, he had as an ideal the housepainter whose application of paint is regular, standardized, and laconic.[1] In fact, Stella worked as a housepainter when he first moved to New York and was struggling to support his art career. Paring down visual elements to simple, rational patterns, the *Black Paintings* feature geometrical schemes of broad black bands painted on raw canvas. Stella let the shape of the canvas guide his designs, and the width of his brush determined the thickness of the dark stripes. Through this straightforward method, Stella avoided using paint to create illusionistic space and instead emphasized the canvas's literal qualities, such as its flatness. The stretcher bars of the *Black Paintings* are unusually thick, so that the paintings push off the wall into the viewer's space, emphasizing that they are objects themselves and not merely surfaces onto which depth is projected.

Like Jackson Pollock before him, Stella used house paint straight from the can rather than artist's oils; unlike Pollock, he approached painting as a routine task, an exercise to be performed. Stella's emotionless way of making art enacts a renunciation of the Abstract Expressionist ethos of individualism, gesture, and affect, and his embrace of an aesthetic of everyday labor inaugurated a culture of "art workers." Stella was one of the first highly successful postwar American artists to come to painting without art-school training. He considered the component crafts of high art—draftsmanship and pigment mixing—irrelevant to his practice. In 1966 he commented, "I didn't want to make variations; I didn't want to record a path. I wanted to get the paint out of the can and onto the canvas. . . . I tried to keep the paint as good as it was in the can."[2]

Given Stella's embrace of industrial paint and impersonality, these early works have a remarkable degree of tactility. The *Black Paintings* are often treated as nothing more than conceptual diagrams, which ignores how interesting they are as visual objects and how much they depend upon paint's materiality. Although in reproduction the *Black Paintings* look severe and mechanical, they have a delicate, handmade quality. As Stella planted his black stripes on unprimed cotton duck, the brush bristles feathered out at the edges, giving each regimented stroke soft, indistinct borders. The dark bars and the light lines flicker and jostle for primacy, setting up a dynamic pattern in which foreground and background oscillate. In some works, faint pencil guide-lines help keep the bands evenly spaced, but even with these guides, the carefully delineated intervals of his patterning are inexact. Stella's adherence to symmetry sometimes veers off course and the stripes go slightly askew. Within their stark confines, the paintings produce visually arresting optical effects that exceed the limitations of Stella's simple tasks.

JBW

1. Jones further comments that Stella's desire to be a worker cannot be separated from his other mythic paradigm, the executive. See Caroline Jones, *Machine in the Studio: Constructing the Postwar American Artist* (Chicago: University of Chicago Press, 1996).

2. Answer to Bruce Glaser in "Questions to Stella and Judd," ed. Lucy Lippard, *Art News* (September 1966); reprinted in *Minimal Art: A Critical Anthology*, ed. Gregory Battcock and intro. Anne M. Wagner (Berkeley and Los Angeles: University of California Press, 1995), 157.

Vito Acconci

American, b. 1940

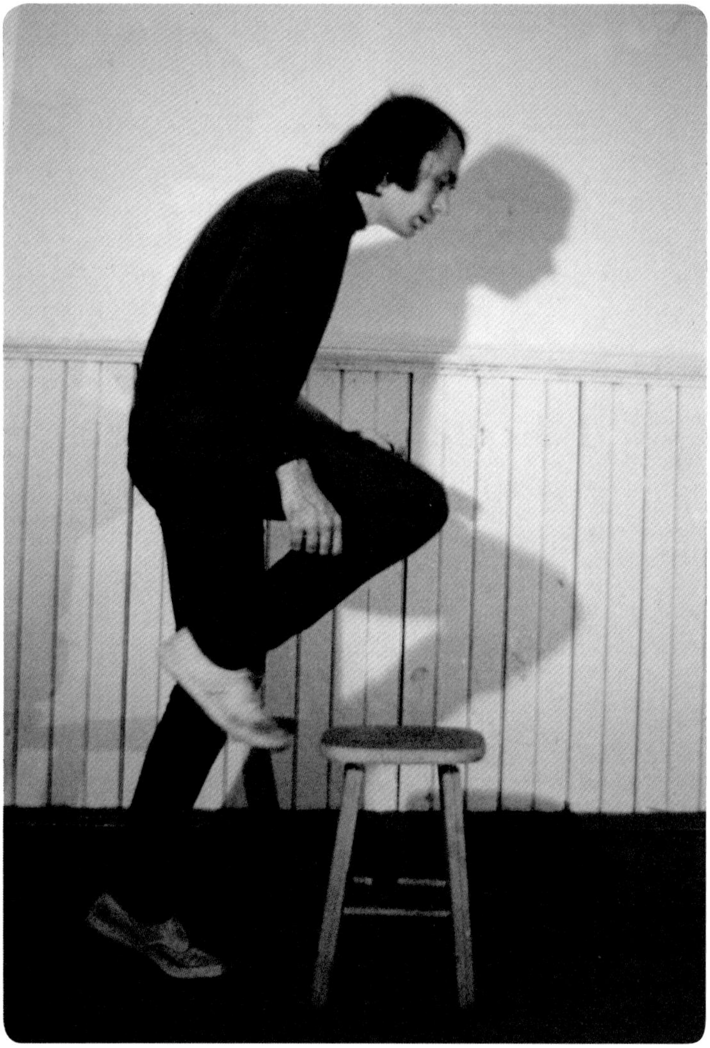

In the late 1960s, Vito Acconci shifted his artistic interest from poetry to performance. Acconci's performances used neither the stage nor any of the skills associated with the performing arts; instead, they tended to be experiments in physical stamina rarely performed for an audience. These performances, or activities, were typically accompanied by short written texts describing the activity and black-and-white documentary photographs. Both the language and the images used to describe and record Acconci's performances are distinguished by a purposeful blandness. This affectless quality stands in stark contrast to the often viscerally charged nature of the activities.

Vito Acconci, *Step Piece,* 1970.

Vito Acconci

STEP PIECE (STEPS: STEPPING-OFF PLACE)

Apartment 6B, 102 Christopher Street, New York City.

February 1-28, 1970; continuing thereafter, indefinitely, every day in alternate months.

8AM each day.

— An 18-inch stool has been set up in my apartment and is being used as a step.

— Each morning, during the designated months, I step up and down the stool at the rate of 30 steps a minute; each time, the activity lasts as long as I can perform it without stopping.

— At the end of each performance-month, a chart will be sent out — noting the results of the repeated activity, the course of changes in duration.

— There will be a month's layoff, after each performance-month, before the next series of performances.

(The public can see the activity performed, in my apartment, any morning during the performance-months. Whenever I cannot be home, I will attempt to perform the activity wherever I happen to be.)

Acconci's texts function simultaneously as an instruction for an activity to be performed and a description of an activity performed. While the photographs of Acconci's performances connote past activity, the texts do not. For instance, in *Step Piece* (1970), Acconci's text can be read as both a scenario and a record:

An 18-inch stool has been set up in my apartment and is being used as a step.
Each morning, during the designated months, I step up and down the stool at the rate of 30 steps a minute: each time, the activity lasts as long as I can perform it without stopping.

At the end of each performance-month, a chart will be sent out—noting the results of the repeated activity . . .

Here Acconci conflates several aspects of work and artwork. The space of home as a site of rest is suspended, as it becomes both the studio space (where art is made) and the exhibition space (where art is seen). All in all, Acconci actually triples his "workload." Not only does he have to "make" the art (stepping on the stool), but he also has to send out a press release of sorts, the labor more traditionally associated with the gallery; moreover, because there is no object per se, what is offered instead are the "bureaucratically-styled 'progress-reports.'"[1]

No particular set of skills is required for *Step Piece*, yet the piece adopts the language and structures of managerial and manual labor. Acconci acts like a manager as he decides upon a task, performs it at designated times, monitors and records it, and finally shares the results with a limited public. Acconci represents the role of the manual laborer as well, however—particularly one who works to the very limits of his body's physical capabilities. In *Step Piece*, the historically tense relationship between the logic of management and the physical endurance required in manual labor is played out on one body—that of the artist. Acconci's body comes to replace the traditional art object, even as it anxiously performs the disappearance of a "productive" laboring body. HM

1. Frazer David Ward, "False Intimacies, Open Secrets: Public and Private in the Performance Art of Vito Acconci and Chris Burden" (Ph.D. diss., Cornell University, 2000), 104.

William Anastasi
American, b. 1933

Since the 1960s, William Anastasi has produced a series of drawings in which he utilizes his body as an instrument of movement, measurement, and time. Influenced by the works of composer John Cage, Anastasi establishes situations that depend upon chance and game-like systems of rules. With these strategies he explores issues of authorship and the contemplative qualities of mark making. The *Subway Drawings* chronicle Anastasi's rides in the New York City subway system. Beginning in the early 1970s, Anastasi

William Anastasi, *Blind Drawing,* 1988.

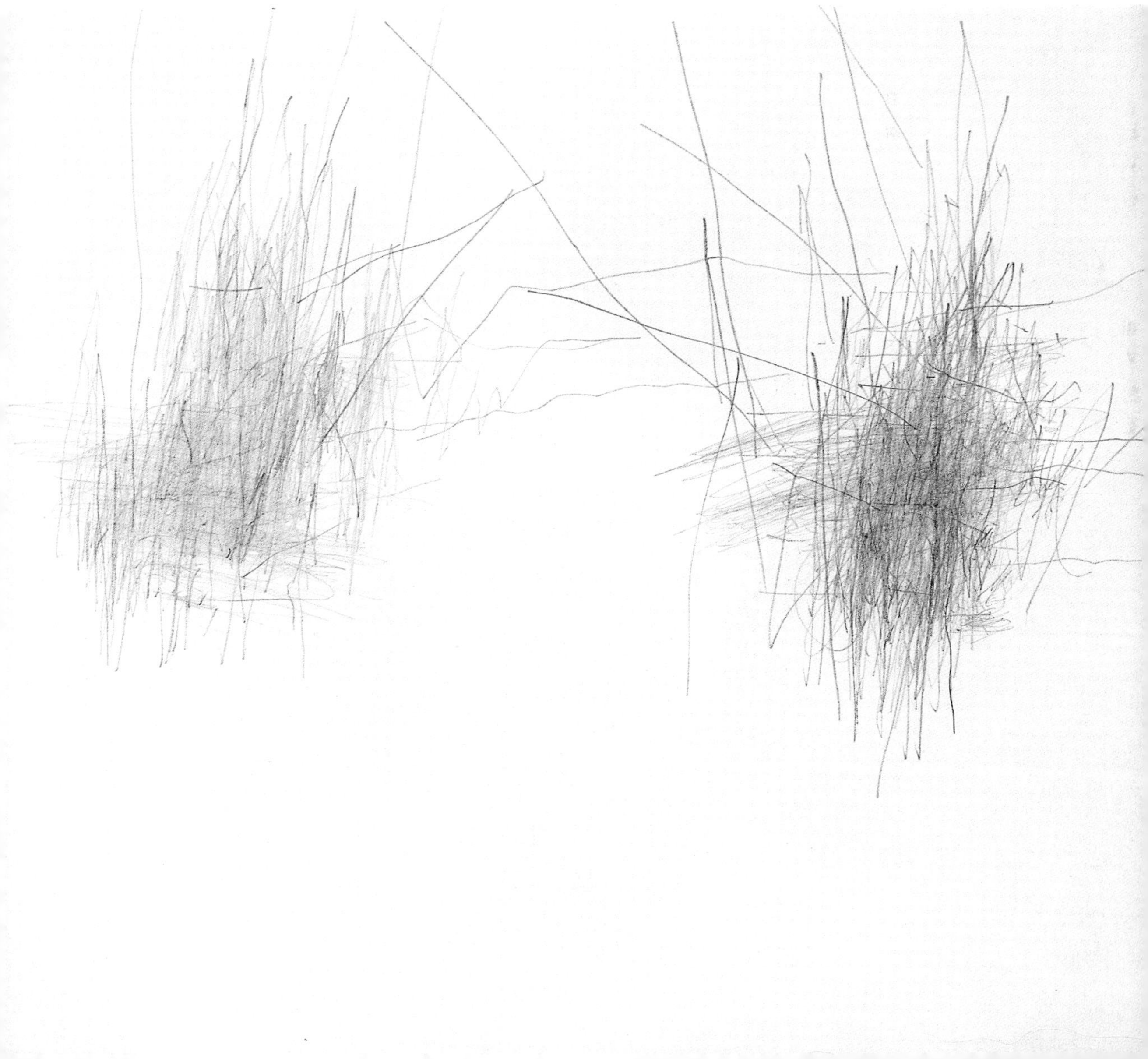

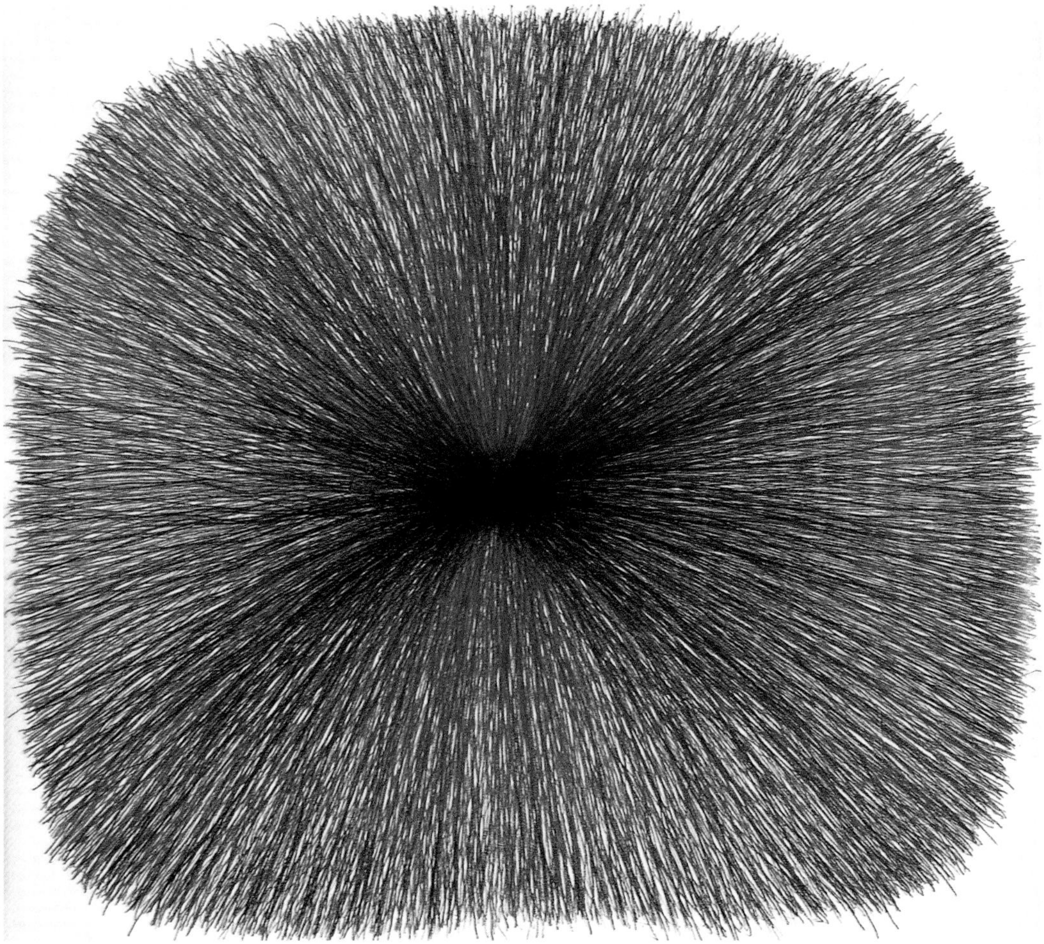

William Anastasi, *Without Title (60 Minute Drawing)*, 1999.

would take a seat on the train, often on the way to a weekly chess game with Cage, place a sketchpad on his lap, hold a pencil in each hand, and close his eyes. He also wore heavy-duty headphones to block out sounds so as to heighten his sensory deprivation and reach a meditative state.

During these sightless journeys, Anastasi let his body sway with the subway. As the train pitched through underground passages, the pencils skimmed the surface of the paper, registering the car's abrupt movements with varying intensities of line. Anastasi's pencil marks mirror the jerky swerves and sudden accelerations of the subway's turns and stops. The scrawls and scribbles cluster into complex knots as the lines skid in unforeseen directions. Like a seismograph, Anastasi's body serves as an implement that absorbs and relays motion, imprinting the surface of the paper with a nuanced record of his travels in New York. By giving up control of his movements and letting his pencils move with the rocking of the subway, he abdicates authorial responsibility for his art.

Rather than using vision to generate his work, Anastasi produces art through physical measurements and arbitrary limits. In *Without Title* (*60 Minute Drawing* [1999]), he drew as many lines on a piece of paper as he could within one hour. The *Blind Drawings*, done on large sheets of paper, were made as Anastasi (again with eyes shut, again with pencils in both hands) rotated his arms as far as he could, thereby tracing the arcs of his own arm-span, displaying his range of motion and capabilities. The erratic inscriptions document his activity. The paper becomes almost textured as the pressure of the pencils begins to erode the smooth surface. Sometimes the marks are so heavy and purposeful that the pencil gouges the paper with ruts or punctures the surface. The lines build up a certain density, becoming glossy with reflective graphite. Like many process-driven drawings, the works register the artist's performance of simple tasks or rudimentary gestures. By drawing blind and using chance, Anastasi's art subverts the long tradition of drawing as the supreme fusion of vision, knowledge, and manual dexterity.

JBW

Robert Morris

American, b. 1931

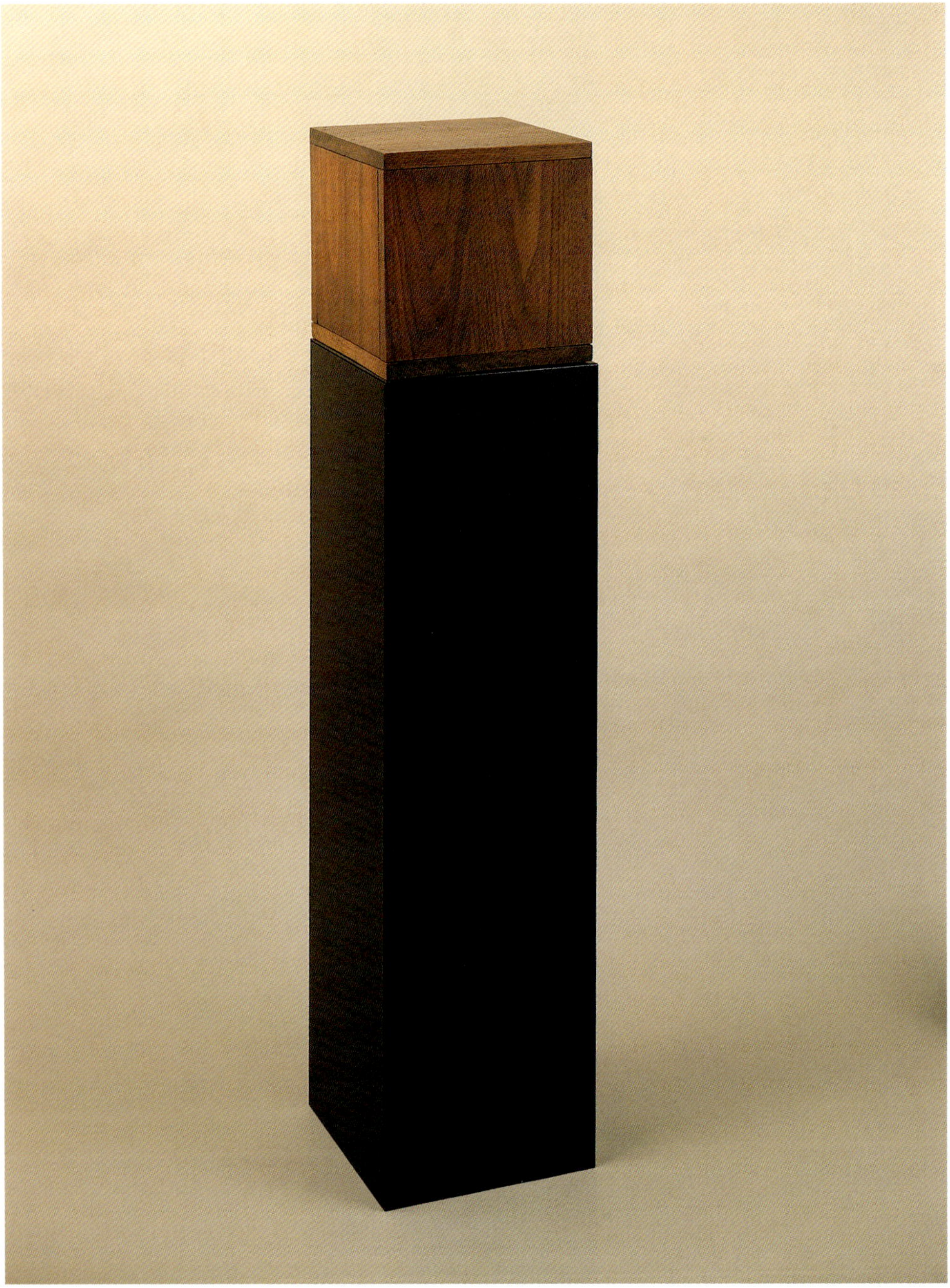

Robert Morris, *Box with the Sound of Its Own Making,* 1961.

In the early 1960s, Robert Morris began investigating the conceptual implications of making art out of task-like activities. *Box with the Sound of Its Own Making* (1961), for example, is a sculpture that presents itself as an account of elementary work. As Morris built a small walnut box, a tape recorder captured the noises of his construction: sawing, drilling, and nailing. The process took more than three hours, and after it was completed, Morris placed a tape player inside the cube that continuously played the recorded sounds. By emitting the sounds of its production, Morris's box makes us aware of how it was made, revealing artistic creation to be a straightforward matter of carpentry.

Box with the Sound of Its Own Making is an early example of Minimalist art, art that utilized simplified, often geometric, shapes. It could be understood as a prescient rebuttal to Richard Wollheim's famous 1965 critique of Minimalism. Wollheim believed that "[Minimalist] objects fail to evince what we have over the centuries come to regard as an essential ingredient in art: work, or manifest effort."[1] Though he was not speaking of Morris's work in particular, Wollheim generally argued that Minimalist objects do not demonstrate their maker's skill or labor but instead are merely declared—with "minimal" work—to be art.[2]

In contrast, Morris's piece offers a record of the time and effort that went into its making. *Box with the Sound of Its Own Making* is an object whose man-made assembly is plainly evident. Surfaces are unpainted, joints are rough, the wood's edges are not cut with factory precision, and the nails are fully visible. Only nine inches cubed, its intimate scale emphasizes its handmade character. The taped sounds are on a loop, and their persistence implies that the work of this piece is ongoing—possibly a function of the specific interaction among the object, space, and the audience. Indeed, this sculpture is also a performance. When Morris first showed it to composer John Cage, Cage obligingly listened to the three-and-a-half-hour tape from beginning to end.

Through its emphasis on process and workmanlike gestures as well as its sound element, the "work" of the piece is seemingly made transparent. *Box with the Sound of Its Own Making* is Morris's attempt to create an object that retains evidence of its manufacture. Viewed in the broad perspective of Marxist thought, Morris's endeavor takes on an added significance. Marx wrote that the exchange of commodities relies upon an effacement of the work that went into making them. Morris tried to build an object that would retain and inscribe his efforts; unlike a commodity fetish, the sculpture does not wipe out or abstract away the labor power that made it. In a passage from *Capital,* Marx imagines what commodities would say if they could talk among themselves: "Our use value may be a thing that interests men. It is no part of us as objects."[3] *Box with the Sound of Its Own Making* is a commodity that literally speaks to those who might own it. By creating a piece that is inseparable from the chronicle of its production, Morris disputes the capitalist drive to force the separation between a thing and its maker.

JBW

1. Richard Wollheim, "Minimal Art," *Arts Magazine* (January 1965); reprinted in *Minimal Art: A Critical Anthology,* ed. Gregory Battcock and intro. Anne M. Wagner (Berkeley and Los Angeles: University of California Press, 1995), 395.

2. Wollheim was particularly concerned with the lack of work in Duchamp's appropriated readymades.

3. Karl Marx, "The Fetishism of Commodities and the Secret Thereof," in *Capital: A Critique of Political Economy, Volume 1,* trans. Ben Fowkes (New York: Vintage Books, 1976).

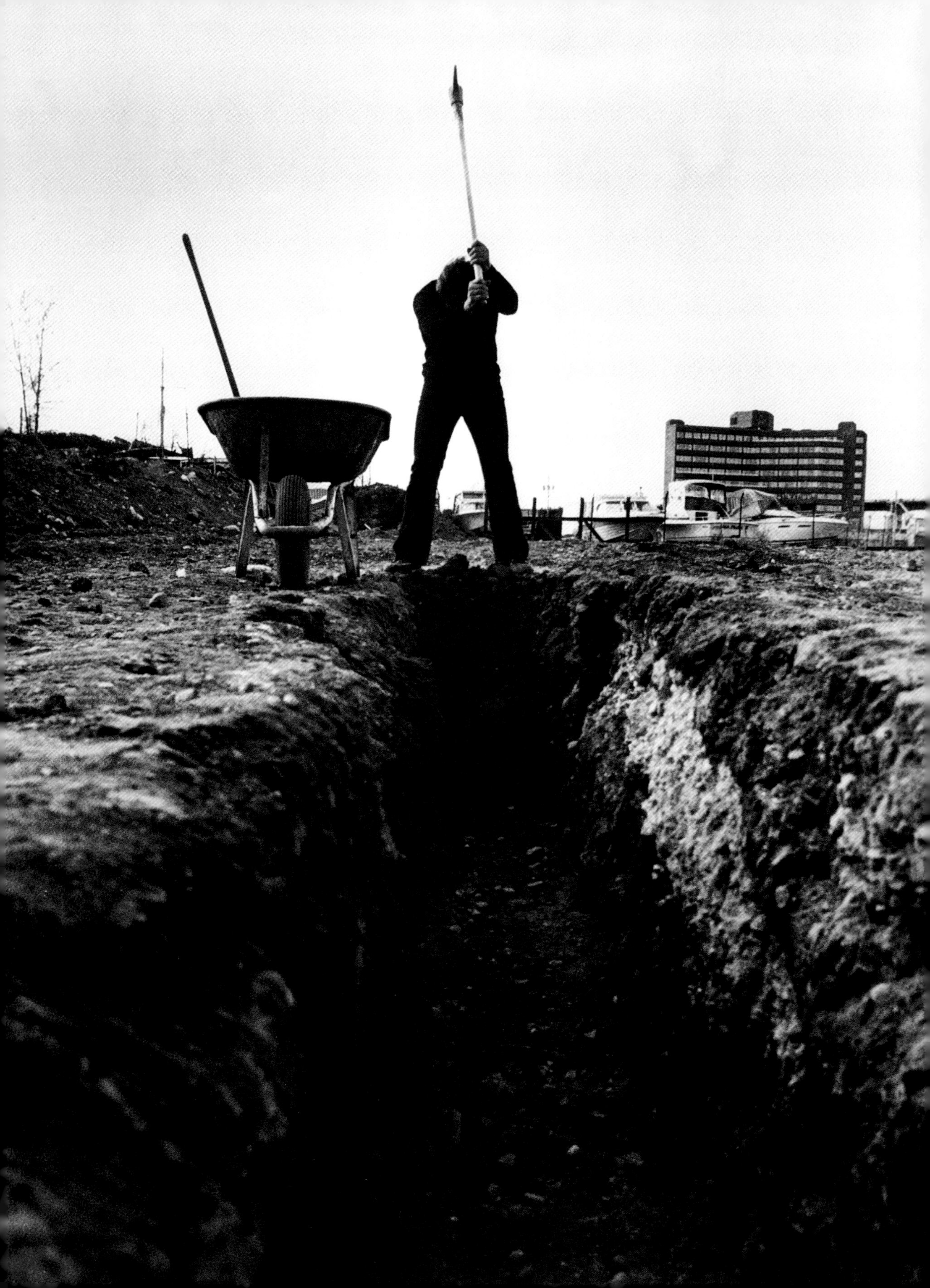

Chris Burden

American, b. 1946

Chris Burden devised and performed a variety of activities throughout the 1970s. Many of these works tested the limits of Burden's own body, particularly his threshold for pain. In *Shoot* (1971), he had himself shot; in *Five Day Locker Piece* (1971), he was locked in a locker for five days; and in *Transfixed* (1974), he was nailed, crucifix-style, to the top of a Volkswagen Beetle. Burden's performances were almost always documented photographically, and, as is typical of much Conceptual art, the black-and-white photographs are flatly descriptive. Each performance was also accompanied by a text that functions like an extended photographic caption. Sometimes the performances would produce a "relic"—an artifact retained from the performance (e.g., the nails from *Transfixed*) presented as a precious object.

Given Burden's interest in performance, he was often asked to "do something" as opposed to "showing something." In *Garçon!* (1976), he served coffee at the Hansen-Fuller Gallery in San Francisco; at the University of Maryland, he performed *Working Artist* (1975), in which he sat in a room at a typewriter, surrounded by images of previous performances. Many of his performances intertwined conventions of blue-collar and artistic labor. In *Honest Labor* (1979), Burden played most explicitly with the conventions of the recently professionalized artist. When the Emily Carr College of Art and Simon Fraser University in Vancouver invited Burden to come and speak as a "visiting artist," he refused. He said instead (in a short text that would subsequently accompany the activity), "Rather than meet with students to present and discuss my past work in a teaching context, I requested that I be provided with a wheel barrow, a shovel, and a pick ax."[1] When Burden states that during his four days he is going "to dig a straight ditch about 2½ feet wide and 3 feet deep . . . from 9 A.M. until 5 P.M.," he offers a distinctly "skill-less" and backbreaking form of blue-collar manual labor in place of the mental or white-collar labor of the visiting artist. Burden's replacement of mental labor with manual labor counters both the logic of Conceptual art and the tasks of the professional visiting artist. Yet there is a further irony: while *Honest Labor* plays on a truism about hard physical labor (an honest day's work), the result is a ditch built for no purpose. Historically, the Modernist art object was prized for its uselessness, yet is Burden's ditch to be prized for its lack of purpose? It seems not, as Burden recounts in a deadpan voice: "Occasionally, someone would offer to dig for me, but after trying it for a few minutes they would return the job to me."[2] Useless backbreaking labor simply remains useless. No longer a participatory artwork, digging a ditch was a job for Burden alone.

HM

1. The text for *Honest Labor* is reprinted in *Chris Burden: A Twenty-Year Survey*, exh. cat. (Newport Beach, Calif.: Newport Harbor Art Museum, 1988), 162–63.

2. Ibid.

Chris Burden, *Honest Labor*, 1979.

Tom Friedman
American, b. 1965

Tom Friedman, *1000 Hours of Staring,* 1992–97.

Tom Friedman's art often combines extreme verisimilitude, obsessive facture, and a literalness that sometimes has comic undertones. He has sharpened a pencil into one intact pencil shaving and he has crumpled two sheets of paper in an identical manner. While his works are wondrous, they are created through extraordinary patience and control rather than a specific set of learned skills.

Friedman borrows the literal quality of much Conceptual art but does so in the service of producing tangible art objects. The viewer of *1000 Hours of Staring* (1992–97) is confronted with a blank sheet of white paper. It is only upon reading the title that the viewer can grasp the work of the piece. After an understandable outburst of laughter, viewers often experience a crisis of faith: Did the artist do what he says he has done? There is, of course, no way to prove the veracity of the artistic claim. If we accept that the activity has occurred, then we must also acknowledge that the specificity of the viewer's role has been usurped by the artist. Does he look so the viewer does not have to, hence eliminating the "work" of the viewer? Or does the work suggest that the labor and/or leisure of the viewer should be the same as the artist's? Contradictorily, the labor of staring at a piece of paper for one thousand hours over the course of five years is clearly arduous, but its difficulty is not bound up in skill. (Anyone can stare, making Friedman's piece utterly democratic.) While Friedman—like many of his Performance art predecessors—established and performed this task, there can be

Tom Friedman, *Everything,* 1992–95.

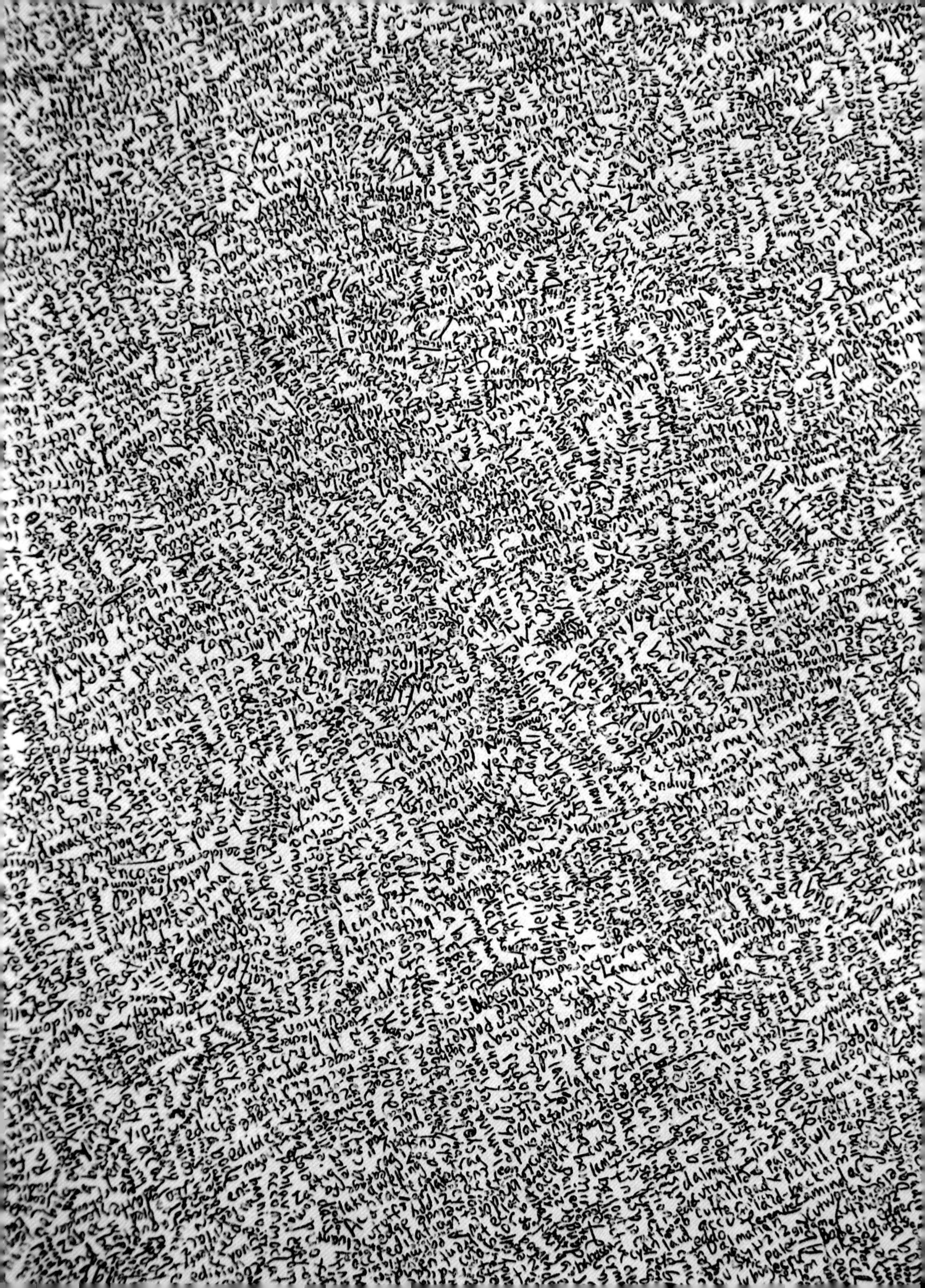

Tom Friedman, *Everything,* 1992–95 (detail).

no adequate recording of such labor. Yet as a rejoinder to his own argument, Friedman nearly contemporaneously produced *Everything* (1992–95), in which he transcribed all of the words in the dictionary on a sheet of paper—paper the same size as that used for *1000 Hours of Staring.* In *1000 Hours,* Friedman suggests that the artist's labor is impossible to monitor; in *Everything,* he intimates that part of the contract between artist and viewer is that occasionally an artist must show his hand and render the process and product of his labor self-evident. HM

Hugh Pocock

American, born New Zealand, 1963

Hugh Pocock's *Drilling a Well for Water* (2003) is simultaneously a sculpture, a performance, an activity, and an exploration. Commissioned by The Baltimore Museum of Art for the *Work Ethic* exhibition, it is also an instance of site-specific art. The project entails the artist establishing a well in the Museum's sculpture garden, retrieving water, bottling that water, and ultimately adding the water to the Museum's heating and cooling unit such that a percentage of the air in the Museum becomes part of Pocock's sculptural project, subsequently titled *Volume*.

The work operates on several levels. It partakes in the history of physically arduous performances from the 1960s and 1970s in which artists set themselves a task and completed it. Pocock differs from his predecessors, however, as he is interested in the labor of art producing something useful: water. Pocock's search for water begins with geological surveys of the area and culminates in his drilling for water in a highly public manner, illuminated by theatrical lights while the activity is being videotaped. Easy and unfettered access to water is one of the monumental advances and privileges of developed countries. Pocock excavates an obsolete form of labor by digging for a well. His insistence that the water subsequently be useful to the institution from which it comes is born of a concern for exposing the radical interconnectedness of cultural institutions and natural processes—an interdependence too often occluded by the immediacy of our access to the natural resources upon which all life depends.

Drilling is also concerned with the formal problems of sculpture, the relationship of solids and voids. Its location in the sculpture garden is a sly rejoinder to the history of monumental vertical outdoor sculpture—offering instead a kind of "sculpture in reverse." Similarly, by using water as a medium for sculpture, Pocock is able to make a work of art that exists in all three states of matter: liquid (as the water is taken from the earth), solid (as the water freezes in the cooling unit), and gas (as the water becomes part of the air of the Museum).

Yet one of the most interesting (and hidden from view) parts of *Drilling* is the way in which the project cut across the division of labor within the Museum itself. Meetings about *Drilling* routinely included people from the Installation, Security, Facilities, and Finance departments as well as registrars, groundskeepers, technicians, the curator, and the artist. In each meeting, the division of labor was evident, yet the standard division between mental and manual labor was often suspended or even rendered null and void as *Drilling* became an elaborate form of institutional problem solving, one in which each person's expertise came to bear on the creation of a final process/product. By insisting upon the cycles of dependence between institutions and the earth, Pocock's *Drilling* momentarily transformed the Museum from an institution structured by a stagnant division of labor to a laboratory environment dedicated to the creative production of new culture.

HM

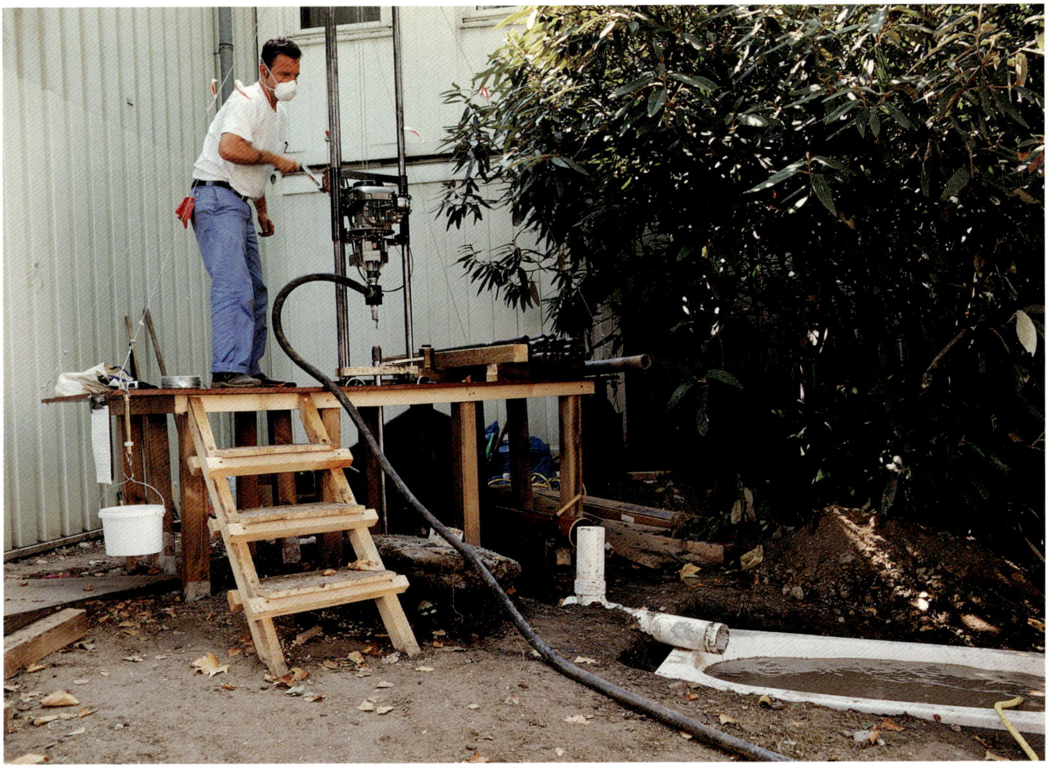

Hugh Pocock, *Drilling a Well for Water,* 2001. Portikus Museum, Frankfurt, Germany.

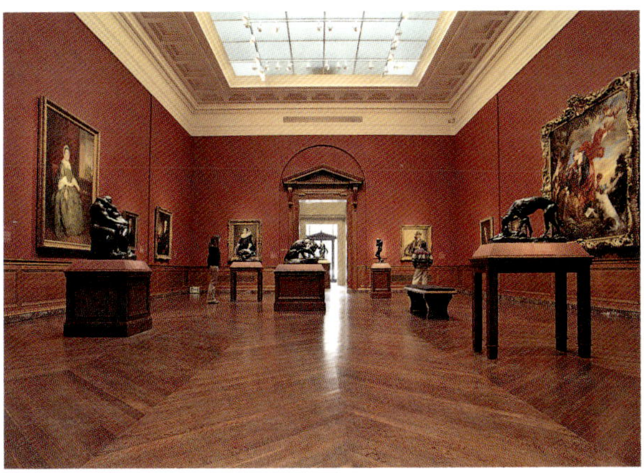

Hugh Pocock, *Volume,* 2003. The Baltimore Museum of Art.

PERFORMANCE

The subject of countless exhibitions, articles, and scholarly publications, "performance" nonetheless remains a troublesome term. Much of this difficulty stems from the fact that performance upsets the conventional categories of art history. Performance is not a movement or a school with an identifiable set of practitioners; instead, it is a strategy adopted by a range of artists who interpret it in vastly different and even contradictory ways. Performance is not a medium but hybridizes different media, thus challenging the very notion of a medium. It is not a distinct discipline but breaches disciplinary boundaries—from music and film to literature—to participate in the broader interdisciplinary turn of the humanities in the sixties. Rather than a fixed idea, performance raises complex interpretive questions regarding the ongoing transformations of the nature of art in the postwar period.

In the critical literature, the most dominant understanding of performance entails the displacement of material objects by the execution of actions on the part of the artist: the immediacy of bodily presentation undermines the intermediary nature of representation. By foregrounding the ephemerality of the event and the significance of a live witness, performance is intimately linked to the temporal present and, more broadly, to a concern with time. Traditionally, art objects are understood to be "timeless"—not only literally, as static things, but also conceptually, in the sense that the meaning of art is thought to be unchanging over time. Through different performance structures, many artists expressly challenged both these ideals. Robert Morris's *Box with the Sound of Its Own Making,* for example, wryly comments on the duration of its own making as well as the "time" or experience of viewing/hearing as integral to an understanding of a "completed" object.

Through the temporality of performance, the artwork itself is also redefined, transformed from an *object* into an *event.* On the one hand, this shift introduces the possibility of art's disappearance or "dematerialization," to use the term coined in the sixties by critics Lucy Lippard and John Chandler, who identified performance as one example of art's decommodification, in which the production of lasting, exchangeable things was rejected. On the other hand, performance's event structure spurns the development of alternative formal strategies. In Eleanor Antin's *Carving,* for example, the artist's daily weight loss is captured through a serial production of photographs subsequently presented in a chronological grid. In other examples, time is figured not as linear and ephemeral but as ongoing and repetitive, as in the "maintenance" project of Mierle Laderman Ukeles or the sanitation performance of the collective Hi Red Center, in which time is thematized as the endlessness of domestic labor.

The "medium" of performance is often thought to be the body, given its prevalence in much performance work (replacing such traditional materials as paint, for instance). But the significance of the body was by no means universal for artists working in the sixties. Most prevalently, women artists, working within the political feminist movement, incorporated their bodies in performances, actions, and sculptural works in order to call attention to how the body is culturally "marked" with differences such as gender. Subsequently, the nature of bodily identity was further differentiated to include class, race, and sexuality. The significance of the body in performance, therefore, moves beyond the privacy of the artist's singular identity to engage the "social body," opening up a larger theoretical project of the late sixties in which the body is under-

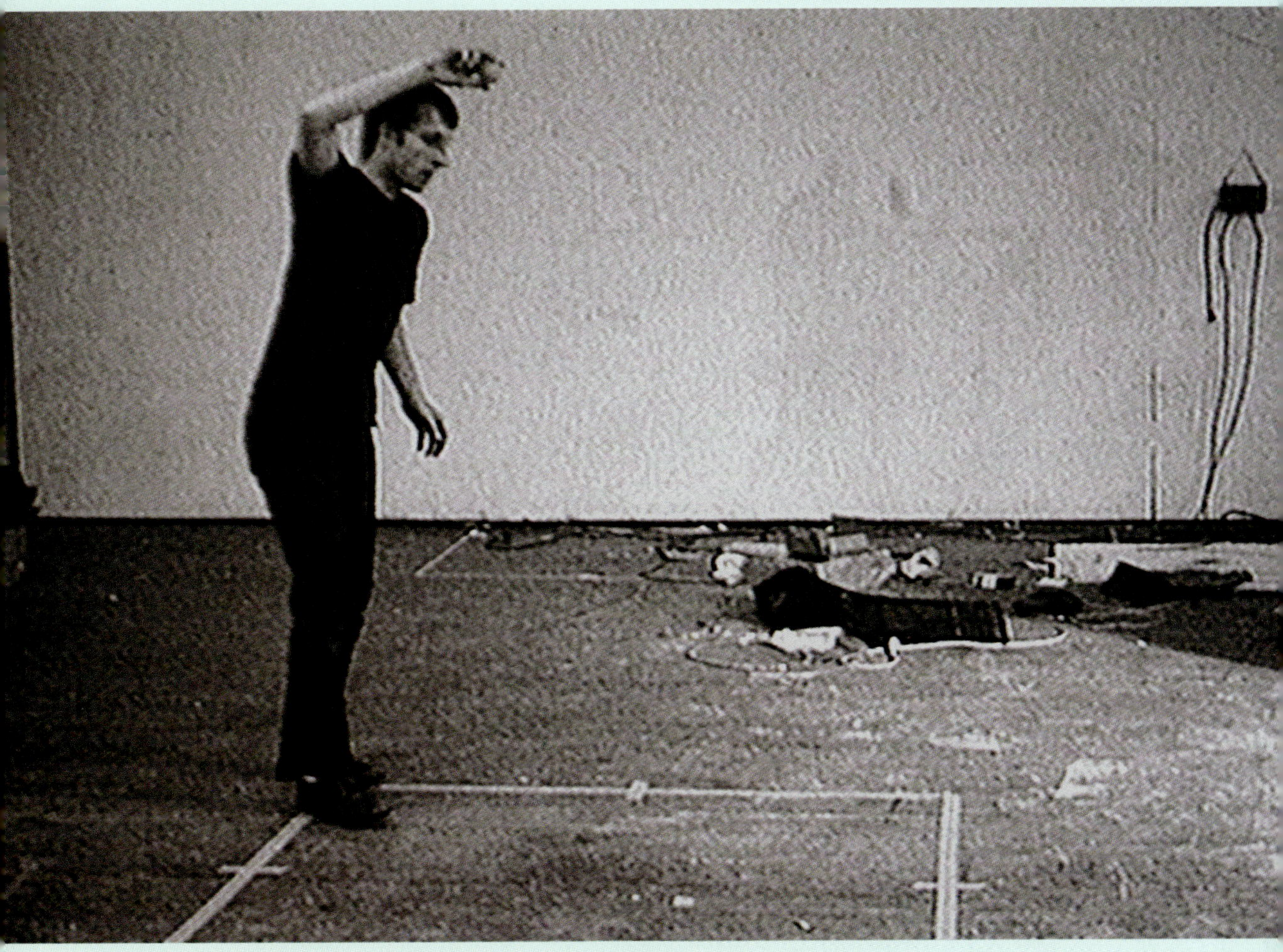

Bruce Nauman, *Bouncing Two Balls Between the Floor and Ceiling with Changing Rhythms,* 1967–68.

stood not as a natural, biological entity but as a socially determined object.

While the proximity of performance to themes of time and the body seems evident, its crucial role in the emergence of language-based practices in the art of the sixties is often overlooked. Performance and language merge through the linguistic concept of the *performative utterance* or the *speech act,* which emphasizes the relationship between words and action. The instruction or proposal work, one of the most ubiquitous textual forms in art of the late sixties, exemplifies this notion of performativity. In these works, which first systematically appear in Fluxus art and then are further investigated in

Hi Red Center, *Cleaning Event,* 1964. Photograph: Minoru Hirata.

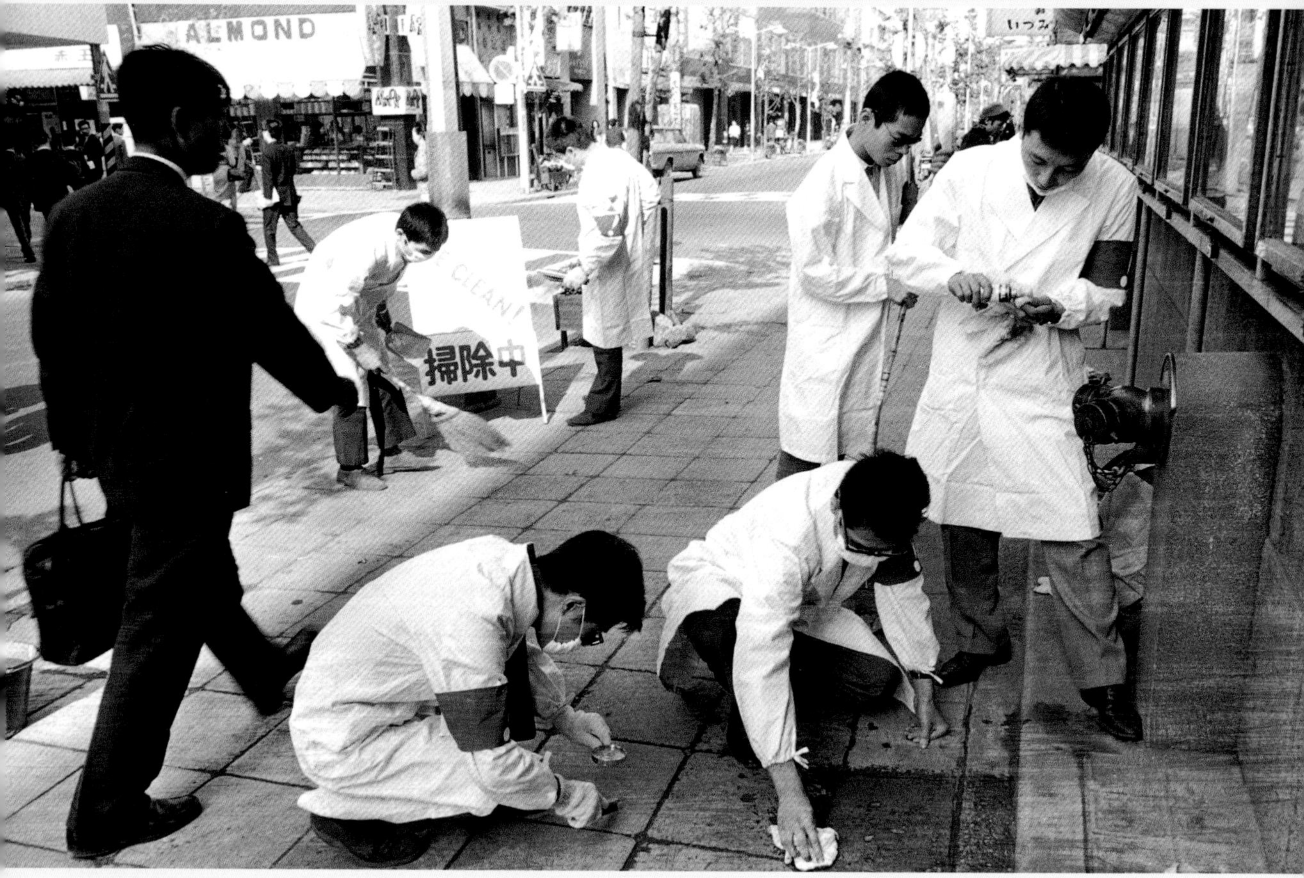

Conceptual art, performances are represented as sets of instructions, which may or may not be executed and thus may or may not acquire other material forms. Often, however, the ambiguous nature of both the art object and the very premise of "materiality" is foregrounded. Robert Barry's *Closed Gallery,* for example, can be seen as exemplifying Conceptual art's resolute immateriality—nothing, ostensibly, is produced. An event occurs, nonetheless, in that the exhibition as a "non-exhibition" is realized through the circulation of a linguistic statement on announcement cards. In Alison Knowles's *Make a Salad,* on the other hand, the performativity of the instruction piece undermines the status of performance as a single, nonrepeatable event: the linguistic instruction bears the potential for an infinite chain of like performances.

As the above discussion demonstrates, the interdisciplinary nature of performance perhaps represents its most crucial contribution. Indeed, for many artists, performance provides a means of looking outside the limited framework of the visual arts into other disciplines, including the performing or "temporal" arts (i.e., theater, music, film, and

Eleanor Antin, *Carving: A Traditional Sculpture,* 1972.

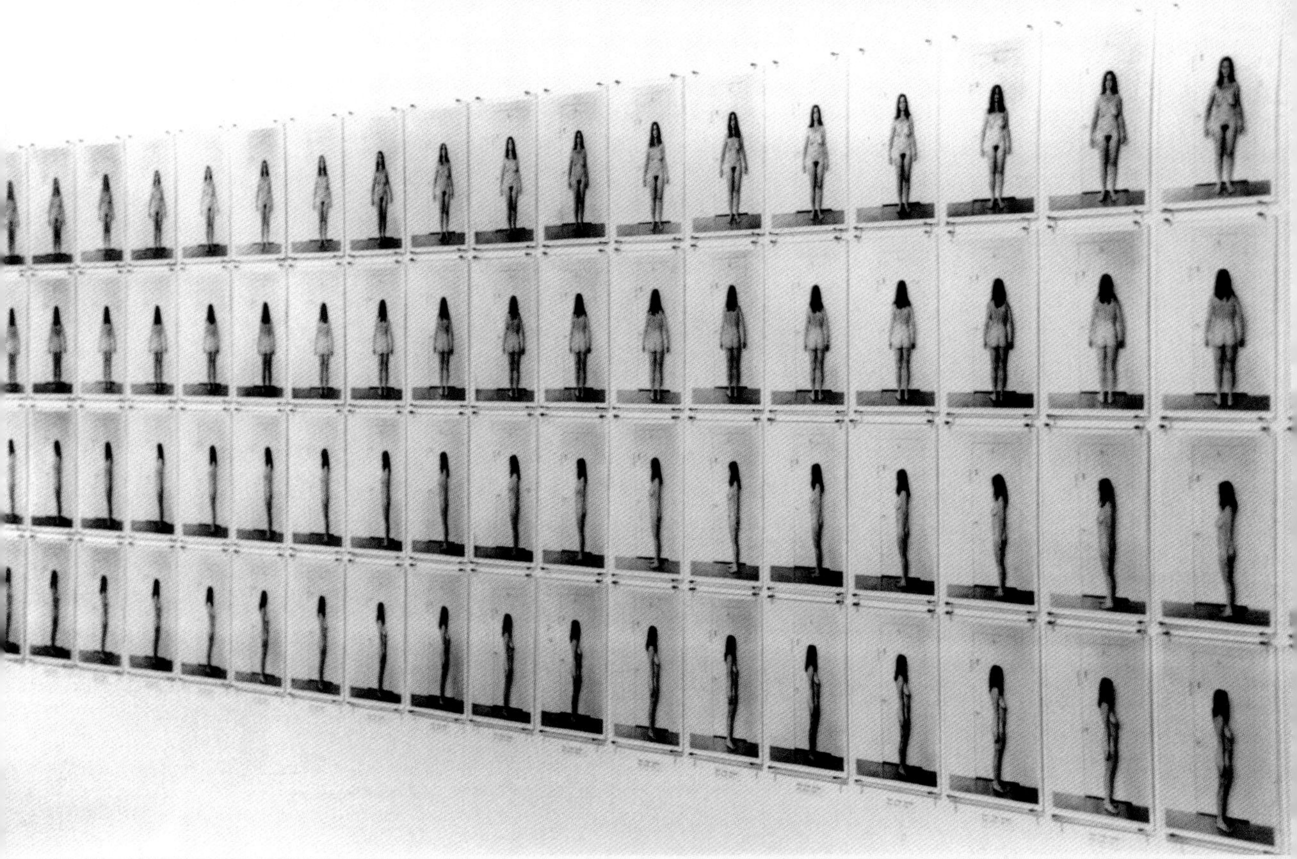

dance). For example, artists associated with Happenings and Fluxus art drew upon experimental theatrical practices of such playwrights as Bertolt Brecht and Antonin Artaud, creating performance pieces in which audience members functioned as active participants rather than mute witnesses. Similarly, in Yoko Ono's *Cut Piece,* audience involvement is explicitly solicited; it assumes, however, a confrontational stance, forcing the audience to face ethical questions regarding the consequences of its actions.

The composer John Cage looms as a major reference in the development of diverse performance practices in the sixties. A number of artists had personal contacts with Cage through his now-famous classes at the New School for Social Research (1956–60). The composer's ideas were also widely disseminated: the consideration of found sounds and noise as "musical" elements (thereby expanding the range of legitimate artistic materials and forms of labor) and the examination of the structure of the performance event, the audience, and the role of the musical score were addressed and expressed in the framework of performance. JK

Bruce Nauman
American, b. 1941

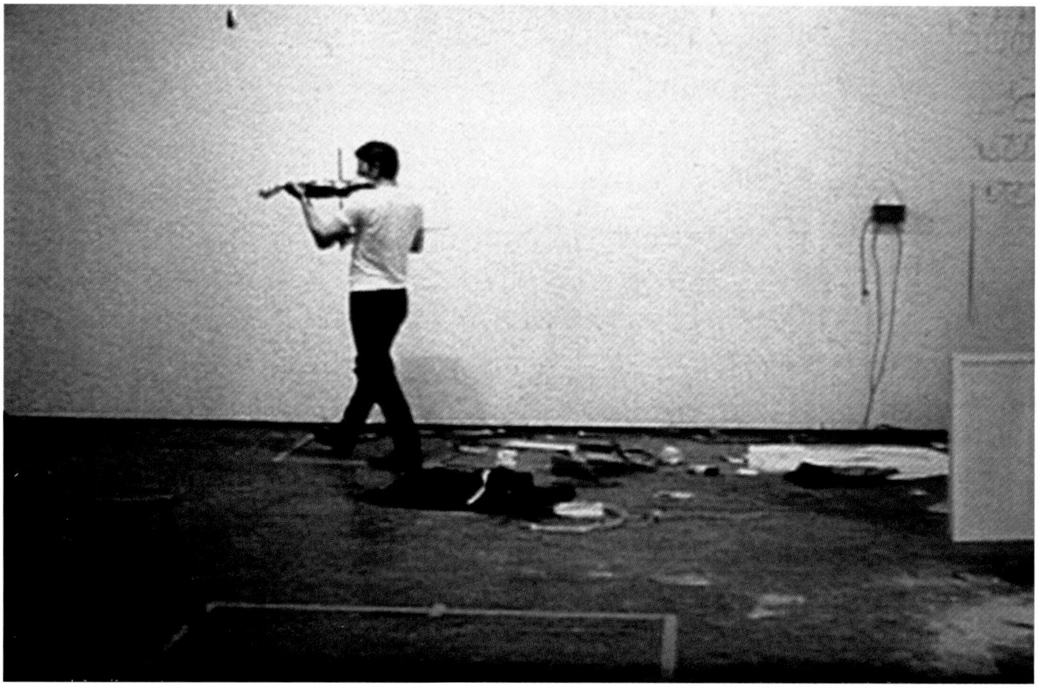

Bruce Nauman, *Playing a Note on the Violin While I Walk Around the Studio,* 1967–68.

Bruce Nauman's four studio films (1967–68)—*Bouncing Two Balls Between the Floor and Ceiling with Changing Rhythms*, *Playing a Note on the Violin While I Walk Around the Studio*, *Walking in an Exaggerated Manner Around the Perimeter of a Square*, and *Dance or Exercise on the Perimeter of a Square*—represent an important stage in the artist's investigation and transformation of sculpture. "If you can manipulate clay and end up with art," the artist once remarked, "you can manipulate yourself in [art] as well. It has to do with using the body as a tool, an object to manipulate."[1] In the mid-sixties, Nauman began to experiment with his body, staging it in various situations to be photographed or treating it as a machine-like tool that performs mundane tasks or manipulates objects. In using his own body, Nauman's intent was not to explore himself as a psychological being but to raise a central question: What does an artist do? "[I]t turned out that I was pacing around the studio a lot," he observes, "so that was an activity that I did so I filmed that, just this pacing."[2] The studio films represent the culmination of this experimentation, in that sculptural materials (including nontraditional ones) are completely displaced by a series of predetermined bodily actions, rendering the artist's movements both the medium and subject of the work. Short in length (about ten minutes), limited in scope, with a single task (pacing, bouncing balls, and the like) repeatedly executed, the four films were originally intended to be screened individually as loops, yielding a sense of never-ending duration.

In each film, the artist is pictured in the isolation of his dusty studio, which, with bare walls and little furniture, appears to be a mere background for his performance. But during the course of the films' playing, the unremarkable studio begins to gain importance. In three of the films, for example, Nauman's body completely disappears from the film's frame, leaving the viewer to stare at a still picture of the seemingly "empty" studio, now devoid of any activity—and thus putatively of any interest. The composer John Cage (an important precedent for Nauman) famously demonstrated in his "silent" composition, *4′33″*, however, that the removal of properly musical sound allowed otherwise overlooked sounds—i.e., those in the everyday world—to be noticed. Likewise, in the studio films, the recording camera is fixed on a tripod rather than mobile, intermittently eliminating the central action (i.e., Nauman's bodily movements). As a result, the spectator becomes attentive to previously unnoticed details and elements: piles of detritus lying haphazardly about; the white square, taped to the floor, which is used in two of the films as a choreographic template; and, in particular, the sounds that are byproducts of Nauman's performed actions. From the dissonant notes of the violin and the rhythmic pattern of balls striking the floor to the artist's incessantly tapping feet, the studio films are as much *sonic* works as *visual* ones. Following Cage's example, Nauman's films present the body as an *instrument:* that is, something capable not just of demonstrating gesture and movement but also of producing sound. JK

1. Cited in Coosje van Bruggen, *Bruce Nauman* (New York: Rizzoli International Publications, Inc., 1988), 109.

2. Bruce Nauman, interview by Lorraine Sciarra (1972), in *Please Pay Attention Please: Bruce Nauman's Words: Writings and Interviews*, ed. Janet Kraynak (Cambridge: The MIT Press, forthcoming).

Richard Serra
American, b. 1939

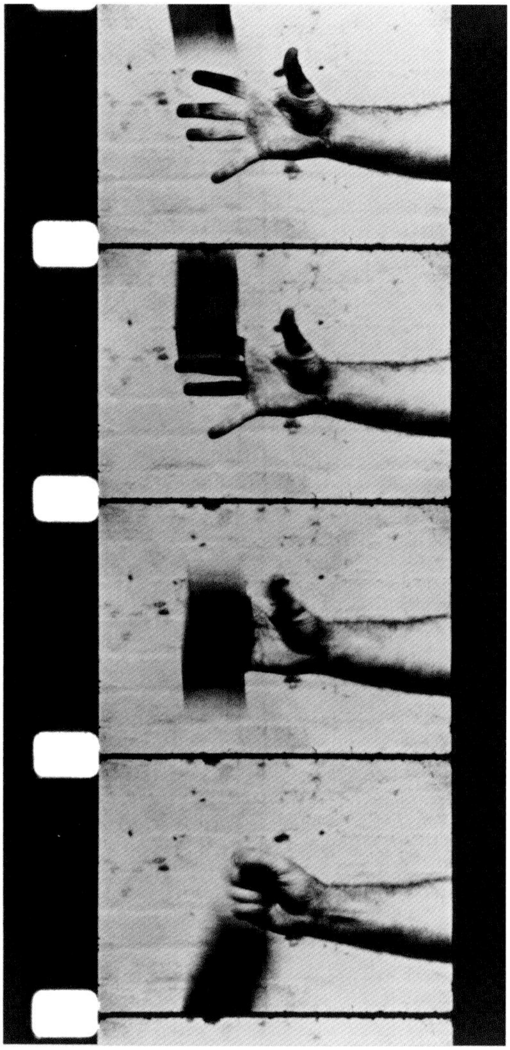

Richard Serra, *Hand Catching Lead,* 1968.

"To drop, to remove, to simplify, to differ, to disarrange": these are just a few of the actions enumerated in Richard Serra's litany-like *Verb List* (1967–68). The list sounds like an abbreviated how-to guide for post-Minimal practice, which was concerned with process and the physical qualities of materials. Presented as infinitives, the verbs in the two-page list are severed from their nouns and read like a list of possibilities for action. The *Verb List* was first written in one of Serra's notebooks, and it generates suggestions for what the tasks of the sculptor might be. As a teenager in California, Serra worked in steel mills, where he "saw steel being bored, cut, rolled, stacked, craned, fitted, reamed, riveted, tooled."[1] His description of the production of steel echoes the staccato rhythm of the *Verb List.*

Serra made films in the late 1960s that seem to obey the commands implicit in the *Verb List:* to drop, to catch, to dig, to remove. In his three-minute 16 mm film *Hand Catching Lead* (1968), small lead strips are dropped from beyond the frame of the camera as a hand tries to halt their downward path. The outstretched hand flexes and grasps, closes and releases. Most of the time, it fails to catch the lead. When the hand does enclose the metal, it registers no victory but lets it go, only to try to catch another fast-approaching strip. The grasping is a repeated motion with no apparent beginning and no end. The film—one long take—resists any narrative arc or climax but instead depicts a cycle of drops and attempts. The hand reacts with such intense regularity as the lead falls that it seems almost like an exercise or a drill. But if this is training, it is pointless, for the hand gets no better at catching the strips as the short film progresses. Primarily known for his large-scale sculpture, Serra explored in the late 1960s the properties of metals, using heavy, prefabricated slabs of iron, steel, and lead, often in repeated, simple shapes that were propped or grouped together. *Hand Catching Lead* can be viewed as a distillation of much of Serra's sculpture, with its emphasis on seriality, gravity, and de-skilled artistic production—that is, a deemphasis on specialized knowledge or craft. For while the hand is fully engaged in its work, it does nothing to transform, carve, or mold the lead.

Hands Scraping (1968) is a three-minute film that shows two pairs of hands—Serra's and the composer Philip Glass's—furiously scratching at a wood floor, as if with their frantic motion they could claw the paint right off the boards. This frenzy looks like a primitive gesture of group labor; here, hands toil without proper tools. As in the *Verb List* and *Hand Catching Lead,* the process itself is more important than the end point or outcome. The hands' purposeful work acts as an allegory for the classical sculptural methods of removing or chipping away. But in this film, the scraping does not yield a cleaned surface, nor does it unearth some hidden treasure. Instead, the hands are absorbed by their own futile, laborious movement. JBW

1. "Sight Point '71–'75/Delineator '74–'76," interview with Liz Bear, *Art in America* (May/June 1976); reprinted in *Writings, Interviews*, by Richard Serra (Chicago: University of Chicago Press, 1994), 35–42.

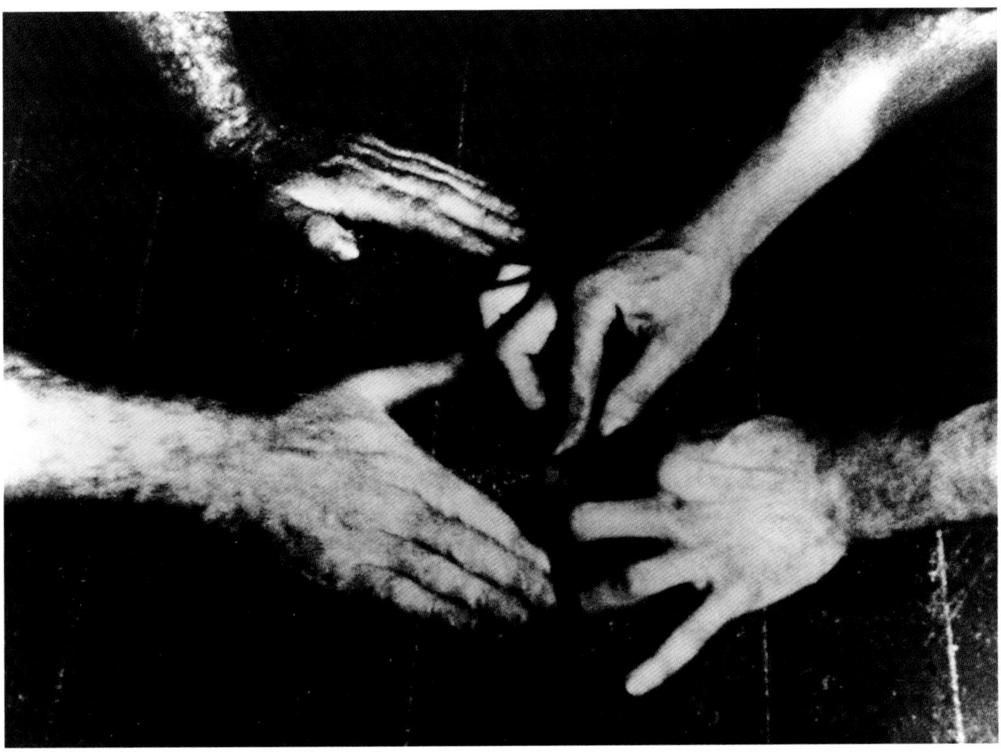

Richard Serra, *Hands Scraping,* 1968.

FEMINISM

Although the problem of gender inequality within the realm of labor had been voiced by such eighteenth- and nineteenth-century thinkers as Mary Wollstonecraft, John Stuart Mill, and Friedrich Engels, the 1960s saw an upsurge of critical thinking and political activism around questions of women's work. Taking cues from the civil rights movement and often developing as an outgrowth of the New Left, feminism emerged in the sixties as a major social movement that sought nothing less than a total reevaluation of how the sexes were differently treated, judged, and paid. Feminists contended that inequality determined women's everyday lives, and they began to examine the ways in which the private and public spheres established and enforced women's subordinate position. Of the many areas examined with a feminist lens, two broadly defined issues emerged that specifically focused on women's work: comparable worth and unpaid domestic labor.

Movements for comparable worth, or pay equity, agitate to reconcile the large disparity between what men and women earn in the workplace. This wage gap, it is argued, occurs because the skills intrinsic to conventionally female occupations such as nursing, providing child care, and secretarial work are vastly undervalued and underpaid. Although critics of feminism say that women choose to enter these lower-paid, female-dominated professions, supporters of pay equity point to the social denigration of vocations such as clerical work or caregiving.

Comparable worth was a mainstay of feminist thought in the sixties. The original platform of the National Organization for Women, founded in 1966, included "equal pay for equal work." But the decade between 1972 and 1982 saw the most intensive activism around this issue, and it continued to dominate feminist discussions throughout the eighties.[1] From 1972 to 1982, feminists campaigned to have the states ratify the Equal Rights Amendment, a proposed constitutional amendment that would, in theory, help close the gendered wage gap. Research showed that for every dollar a man earned, a woman with a similar level of experience would receive fifty-nine cents. So familiar and politically meaningful was this number that some pro-ERA buttons simply read "59¢." Wage discrimination continues to be a problem. The pay gap between women's and men's work has barely decreased in the past few decades, and the pay differential between white men and people of color (men and women) is vast.

By critically theorizing the sexual division of labor in the public sphere, feminists showed how gender and class are mutually implicated in capitalist economies that underpay women's work at the office and at home. And galvanized by the rallying cry "the personal is political," women increasingly saw how their individual circumstances might relate to wider problems of inequality. Feminists noted that within the home, women do much of the work that sustains the family (and, arguably, all of society), such as cleaning, cooking, and raising children. These unpaid duties are part and parcel of an ongoing system that refuses to recognize that women shoulder a disproportionate amount of the world's total labor and instead views household work as easy or trivial. In an influential 1970 essay, "The Politics of Housework," Pat Mainardi challenged this line of thought by asserting, "Housework trivial? Not on your life! Just try to share the burden."[2]

Some radical feminists go further than a call for equity in housework by demanding actual wages for housewives and stay-at-home mothers. Rather than regarding the home as the "natural" purview of women, they understand domestic labor as part of the larger sociopolitical structures that oppress women. Domestic work, they reason, should be compensated like any other work. "If women were paid for all they do, there'd be a lot of wages due," states the global coalition still actively fighting for housework wages. More recently, feminist discussions of labor in the United States have taken up the corporate "glass ceiling" that prevents women from rising to executive positions and the exploitation of undocumented immigrant women working as maids, cooks, and nannies. JBW

1. For a broad history of women's wage labor, see Alice Kessler-Harris, *A Woman's Wage: Historical Meanings and Social Consequences* (Lexington: The University Press of Kentucky, 1990). An in-depth look at the comparable worth movement in the United States can be found in Linda M. Blum's *Between Feminism and Labor: The Significance of the Comparable Worth Movement* (Berkeley and Los Angeles: University of California Press, 1991).

2. Reprinted in *Sisterhood Is Powerful,* ed. Robin Morgan (New York: Vintage/Random House, 1970), 447–554.

Eleanor Antin
American, b. 1935

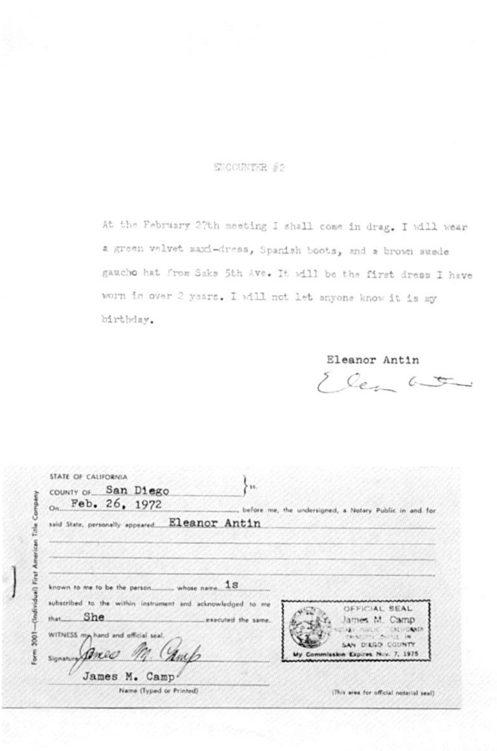

ENCOUNTER #2

At the February 27th meeting I shall come in drag. I will wear a green velvet maxi-dress, Spanish boots, and a brown suede gaucho hat from Saks 5th Ave. It will be the first dress I have worn in over 2 years. I will not let anyone know it is my birthday.

Eleanor Antin

Form 3001—(Individual) First American Title Company

STATE OF CALIFORNIA
COUNTY OF San Diego } ss.
On Feb. 26, 1972 before me, the undersigned, a Notary Public in and for said State, personally appeared Eleanor Antin
known to me to be the person whose name is subscribed to the within instrument and acknowledged to me that She executed the same.
WITNESS my hand and official seal.
Signature
James M. Camp
Name (Typed or Printed)

OFFICIAL SEAL
James M. Camp
SAN DIEGO COUNTY
My Commission Expires Nov. 7, 1975

(This area for official notarial seal)

Eleanor Antin, *4 Transactions,* 1972.

Like many artists involved in performance, Eleanor Antin often focused on her body and her own actions in place of producing a traditionally defined art object. In *Carving: A Traditional Sculpture* (1972), one of her best-known works, this substitution is made particularly explicit. One hundred forty-eight black-and-white photographs, hung in a grid, document Antin's weight loss over a thirty-six-day period. Parodying one of the myths of sculpture—that a sculptor seeks to uncover a true form somehow hidden in the stone or wood, a form discovered through the sculptor's carving—Antin replaces the skill of the sculpture with an activity anyone can do: dieting.

Although a number of her male Conceptualist counterparts explored acts of physical endurance, they often did so in a putatively nonideological manner. Antin's *Carving* stages the problem of labor (and artistic labor in particular) within a feminist context. She uses Conceptualist strategies to critique the myths of art; likewise, she uses feminism to critique the apolitical nature of much Conceptual and Performance art. Here, then, the managerial impulse to document and survey is shown to permeate women's lives differ-

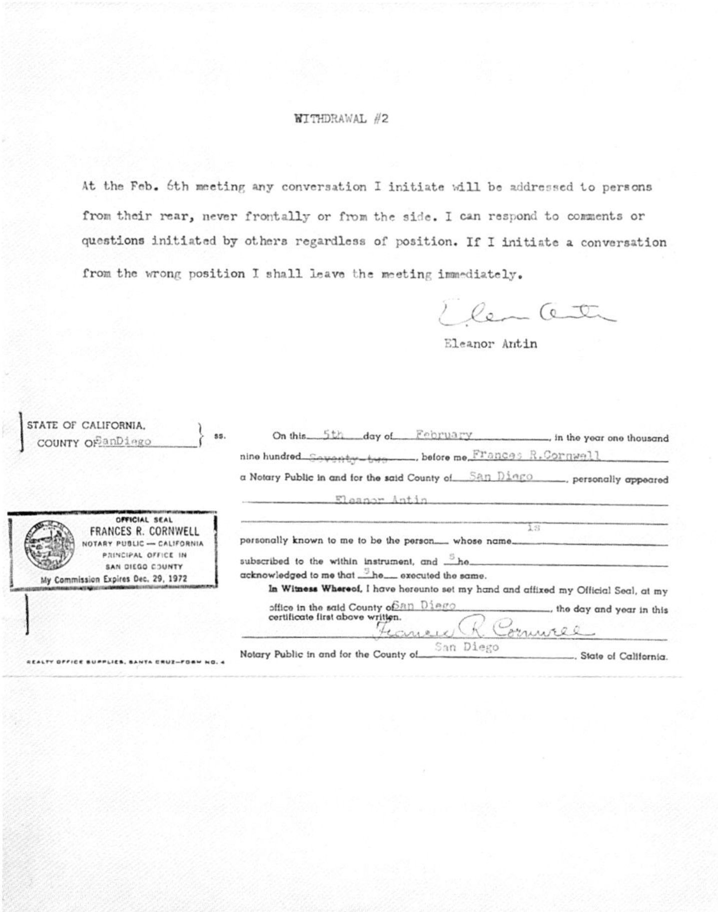

WITHDRAWAL #2

At the Feb. 6th meeting any conversation I initiate will be addressed to persons from their rear, never frontally or from the side. I can respond to comments or questions initiated by others regardless of position. If I initiate a conversation from the wrong position I shall leave the meeting immediately.

Eleanor Antin

STATE OF CALIFORNIA, COUNTY OF San Diego } ss.

On this 5th day of February, in the year one thousand nine hundred Seventy-two, before me, Frances R. Cornwell a Notary Public in and for the said County of San Diego, personally appeared Eleanor Antin personally known to me to be the person whose name is subscribed to the within instrument, and she acknowledged to me that she executed the same.

In Witness Whereof, I have hereunto set my hand and affixed my Official Seal, at my office in the said County of San Diego, the day and year in this certificate first above written.

Frances R. Cornwell

Notary Public in and for the County of San Diego, State of California.

OFFICIAL SEAL
FRANCES R. CORNWELL
NOTARY PUBLIC — CALIFORNIA
PRINCIPAL OFFICE IN
SAN DIEGO COUNTY
My Commission Expires Dec. 29, 1972

REALTY OFFICE SUPPLIES, SANTA CRUZ—FORM NO. 4

ently, bound as it is to the production of women's bodies as a consumable commodity.

Antin also used a task-based performance strategy to critique the mores of bourgeois feminism as well as traditional art production. In *4 Transactions* (1972), Antin prescribed behaviors that she would engage in at a women's encounter group. In one transaction, she would only address people from behind; in another, she would wear a dress for the first time in two years and attend the meeting "in drag." Each activity or "transaction" was typed up and notarized but was known only to Antin herself. Each behavior was designed to interrupt the smooth functioning of the women's encounter group and to disturb notions of proper feminist behavior. Unlike *Carving*, in which Antin subjects herself to the monitoring of women's bodies by an image regime, in *4 Transactions* she ridicules the behavioral monitoring of social groups. In this regard, Antin's use of the managerial strategies of Conceptual art highlights the similarities between leisure (a voluntary women's group) and work (a voluntary diet): each activity, as well as the art made about it, is suffused with the managerial logic of proper forms of behavior adequately documented.

HM

Mierle Laderman Ukeles

American, b. 1939

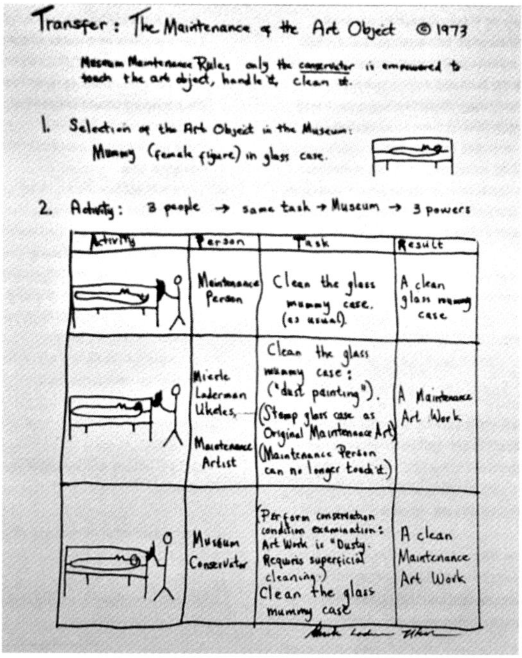

Mierle Laderman Ukeles, *Transfer: The Maintenance of the Art Object,* 1973.

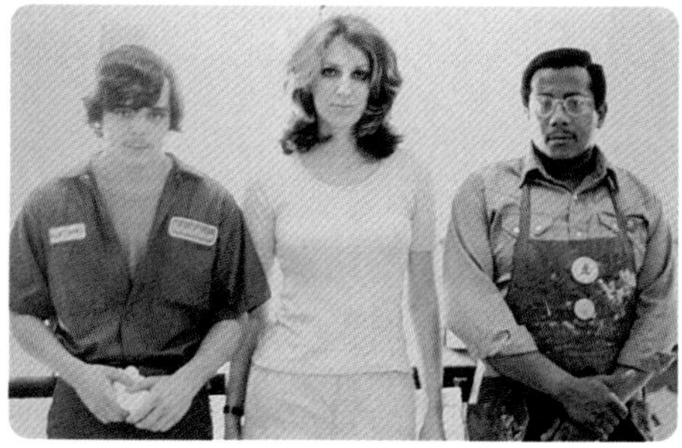

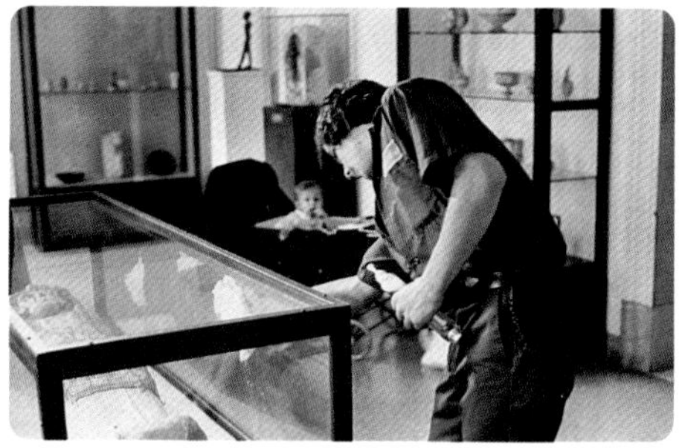

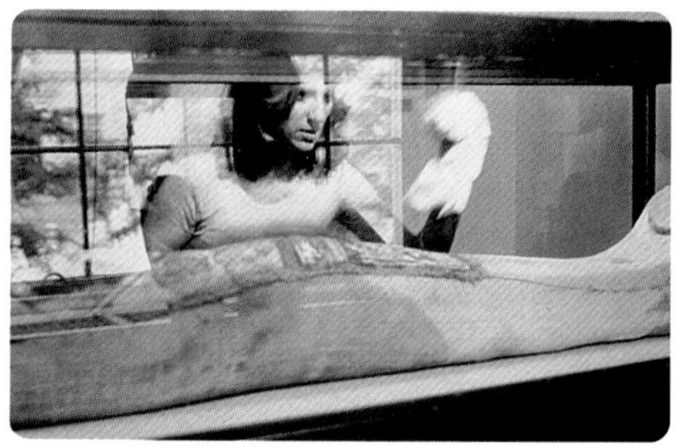

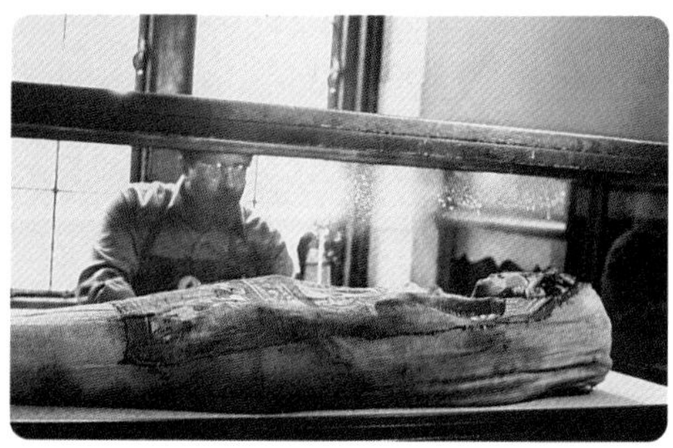

In her "Maintenance Art Manifesto" of 1969, Mierle Laderman Ukeles stridently argued that maintenance labor is equally composed of everyday domestic activities, such as cleaning, cooking, and child rearing, as well as janitorial duties such as "keep[ing] the dust off the pure individual creation"[1] in museums. Maintenance labor, she contends, is the invisible work that makes all other forms of work possible. In 1973, Ukeles staged four *Maintenance Art Performances* at the Wadsworth Atheneum. In *Hartford Wash: Washing Tracks, Maintenance Inside* and *Hartford Wash: Washing Tracks, Maintenance Outside*, Ukeles mopped and scrubbed the interior galleries and exterior steps of the museum, respectively, and in *Keeping of the Keys*, Ukeles took over the task of securing the galleries. Yet the work that most thoroughly explores divisions of skilled and nonskilled labor is *Transfer: The Maintenance of the Art Object.*

In *Transfer*, Ukeles selected a mummy housed in a glass case in the Wadsworth's collection. Within the normal museum hierarchy, it is the janitor's job to keep the casework clean and the conservator's job to keep the artwork clean. Ukeles took on the janitor's labor by cleaning the mummy case as a piece of "maintenance art," and she then proclaimed her cleaning to be art, her cleaned mummy case a "dust painting." Upon the completion of her dust painting, the artist stamped the case and the cleaning rag with a rubber stamp. In an event staged for the camera, the stamped rag and cleaning fluid were handed to the conservator, as the case, now an artwork, could only be cleaned by him. The photographs of *Transfer* are accompanied by a hand-drawn diagram resembling a low-tech flowchart and documents how one job (cleaning) had become the province of three different professionals: janitor, artist, and conservator. The stick figures on the chart lend a goofy air to the work, offering a send-up of the often clinical "aesthetic of administration" put forth by many of Ukeles's Conceptual artist counterparts. Yet the silliness of the piece hardly mitigates the incisiveness of the critique of the modern organization of work, as the diagram satirizes the managerial desire to divide labor and in so doing assigning it different types of value. While the performance exposes the division of labor within institutions, it also highlights the division of labor that supports the aura of the artist's signature (only special people like conservators can clean up after artists). In *Transfer*, though, anyone can use the maintenance art stamp, potentially compromising the privileged status of artistic labor.

Ukeles's investigations of institutions also include the nuclear family. In *Private Performances of Personal Maintenance as Art* (1970–73), she obsessively documents, sometimes minute by minute, her labor as a mother and wife. Under capitalism, this labor (which is not subject to the laws of wage labor) goes unremunerated because the labor of mothering is deemed "natural" and hence not truly "work." By documenting her domestic labor as maintenance art, Ukeles, the artist, is able to transform it into art, claiming for it a value it does not have otherwise. HM

1. Mierle Laderman Ukeles, "Maintenance Art Manifesto" (1969); reprinted in *Documents* 10 (Fall 1997): 6.

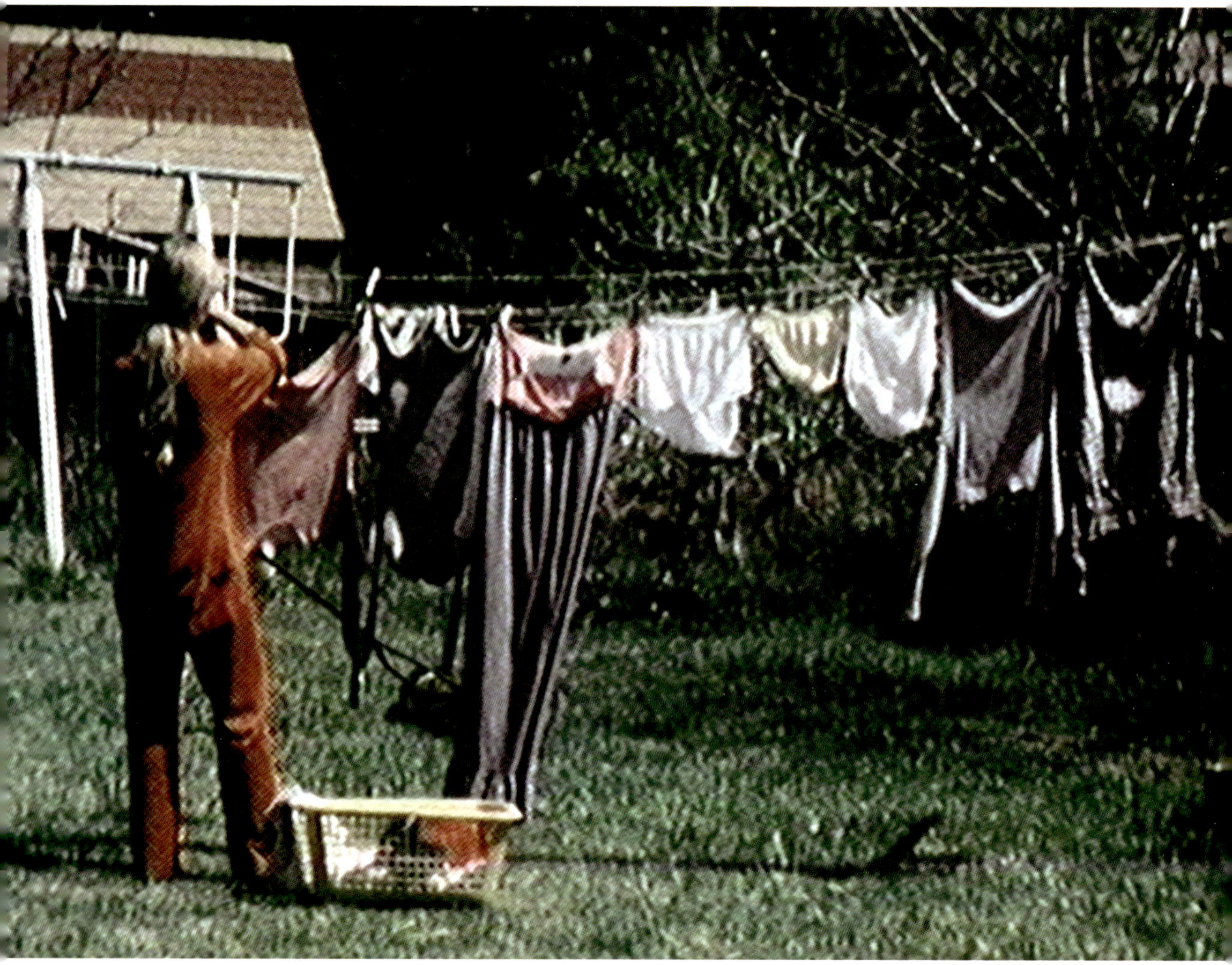

Martha Rosler, *Backyard Economy I*, 1974.

Martha Rosler
American

Martha Rosler has been committed throughout her career to making art in everyday formats and accessible media, such as Super 8 film, photography, and video, all of which are available to everyday folks as well as artists and all of which are relatively inexpensive to produce and easy to distribute and disseminate. Despite this, Rosler's work has often been difficult to see in mainstream art institutions. Informed early on by Conceptual art's "do-it-yourself" aesthetic and a Marxist-inspired suspicion of art as a luxury commodity, her influence, however, has long been felt among artists and critics, and her particular blend of Marxism and humor was especially important in the formation of the highly fractured and contestatory field of Feminist art.

During the 1970s Rosler consistently took domesticity and traditional forms of women's labor as her subject matter. In works such as *A budding gourmet* (1974), a serial postcard novella, and *Semiotics of the Kitchen* (1975), a videotape, she examined the space of the kitchen and cooking as forms of social aspiration and entrapment, respectively. It wasn't long before Rosler started to situate the domestic labor of cooking and women's work generally within a larger sociopolitical landscape. In the serial postcard novels *McTowers Maid* (1975) and *Tijuana Maid* (1975), Rosler identified the underpaid labor of migrant women as part and parcel of a larger domestic economy with national and global ramifications. Cooking is seen in both works as a form of unpaid or underpaid labor, but it is also seen as embodying the pleasure and aspirations of millions of women. It is precisely this kind of dialectical approach to the economic and psychological issue of women's labor that makes Rosler's work sympathetic as well as incisively critical.

In *Backyard Economy I* and *II* (1974), we see the artist at work in her backyard. She waters the plants, mows the lawn, and hangs the laundry. It appears to be a lovely day, with a brilliant blue sky, lots of sunshine, and blooming flowers. While on the one hand these short Super 8 films depict the banality of housework with its endless cycles of repetition and its steady tedium, on the other hand, they also offer an idyllic image of the simple pleasures of everyday life, the space of the garden, and the comforts of home. This ambivalence is doubled by the fact that Rosler has turned her everyday chores into a work of art by filming them in her role as "the artist." Like many Feminist artists of her generation, Rosler insists that these everyday jobs perform double duty inasmuch as they stand as both housework and artwork. HM

WAGE LABOR

In his 1847 essay "Wage Labor and Capital," Karl Marx outlines his theory of for-wage work, a concept that is central to his entire analysis of human exploitation in capitalism. Wage labor is the process by which workers sell their labor power to capitalists for a predetermined price, usually in blocks of time such as hours or weeks. Marx wrote, "wages are the sum of money paid by the capitalist for a particular labor time or for a particular output of labor. . . . The capitalist buys this labor power for a day, a week, a month, etc."[1] Workers, in effect, merely auction off their days, which are then "owned" and put to someone else's use. Because workers labor only to subsist, they have no real connection to the work they do, the products they create, or the services they render:

> The worker works in order to live. He does not even reckon labor as a part of his life; it is rather a sacrifice of his life. It is a commodity which he has made over to another . . . what he produces for himself is not the silk that he weaves, not the gold that he draws from the mine, not the palace that he builds. What he produces for himself is wages.

By selling their labor power, workers become commodities themselves, little different from the objects that they make. This is foundational to Marx's conception of alienation, which means people's estrangement not only from their work but also from each other—and, ultimately, from themselves.

Marx understood work as necessary for human self-actualization; labor is, in fact, the "essence" of what separates people from animals. Yet capitalism and its dependence on wage labor has warped work in such a way that humans no longer feel alive and purposeful when they do it. Wage labor is, on the contrary, deadening and repulsive because it has no meaning to those performing it other than the acquisition of a meager salary. Capitalists seek to increase profits even more by paying workers as little as possible. Marx often contrasts this grim cycle of wage labor to the supposedly "free labor" of artistic creation, but this is a questionable distinction. In Marx's idealized view, artistic labor is unfettered from the relentless pace of capitalism that demands constant toil.

More recent characterizations of art and work echo Marx. Artists are popularly believed to be "off the clock," unmonitored and unregulated agents of free will, subject only to their own whims and desires. Instead of being trapped by the grind of wage labor, artists work when they feel like it—when inspiration hits—and are reimbursed, if they are successful, for the pieces they create. There is some historical precedent to this lasting fiction. Jackson Pollock, for instance, was paid a modest monthly salary by Peggy Guggenheim. This freed him from having to hold a time-consuming job, allowing him to focus primarily on painting. For contemporary artists, however, especially those living in countries with little state support for the arts, the reality is quite different. They do not know if their work will sell or where art materials (much less rent) will come from. Dependent upon the ever-shifting criteria and tastes of grant-making agencies and gallerists, contemporary artists are often under the thumb of the market in an especially intense way. Many artists, of course, support themselves with teaching or other jobs but receive little or no compensation for the hours they spend making art.

While artists usually calculate the prices of their pieces in relation to their own time and expertise, these prices are meaningless if their work does not sell. A group active in the late 1960s called the Art Workers' Coalition suggested that all artists should receive wages, regardless of how much art they sold. This was seen as particularly urgent for artists whose works did not take the form of tangible objects and whose labor might therefore be difficult to "see." How might artists seek remuneration within an economy that values only the completed product? To put it more pointedly within the context of wage labor: What is an artist's time worth? A number of artists have broached this question as they attempt to legitimate their own work hours by proposing a system of wage labor. Although Marx saw it as the root of workers' problems, such a system could still present itself as a more appealing alternative to having artistic labor go unpaid.

The sculptor Ed Kienholz, for instance, in his *Concept Tableaux* (1963–67), sold written descriptions of large-scale works and would only execute the pieces if the collector agreed to pay for materials and an hourly wage. Working under the logic of wage labor means that artists structure their art making within the regime of the pay scale, demarcating and accounting for the time they spend on a piece. Marx notes that an hour of labor power is a commodity, just like a pound of sugar: "one is measured by the clock, the other by the scales." The measurement of labor by the clock is manifested most visibly in Tehching Hsieh's yearlong performance, *Time Piece* (1980–81), in which Hsieh punched a time clock on the hour every hour for a full year. Hsieh mimes the empty rituals of work, turning clock punches into his only act of labor—one whose very frequency renders any other type of work impossible. Hsieh's work makes clear that the flip side of not ever going to work is, of course, that you are never *off* work, either; the workday expands to fill every minute. Who pays for these hours logged?

JBW

1. All quotations are from Marx's "Wage Labor and Capital," first presented in lectures in 1847 and published in *Neue Rheinische Zeitung* in 1849. A later version, edited by Friedrich Engels, clarified the distinction between "labor" and "labor power." A translation of this edited essay appears in *The Marx-Engels Reader*, ed. Robert C. Tucker (New York: W. W. Norton, 1978), 203–17.

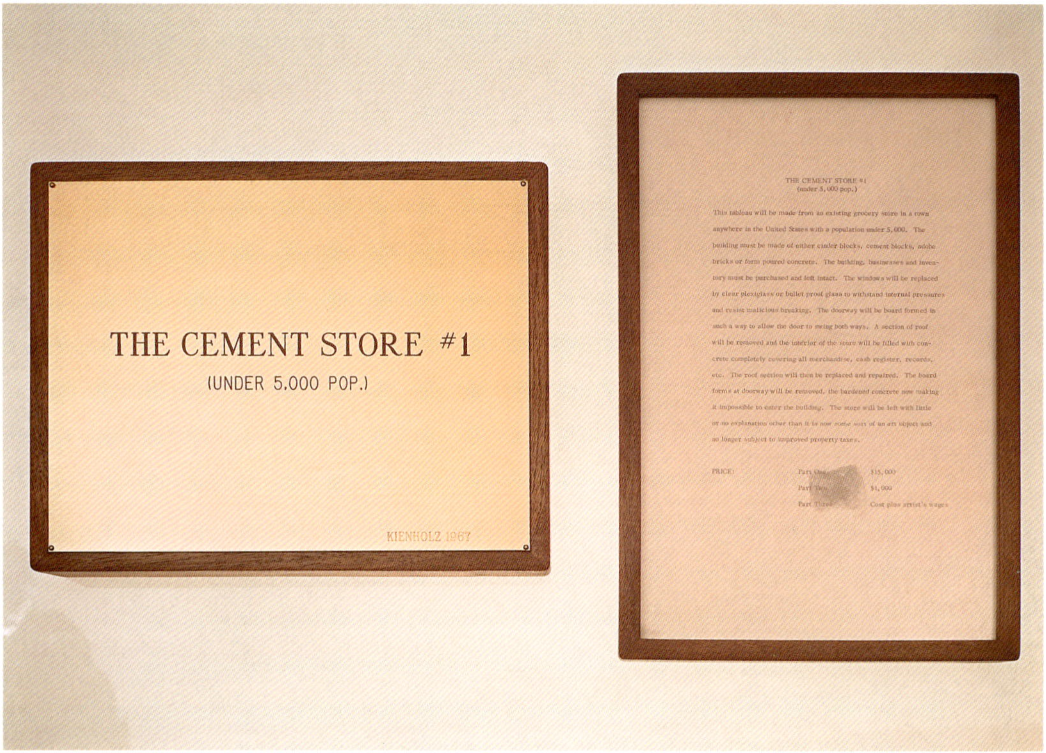

Edward Kienholz, *Concept Tableaux,* 1963–67.

Edward Kienholz

American, 1927–1994

Edward Kienholz was an assemblage and installation artist associated with the Ferus Gallery in Los Angeles in the late 1950s. He was included in the important *The Art of Assemblage* at The Museum of Modern Art and by 1966 had a controversial one-person exhibition at the Los Angeles County Museum. Known for acerbic, bawdy, and humorous works, Kienholz's oeuvre was distinguished by the use of discarded objects, viscous painted surfaces, and sharp social commentary. As Kienholz's ambition and career grew, so did the scale of many of his installation works, called "tableaux." Often life-sized and highly theatrical, the tableaux were labor intensive and expensive to produce.

From 1963 to 1967 Kienholz made a series of proposals collectively entitled the *Concept Tableaux*. Although the term "Conceptual art" is difficult to date precisely, Kienholz's *Concept Tableaux* demonstrate an early instance of the term "concept" being used in conjunction with an art object. With the *Concept Tableaux*, Kienholz astutely divided the labor of the artist into three distinct categories, each of which necessitated a different engagement with the collector/buyer of the work. The first step was a plaque with a detailed description of the work—the idea—which could be purchased simply as a proposal. In the second step, Kienholz produced a preparatory drawing for the tableau, which could be purchased for an additional sum. Should a committed-enough buyer be secured, the final step was the construction of the tableau, at which point the buyer would be charged for parts and an hourly wage for the artist. Kienholz here has separated the mental and manual functions of the artist, placing drawing as an intermediary step—one shared by artists and skilled craftsmen and laborers alike. In a unique gesture, however, Kienholz made evident the differing values produced by this division of labor. While many artists of the period staged the division of labor, few embraced the concept of wage labor in art. Traditional Marxist economic theory held that the production of art was radically different from production under wage labor. Wage labor, the selling of one's time on the open market as if it were a commodity, was understood to produce a profound sense of objectification and alienation. By contrast, the creation of art was thought to have liberatory potential, coming as it does from a person's sense of humanity. In the *Concept Tableaux*, Kienholz seems to take issue with this idea, implying that an artist's time is as bound to the logic of the market as that of any other laborer. To pretend otherwise potentially robs the artist of the value—both economic and philosophical—of his work and time. If art, too, depends upon the division of mental and physical labor, then Kienholz wanted to be paid for both. HM

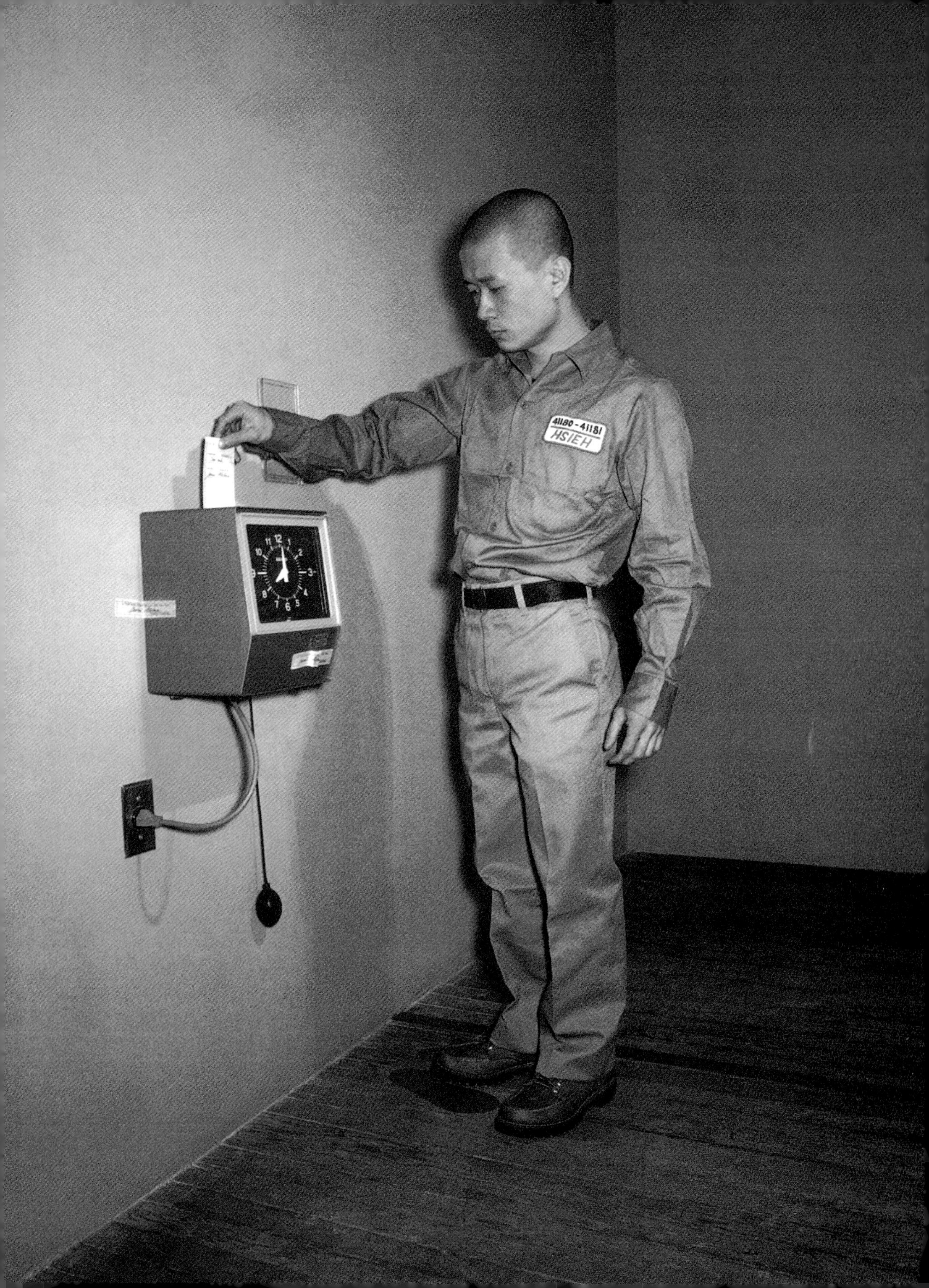
41180 - 41181
HSIEH

Tehching Hsieh
Taiwanese, b. 1950

From April 11, 1980 to April 11, 1981, every hour on the hour, Tehching Hsieh punched a time clock installed in his New York City studio. Setting an alarm to make sure he punched his card punctually, he could not sleep through the night. He also limited his activities to the area around his loft, so that if he left, he could return within the hour. Hsieh's commitment to this work was absolute: out of 8,760 required punches, he only missed 134. Informally known as *Time Piece*, this was the second of a series of year-long performances in which Hsieh subjected himself to extreme conditions. The first involved living for a year entirely within a cage (a paid assistant brought him food and water); in another, he lived outside for the duration of the performance, never stepping inside a building or even under an awning.

In *Time Piece*, Hsieh enacts a slavish adherence to the arbitrary workday clock. Time clocks act as instruments of demarcation, distinguishing work time and leisure time, calculating with precision the hours, minutes, and seconds one is on the job. Hsieh's monotonous task takes up his entire life, consuming it until there is no longer a distinction between work and life, public and private time. *Time Piece* hyperbolizes the mechanization and relentless repetition of modern labor. Forced to strive for ever-increasing efficiency, people are subject to tighter schedules and heightened surveillance; such regulations are taken to excess in Hsieh's performance.

Time Piece is accompanied by abundant documentation. Hsieh set up a film camera to take a single frame of every punch of the clock, representing this year of his life as nothing but the moments he inserted his cards. In this compressed record, the year passes in about six minutes. As the clock hands rapidly twirl and his body in its plain uniform lurches and twitches with each snap of the shutter, his face remains expressionless. He shaved his head at the beginning of the year so the film would more concretely record the progression of time passing, and by the end of the movie, it is shoulder-length. Hsieh collected every punch card and had them notarized by a witness at the end of each day. These were then kept in a series of notebooks as a testament to his diligence. Even though the documentation points to Hsieh's assiduousness, it also betrays an anxiety about questions of evidence. His paper trail exaggerates bureaucratic demands for strict information management and record keeping.

Time cards are tangible registers of bodily presence used in the workplace to monitor employees at the threshold of unregulated and regulated time. As a self-manager without the pressure of a system of rewards and punishments, Hsieh nonetheless makes himself into a perpetual work machine, perfect in every way save one. He does not produce any commodity or work in the usual sense, cycling instead through his rapid one-hour shifts. His action generates *nothing but* indexical traces, time cards and film frames, as well as one involuntary, passive, material by-product: his grown-out hair. JBW

Tehching Hsieh, *One Year Performance 1980–1981 (Time Piece), 11 April 1980–11 April 1981.* Photograph: Michael Shen.

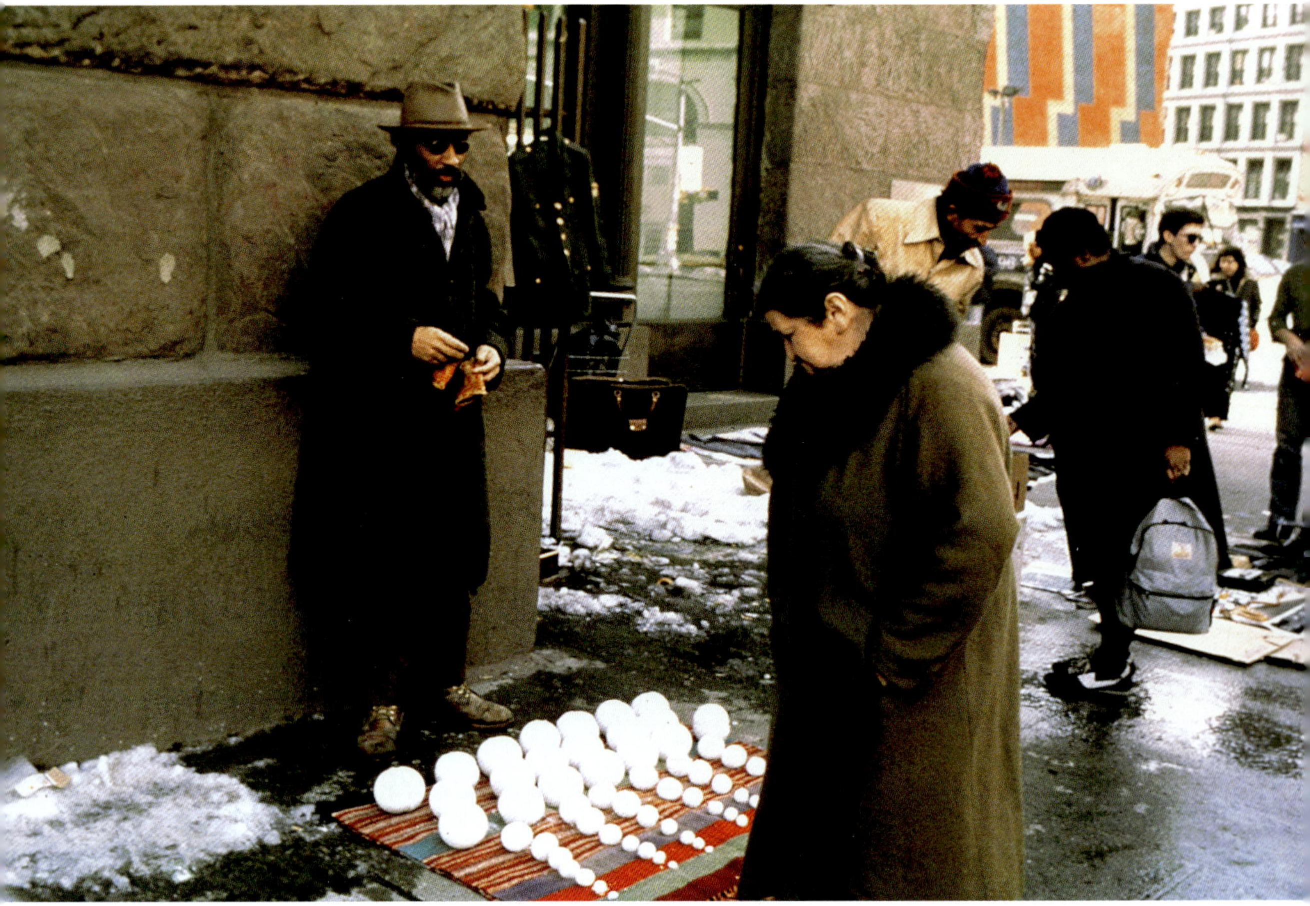

David Hammons, *Bliz-aard Ball Sale,* 1983.

David Hammons

American, b. 1943

All that remains of David Hammons's *Bliz-aard Ball Sale* (1983) are photographs of the artist selling snowballs on a Manhattan street corner. In one image, we see the artist interacting with his discerning customers; in another, a woman laughs into the camera; in yet another Hammons leans nonchalantly on a building wall, sporting a Mona Lisa smile. The snowballs themselves are well organized, moving from small to grapefruit-sized in an orderly progression. So, too, they appear to be remarkably well made: round, smooth, and compact. This is notable, as little actual snow appears to be on the street surrounding the artist. The quantity and the variety of snowballs suggest that they took real tenacity to make.

Bliz-aard Ball Sale is an homage to the spirit of Dada's provocations of bourgeois norms, Fluxus's goofball sense of humor, and John Cage's Zen-like pursuit of the perfection of nothingness. Hammons humorously channels the American huckster spirit of P. T. Barnum and stages the lively mixture of banter, suspicion, and admiration that is a hallmark of New York City street life. As witty as *Bliz-aard Ball Sale* is, it also mounts a devastating critique of art as private property. Long after Duchamp had established that the idea of the artwork was more important than the final product, the art world's demand for a sellable commodity object reigned supreme, particularly in the boom days of the 1980s in New York. Hammons cleverly provides a product but supplants the role of the gallery by selling the snowballs himself—in essence, doubling his labor. Yet the labor of making snowballs and the work of selling them are offered in a highly tongue-in-cheek manner. Making snowballs, while it requires skill, is a democratic, "anyone can do it" activity. Salesmanship, too, is both skilled and unskilled labor.

Ultimately, Hammons appears to be more interested in the process of making snowballs and selling them than in the final product, a disappearing object. In this regard, Hammons is operating in the tradition of Process artists, who were fascinated with their own labor. He combines this, however, with the sometimes lazy logic of the Duchampian readymade. In discussing the found object, he once said: "When you find a found object, the work is halfway complete because the object is talking to you. Whereas everything at Pearl Paint is devoid of spirit; you have to bring everything to it. I'm not working that hard."[1] If many artists in the 1970s used Conceptual and Performance art strategies to engage in both manual labor and its management, then David Hammons's production of a disappearing (found) object seemingly subverts both forms of labor. HM

1. David Hammons and Louise Neri, "No Wonder," *Parkett*, no. 31 (1992): 50. Pearl Paint is an art supply shop located in the heart of New York's SoHo art district.

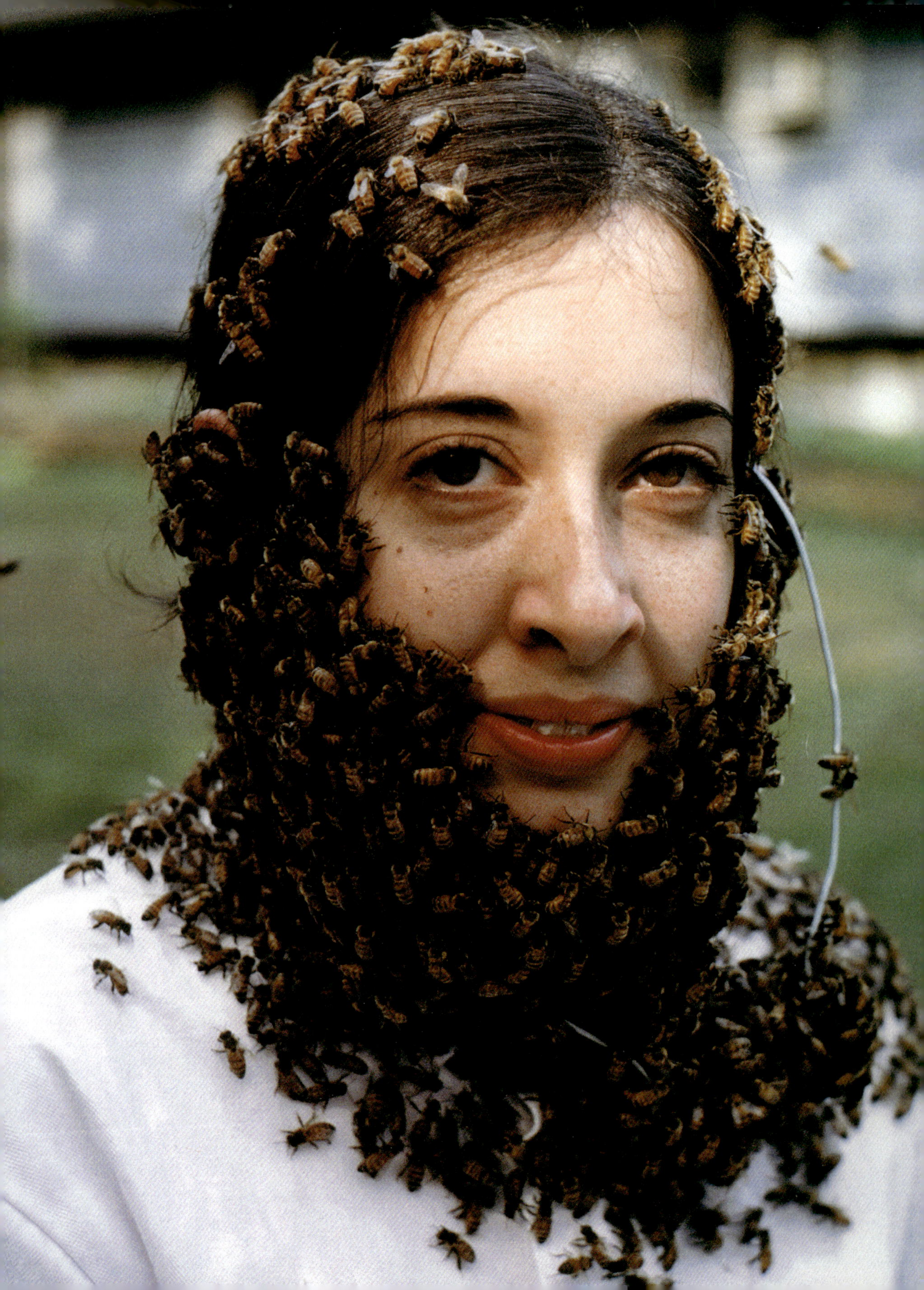

Hope Ginsburg

American, b. 1974

Hope Ginsburg's artwork takes numerous forms. She worked with a beekeeper learning how to make honey; she auditioned to be a saleswoman on the QVC television network; she has made handmade felt mittens; she works in a design firm; and, recently, she produced small novelty items, such as temporary tattoos. As disparate as this list might appear, issues of performance crop up consistently in Ginsburg's oeuvre. She is always a primary actor/figure in her work, which itself is an ongoing exploration of the porous boundary between art and life.

The *Bearded Lady* project began in 1998 when Ginsburg, professing a lifelong love of bees, found a mentor in beekeeper Francis Bowen. As Bowen's apprentice, Ginsburg assisted him at lectures, at state fairs, and in the garden. As trust and friendship grew between them, Ginsburg began to inquire about the phenomenon of bee beards—an old American picnic or state fair trick in which a swarm of bees forms a beard on a performer's face. A bee beard is made by suspending the queen bee from a cage on the performer's chin. The bees will swarm to protect the queen of their hive, and once attached to the cage, they form a protective phalanx or "beard." Ginsburg worked with Bowen and apiarist Jim Gray on developing the proper antibodies for bee stings (which requires being stung repeatedly over time) so that she could perform the Bearded Lady trick. Recorded on video, and subsequently rendered into a lovely faux-Victorian label for her own brand of honey ("Bearded Lady"), Ginsburg's "performance" culminated in a successful bee beard. The work is ongoing: Ginsburg still produces Bearded Lady honey, which can be purchased directly from the artist or in gift shops in institutions where the artist exhibits her work.

Bearded Lady can be understood within the tradition of task-based performance inasmuch as the artist is led by her own desires and interests to create a task for herself, which she subsequently completes. Historically, artists interested in task-based performances treated their artistic process as vastly more interesting and important than the final product or result. Ginsburg does, however,

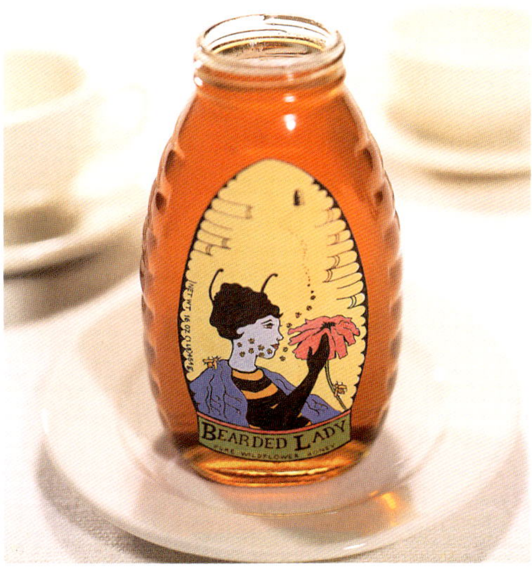

Hope Ginsburg, *Bearded Lady,* 1998–2000.

produce a product, one readily bought and sold on the market, and one that is a usable commodity: honey. Traditionally, Process art was conceived of as a way to undermine the capitalist demand for art to be a profitable product. In the *Bearded Lady* project, Ginsburg tackles this demand from a different angle. Given that so much task-based work and Process art of the 1960s was subsequently commodified through the production of relics and documentation, Ginsburg's production of a commodity acts as a sort of "first strike." Here the artist offers up a handmade commodity, one meant to be ingested by the viewer, as a kind of homeopathic remedy for the inevitable commodity status of art.

In her exploration of the performative quality of art and the slippage between the spaces of art and everyday life, Ginsburg is currently at work producing small novelties of the sort found in Cracker Jack boxes. Entitled *The Novelty Project* (2002–2003), the first works are temporary tattoos designed to be purchased at a nominal cost and worn by the viewer. The *Little Black Moustache* is a pencil-thin vaudevillesque moustache tattoo. Clearly a play on Coco Chanel's enduring gift to women's fashion, this moustache functions as a playful reconfiguration of face and gender. When it is worn, the viewer/wearer is thrown into a space of heightened self-awareness, open to innumerable questions from friends, family, and mere passersby. The *Little Black Moustache* is accompanied by the *Rosy Red Cheek* tattoos, bright red circles in the vein of Raggedy Ann. Ginsburg advises, "They're for flirty days, when the elegance of the *Little Black Moustache* is too severe."[1] HM

1. Hope Ginsburg, correspondence with the author, Summer 2002.

Francis Alÿs

Belgian, b. 1959

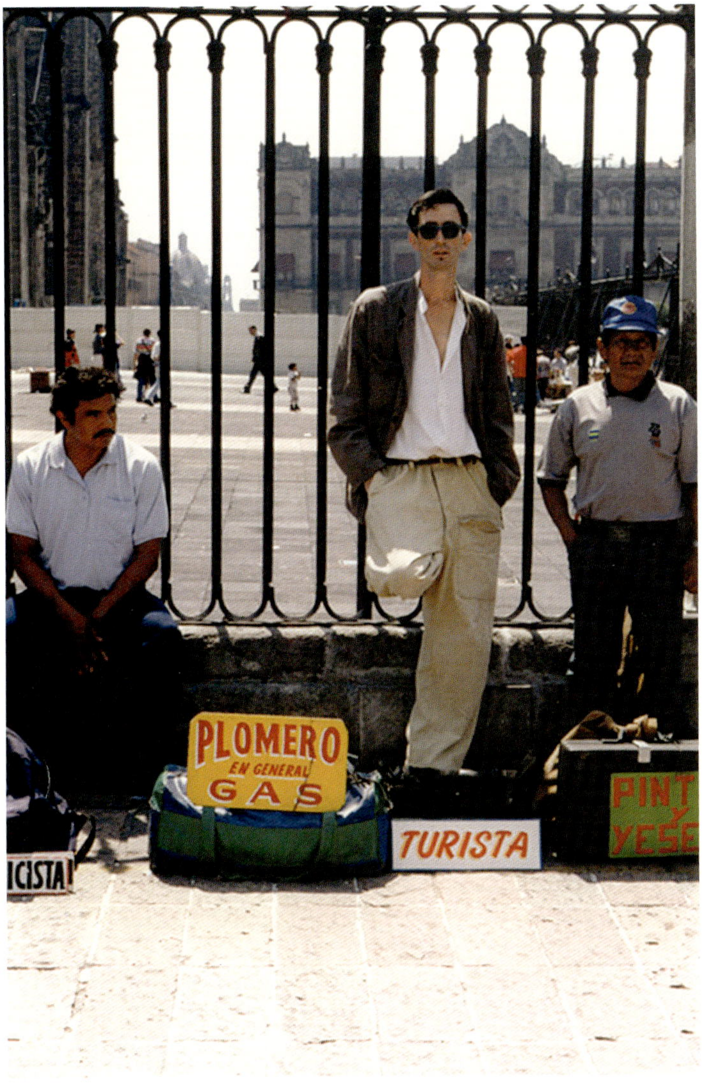

Francis Alÿs, *Turista,* 1997.

Francis Alÿs is a Belgian native who lives and works in Mexico City. The intense urban street life of his adopted hometown serves as both the backdrop and the medium for much of his work, which engages various aspects of time and labor unique to the urban environment. In *Paradox of Praxis 1: Sometimes Doing Nothing Leads to Something* (1998), for instance, the artist pushed a large block of ice through the city streets until it melted completely. This activity, documented on videotape, took the length of an average workday, as he began in the morning and was finished by the late afternoon. At first, the task looks quite arduous and "normal," inasmuch as Alÿs looks like a worker moving a block of ice from one place to another. By the end of the piece, however, the artist is seen playfully kicking a diminishing piece of ice as if it were a soccer ball. Here the logic of the workday and its supplementary other—the realm of play—are both condensed and mapped onto one another, as moving the ice is never strictly work, nor is kicking the ice merely play. Alÿs has been described as an artist "intent on concentrating and expanding the anti-logic of resistance to global cultural and economic homogenization."[1]

In *Turista* (1997), we see a photograph of several men lined up, their backs against a wrought-iron fence. No one seems particularly aware of or concerned about the presence of the camera. Each man has in front of him a hand-painted sign: electrician, plumber, tourist. It is clear that the men with signs that list occupations like "electrician" are available to be hired. But what of Francis Alÿs, the artist with his "tourist" sign? Standing among men who are waiting for employment dependent upon their particularized sets of skills, artist Alÿs waits instead for someone to hire him to be a tourist. Here the artist aligns himself (literally) with manual laborers who offer a service as opposed to a product. Yet the service offered by Alÿs is the unskilled "labor" of being a tourist. One of the salient features of late capitalism has been the increasingly blurred boundaries between work and leisure: both share a highly administered and regimented logic. Alÿs is willing to do the work of the tourist for an employer, yet the very proposition is so paradoxical as to provoke hilarity. Is being a tourist really work (it is exhausting, it comes with highly prescribed forms of behavior)? And furthermore, shouldn't the artist be "working" and making art rather than selling his time for the performance of leisure activities? On the other hand, Alÿs is participating in the long-standing tradition of the artist as a *flâneur*, the nineteenth-century subject who roams the city streets open to any and all experiences. The *flâneur* and the artist share a mythology: that their work (on the part of the artist) or lack of work (on the part of the *flâneur*) is ultimately unalienated. Both are motivated by genius as opposed to sustenance, and thus they cannot be alienated from the final product of their work. In *Turista*, however, Alÿs renders transparent the fact that an artist always serves the pleasure of another—once a church or aristocratic patron, then the emergent bourgeois class, and now a globalized luxury economy in which tourism and the arts are intimately linked. *Turista* radically reverses the traditional roles. Instead of the art lover/patron traveling to a foreign city to see art (in, say, a museum or an international biennial), Alÿs suggests that the patron should enable the artist to have the same tourist experience. What remains unclear in such a transaction is who is working—and who is not. HM

1. Cuauhtemoc Medina, "Action/Fiction," in *Francis Alÿs*, exh. cat. (Antibes, France: Musée Picasso, 2001), 24.

IN 1964 ALLAN KAPROW, the inventor of "Happenings," published "Should the Artist Become a Man of the World?" in *ArtNews*.[1] The article was an attack upon the Abstract Expressionists, who, Kaprow argued, stood apart from society, treating their studios as sacred spaces. Kaprow claimed by contrast that the artist had now "entered into the social mainstream as a professional like any other." If the artist is a professional "like any other," then what similarities can be found between artists of the 1960s and their professional contemporaries in other fields? The most dramatic shift in the labor force of the United States in the decade following World War II was a striking enlargement of the management and service sectors, accompanied by an equally steady decline in the manufacturing base. This shift from blue- to white-collar labor transformed American

THE ARTIST AS MANAGER

The Artist Sets a Task for Others to Complete

Robert Rauschenberg
Andy Warhol
Sol LeWitt
Mel Bochner
Donald Judd
John Baldessari

daily life as it altered ideals of masculinity and family life, aided the rise of the suburbs, and helped change the definition of leisure time. So, too, the emergence of a dominant managerial class was to have a definitive impact on post-1960s art.

The development of Minimalism and Conceptual art relied upon the delegation of artistic activity by the artist to another person—either in the form of plans sent to a factory to be transformed into Minimalist sculpture (Donald Judd), or in Conceptual art's use of a bureaucratic aesthetic of typewritten documents (Sol LeWitt) and the newly developed Xerox machine (Mel Bochner). Art historian Benjamin Buchloh has gone so far as to call this phenomenon the "aesthetic of administration." What is of crucial importance is that in these works the artist conceives of himself as an intellectual rather than a manual laborer. Historically, the artist had embodied both forms of labor: he was both inventor and fabricator. Now, however, a higher value was placed on mental labor, so much so that the artist no longer needed and/or wanted to be personally involved in the fabrication or making of the objects. Sometimes referred to as "post-studio art," this development signaled a major attitudinal shift among artists engaged in performative acts dedicated to the exploration of process for its own sake in their studios.

Increasingly, post-studio artists provided instructions or directions for studio assistants or industrial fabricators who would then produce the works. The work of having an idea and the work of making a product were presented, then, as radically separate. In making this distinction, artists exemplified an important theoretical shift in relation to their role. The

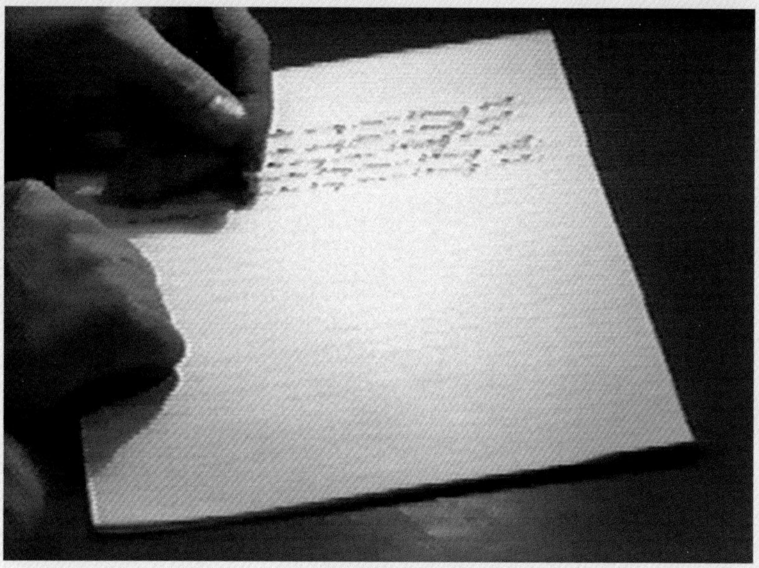

John Baldessari, *I Will Not Make Any More Boring Art,* 1971.

artist was typically seen as the primary generator of the meaning of the work of art. French theorist and critic Roland Barthes, however, was to offer a different account of artistic meaning. Proclaiming the "death of the author," Barthes surmised that it was in fact the reader/viewer who provided the meaning of the work. The desire on the part of the artist to remove any trace of his or her manual labor or artistic subjectivity from the work of art was motivated by a desire to avoid the fetishism of the art object—and to escape the myth of the artist, in particular, as a primary arbiter of meaning. Indeed, artists' ability to remove themselves from the production process was partly bound up with their sense of themselves as being professionals like any others. But as artists increasingly abdicated traditional skills such as drawing and sculpting in favor of paid assistants and fabricators, their own artistic labor was radically reorganized. So although Sol LeWitt was to say that "in conceptual art the idea or concept is the most important aspect of the work,"[2] in actuality, this "de-skilled" work—work performed by someone other than the artist—had to be accompanied by certificates that would confirm the work's authenticity. In this way, Conceptual art showed art to be a legal and contractual category as opposed to a purely aesthetic one. The newly articulated legality of art furthered the rise of the managerial artist, as artists would now routinely participate in the social codes once associated with white-collar professionals such as lawyers, doctors, and small business owners. HM

1. Allan Kaprow, *Essays on the Blurring of Art and Life* (Berkeley and Los Angeles: University of California Press, 1996).

2. Sol LeWitt, "Sentences on Conceptual Art," *Art-Language* 1, no. 1 (May 1969): 11–13.

Robert Rauschenberg

American, b. 1923

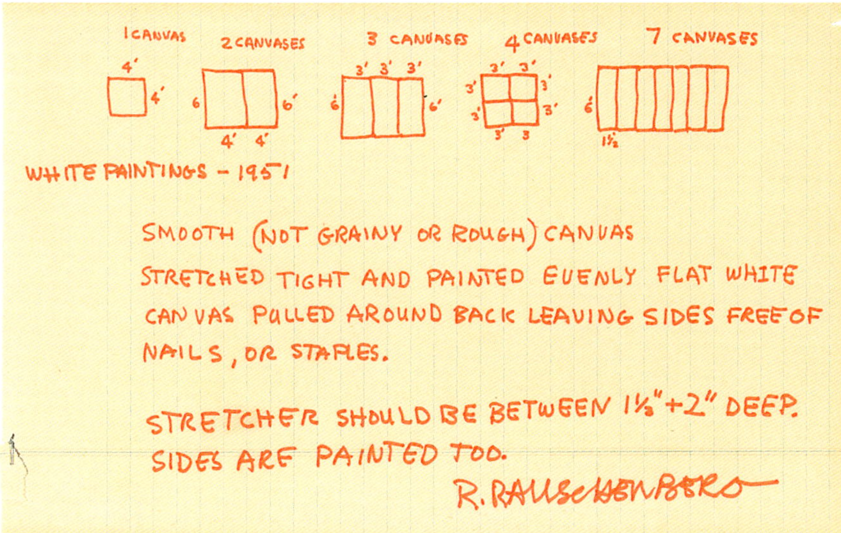

1 CANVAS 2 CANVASES 3 CANVASES 4 CANVASES 7 CANVASES

WHITE PAINTINGS – 1951

SMOOTH (NOT GRAINY OR ROUGH) CANVAS
STRETCHED TIGHT AND PAINTED EVENLY FLAT WHITE
CANVAS PULLED AROUND BACK LEAVING SIDES FREE OF
NAILS, OR STAPLES.

STRETCHER SHOULD BE BETWEEN 1½"+2" DEEP.
SIDES ARE PAINTED TOO.

R. RAUSCHENBERG

Robert Rauschenberg, instructions for *White Paintings,* 1965.

First painted in the summer of 1951 while Robert Rauschenberg was studying at Black Mountain College in North Carolina, the *White Paintings* are a suite of five purely white works. The smooth canvases, painted in house paint with a roller in order to eliminate brushwork and minimize visual incident, interact with viewers who can see their own muted shadows on the paintings' uniform surfaces. In this, they reflect back fleeting moments and capture the ephemerality of time. "I don't want their past to be a mark on them," Rauschenberg has said.[1] This comment indicates that he understands the works' impeccable whiteness to be a measure of their "presentness," regarding them not as unique objects that accrue value as they grow old but as iterations of a conceptual idea. A letter to his dealer, Betty Parsons, written soon after he first made the *White Paintings*, shows that he was quite conscious of the consequences of his decision: "It is completely irrelevant that I am making them—*Today* is their creator."[2]

The *White Paintings*, with their pristine, unadorned faces, negate the primacy of the "artist's hand." From the beginning, Rauschenberg recognized that their monochrome simplicity enacts an erasure of his own role as singular creator. Over the years, Rauschenberg has replenished his stable of *White Paintings* by having his studio assistants (re)create the canvases. His specifications, along with measurements and directions for stretching, state the importance of the evenness of the surface. The paintings were first remade according to his written instructions

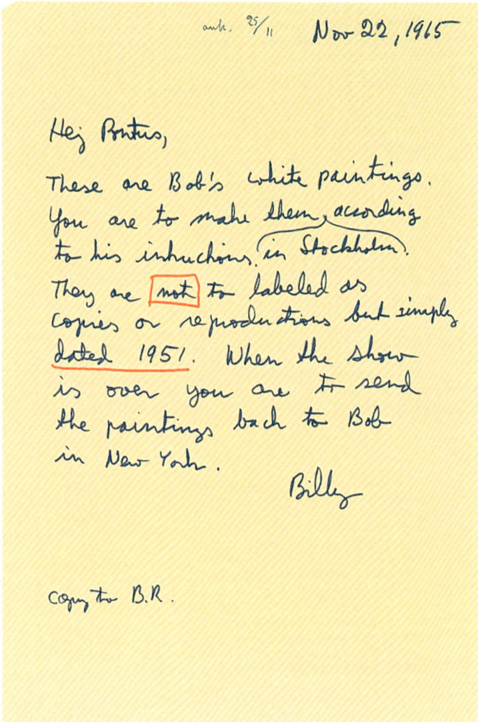

ank. 25/11 Nov 22, 1965

Hej Pontus,

These are Bob's white paintings. You are to make them according to his instructions in Stockholm. They are not to labeled as copies or reproductions but simply dated 1951. When the show is over you are to send the paintings back to Bob in New York.

Billy

Copy to B.R.

Letter from Billy Klüver to Pontus Hulten regarding Rauschenberg's instructions for *White Paintings.*

for a 1965 exhibition in Stockholm, and he has since authorized his assistants to make entirely new paintings if the ones currently in circulation became dingy. Since 1951, the *White Paintings* have been remade several times so they retain a newly painted purity. Rauschenberg insists that each new set of paintings is not an edition of the original but a further instantiation of the 1951 series.

The *White Paintings* play a significant role not only in Rauschenberg's development but also in the history of avant-garde performance. Although the exact details are not fully known, some of the paintings were hung from the rafters of Black Mountain College's dining hall as a visual component of John Cage's *Theater Piece #1*, an event often noted as an influential precursor to Happenings. Performed in the summer of 1952, *Theater Piece #1* featured, among others, dancer Merce Cunningham, pianist David Tudor, and Rauschenberg himself in a semi-structured, multimedia evening that blurred the boundaries between performers and spectators. The paintings literally set the stage for the participatory and improvisational tenor of this art. Cage later cited the *White Paintings* as a major inspiration for his composition *4′33″*—a work that accomplishes, as a musical piece, similar effects of audience incorporation by means of silence or blankness. With the *White Paintings*, viewers realize that a seemingly "blank" canvas flickers with a play of light and shadows. Likewise, during Cage's four and a half minutes of silence, listeners become aware of the ambient sounds around them. JBW

1. Walter Hopps, *Robert Rauschenberg: The Early 1950s* (Houston: The Menil Collection/Houston Fine Art Press, 1991), 66.

2. Ibid., 230 (from a letter dated October 18, 1951).

Robert Rauschenberg, *White Painting* (one panel), 1951.

Andy Warhol

American, 1928–1987

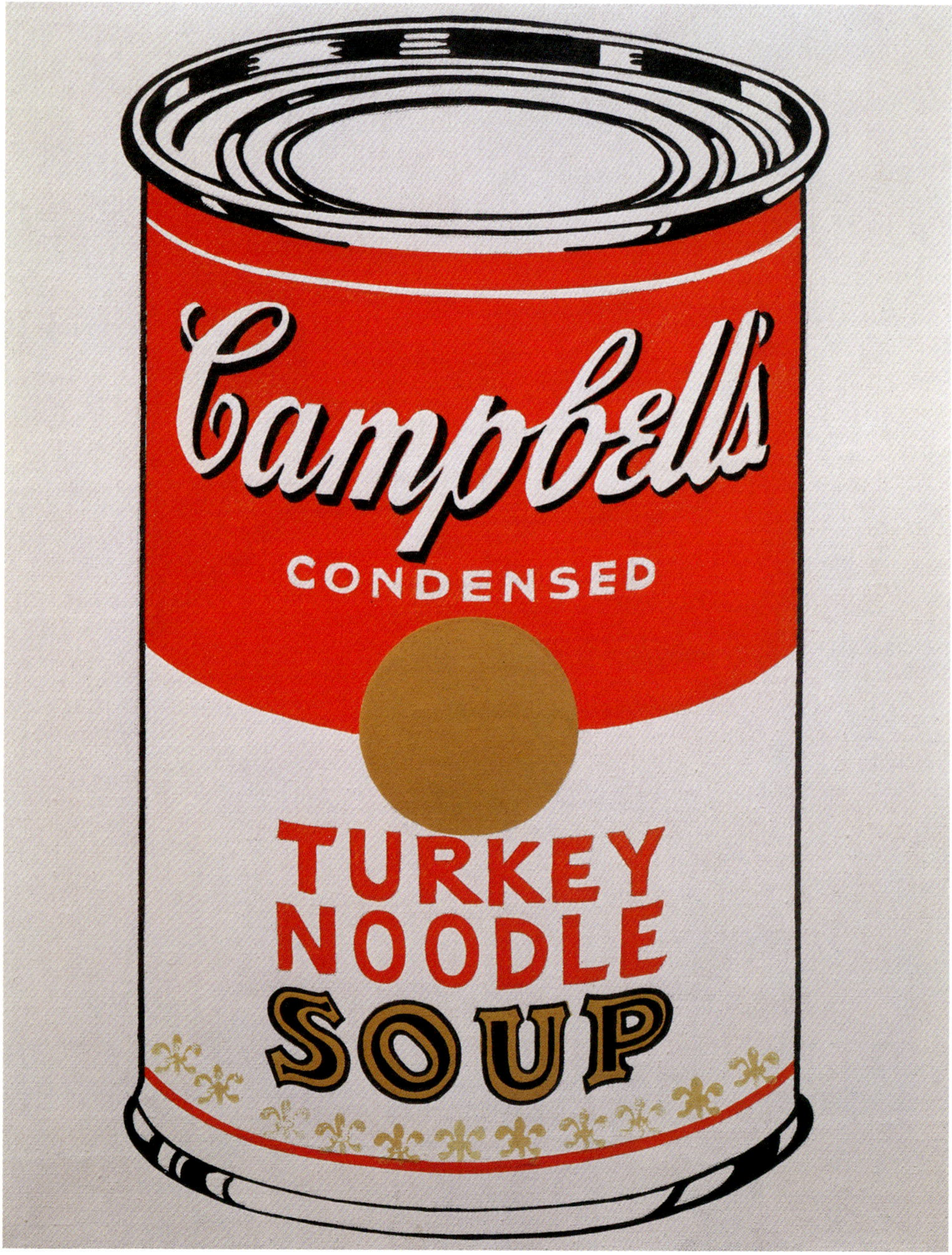

Andy Warhol, *Campbell's Soup Can (Turkey Noodle)*, 1962.

Andy Warhol began his career as a commercial artist, producing hand-drawn advertising images. Successful in the field, he nonetheless wanted to become an art-world artist instead. Certainly, as a commercial artist, Warhol was well versed in the division of labor: mental and manual, skilled and unskilled, image and product. And his early artistic production took the form of somewhat sentimental still-life paintings of mass-produced commodities and images. Soon, however, he abandoned any trace of an explicitly painterly mark in his art, opting instead for the quasi-mechanical production of silk-screening. The silk-screening took place in a studio that Warhol dubbed The Factory, a loft once used for light industry. Addressing both the use of silk screen and the space of The Factory, Warhol stated: "Factory is as good a name as any. A factory is where you build things. This is where I make or *build* my work. In my artwork, hand painting would take much too long and anyway that's not the age we live in. Mechanical means are *today*, and using them I can get more art to more people. Art should be for everyone. . . . Silkscreen work is as honest a method as any, including hand painting."[1]

One of the most definitive aspects of Warhol's repetitive silk screens of ready-made images was a de-skilling of artistic activity, paralleled perhaps only by Frank Stella's stripe paintings. The mass-produced image, combined with its mechanical means of production, meant that Warhol's early work had a notable "anyone can do it" quality. This was made explicit in his *Dance Diagrams* (1962) and *Do It Yourself* (1962) canvases, both of which presented putatively creative endeavors—ballroom dance steps or painting-by-numbers—rendered available to anyone through mechanical means.

Whether Warhol made all of his works or oversaw their production is the subject of art-historical debate. Benjamin Buchloh has suggested that "again and again, Warhol tantalized collectors, curators, and dealers by generating doubts about the authenticity and authorship of his work."[2] In this regard, definitively ascertaining whether Warhol or his studio assistant, Gerard Malanga, made the paintings is slightly beside the point. Warhol's elision of a "factory" and an artist's studio seems to highlight the intensity of the early 1960s as a transitional moment from a high Modernist mode of production, one utterly dependent upon authorial gesture, to a more diffused form of production under late capitalism. Ironically, Warhol revived the studio system in which the "master" worked with apprentices and assistants to produce art in which the artist's aura reigns supreme even if the artist is not the actual fabricator of the work. While many of Warhol's peers would subsequently thematize the division of artistic labor in their work, Warhol played out (and with) the tension of the audience's expectations of artistic labor. He did so with a canny understanding that what the art audience wanted most, perhaps, was an art that offered a comforting nostalgia (the master artist) while simultaneously embodying the most troubling aspects of contemporaneity.

HM

1. Douglas Arango, "Underground Films: Art or Naughty Movie," *Movie TV Secrets* (June 1967), quoted in Benjamin H. D. Buchloh's "Andy Warhol's One-Dimensional Art: 1956–1966," in *Andy Warhol: A Retrospective*, exh. cat., ed. Kynaston McShine (New York: The Museum of Modern Art, 1989), 40.

2. Buchloh, "Andy Warhol's One-Dimensional Art," 56.

Sol LeWitt

American, b. 1928

"The idea becomes the machine that makes the art," wrote Sol LeWitt in 1966.[1] This assertion is best embodied in LeWitt's wall drawings, in which assistants draw webs of lines directly on the wall using his written instructions as guides. For LeWitt, the artist need only generate the concept; execution is a matter of delegation. The wall drawings eradicate the artist's personal touch, as the artist does not make the art himself. In fact, LeWitt's work challenges many conventions of art making, such as the unique, precious object. Instead, he embraces repetition: the same wall drawing can be made over and over. When buyers purchase a wall drawing, they in essence buy only the sets of rules and diagrams. If they move or lend the work to a museum show, the piece is simply redrawn in the new location.

LeWitt's first wall drawing was completed in 1968 at the Paula Cooper Gallery in New York City as a part of an antiwar benefit. Using thin sticks of graphite, LeWitt drew horizontal, vertical, and diagonal lines straight on the wall. His flat geometric patterns merged with the architecture in a manner recalling classical frescoes. After the show closed, the walls were painted over and the works erased at his request. LeWitt made his first wall drawing himself, but he soon realized that because his drawings were based on easily schematized patterns, he could merely write out a plan and have others put their pencils to use. "Lines in four directions, each in a quarter of a square," reads a typical early LeWitt instruction. He issues his directives both as written descriptions and as sketches, leaving the painstaking work of producing his drawings—often physically exhausting labor because of the density and precision of the marks as well as the sheer scale of the art—to workers he names his "draftsmen." LeWitt scales his work to fit the designated wall, and the wall drawings are often so large and intricate that they require teams of assistants to complete them.

As much as LeWitt's ideas might be the motor of the art-producing machine, that machine does not work with industrial exactness. Material marks need human bodies to realize them, and every draftsman has a different type of touch. Although his instructions are straightforward and explicit, they leave some room for variation. LeWitt savors the aspects of chance in his wall drawings as he allows for the diversity of his draftsmen's interpretations and abilities. As he noted on the side of one instruction sketch, "The lines should be made as close together as possible. They do not have to be regular but would differ with each person who does them."[2] For LeWitt, the draftsmen are not faceless drones; he insists that their names be listed in exhibition catalogues, acknowledging their labor and recognizing the collaborative art process.

LeWitt has long investigated the ways in which rational systems might be made to unravel. Although his drawings seem to be quasi-scientific formulations, he allows intuition and the irrational to enter his working process. LeWitt insists that making the wall drawings is an absorbing exercise that verges

Sol LeWitt, *Wall Drawing #280,* 1976.

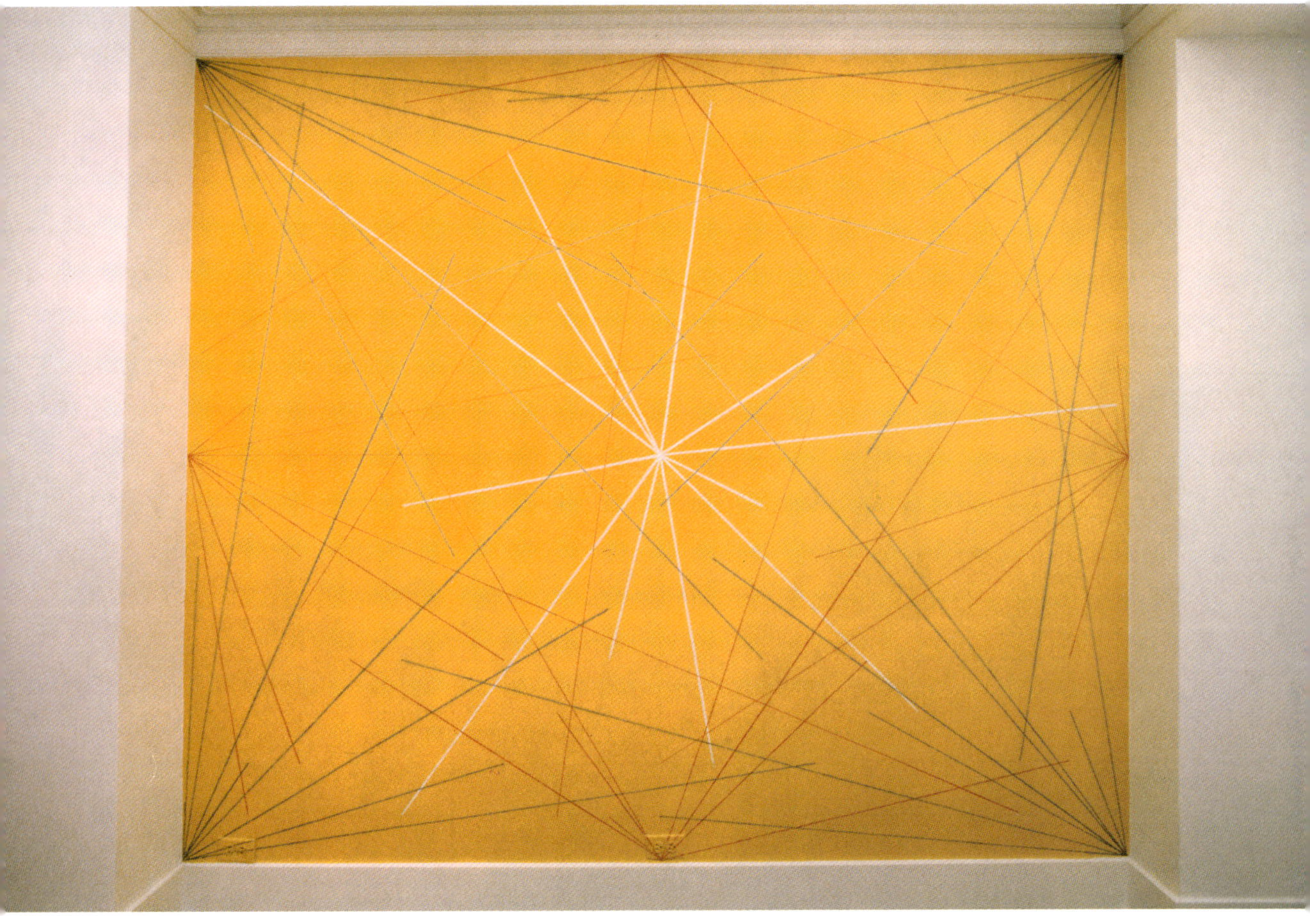

on Zen meditation. As he has commented, "The draftsman and the wall enter a dialogue. The draftsman becomes bored but later through this meaningless activity finds peace or misery."[3]

LeWitt's sanguine assertions about the mental and spiritual benefits of making his work are perhaps overstated—this art involves tedious, hand-cramping labor. But his open managerial style invites draftsmen and viewers alike to understand his art as generated not by rote mechanics but by individual touches.

JBW

1. Sol LeWitt, "Paragraphs on Conceptual Art," *Artforum International* 5, no. 5 (1967): 80.

2. *Wall Markings* (1968). Reproduced in *Sol LeWitt, Drawings, 1958–1992* (The Hague: Hags Gemeentemuseum, 1992), 109.

3. Quoted in *Sol LeWitt*, exh. cat. (Pasadena, Calif.: Pasadena Art Museum, 1970).

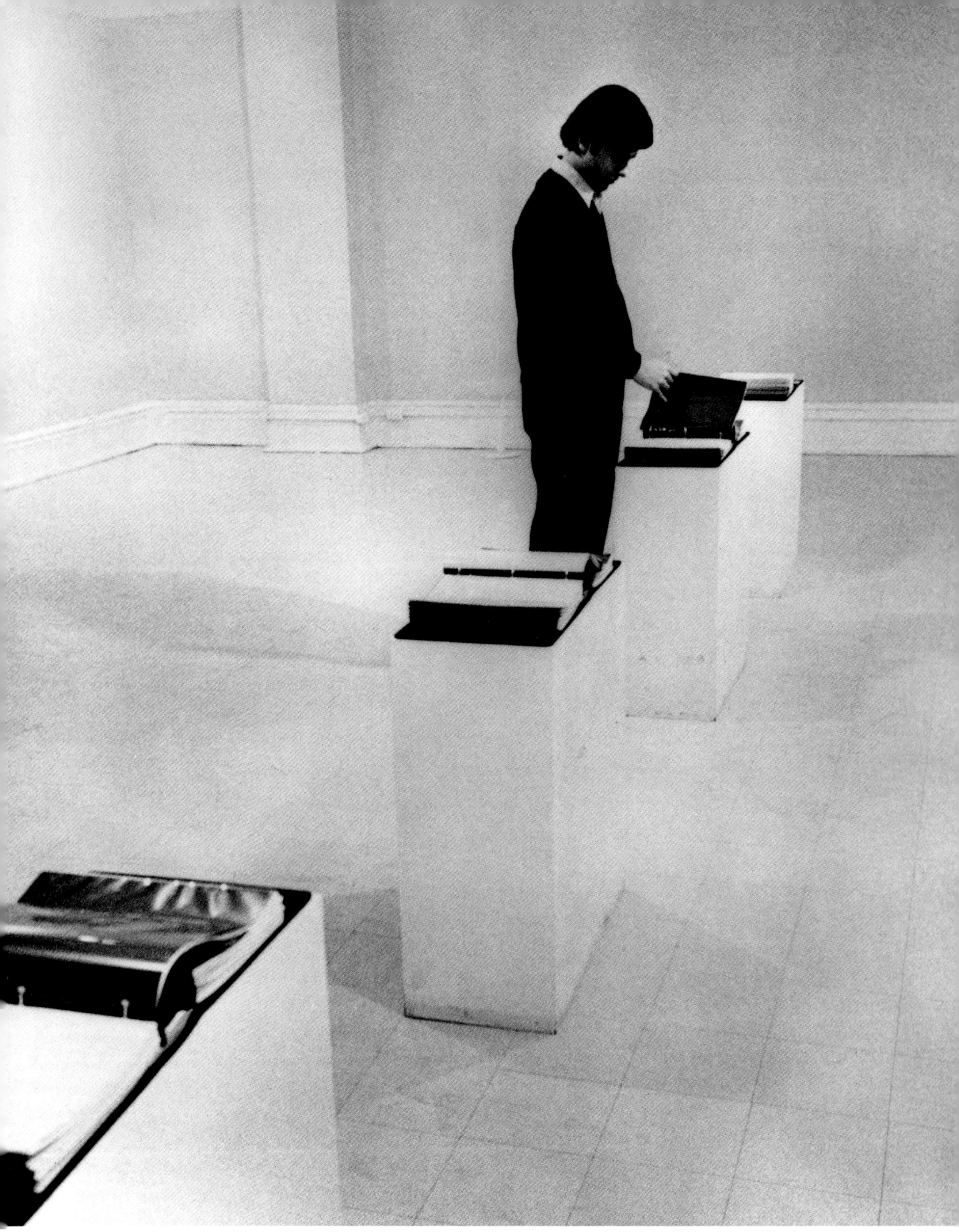

Mel Bochner, *Working Drawings and Other Visible Things on Paper Not Necessarily Meant to Be Viewed as Art,* 1966.

Mel Bochner
American, b. 1940

Asked to organize an exhibition of drawings for the gallery at the School of Visual Arts (SVA) in 1966, Mel Bochner gathered working drawings from artist peers such as Donald Judd, Eva Hesse, Carl Andre, and Sol LeWitt, among others. The drawings procured were not necessarily "art" but were rather "working drawings" and proposals for projects—which meant that they weren't necessarily "not-art," either. Given the limited funds of the SVA gallery, Bochner decided that rather than framing the drawings, he would reproduce them on the then new technology of the Xerox machine, which allowed him to produce them on paper of a uniform size. The drawings were subsequently arranged in alphabetical order, according to the makers' names, and they were mixed in with working drawings and notations from other "intellectual workers,"[1] such as musicians, scientists, and engineers. The authored works were in turn equally interspersed with anonymous material (most notably, perhaps, on the final page of the book, an assembly diagram for a Xerox machine). All of the images were copied four times and placed in identical notebooks that were set upon identical white plinths in the gallery. Titled *Working Drawings and Other Visible Things on Paper Not Necessarily Meant to Be Viewed as Art*, the work permitted viewers to flip through the pages of the loose-leaf binders.

By placing the notebooks on pedestals, Bochner was clearly engaging the new language of Minimalist sculpture, with its insistence on seriality, authorial detachment, and an engagement with the body of the viewer. So, too, Bochner's Minimalist counterparts had begun to experiment with the industrial fabrication of their work. According to art historian James Meyer, "one of the most remarkable items"[2] to be found in *Working Drawings* is an invoice to Donald Judd from his welder billing him for numerous recently completed works.

By eliding the working drawings of artists, fabricator receipts, and the diagrammatic internal workings of new technology, Bochner articulated an explicit continuity between the working methods of artists and other intellectual and creative professionals. Here intellectual work was seen as an elaborate form of problem solving, be it untangling a mathematical equation, constructing a seamless cube, or troubleshooting a stalled Xerox machine. Each operation was a mental one first, a manual one second. Although Bochner did not perform the role of manager whose duty it is to establish a plan for another to execute, he did take up a crucial managerial strategy: the dual ability to represent labor (often in the form of charts and graphs) and to compile and organize those representations. Hence, the use of the Xerox machine in *Working Drawings* (one of the first instances of Xerox "art") is extremely telling. The infinite reproducibility of information was to become a hallmark of contemporary bureaucratic life, and so, too, reproducibility, seriality, and repetition would become the dominant paradigm of the successful working artist. HM

1. The phrase is James Meyer's. See his "Second Degree: *Working Drawings and Other Visible Things on Paper Not Necessarily Meant to Be Viewed as Art*" in *Mel Bochner: Thought Made Visible, 1966–1973*, exh. cat., ed. Richard S. Field (New Haven: Yale University Art Gallery, 1996), 95–96.

2. Ibid., 98.

Donald Judd

American, 1928–1994

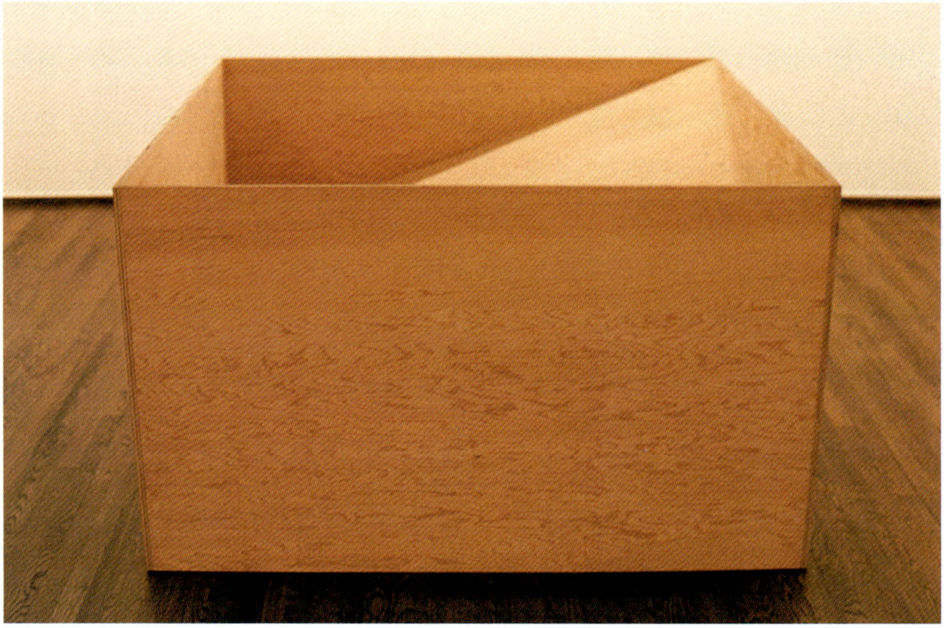

Donald Judd (along with Carl Andre and Dan Flavin) was one of the preeminent artists associated with Minimalism, and he helped introduce the concepts of seriality, repetition, and the use of industrial materials and factory fabrication to 1960s art. Like many artists of his generation, Judd sought to free his art from symbolic emotional content and bourgeois pretensions about art's transcendental quality. Stating an opposition to artwork that presented itself as embodying a rational totality, Judd was to insist instead that "the parts are always more important than the whole."[1]

The use of new industrial materials, such as Plexiglas, aluminum, and rolled steel—rather than high-art materials such as marble and bronze—meant that Judd placed his work in a continuum with the mass-produced commodity object as opposed to the history of sculpture. His production methods often involved sending diagrams and drawings to industrial fabricators requiring them to fabricate the work completely. While artists have long relied upon the skill of trained craftsmen and other professionals, Judd's particularly taciturn objects provoked sharp dissent. For instance, Mark di Suvero was to say: "I think my friend Don Judd can't qualify as an artist because he doesn't *do* the work. A man has to make a thing in order to be an artist."[2] Judd's working methods were to cause a controversy later in his career as well. When the Italian collector Giuseppe Panza authorized the fabrication of sculptures from Judd drawings in his possession, without explicit permission of the artist, Judd declared these pieces "forgeries," insisting that his presence and oversight were required in the fabrication of his artwork.[3]

Judd's use of new materials and factory-style production techniques makes him exemplary as an artist who transplanted managerial labor into the sphere of art. While such working methods may have troubled some artists and collectors, they clearly enthralled and liberated others. Fellow artist Robert Smithson's assessment of Judd's work is emblematic of the sense of permission Judd gave to a subsequent generation of artists: "He may go to Long Island City and have the Bernstein Brothers, Tinsmiths, put 'Pittsburgh' seams into some (Bethcon) iron boxes. . . . Or maybe he will travel to Hackensack, New Jersey, to investigate a lead he got on a new kind of zinc-based paint called Galvanox, which is comparable to 'hot-dip' galvanizing. These procedures tend to baffle art-lovers. They wonder where the 'art' went or where the 'work' went or both. It is hard for them to comprehend that Judd is busy extending art into new media."[4] It seems inevitable that such new media would engender equally new modes of artistic production. Judd, in his enthusiasm for new materials, functioned much like his Research and Development analogue in the corporate sector, discovering new uses for new materials while also deploying a management strategy of delegation and oversight.

HM

1. Bruce Glaser, "New Nihilism or New Art? Interview with Stella, Judd, and Flavin" (1964); reprinted in *Minimalism*, by James Meyer (London: Phaidon Press, 2000), 198.

2. From the transcript of a symposium on "The New Sculpture" with Mark di Suvero, Donald Judd, Kynaston McShine, Robert Morris, and Barbara Rose, reprinted in Meyer's *Minimalism*, 221.

3. For an elaborated account of this controversy, see Susan Hapgood, "Remaking Art History," *Art in America* (July 1990): 114–17.

4. Robert Smithson, "Donald Judd," in *7 Sculptors* (Philadelphia: Institute of Contemporary Art, 1965); reprinted in Meyer's *Minimalism*, 210.

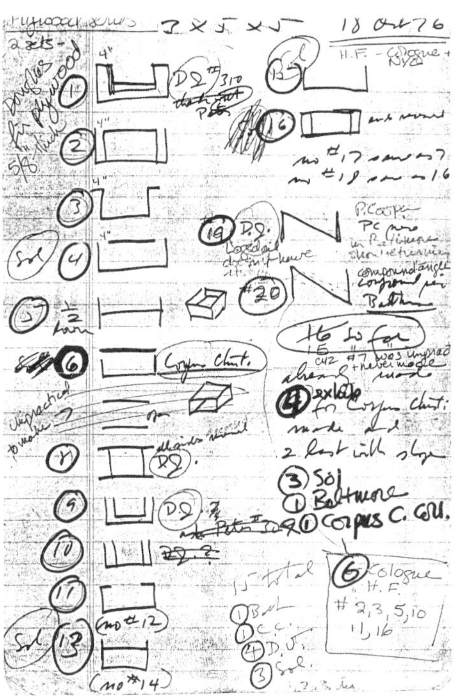

(opposite page) Donald Judd, *Untitled*, 1976.

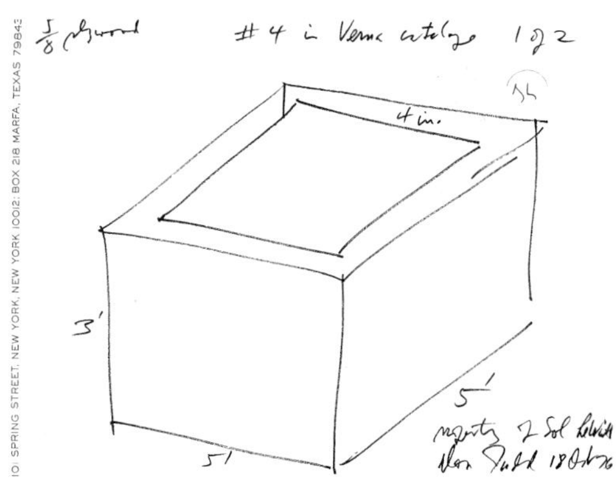

Donald Judd, working drawings for *Untitled Cube*.

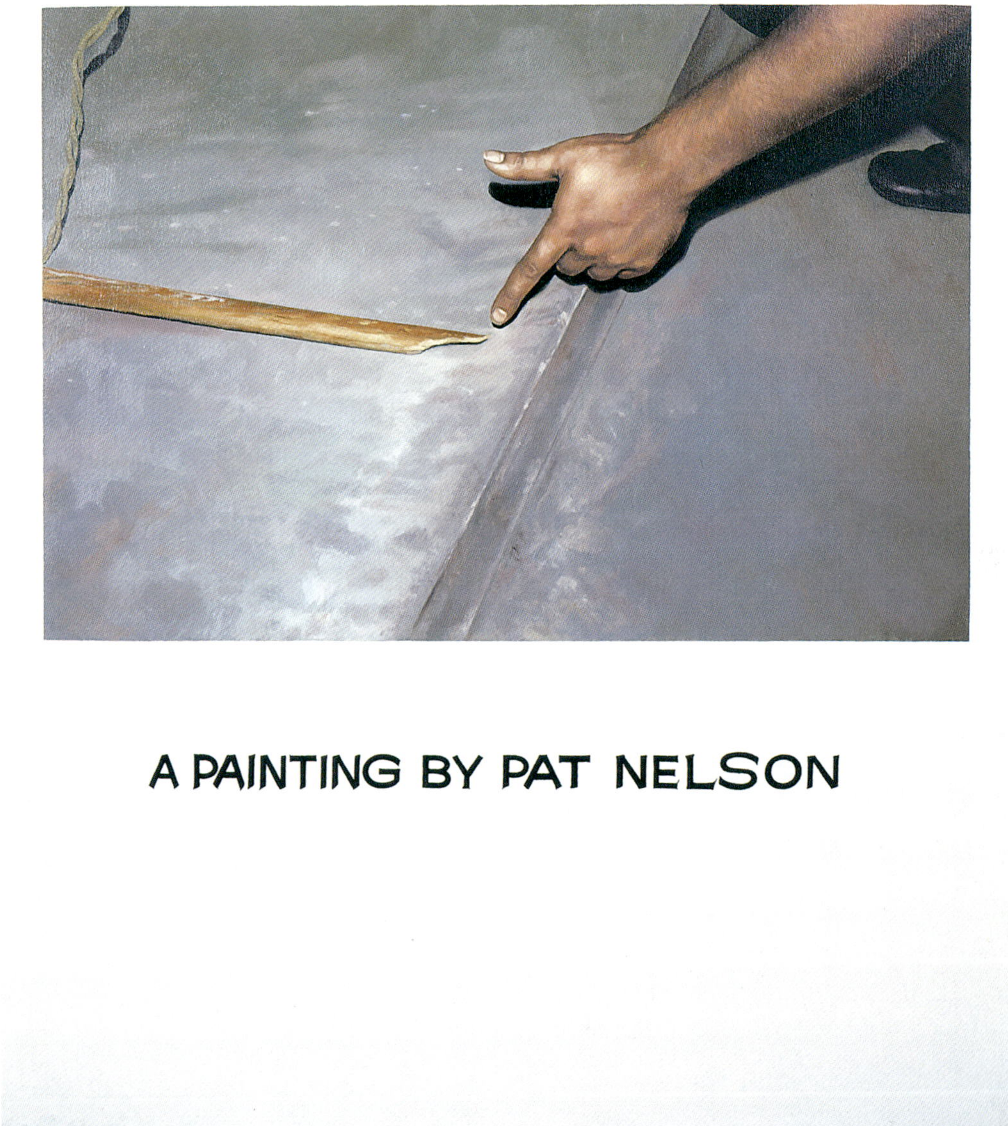

John Baldessari, *Commissioned Painting: A Painting by Pat Nelson,* 1969.

John Baldessari

American, b. 1931

During the late 1960s, John Baldessari made paintings composed entirely of phrases taken from books and painted by a professional sign painter as well as paintings in which photographic images were placed on canvases through a photo emulsion process. In both instances, Baldessari sought to remove all traces of self-expression from the work, enacting a version of what Roland Barthes would come to call "the death of the author." Baldessari's refusal of traditional artistic skills is particularly pointed: he went to great pains to learn how to draw, only to abandon it willfully in an attempt to separate his artwork from his person.[1]

In a set of fourteen paintings called *The Commissioned Paintings* (1969–70), Baldessari further elaborated this systematic self-erasure from the production process. Each *Commissioned Painting* adheres to the same strict format: in the upper two-thirds of the painting is a painted copy of a mundane photograph, and underneath each image, a sign painter paints a caption that states the name of the painter of the image. The images themselves are striking in their utter banality: each shows an outstretched index finger pointing at something (a kitchen stove, a bare light bulb). Describing the process of taking these photographs, Baldessari said, "I was having a friend of mine, George Nicolaidis, walk around and point things out in a visual field that jumped out at him. . . . As he pointed, I would photograph him."[2] Baldessari subsequently took these snapshots to various Sunday painters he had discovered through numerous trips to art shows at county fairs. Baldessari asked the artists to choose an image and paint it as faithfully as possible. The painting was then taken to a sign painter who painted the title of the work—*A Painting by* [person's name]—directly onto the canvas. The completed work was then signed on the back by Baldessari.

Baldessari "concertedly exempted himself from being their fabricator and furthermore, excluded himself from the process of choosing the objects represented"[3] as a way to problematize the authority and intention usually ascribed to the great artist. He did so in a way that effectively divided the labor of the artist into two fundamental phases: the idea and its execution. In doing so, he established the space of ideas as the exclusive property of professional artists and relegated amateurs and craftsmen to the manual labor of execution. Yet Baldessari's elimination of himself as a "supposed inspired inventor of images and compositional form"[4] suggests that the role of the artist may not even be privileged at the level of ideas; like many successful managers, the artist may be merely an avatar of a professionalized system, an effective organizer of the labor of others. HM

1. See the interview with Baldessari by Hugh Davies and Andrea Hales in *John Baldessari: National City*, exh. cat., ed. Hugh M. Davies and Andrea Hales (San Diego, Calif.: Museum of Contemporary Art, 1996), 85–104.

2. Ibid., 97.

3. Anne Rorimer, *New Art in the 60s and 70s: Redefining Reality* (London: Thames and Hudson, 2001), 131.

4. Anne Rorimer, "John Baldessari: The National City Period: 1966–70," in *John Baldessari: National City*, ed. Davies and Hales, 31.

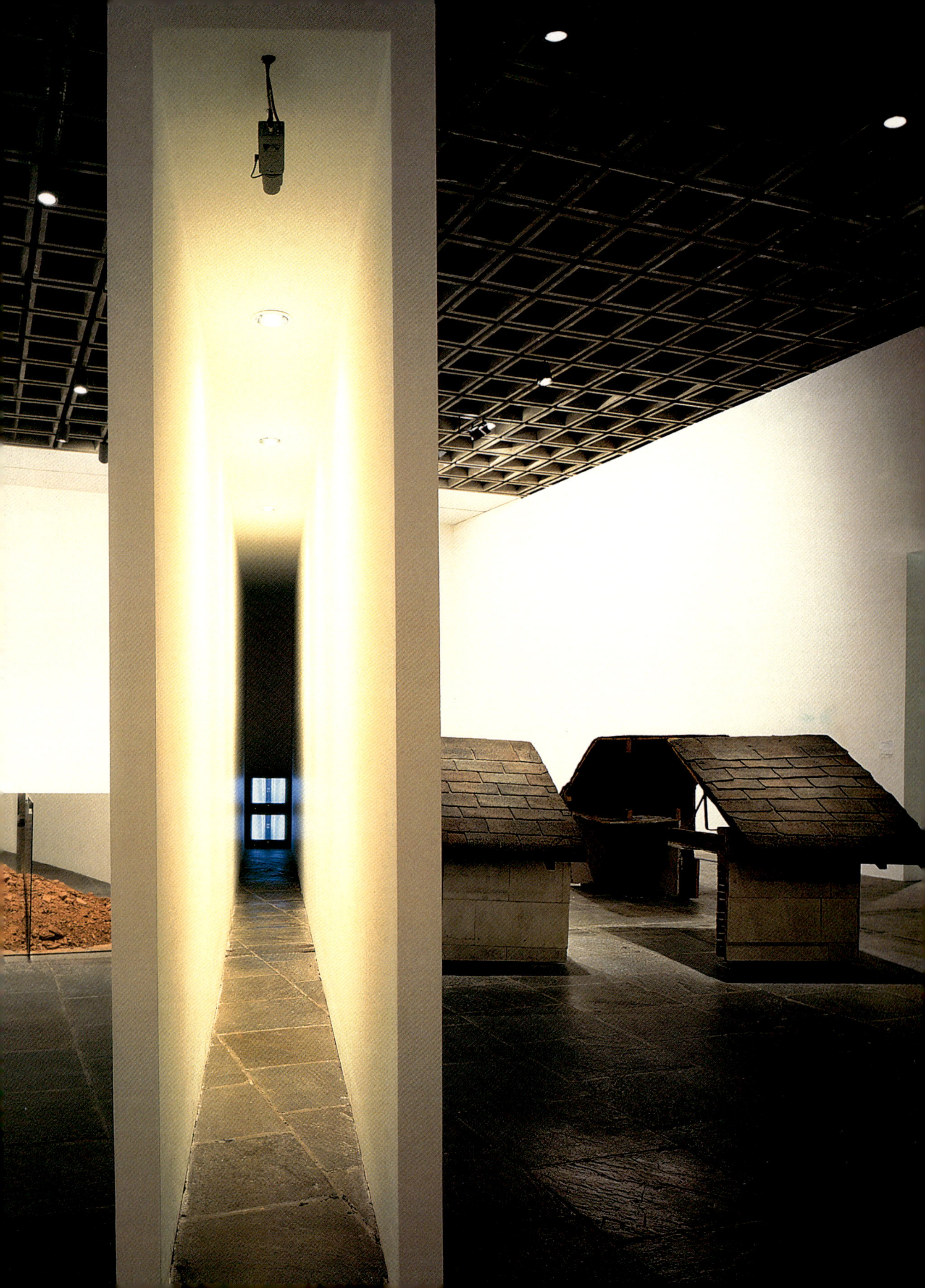

TRADITIONAL ART, SUCH AS perspectival painting, historically imagined a stationary and contemplative viewer. So, too, the museum and the concert hall have requested that viewers be quiet and respectful, the passive recipients of the artist's offering. During the 1960s this conception of the audience changed dramatically. As early as 1952, John Cage scored *4'33"*, a musical work in which the pianist sits on the stage, hands in his or her lap, for four minutes and thirty-three seconds. The "music" is the sounds produced by the audience. Cage's work signaled a significant break with prior forms of art. Here was an artwork, a piece of music, dependent almost exclusively on the audience. When confronted with this new responsibility, many audience members experiencing *4'33"* rebelled—yet even their protestations were transformed into music.

THE ARTIST AS EXPERIENCE MAKER

The Audience Completes the Work

John Cage
Allan Kaprow
Yoko Ono
Valie Export
Fluxus
George Maciunas
Alison Knowles
Zen
George Brecht
Mieko Shiomi
Play
Felix Gonzalez-Torres
Erwin Wurm
Gabriel Orozco

In keeping with Barthes's notion of "the death of the author," a number of artists began to conceive of art as an interactive experience rather than a discrete object. The viewer was no longer seen as a potential passerby but as a necessary agent for the completion of the work. The desire for experience over object has many causes. For some artists, it was a way for art to negate its own luxury status, inasmuch as art was not a commodity object to be bought or sold but a temporal event liberated from the demands of the market. Alison Knowles's *Make a Salad* (1962) is a particularly strong iteration of this idea. The work exists as a concept ("make a salad"), as an instruction ("make a salad"), and as the actuality of anyone, anywhere, making a salad and conceiving of it as art. This artwork depends entirely upon the viewer and is utterly uncommodifiable.

For other artists, participatory works were designed to liberate the creative impulses of the audience. Many artists of the 1960s wanted to counter the idea that artists were a special class of creative people. Rather, they found that "creative activity is immanent in each man and . . . the work of art or the artist happens to be moments of this activity."[1] The idea that art was an activity that everyone could participate in and generate found its strongest advocate in the German philosopher Herbert Marcuse. Marcuse's widely read *Eros and Civilization* (1955) and *An Essay on Liberation* (1969) both argued that human beings are fundamentally creative and that a true state of freedom existed not only in a freedom from need (a society committed to providing housing, food, health care, and a living wage for its citizens) but also in the freedom to explore one's creative

Bruce Nauman, *Live-Taped Video Corridor*, 1970.

potential, in whatever guise that might be expressed. Marcuse's radical utopianism infused the free speech, student, and antiwar movements of the period, and he was important for artists as well: in his analysis, art is not a by-product of culture but actively helps produce it. Hence art is not solely individual or solipsistic (for either the maker or the viewer). Rather, the democratization of the creative act contributes to the communal production of freedom.

While Marcuse offered a politics of liberation that rhymed with much of the revolutionary spirit of the period, for other artists and thinkers, the realm of politics was bound up with the problem of ethics and the public sphere. Some did not see audience participation as exclusively playful or liberatory. Rather, the public sphere is constructed as a site where equals come together to debate.[2] Indeed, some artists placed the audience in a precarious position. If Yoko Ono allows viewers to cut off pieces of her clothing in *Cut Piece* (1964), does the audience have the right to abuse that offer? Can participants take all of her clothing? Similar questions have arisen more recently, as when Felix Gonzalez-Torres gives the gift of free posters and candies. How many can we take? What is our obligation to the objects and the artist once we have taken a gift from him?

Ironically, while audiences were increasingly offered art as an anticommodity, ludic, or ethical experience, they were also asked to do the "work" of completing it. By disallowing passive viewership, the new participatory works pressed their audiences into service, asking them to "work" for their art; in doing so, they both mirrored and created yet another moment where the traditional boundaries between work and leisure were blurred. While many artists desired this blurring, they may have unwittingly taken part in the larger cultural shift at hand: artists, too, were becoming service providers as opposed to object makers, mirroring the larger societal transformation from a manufacturing to a service-based economy.

HM

1. Ursula Meyer, "The Eruption of Anti-Art," in *Idea Art*, ed. Gregory Battcock (New York: E. P. Dutton, 1973), 126.

2. This version of the public sphere is articulated most fully by Jürgen Habermas, *The Structural Transformation of the Public Sphere: An Inquiry into a Category of Bourgeois Society*, trans. Thomas Burger (Cambridge: The MIT Press, 1992).

John Cage

American, 1912–1992

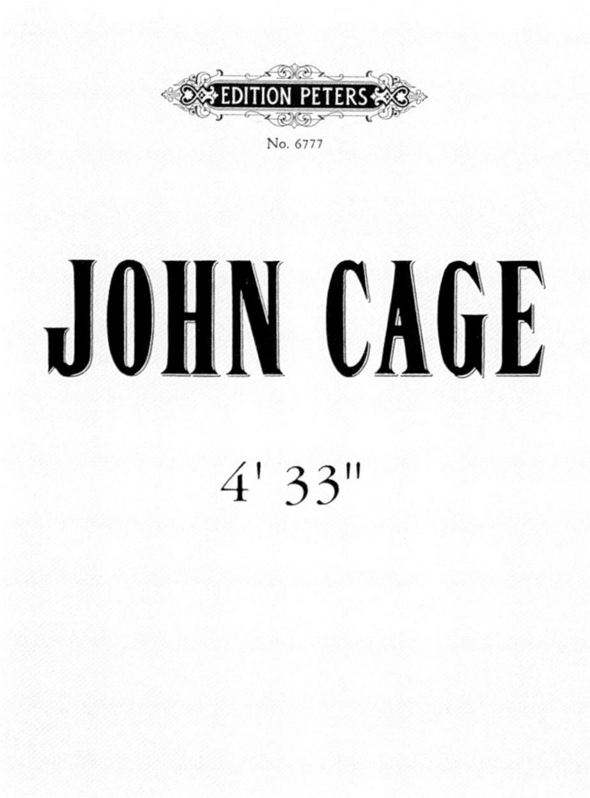

John Cage, *4′33″*, 1952.

Although John Cage was a musician and composer, his influence was strongly felt in the 1960s art world. His friendship with Marcel Duchamp, his studies with the widely regarded Zen teacher D. T. Suzuki,[1] and his experiments with chance operations had lasting effects on the visual and performing arts. This influence began, in part, at the experimental Black Mountain College, where Cage met Robert Rauschenberg and saw his *White Paintings* (c. 1951)—stark, white canvases painted with house paint and a roller. As influential as Cage was, he was also quick to admit that influence ran in both directions. In the introduction to his important essay on Rauschenberg, he wrote: "To Whom it May Concern: The white paintings came first; my silent piece came later."[2]

The "silent" piece to which Cage refers is perhaps his most important and (in)famous composition, *4′33″*, which premiered in 1952 at the Maverick Concert Hall in Woodstock, New York. The title describes the duration of the piece—four minutes and thirty-three seconds. (Although Cage liked the potential spatial reading as well: four feet and thirty-three inches.) *4′33″* was performed by David Tudor, a young experimental pianist with whom

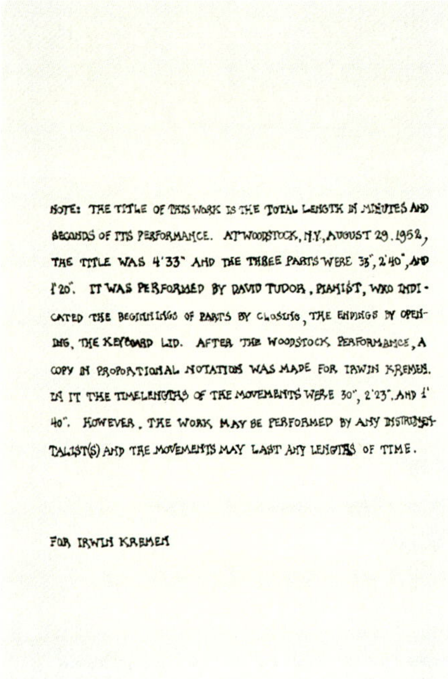

NOTE: THE TITLE OF THIS WORK IS THE TOTAL LENGTH IN MINUTES AND SECONDS OF ITS PERFORMANCE. AT WOODSTOCK, N.Y., AUGUST 29, 1952, THE TITLE WAS 4'33" AND THE THREE PARTS WERE 33", 2'40", AND 1'20". IT WAS PERFORMED BY DAVID TUDOR, PIANIST, WHO INDICATED THE BEGINNINGS OF PARTS BY CLOSING, THE ENDINGS BY OPENING, THE KEYBOARD LID. AFTER THE WOODSTOCK PERFORMANCE, A COPY IN PROPORTIONAL NOTATION WAS MADE FOR IRWIN KREMEN. IN IT THE TIMELENGTHS OF THE MOVEMENTS WERE 30", 2'23", AND 1'40". HOWEVER, THE WORK MAY BE PERFORMED BY ANY INSTRUMENTALIST(S) AND THE MOVEMENTS MAY LAST ANY LENGTHS OF TIME.

FOR IRWIN KREMEN

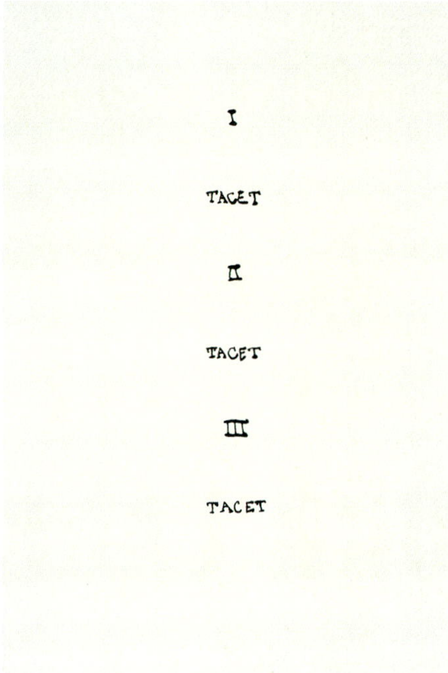

I

TACET

II

TACET

III

TACET

John Cage, *4′33″*, 1952.

Cage had formed an important friendship. It was Tudor, apparently, who solved the problem of how to perform four minutes and thirty-three seconds of silence, given that the work was divided into three movements and there were no notes to be played. Tudor decided to close "the cover of the piano keyboard at the start of each movement and [open] it at the end of the specified time. Aside from these actions he did nothing but sit on his bench, immobile but intent."[3] In *4′33″* the audience hears the sounds of itself and its surroundings, and thus the piece never sounds the same twice.

Cage intimated that there is no such thing as silence. Rather, the world is filled with ambient sounds; one need only pay attention to them. Cage's entire oeuvre was an attempt to remove himself and his own taste from the production of music. To this end, he developed elaborate systems of chance to determine notes and their duration, used a wide variety of everyday objects to make sounds, and modified pianos (again with everyday objects from the hardware store, especially nuts and bolts) as a way to defy any incursion of his own preferences into the final composition. No work achieved this more successfully than *4′33″*. Here the removal of authorial intention also meant a nearly complete abdication of traditional forms of creative labor. Cage the composer does nothing, and the "music" is subsequently "made" by the audience. Only David Tudor works, performing silence for the crowd. HM

1. For more on Cage and D. T. Suzuki, see Judith Rodenbeck's entry on Zen in this volume.

2. John Cage, *Silence* (Middletown, Conn.: Wesleyan University Press, 1961), 98.

3. Calvin Tomkins, *The Bride and the Bachelors: Five Masters of the Avant-Garde* (Middlesex, England: Penguin Books, 1976), 118–19.

Allan Kaprow

American, b. 1927

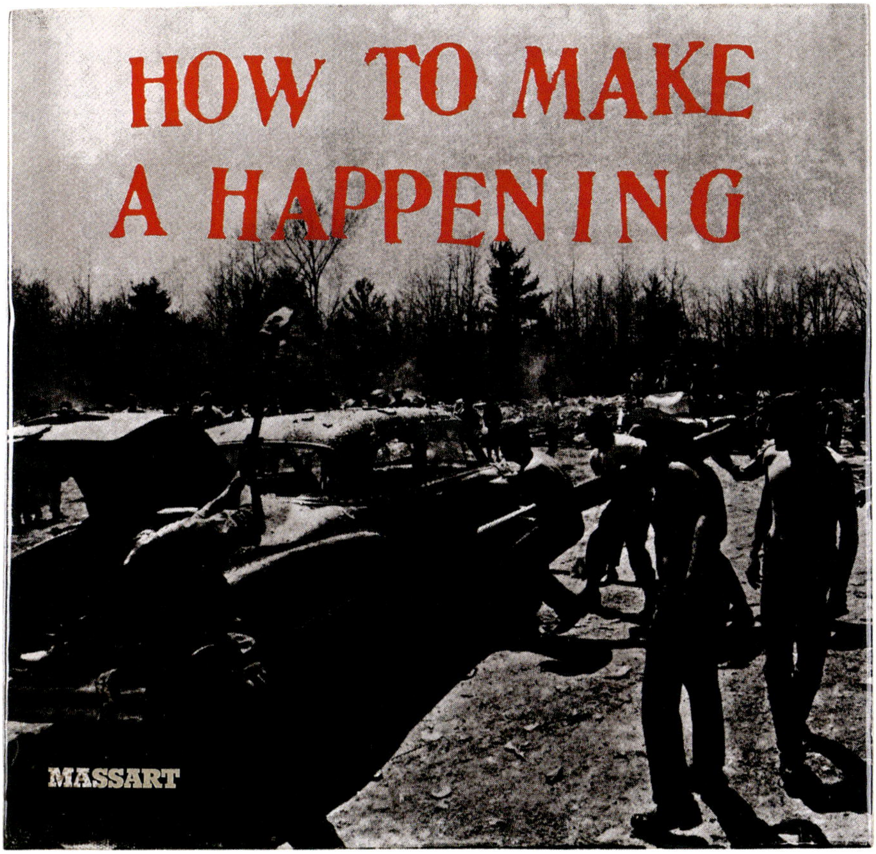

Allan Kaprow, *How to Make a Happening,* 1966.

Since the mid-1950s, Allan Kaprow has explored the breakdown of rigid distinctions between "art" and "life"—what Kaprow himself might call the disappearance of "art." Kaprow began his career as an expressionist painter in the early 1950s, but he very quickly found the idiom uninteresting. Instead, he said, "we must become preoccupied with and even dazzled by the space and objects of our everyday life."[1] So Kaprow extended the painted arena into space, then began con-

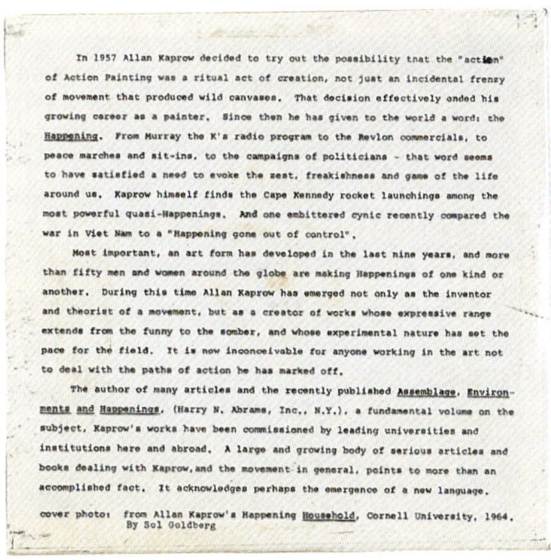

In 1957 Allan Kaprow decided to try out the possibility that the "action" of Action Painting was a ritual act of creation, not just an incidental frenzy of movement that produced wild canvases. That decision effectively ended his growing career as a painter. Since then he has given to the world a word: the Happening. From Murray the K's radio program to the Revlon commercials, to peace marches and sit-ins, to the campaigns of politicians - that word seems to have satisfied a need to evoke the zest, freakishness and game of the life around us. Kaprow himself finds the Cape Kennedy rocket launchings among the most powerful quasi-Happenings. And one embittered cynic recently compared the war in Viet Nam to a "Happening gone out of control".

Most important, an art form has developed in the last nine years, and more than fifty men and women around the globe are making Happenings of one kind or another. During this time Allan Kaprow has emerged not only as the inventor and theorist of a movement, but as a creator of works whose expressive range extends from the funny to the somber, and whose experimental nature has set the pace for the field. It is now inconceivable for anyone working in the art not to deal with the paths of action he has marked off.

The author of many articles and the recently published Assemblage, Environments and Happenings, (Harry N. Abrams, Inc., N.Y.), a fundamental volume on the subject, Kaprow's works have been commissioned by leading universities and institutions here and abroad. A large and growing body of serious articles and books dealing with Kaprow, and the movement in general, points to more than an accomplished fact. It acknowledges perhaps the emergence of a new language.

cover photo: from Allan Kaprow's Happening Household, Cornell University, 1964.
By Sol Goldberg

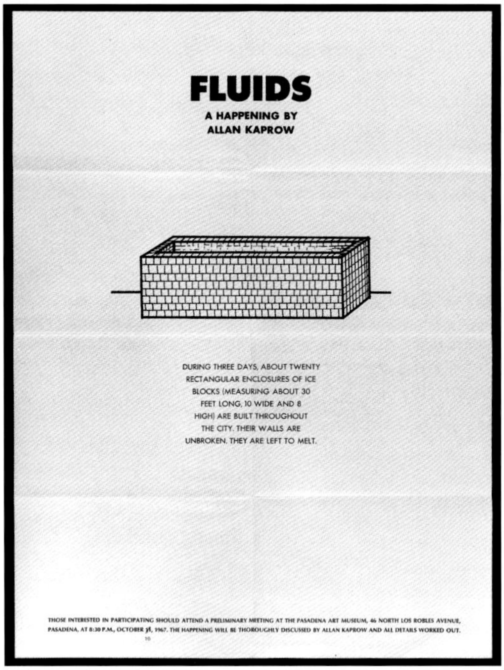

structing environments, and finally developed the time-based pieces known as "Happenings." From 1958 on, Kaprow's work has taken the form of making things happen, either in Happenings or in the more simplified and do-it-yourself form he devised in the mid-1960s and called "activities."

For Kaprow, art of the sixties found its greatest energies "gathering in the crossovers, the areas of impurity, the *blurs* which remain after the usual boundaries have been erased."[2] The resulting works—temporary environments, Happenings, and smaller-scale activities—were all intentionally ephemeral in nature. Emerging from his study of collage principles and his earlier practice as an action painter, they were fundamentally experiential works designed for active participation. What remains of them are only their dispersed traces: hearsay and gossip, reminiscences, a few photographs and documents, and the "recipes" Kaprow has saved.

Significantly, for Kaprow a piece doesn't exist as a happening without its performance. His work is thus distinct from other, more conceptually based works that didn't insist on performance. In the increasingly simplified instructional form he adopted, it was important, first, that the tasks could be performed by anyone and required no expertise, and second, that these tasks would derive from habitual practices like shaking hands or looking in a mirror. "Experience, I believe, is physical, not intellectual," Kaprow wrote, adding, "an experience is thought which has been 'incorporated,' on a muscular, neural, even cellular level, into the body."[3]

Early Happenings had rather extensive notation, but by the time Kaprow recorded *How to Make a Happening*, he had pared down these scripts to a shorter poetic form. Not much later, as he developed activities, he would adopt a photo-text format based on instruction manuals. The LP ironically emphasizes the "oral tradition" of Happenings as well as the instructional format. The A side presents Kaprow reading a lecture, only partially tongue-in-cheek, of a ten-point program on what Happenings should be, while the B side describes some recent Happenings and ends with a reading of a haiku-like recipe, *Raining* (a Happening for Billy Klüver).

Fluids was a commission for a museum retrospective and as such, in principle, contradicted everything Kaprow had said to date about the "museumification" of Happenings. *Fluids* involved the construction of identical rectangular enclosures using fifty-pound blocks of ice. The minimalist structures were assembled by hand by participants; once built, they would be left to melt. The result, communally constructed and labor intensive, was a set of carceral yet semitransparent vanishing buildings that Kaprow called

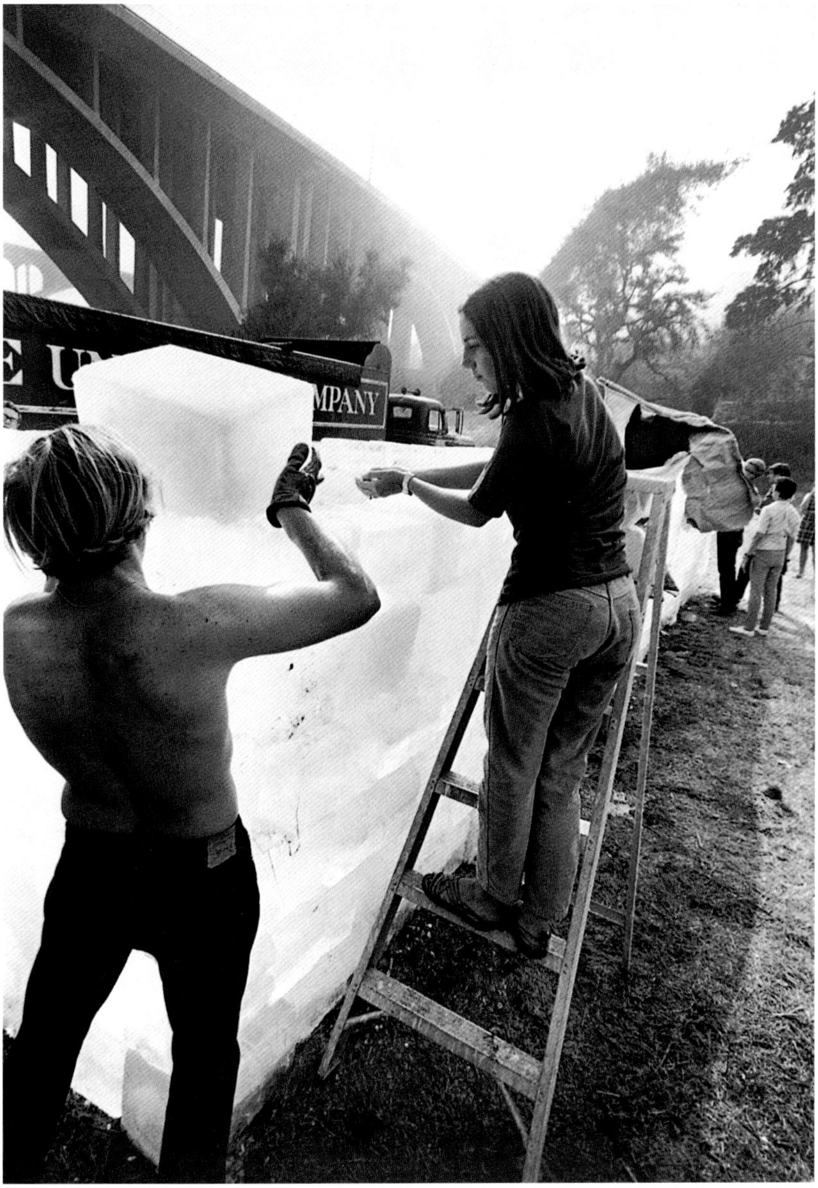

Allan Kaprow, *Fluids,* 1967. Photograph: Bruce Breland.

"throw-away architecture." *Fluids,* he said, "was a reflection—an ironic and humorous one, perhaps poignant of our whole culture, which is sustaining itself by increasing, each decade, the number of its obsolescent functions."[4]

JR

1. Allan Kaprow, "The Legacy of Jackson Pollock," in *Essays on the Blurring of Art and Life* (Berkeley and Los Angeles: University of California Press, 1996), 7; the essay was originally published in *Art News* (October 1958): 24–60.

2. Barbara Rose and Irving Sandler, "Sensibility of the Sixties," *Art in America* (January/February 1967): 45.

3. Allan Kaprow, *7 Environments* (Naples and Milan: Studio Morra and Mudima, 1992), 25.

4. Allan Kaprow, "La Sfida del Sistema," *Metro* (Venice) 14 (June 1966): 41.

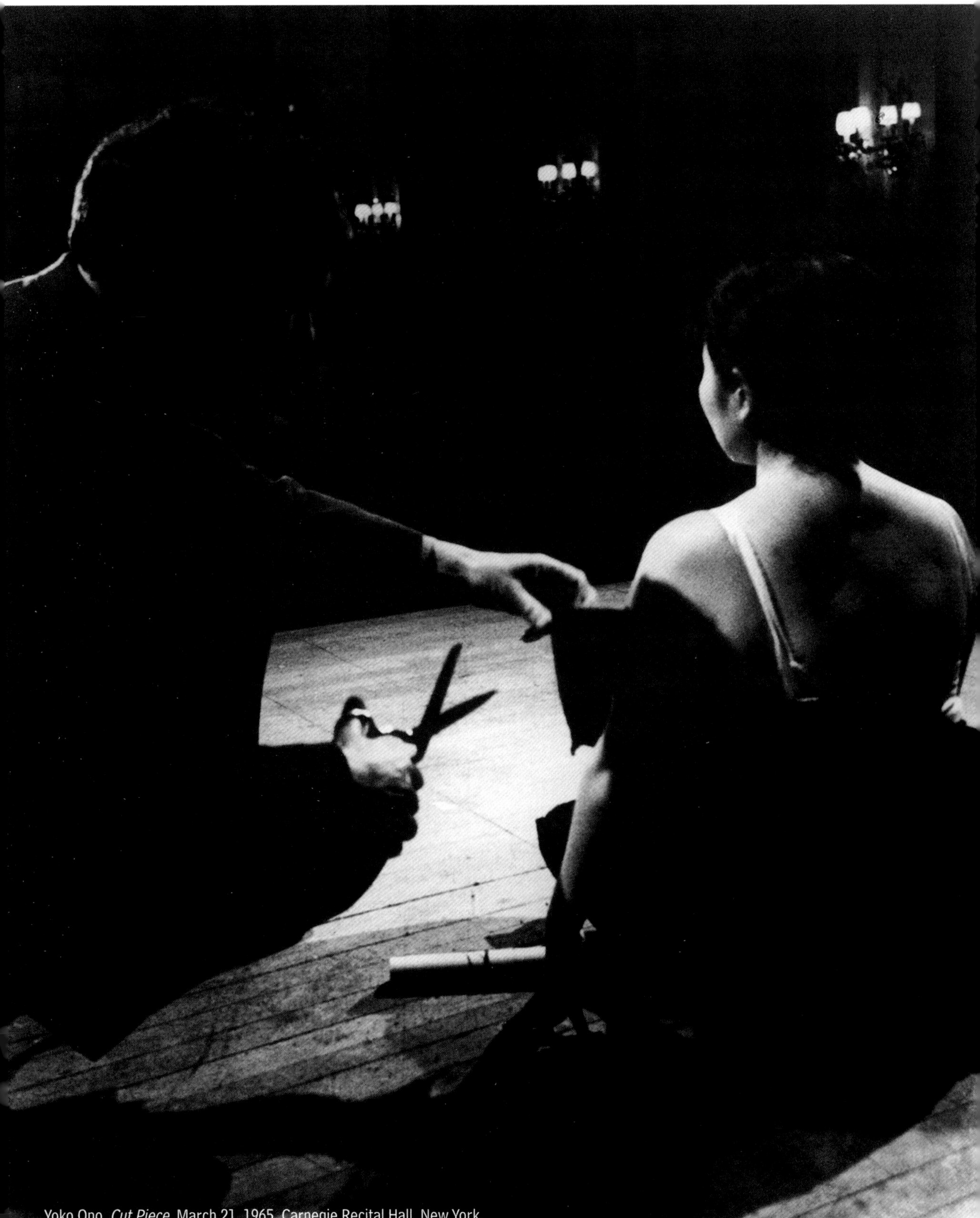

Yoko Ono, *Cut Piece,* March 21, 1965, Carnegie Recital Hall, New York.

Yoko Ono

Japanese, b. 1933

Associated with avant-garde music circles in the early 1960s, Yoko Ono began her artistic career as a composer deeply interested in audience participation. As her compositions grew increasingly visual in nature, she started writing instructions for viewers to perform. These scores were first handwritten in Japanese script and later typed in English and published in her book *Grapefruit.* Ono's instructions were some of the first Conceptual pieces to rely wholly upon linguistic propositions. For the most part, the scores require fanciful mental work for the audience. In *Painting to Be Constructed in Your Head* (1962), for example, Ono exhorts readers to imagine and then fuse three paintings. By leaving room for the audience's interpretation and transformation, Ono treated her instructions as a way to democratize art practice. "Soon," she wrote, "there will be no need for artists, since people will start to write their own instructions."[1] She emphasizes that art is an irrational, liberating encounter with the world; her *Map Piece* (1964) asks readers to draw a map to lose rather than to orient themselves.

In addition to her instructions, Ono made objects that relied upon audience interaction. In *Painting to Hammer a Nail* (1961–66), Ono offers a jar of nails and a blank white canvas with a hammer attached to it. She asks the audience to use the hammer to drive nails into the work and then to tie strands of their own hair around the nails. The work, a combination of painting and sculptural relief, has a performance aspect as well. It is incomplete without the labor of the viewer who follows Ono's instructions. In this case, she calls for a literal act of construction. Unlike most performance art, however, her scores engage the spectator's body, not the artist's. In fact, Ono was invested in dismantling the binary of the viewer and the viewed in order to trouble assumptions about passive spectators and active performers.

Nowhere is this blurring of artist and audience clearer than in Ono's *Cut Piece*, performed in Kyoto, Tokyo, London, and New York between 1964 and 1966. During *Cut Piece*, Ono knelt on a stage with a pair of scissors and invited the audience to cut off pieces of her clothing. *Cut Piece* asked the viewers to renounce their conventional invisibility and mount the stage while she herself remained still. This reciprocity between the artist and the viewer invokes the rhetoric of the gift.[2] In fact, Ono has stated that she always wore her best outfit in order to underscore her artistic offering. Like her instruction works, *Cut Piece* was written as a score, and it has since been performed by many others. (Avant-garde cellist Charlotte Moorman claimed to have enacted it more than a thousand times.)

Ono takes a feminist attitude toward artistic labor as she uses her own body as an object of investigation. She also challenges notions of the artist's authority by holding no strict claim or ownership over her ideas. Instead, she emphasizes the ease with which they can be repeated and adapted. JBW

1. Yoko Ono, "Letter to Ivan Karp, 1965," in *Grapefruit: A Book of Instructions* (New York: Simon and Schuster, 1970), unpaginated.

2. See Miwon Kwon's essay in this volume; see also my "Remembering Yoko Ono's *Cut Piece*," *Oxford Art Journal* 26 (Spring 2003): 99–123.

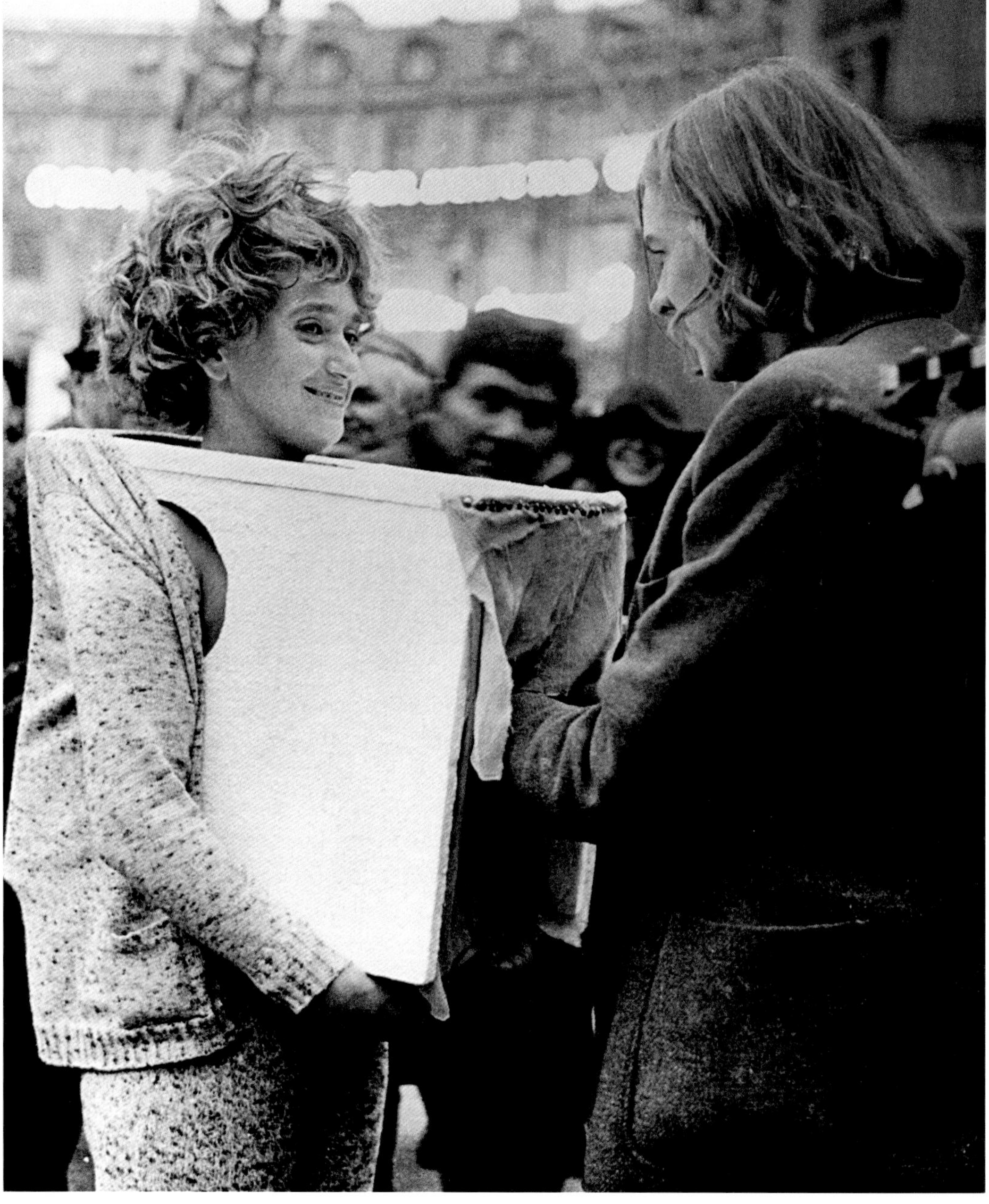

Valie Export (with Peter Weibel), *Tapp und Tastkino (Touch Cinema),* 1968. Photograph: Werner Schulz.

Valie Export
Austrian, b. 1940

Affiliated with Viennese Actionism in the early 1960s, Austrian artist Valie Export has been at the forefront of a highly political brand of Feminist art. In her "expanded cinema" projects, Export confronts media representations of women: she has argued that "women must make use of all media as a means of social struggle and social progress in order to free culture of male values."[1] Using video, film, and—most provocatively—her own body in street performances, Export often confronts audiences directly, challenging the systems that reduce women to mere objects. She makes the female body physical and real in an attempt to vivify it from its flattened screen representations.

In her 1968 *Tapp und Tastkino (Touch Cinema)*, Export constructed a small mock-up of a theater, complete with cloth curtains, that she strapped to her chest. She wandered the streets of cities such as Vienna and Munich with this appendage on her body while her collaborator, Peter Weibel, summoned curious passersby to "visit the cinema" for five minutes by parting the curtains and touching her naked breasts. Instead of offering up a highly sexualized female body to be viewed, this work solicits touch. As Export has explained, "The curtain, hitherto raised only for the eyes, is, at long last, raised for the hands as well."

Export inverts the workings of film, in which the pleasure of the gaze substitutes for physical contact. In *Touch Cinema*, the audience experiences the performance via the hand, complicating the notion that the relation between object and subject is structured solely by vision. The erotics of this exchange are called into question by virtue of their public context. The touching happened on the street, a space where such contact is normally prohibited, and yet only one person at a time could take part in this live, peripatetic "movie."

The box buckled to Export's torso was handmade and portable. She made her first "cinema" out of Styrofoam; that version was destroyed after her first two performances of *Touch Cinema*. It was redesigned and remade in aluminum for further performances, including one at the 1969 "Underground Explosion" in Essen, Germany. Always controversial, *Touch Cinema* was a particularly incendiary presence at the Essen festival: it sparked a riot in which Export sustained a head injury.

In performances of *Touch Cinema*, viewers are not held at a conventional, removed distance; instead, they are placed face-to-face with the performer. Photographs that document the action show people sheepishly reaching for Export's flesh as she stares right into their eyes. (There is also video footage of the performance that was shot for Austrian television.) Export compels viewers to become actors in her "movie," and she turns the usually passive role of the viewer into one of active participation. In order to have access to her body, the audience must do some work.

JBW

1. Valie Export, "Women's Art: A Manifesto" (March 1972), *Neues Forum* 228 (January 1973): 47. The manifesto, translated by Regina Haslinger, is reprinted in *Theories and Documents of Contemporary Art: A Sourcebook of Artists' Writings*, ed. Kristine Stiles and Peter Selz (Berkeley and Los Angeles: University of California Press, 1996), 755–56.

FLUXUS

"Fluxus" was proposed by George Maciunas in 1961 as the name of a magazine devoted to advanced experimental and intermedia arts, including performance, music, and poetry as well as objects and images. Fluxus also provided the name for a group of artists that was then loosely cohering around these common interests. With Maciunas as its impresario, Fluxus was characterized by easily packed and mobile productions, true internationalism, and the high seriousness of its irreverence. Neither a movement nor, properly speaking, a collective—and definitely not a cooperative—Fluxus was a quasi-collaborative, quasi-anarchist effort to redefine the field of artistic production.

Maciunas cited a number of historical sources, from the collective idealism of the Soviet avant-garde and Dada anti-art to the chance operations of the Duchampian readymade and Cageian Zen. In what is perhaps the best-known formulation of Fluxus, he wrote:

> FLUXUS *objectives* are *social* (not aesthetic). They are connected to the [NOVY] LEF group of 1929 in Soviet Union (ideologically) and concern itself [*sic*] with: Gradual elimination of fine arts (music, theater, poetry, fiction, painting, sculpture, etc., etc.). This is motivated by desire to stop the waste of material and human resources (like yourself) and divert it to *socially constructive ends.*[1]

Maciunas had a strong interest in both early and contemporary music, which had initially drawn him toward the new kind of score-based art then being produced in lofts and alternative galleries. Several of the original members of Fluxus (George Brecht, Dick Higgins, Toshi Ichiyanagi, Alison Knowles, Jackson MacLow, Yoko Ono, Robert Watts) had met in the late 1950s through John Cage's class in experimental composition. Music provided a model of ensemble work or collective interpretive activity, and early Fluxus manifestations took the form of "Fluxus concerts." In 1962–63, while working for the U.S. Army in Germany, Maciunas organized a series of "concerts" of experimental compositions using nontraditional "instruments" or abusing traditional ones. The first, in Wuppertal in June 1962, was broadcast on German television, and the success of this event was such that three months later, in Wiesbaden, he staged a much more ambitious production, a "Festum Fluxorum." By 1963, Maciunas was back in New York, but Fluxus had established an international network.

Late in 1964, a number of Fluxus artists took part in a production of Karlheinz Stockhausen's theater event, *Originale,* which was being directed by the artist Allan Kaprow as part of the Second Annual New York Avant-Garde Festival. Contending that Stockhausen and his work represented the worst of elitist, Eurocentric culture, Maciunas and his colleague Henry Flynt staged a vigorous (but in the end somewhat pathetic) picket. Kaprow recalls:

> I said [to Maciunas], "Don't do it!" And he said, "Why not?" I said, "Because the press and all the public will think it's part of the piece!" . . . [The picketing] was only during the intermissions between parts of the piece . . . and after the first intermission I went down there and joined in the picket line just to make sure that my prophecy would be indeed fulfilled. And George was hissing at me; he said, "Go away! Get away!" And I hissed back, I said, "Why? It's a free country."[2]

The picket had been prompted by a hard-line ultra-left position, and it proved a watershed moment. Several key Fluxus artists distanced them-

James Riddle, *E.S.P. Fluxkit (DOP),* 1966.

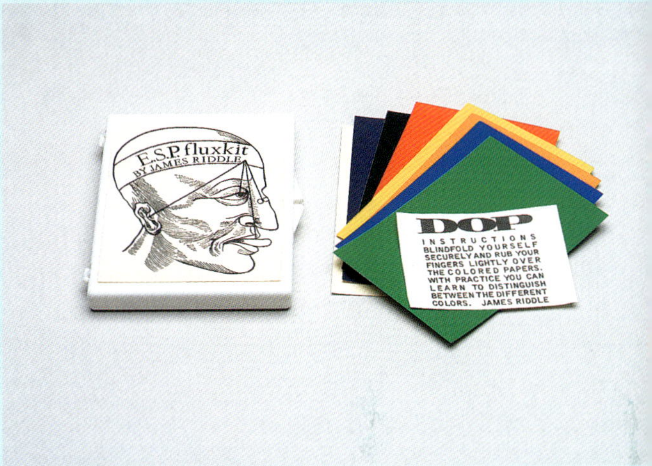

selves from Maciunas, Flynt, and Fluxus itself as a result of it. But if Fluxus could not sustain a party line, its commitment to certain modes of alternative artistic production was nevertheless crucial, and an unofficial compromise was struck. George Brecht explained, "In Fluxus there has never been any attempt to agree on aims or methods; individuals with something unnameable in common have simply naturally coalesced to publish and perform their work."[3]

Fluxus performances were naturally collaborative. The ruling model was low theater, cheap entertainment, carnivals—popular forms with an emphasis on humor and physical one-liners, immediate and concrete in their apprehension. Fluxus was anti-professional, for courting what Maciunas called the "nonpersonal" meant the elimination of virtuosi. Scores for events were not so much instructional as directive, performative, and indeterminate. Anyone could perform Alison Knowles's *Proposition #1,* the score for which reads: "Make a salad." And personal events (weddings, divorces, and so on) could be performed as vaudevillian Fluxus events. Such performances opened conventional ceremonies to critique even as they provoked a deeper analysis of the impersonal social needs addressed by such ritualized events. By the same token, Fluxus pieces could be performed in ways that implicitly critiqued the impersonal conventions of the concert performance and the compartmentalization of everyday life (Knowles carried her infant on stage, for example). Brecht quoted Dadaist Tristan Tzara: "Art is not the most precious manifestation of life. Art has not the celestial and universal value that people like to attribute to it. Life is far more interesting."[4]

The word "fluxus" denoted a Heraclitean concept of temporal flow that was demonstrated in the process-oriented production and performance of scores designed to guarantee an indeterminate outcome. But Fluxus also implied the repetitive, nearly mechanical processes of digestion and excretion, and this connotation dominated the Fluxus system of object production. For in Fluxus, a kind of Brer Rabbit strategy of cultural affirmation characterized the relationship of Fluxus "goods" to the efficient cycles of production, exchange, and consumption—the "digestive" system—of the art market.

Fluxus expanded the notion of "publication" and "edition" in its production, promotion, and sale of the trivial, the incidental, and even the immaterial. Under the persnickety guidance of Maciunas, Fluxus confounded the commercial institutions of the art world through its creative appropriation of serial production, promotion, and distribution techniques, a strategy visible first and foremost in absurdist modifications of use- and exchange-value such as Maciunas's *Ping Pong Rackets* (1965) or Mieko Shiomi's *Endless Box* (1963) and *Spatial Poem No. 1* (1965).

These performative objects and accumulations of ready-made materials were often small-scale, handheld, and sometimes wholly invisible (air, for

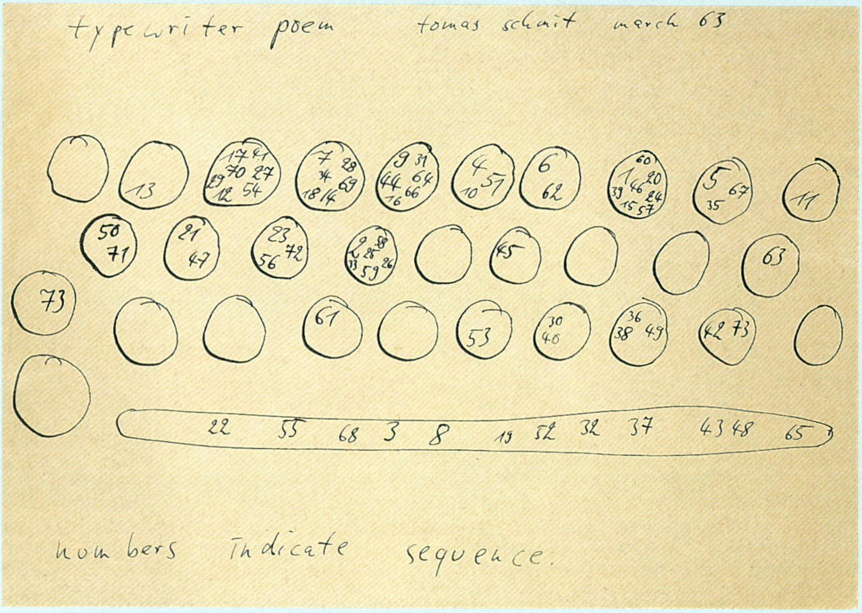

Tomas Schmit, *Typewriter Poem,* 1963.

instance) and were gathered into kits offered for sale. Advertised liberally in Fluxus organs, such collections were assembled laboriously and sold via mail order. The labor-intensive, precise, and significantly anal-retentive operations of producing and documenting these editions and multiples—they exist in proliferating editions and variations—resulted in a practice of dissemination and dispersal that, perversely, precisely because of the logic of dissemination, has been documented by Fluxus and its scholars in exhaustive detail. In this way Fluxus directly indicated the process at work in the kind of fetishism that attaches value to things and produces the kinds of hypervalued collections of the incidental (the "waste of material and human resources") that Fluxus both mimicked and sought to undermine.

Knowles scored one of the most lovely and succinct critiques of this kind of fetishism.

PERFORMANCE PIECE # 8 (1965)

Divide a variety of objects into two groups. Each group is labeled "everything." These groups may include several people. There is a third division of the stage, empty of objects, labeled "nothing." Each of the objects is "something." One performer combines and activates the objects as follows for any desired duration of time:

1. Something with everything
2. Something with nothing
3. Something with something
4. Everything with everything
5. Everything with nothing
6. Nothing with nothing

JR

1. George Maciunas, letter to Tomas Schmit (1964); reprinted in *Theories and Documents of Contemporary Art: A Sourcebook of Artists' Writings,* ed. Kristine Stiles and Peter Selz (Berkeley and Los Angeles: University of California Press, 1996), 726.

2. Allan Kaprow, interview by Judith Rodenbeck, October 29, 1996.

3. George Brecht, "Something about FLUXUS" (1964); reprinted in *An Introduction to George Brecht's Book of the Tumbler on Fire,* by Henry Martin (Milan: Multhipla Edizioni, 1978), 129.

4. Tristan Tzara, quoted by George Brecht in "Paragraphs, Quotations, and Lists" (1961); reprinted in Martin's *Introduction to George Brecht's Book,* 128.

George Maciunas

American, 1931–1978

George Maciunas was the founder, "Chairman," and impresario of the collaborative effort known as Fluxus. He spent the better part of his life giving other people's concepts physical form in the numerous editions of boxes, kits, and publications that he assembled and sold under the imprimatur of Fluxus from 1961 until his untimely death in 1978. Maciunas had a background in art history, architecture, and musicology and worked for many years as a designer. But his primary "job" was as a composer, arranger, and chief promoter for Fluxus. Though he expressly rejected "art" as a profession—he insisted that individuals affiliated with Fluxus have some other productive activity from which they made their living—his output was prodigious and eclectic.

For Maciunas, the primary objectives of Fluxus were social, and these dictated all his

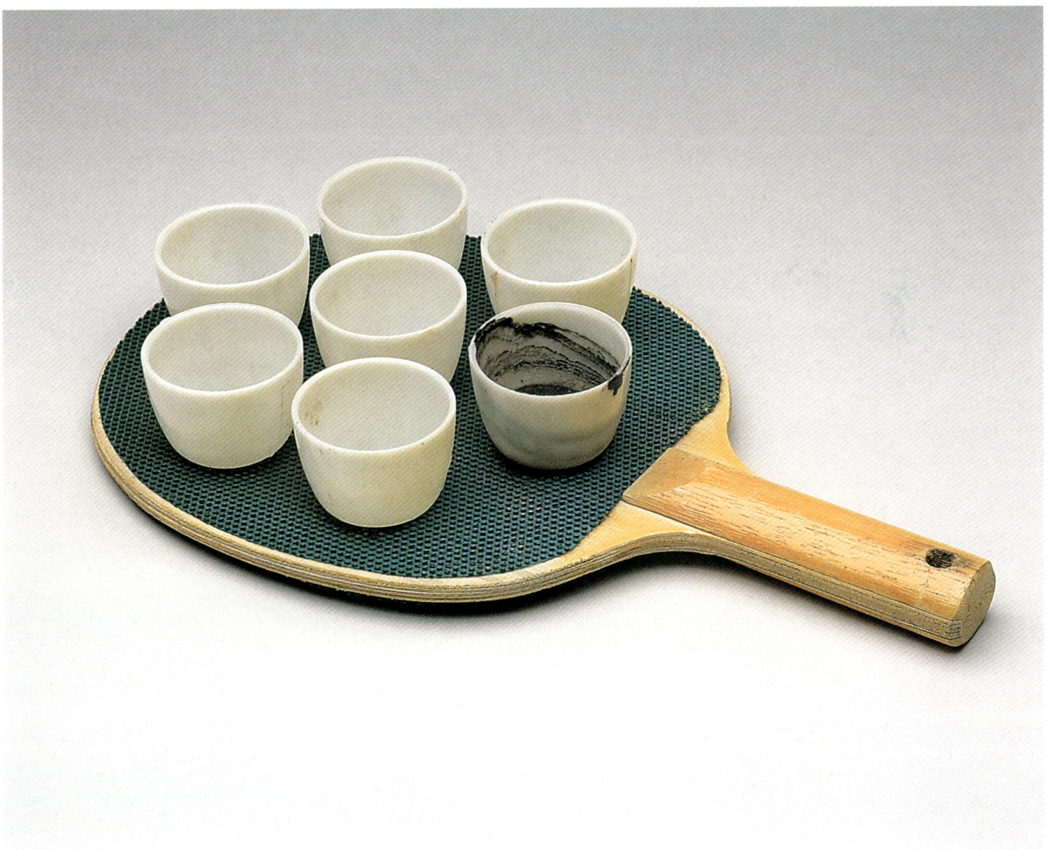

George Maciunas, *Modified Ping-Pong Racket: Concave Racket*, ca. 1970.

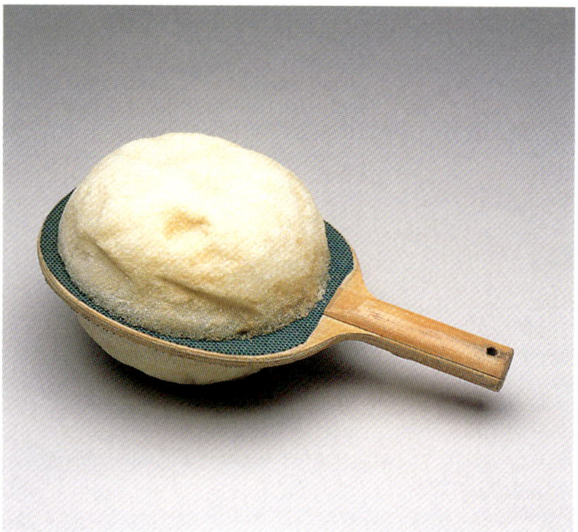 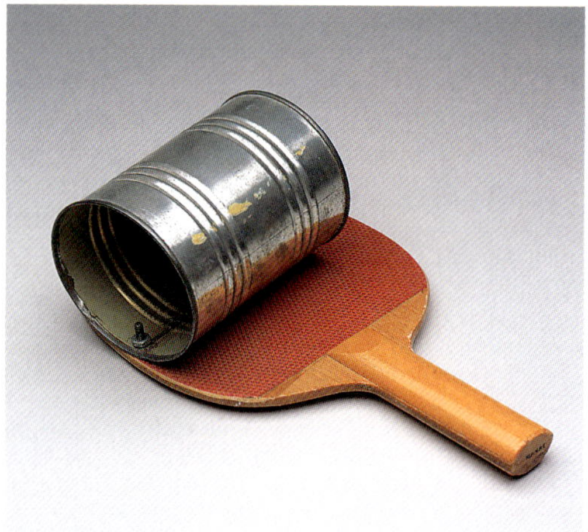

George Maciunas, *Modified Ping-Pong Rackets: Convex Racket; Can of Water Racket; Hole in Center Racket,* ca. 1970.

art activities. "Fluxus art-amusement," he wrote, "is the rear guard without any pretension or urge to participate in the competition of 'one-upmanship' with the avant-garde. It strives for the monostructural and non-theatrical qualities of simple natural events, a game or a gag. It is the fusion of Spike Jones, Vaudeville, gags, children's games and Duchamp."[1] He understood Marcel Duchamp to have democratized the art object radically; John Cage offered a model of rule-based chance operations and indeterminate composition that deemphasized authorial control. Anything could be art and anyone could make it. From these precedents, Maciunas drew several principles: work should be concrete and game-based; it should be simple, humble, and funny, rather than sophisticated and precious; in the ideal, it should be anonymously or collectively produced; and any sincere "playing" of a performance score or game was valid.

Maciunas was particularly interested in organized sports and their structures, and some of his most amusing works consist of modified traditional games and game equipment. Such sports were of interest for several reasons. First, the structure provided by the rules and format of the game serves as a ready-made set of conventions or performative contract—what Maciunas called an "automatic machine" for producing indeterminate results.[2] Second, the equipment for the game is industrially ready-made. Finally, modifying or "assisting" these readymades may make the game nearly impossible to play; its conventions become arduous and self-evidently arbitrary. Essentially, Maciunas said, he was "taking existing sports and preparing them the way Cage prepares a piano."[3]

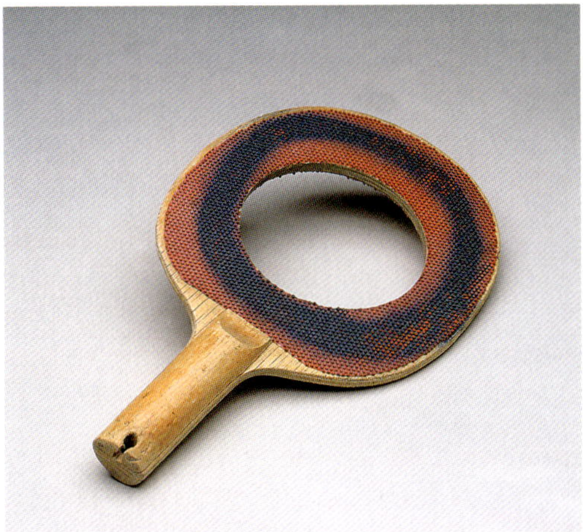

Maciunas first produced his modified Ping-Pong rackets around 1965 for a Fluxus "Olympics." The paddles' humor rests on the implication of their use in a game rather than on any intrinsic formal properties of the paddles as objects. And playing a game of Ping-Pong with them (precisely the kind of literalist follow-through typical of Fluxus) achieves slapstick results. This Fluxus inversion of the possibilities of the readymade—rendering the object "useless" but leaving its original purpose relatively intact—foregrounds the Ping-Pong game and its formalities, which are emphasized as the performative site of an exchange between those players who, no matter how temporarily or provisionally, agree to its conventions.

JR

1. George Maciunas, "Fluxus Art-amusement" (1965), excerpted in *Fluxus*, by Thomas Kellein (London: Thames and Hudson, 1995), 135.

2. That is, results that vary with each performance. George Maciunas, "Neo-Dada in Music, Theater, Poetry, Art" (1962); reprinted in *In the Spirit of Fluxus*, exh. cat., ed. Janet Jenkins (Minneapolis: Walker Art Center, 1993), 157.

3. George Maciunas, interview by William Woods, KRAB-Seattle, September 1977.

Alison Knowles

American, b. 1933

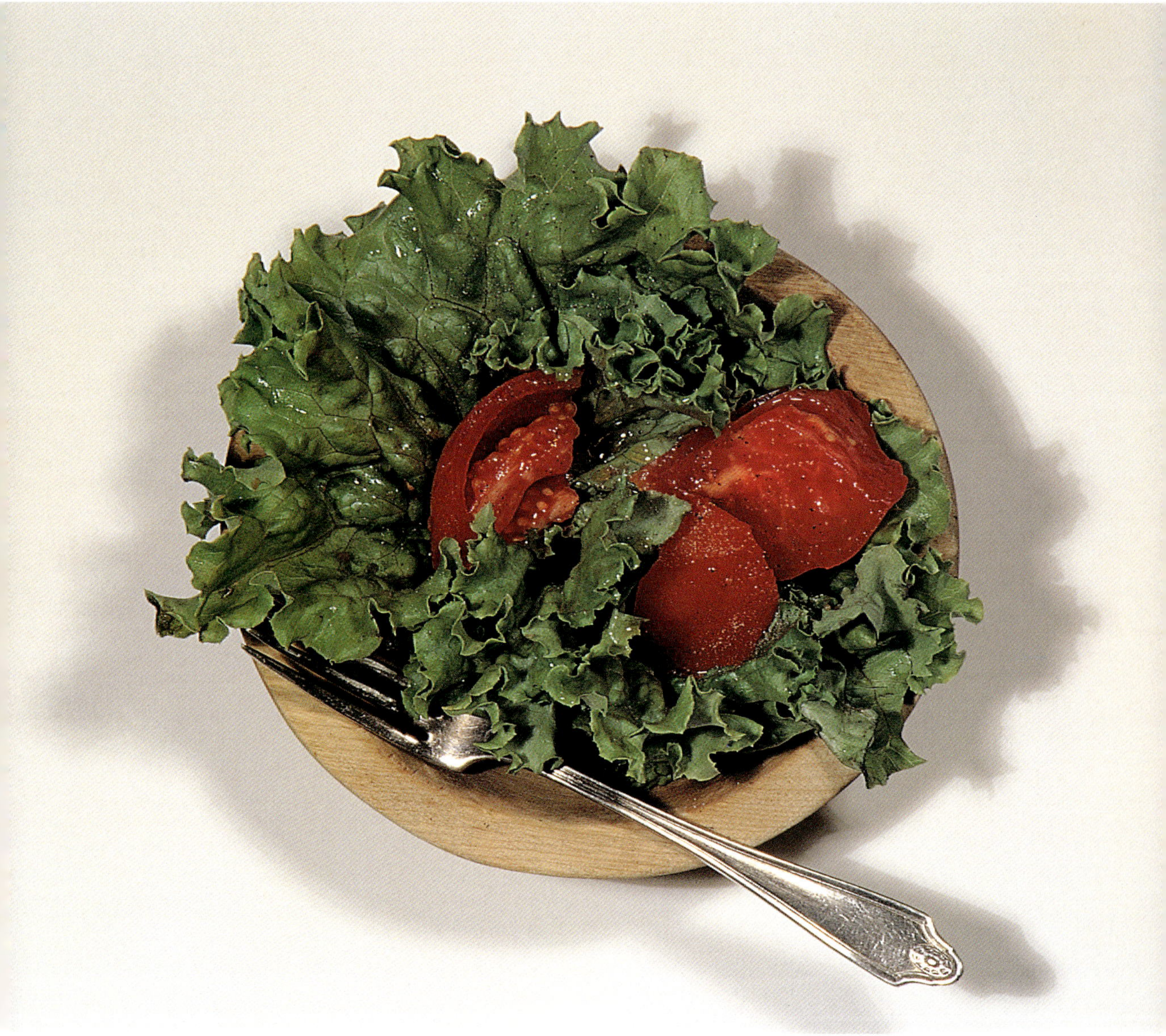

Alison Knowles, *Make a Salad,* 1962.

One of the original members of Fluxus, Alison Knowles came closest to reaching the group's goal, inspired by Zen teachings, of breaking down the separation of the aesthetic and the mundane. In principle this goal entails several things: attention to the moment and the everyday, the rupture of hierarchies and false divisions, and the dissolution of the ego. Knowles's work as an artist and as a performer of both her own and other Fluxus artists' scores is characterized by a concrete and material simplicity, even humility; an emphasis on the nuances of difference that occur within repetitions; and methodical, meditative execution. The Zen principles Knowles adopted might be said in some ways to typify "women's work," understood in its conventional limitation to the domestic sphere. In Knowles's practice, the emphasis on the concrete and mundane at once draws from and revalues such activities, redefining the everyday (and women's work in particular) as productive, meditative, collaborative, interpretive, and even poetic.

Knowles's work mobilizes a tension between ordinary language and everyday activity. An early, important Fluxus work, *Bean Rolls* (1964), which Knowles called "a canned book," consists of small scrolls inscribed with bean-related data—"Early Red Valentines, Early Mohawks, Long Yellow Six Weeks, English Canterburys . . . Bean's insulated Boot Foot Wader (Suspenders extra)"—that are placed in a can. Although *Bean Rolls* presents the names of mundane things, the list is a form of anonymous poetry that is verbal and visual. At the same time, it is a statistical accumulation. Though comprising "facts," the associative chains of the scrolls reveal—and require the reader to repeat—the delicious linguistic labor that accompanies gardening, hybridizing, and canning, the kind of mental meander one might experience while waiting for beans to cook. In *Proposition #1: Make a Salad* (1962), Knowles translated domestic labor into a performance context. The score directs its reader, simply, to "make a salad." The radical brevity suggests that anyone can "play" the score. Indeed, if ordinary life, like language, gains meaning from its use, then one can either make a salad or perform an Alison Knowles piece of "art music." And if the score, in its banal simplicity, nevertheless evokes W. B. Yeats's "fine women [who] eat / A crazy salad with their meat,"[1] this crazy salad could itself be composed of lettuce or music or words.

Pieces such as *Bean Rolls*, *Make a Salad*, or *Identical Lunch* (1969) transvalue the production and consumption of food into art activities—and, in a typical anti-art reversal, recode art action into everyday activity. "I think that many of the pieces are just simple refreshment pieces done for whatever day's work you have to do, supporting occurrences in life," Knowles has said. "Whatever it is you have to touch and work with, you can make a kind of performance of it, but it has to be stripped of the hangings and accoutrements of theatre."[2] But Knowles is not simply challenging the conventional isolation of art from life, for the reversal applied to Knowles's performance practice, too. She often performed, against all concert decorum, with her babies in tow. JR

1. William Butler Yeats, "A Prayer for My Daughter," in *Selected Poems and Two Plays of William Butler Yeats*, ed. M. L. Rosenthal (New York: Collier Books, 1962), 92.

2. Estera Milman, "Road Shows, Street Events, and Fluxus People: A Conversation with Alison Knowles," *Visible Language* 26, no. 1/2 (1992): 103; cited in David T. Doris, "Zen Vaudeville: A Medi(t)ation in the Margins of Fluxus," in *The Fluxus Reader*, ed. Ken Friedman (Chichester, England: Academy Editions, 1998), 108.

ZEN

Zen is a spiritual discipline from Japan with roots in China and origins in the 2,500-year-old religion of Buddhism. Japanese scholar D. T. Suzuki (1870–1966) popularized Zen in the West through a series of accessible books and public presentations, and most important, a series of lectures he gave at Columbia University from 1951 to 1957. Suzuki's version of Zen has had the broadest reception, and it is widely recognized to have had a major impact on the arts of the postwar era.

Structured through a series of paradoxes, Zen is a qualified meditative practice, for it does not recognize a division between action and contemplation. Through the elimination of individual ego, it aims at a kind of individual enlightenment, or *satori,* focused on recognition of and absorption by the natural continuity of the palpable world and the concrete immediacy of the everyday. Zen is anti-habitual, and yet the correct practice of repeated exercises, be they sweeping, painting, or archery, can bring *satori.* "What is the truth?" asks the adept. The monk replies, "Your everyday mind."[1]

Zen influenced postwar art in the West in three ways. First, many of its tenets, if not always its actual practices, seemed to confirm the material scope of postwar artistic practice. Second, its emphasis on the concrete and the everyday was consonant with preexisting homegrown belief systems. Finally, as a private and ethical discipline relatively free from mysticism, Judeo-Christian orthodoxies, and the tainted rationalism of the Western Enlightenment, it provided for some artists an anodyne resting place for their very specifically postwar "spiritual" concerns.

Empiricism, detachment, spontaneity, the elimination of hierarchies, and a radical individualism were the cardinal points of Zen practice. They are also features shared by two of the most prominent Western philosophical positions of the 1950s. According to Suzuki, Zen, pragmatism, and existentialism "all accept experience as the basis of their theorization, and this experience is closely attached to the world of relativities."[2] Where they differ, according to Suzuki, is in their relation to purpose. Zen emphasizes "not leaving any trace behind as one lives one's life," while pragmatism is purposeful. And Zen, unlike existentialism, said Suzuki, refuses fear in the face of "never-ending responsibilities."

Suzuki, who was also a scholar of American pragmatism, freely translated Zen into Emersonian terms. For example, he rendered the statement "Zen is the religion of *tsu-yu,*" in which *tsu-yu* is usually translated as "freedom," as "Zen is the religion of self-reliance." Such shifts eased the transfusion of Zen principles into an American vernacular. And where Suzuki's version of Zen placed particular emphasis on *satori,* the Western reception of this experience, too, mapped readily onto the ready-made aesthetics of postwar art.[3]

Art historian Helen Westgeest has identified five distinct areas of emphasis that Western artistic preoccupations of the 1950s seem to share with Zen: (1) the embrace of emptiness and nothingness (detachment); (2) dynamism and spontaneity; (3) attention to both negative as well as positive space (Japanese *ma,* or "interval"); (4) direct experience of the present (*satori*); and (5) nonhierarchical organization.[4] A direct correspondence between Zen

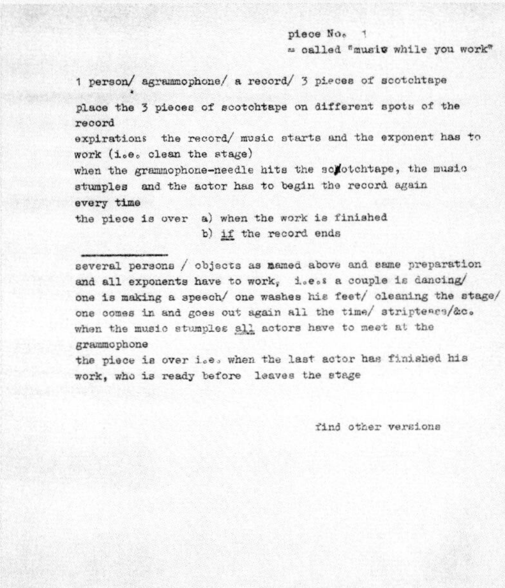

piece No. 1
= called "music while you work"

1 person/ agrammophone/ a record/ 3 pieces of scotchtape

place the 3 pieces of scotchtape on different spots of the record
expiration: the record/ music starts and the exponent has to work (i.e. clean the stage)
when the grammophone-needle hits the scotchtape, the music stumples and the actor has to begin the record again every time
the piece is over a) when the work is finished
b) <u>if</u> the record ends

several persons / objects as named above and same preparation and all exponents have to work, i.e.: a couple is dancing/ one is making a speech/ one washes his feet/ cleaning the stage/ one comes in and goes out again all the time/ striptease/&c.
when the music stumples <u>all</u> actors have to meet at the grammophone
the piece is over i.e. when the last actor has finished his work, who is ready before leaves the stage

find other versions

Arthur Koepcke, *Music While You Work,* 1962.

and Western artistic practice of the immediate postwar era can be drawn at the level of form, especially in painting. Zen has ancient and intimate links with Chinese and Japanese traditions of ink-and-brush painting, and the Zen practice of *sumiye* painting, in its spontaneity, its deployment of the calligraphic mark as both drawing and writing, its nonhierarchical composition, and its implication of gesture before and beyond mark on ground, was of crucial and explicit formal interest to artists in the West. Indeed, in summing up *sumiye,* Suzuki simultaneously described many of the strategic moves identified with postwar abstract painting in both Europe and America: "No deliberation is allowed, no erasing, no repetition, no retouching, no remodelling, no 'doctoring,' no building-up."[5]

Formalists argued that this kind of art making was a rigorous and disciplined exercise in medium-specificity and that viewing such art provided a glimpse of the sublime. But for Suzuki, the emphasis was on the act of painting as much as the result: "Life delineates itself on the canvas called time; and time never repeats: once gone, forever gone; and so is an act: once done, it is never undone. Life is a *sumiye*-painting, which must be executed once and for all time and without hesitation, without intellection, and no corrections are permissible or possible."[6] In the 1950s, more pragmatically inclined artists, under the partial influence of Suzuki's Zen, turned to the strategy of the readymade, adopted a model of artistic production that was multidimensional, open, and immediate, and regarded the resulting art "object" as in some measure a collaborative transaction between maker and user. It is in this latter dynamic understanding that postwar artistic practices and Zen have had the most not to say but to *do* with each other. JR

1. William Barrett, "Zen for the West," in *Zen Buddhism: Selected Writings of D. T. Suzuki,* ed. William Barrett (New York: Anchor Books, 1956; reprint, New York: Doubleday, 1995), xvi.

2. Ibid., 265.

3. George J. Leonard, *Into the Light of Things: The Art of the Commonplace from Wordsworth to John Cage* (Chicago: University of Chicago Press, 1994), 161.

4. See Helen Westgeest, *Zen and the Art of the Fifties: Interaction in Art Between East and West,* exh. cat. (Zwolle: Waanders; Amstelveen: Cobra Museum voor Moderne Kunst, 1996).

5. *Zen Buddhism,* ed. Barrett, 279.

6. Ibid., 130.

George Brecht

American, b. 1926

For George Brecht, art making was largely a question of organization, for which he selected strategies from statistics, physics, and Zen. "The primary function of my art," Brecht wrote, "seems to be an expression of maximum meaning with a minimal image, that is, the achievement of an art of multiple implications, through simple, even austere, means."[1]

Music, which was then undergoing a highly techno-scientific analysis, provided Brecht with a working example of a contemporary artistic practice that matched this criterion. It also provided him with the model of the score, different parameters of which he explored in John Cage's composition class at the New School for Social Research. The score, as Brecht understood it, was important in several ways: it could be read or played by anyone; it was open to interpretation; it could be widely disseminated; and it yielded no singular finished product. The scores Brecht developed in Cage's class assembled ordinary tasks and sonic events in chance-derived durations (e.g., the time it takes a candle to burn). But Brecht soon became dissatisfied with a music that was only "for the ears." Music, he said, "isn't just what you hear or what you listen to, but everything that happens."[2] The "act of imagination or perception is in itself an arrangement, so there is no avoiding anyone making arrangements."[3] Cage's essentially concert-based practice was inadequate to the "total, multi-sensory experience I was interested in."[4] Brecht began to shift his attention to minimalist verbal scores that could be repeated infinitely in open interpretations without spatial or temporal limits. (The score for *Word Event*, for example, reads, in total, "exit.")

The concept of the event—loosely drawing from physics, a change in state—was crucial to Brecht's work and was most sharply demonstrated in *Water Yam*. Realized between 1959 and 1965 and first published in 1962, *Water Yam* was one of the first Fluxus boxes devoted to a single artist and served as a continuously updated repository of Brecht's event scores. The box can be seen in different ways—as a multipart sculptural object, a publication, a collection of scores, a graphic portfolio. *Water Yam* exists in a number of versions as well, each consisting of a box (sometimes wood, sometimes plastic, dimensions variable) containing a (variable) number of printed event scores. The earliest works in *Water Yam*, such as *Time-Table Music* (1959) or *Motor Vehicle Sundown Event* (1960), are indebted to Cage in their aurality and tend to have complex instructions and a polyphonic structure. Later scores are more telegraphic and open in structure, presenting minimal text with maximal differentiation (e.g., "red, green").

Humorous but also poignant, Brecht's pieces often point to ways in which habits and rules constrict our everyday lives. As we read or perform the indeterminate and open scores in a work like *Water Yam*, those habits and rules are doubly emphasized, and we are made aware of their social and conventional dimensions.

Ben Vautier: Why do you work?
George Brecht: No reason.

George Brecht, *Water Yam,* 1963.

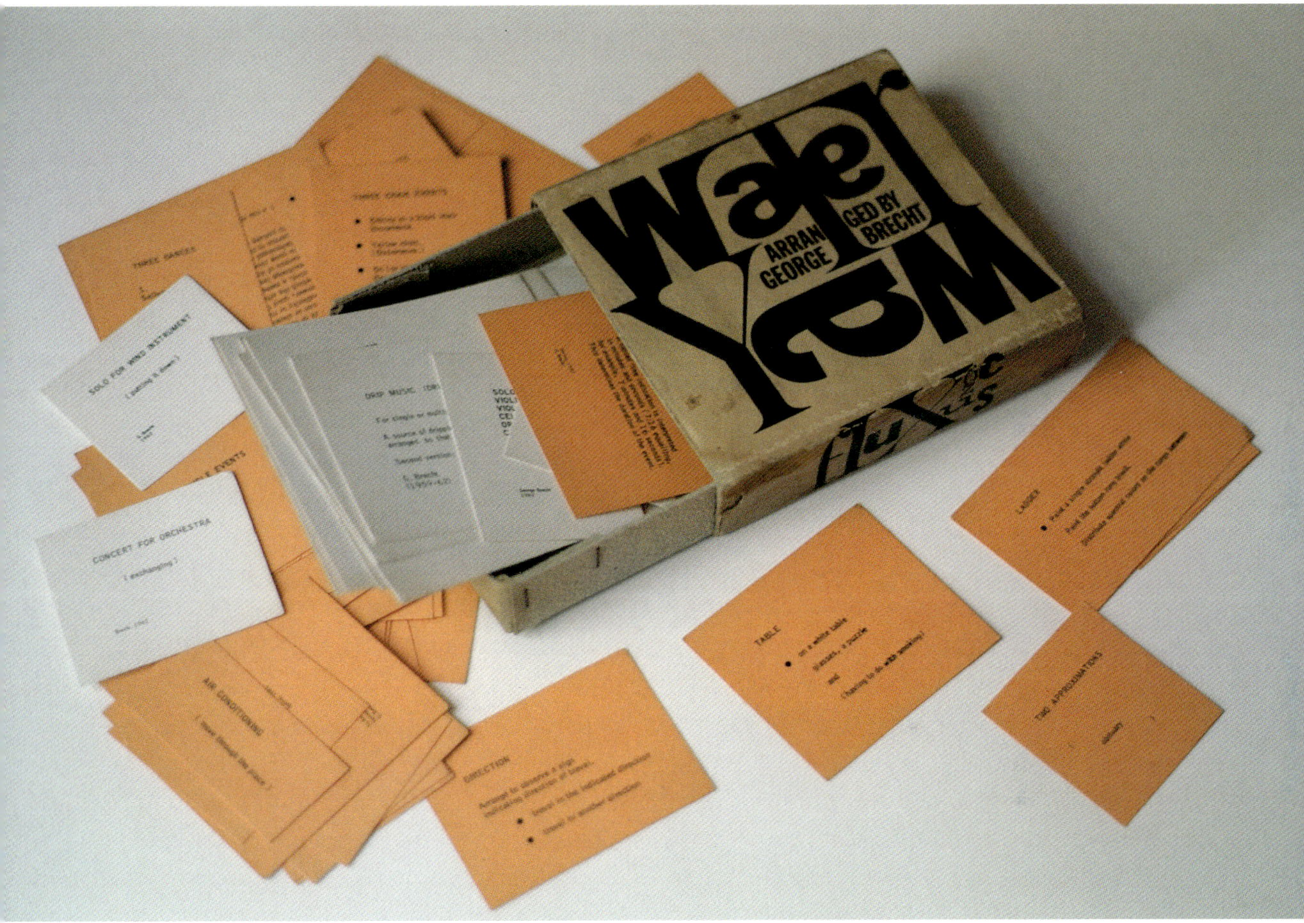

BV: If you don't think of yourself as an artist, how do you think of yourself?

GB: Nothing special. . . . Nothing in particular.[5]

JR

1. George Brecht, from "Project in Multiple Dimensions" (1958); reprinted in *An Introduction to George Brecht's Book of the Tumbler on Fire*, by Henry Martin (Milan: Multhipla Edizioni, 1978), 126.

2. "An Interview with George Brecht by Irmeline Lebeer," trans. Henry Martin, in Martin's *Introduction to George Brecht's Book*, 83. The interview was first published in 1973 in *Art Vivant* (Paris).

3. "Excerpts from a Discussion Between George Brecht and Allan Kaprow Entitled 'Happenings and Events' Broadcast by WBAI Sometime During May," *V TRE* 4 (June 1964): 1.

4. "Origin of Events," cited in David T. Doris, "Zen Vaudeville: A Medi(t)ation in the Margins of Fluxus," in *The Fluxus Reader*, ed. Ken Friedman (Chichester, England: Academy Editions, 1998), 97.

5. Ben Vautier and Marcel Alocco, "A Conversation About Something Else: An Interview with George Brecht," *Identités* (Nice) 11/12 (Summer/Autumn, 1965); reprinted in Martin's *Introduction to George Brecht's Book*, 73.

Mieko Shiomi

Japanese, b. 1938

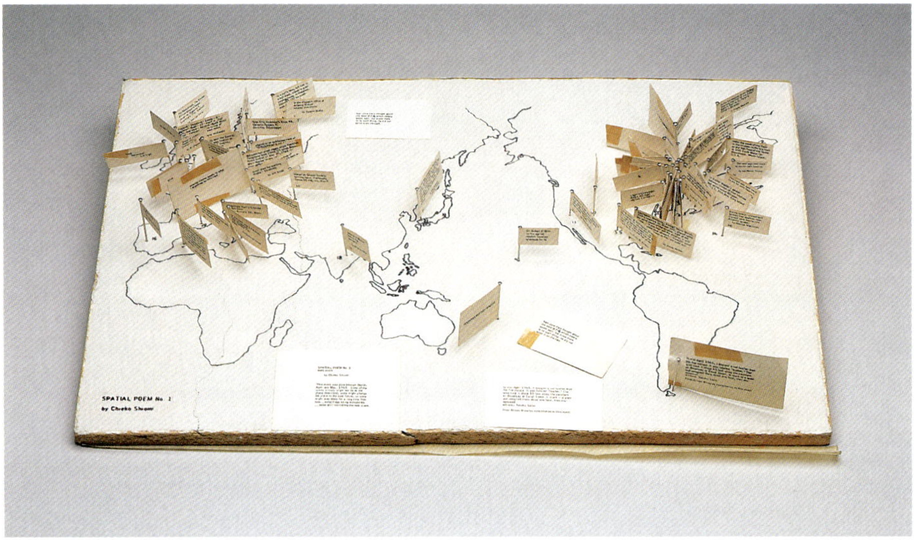

Mieko Shiomi, *Spatial Poem No. 1,* 1965.

Mieko Shiomi was affiliated with the Fluxus movement both while she was living in the United States and after she returned to Japan. Her work, like that of many Fluxus artists, is deeply indebted to the idea of an "event score"—a set of instructions for performance borrowed from the disciplines of music and dance. It is perhaps not surprising that Shiomi—an accomplished, classically trained musician—wrote instructions that follow the logic of a musician's composition or a choreographer's notations for dancers. Her instructions, however, were not designed for trained professionals. Rather, they are actions to be completed by anyone. While actively involved with Fluxus, Shiomi wrote the scores for several important Fluxus events, notably *Water Music* (1964), in which participants were asked to "let the water loose" from a variety of bottled waters, and *Disappearing Music for Face* (1964), one iteration of which was a film by Peter Moore featuring Yoko Ono as the performer. Over the course of twelve minutes, a smile steadily, and in an infinitely sad progression, turns into a non-smile. In both instances, "music" is conceived of as visual as well as aural, typifying the boundary-defying quality of much Fluxus work.

Intimacy distinctly marks Shiomi's oeuvre. After her return to Japan, her instructions were typically sent to friends, acquaintances, and fellow artists. In her *Spatial Poem* series, staged in nine separate versions from 1965 through 1975, she repeatedly sent letters to friends and colleagues inviting them to do an event and document their action, thought, or work in some way. As the responses were mailed back to her, she charted the replies on

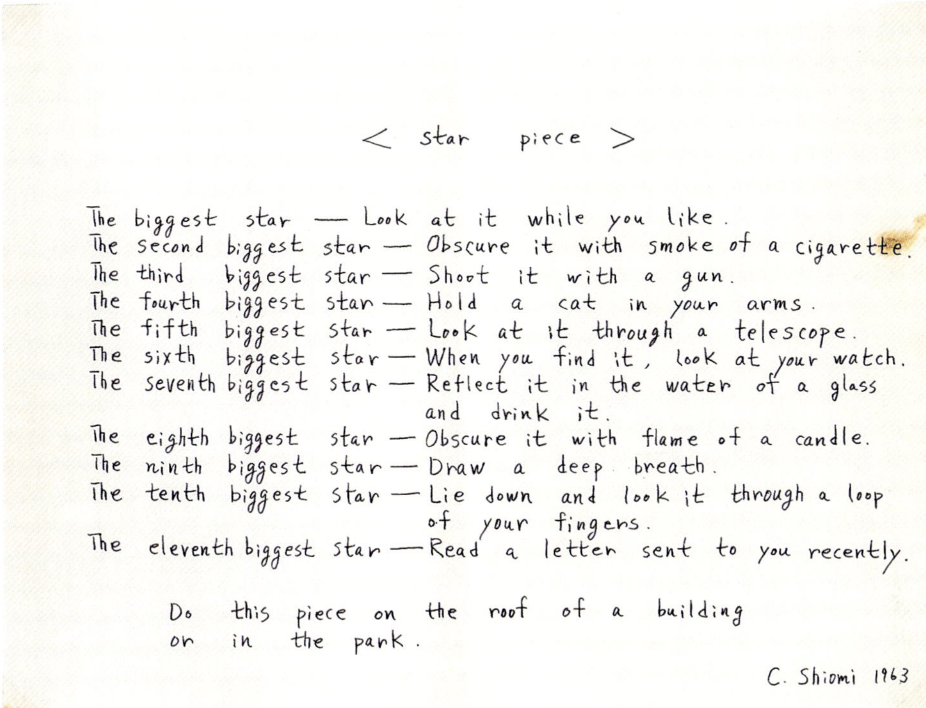

< star piece >

The biggest star — Look at it while you like.
The second biggest star — Obscure it with smoke of a cigarette.
The third biggest star — Shoot it with a gun.
The fourth biggest star — Hold a cat in your arms.
The fifth biggest star — Look at it through a telescope.
The sixth biggest star — When you find it, look at your watch.
The seventh biggest star — Reflect it in the water of a glass and drink it.
The eighth biggest star — Obscure it with flame of a candle.
The ninth biggest star — Draw a deep breath.
The tenth biggest star — Lie down and look it through a loop of your fingers.
The eleventh biggest star — Read a letter sent to you recently.

Do this piece on the roof of a building or in the park.

C. Shiomi 1963

Mieko Shiomi, *Star Piece,* 1963.

a map of the world locating the participants geographically. In *Spatial Poem No. 3* (1968), for example, participants were asked to document any activity having to do with falling. The work was then produced as a multiple and modified by George Maciunas in the form of a "fluxcalendar" in which the days of the year are accompanied by responses ranging from: "July 12, On entering the subway Philip Kaplan dropped his token in the machine. At the same time a bead of perspiration left his beard. They disappeared in three different directions. NEW YORK," to "August 17, 1:10 PM, Stanley Brouwn picked up a clod of earth at point A, then walked to point B and dropped it. AMSTERDAM."

When gathered together, the seemingly banal activities or occurrences create a sense of community, no matter how dispersed its members. Shiomi subverts the managerial logic of documenting and monitoring everyday human minutiae. Instead, her desire to record furthers the aim of multiple friendships rather than the logic of efficiency. So, too, the *Spatial Poem* series seems prescient in its understanding of the newly emergent condition of globalism, a condition where some artists may move about freely, others need to travel to earn a living, and still others remain quite rooted, tracking movement from afar.[1]

HM

1. Jon Hendricks, artist and curator of the Gilbert and Lila Silverman Fluxus Collection, noted that Shiomi had to develop a "kitchen table" art practice that would allow her to continue making art while she performed the more traditional housebound labors of child rearing upon her return to Japan. Hendricks, conversation with the author, Detroit, Spring 2002.

PLAY

No discussion of work can be maintained for very long without registering the concept of play. Do we work in order to play? Do we play as a respite from work? Is making, toiling, and working the existential condition of humankind? Or is the frolic and freedom of play our true essential nature? These questions, despite the subject of their study, have provoked heady discourse. Indeed, Johan Huizinga's *Homo Ludens*, one of the most important and long-lasting books on the subject, opens with: "Play is older than culture."

For Huizinga, true play contains elements of chance and nonseriousness; most important, play is completely voluntary. Play can never be a task or a duty. Huizinga describes play as released from these powerful societal motivators, as a pure instance of freedom. Historically, societies have organized spaces and times for play in order to facilitate and ensure the well-being of the group. While Huizinga traces the concept and evolution of play from so-called primitive societies through the end of the nineteenth century, he ends his book on a somewhat pessimistic note, seeing the functions of play denigrated in the contemporary period. Observing the professionalization of sports and the co-optation of the rhetoric of play by various business entities, he states: "The spirit of the professional is no longer the true play-spirit; it is lacking in spontaneity and carelessness."[1] Specifically, Huizinga describes this condition among artists: "Art is far more susceptible to the deleterious influences of modern techniques of production than is science. Mechanization, advertising, sensation-mongering have a much greater hold upon art because as a rule it works directly for a market and has a free choice of all the techniques available."[2]

In the face of growing pessimism about the increasingly administered nature of contemporary society, many artists aimed to return art to its rightful dimension of play. In 1963 Henry Flynt, a fellow traveler of the Fluxus movement, coined the term "veramusement" and picketed mainstream art institutions, such as Lincoln Center and the Metropolitan Museum of Art, in order to protest what he called "serious culture." George Maciunas's seemingly endless production of game boxes speaks to his desire to use art as a means toward play. But Maciunas's modified Ping-Pong rackets are perhaps his most emphatically playful works. The rackets are so radically transformed that one could never play the game as it is intended: one paddle has a huge hole cut out of the middle, and another is so heavy that it can barely be lifted. Hence a cultural site dedicated to play—Ping-Pong—is made more contingent and less serious than ever. Maciunas's gesture suggests that art might be used as a way to intervene in a "sport" that resists its codification into a regulated form of play.

Contemporary artists operate under an even more highly elaborated market for art than their 1960s predecessors. The increased scale of contemporary art galleries and the highly developed international circuit of biennials mean that artists today are under extraordinary pressures to produce to meet the demand of both collectors and museums. Several artists have responded to this demand by making transitory, site-specific works designed to foil the logic of art as a commodity and/or art as private property. Instead, they offer art as a transitory and playful experience. Erwin Wurm's *One Minute Sculptures* are a perfect example of art that takes nonproductive play as its *modus operandi.* In these works, the artist provides instructions for viewers to perform actions such as "balance two felt-tip markers on your shoes while thinking of Spinoza" for the duration of one minute. Here the art object is not a commodity to be manipulated by the market, nor is the activity purposeful in any specific way. Rather, in a nearly perfect translation of Huizinga's definition of play, the social space of art is used to provide a time-based, nonserious activity open to the whims of chance and dedicated to ensuring the good humor and well-being of the viewer—should she feel free enough to participate. HM

1. Johan Huizinga, *Homo Ludens: A Study of the Play Element in Culture* (Boston: Beacon Press, 1955), 197.

2. Ibid., 202.

Felix Gonzalez-Torres

Cuban-born American, 1957–1996

Like many artists of his generation, Felix Gonzalez-Torres was deeply influenced by Minimalist sculpture. Minimalism's play with endless permutations of serial forms, its reliance upon factory-produced objects, and its concern with the phenomenological relationships between viewers and objects were all extended and challenged by artists at work in the 1990s. If Minimalism portended a high degree of abstraction, partaking of a centuries-long tradition regarding art's autonomy, then artists of the 1990s such as Robert Gober, Gonzalez-Torres, and Cady Noland sought to reinvest Minimalist forms and ideas with explicit social content. The desire to have art speak to political issues as well as more traditionally defined aesthetic concerns was particularly pointed: the late 1980s and 1990s were a period of extreme social crisis, as the government's negligence in regard to AIDS resulted in grave human devastation.

Gonzalez-Torres's work occupies several fields of critical discourse, political activism, and art practice. Known for his activism in collectives such as ACT-UP and Group Material, he also produced a body of highly influential, poetic, and personal work. Almost all of his work exists in multiple and even infinite forms, most notably his stack and candy pieces. The stack pieces are beautifully precise stacks of endless sheets of printed paper. While these works evoke the sculptural forms of Donald Judd, they function completely differently, as viewers are encouraged to take a poster home. The candy pieces piled in corners or laid out in geometric shapes on the floor function similarly: viewers are permitted and encouraged to take one of the shiny cellophane-wrapped sweets. Both the stack and candy pieces rely heavily upon the logic of the gift, with the artist playing the role of a benevolent dispenser of a democratized luxury item. The pieces also replicate the function of the souvenir. In Gonzalez-Torres's work, there is no need for a souvenir of the art experience, because the work is its own souvenir. So, too, the works understand the relation between the souvenir and the *memento mori*, as the offering, through its perpetual disappearance, is a subtle reminder of both the viewer's mortality and the hubris of the museum's belief in timeless perpetuity. His works require viewer engagement to complete their logic, and they also make specific demands upon their owners. As the works are available to be taken at will, they exist in a state of perpetual diminishment. Gonzalez-Torres stipulates in the contract accompanying each work, however, that its owner must be responsible for continually replenishing it. While numerous artists order their materials from various manufacturers and ask the viewer to complete their works, only Gonzalez-Torres extends the labor of the artwork to include the collector and museum by insisting that owners are responsible for the management of inventory. HM

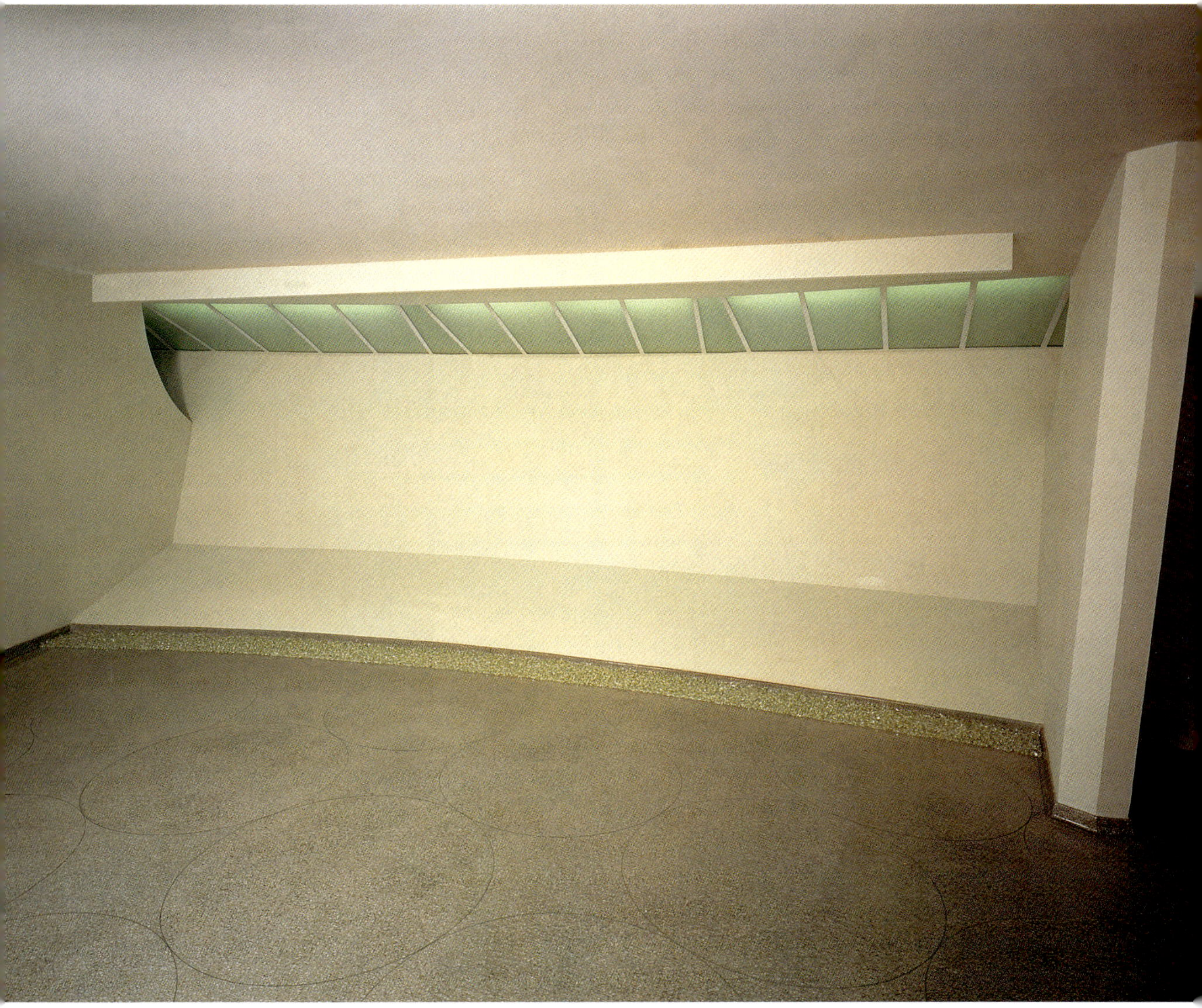

Felix Gonzalez-Torres, "Untitled" (Rossmore II), 1991.

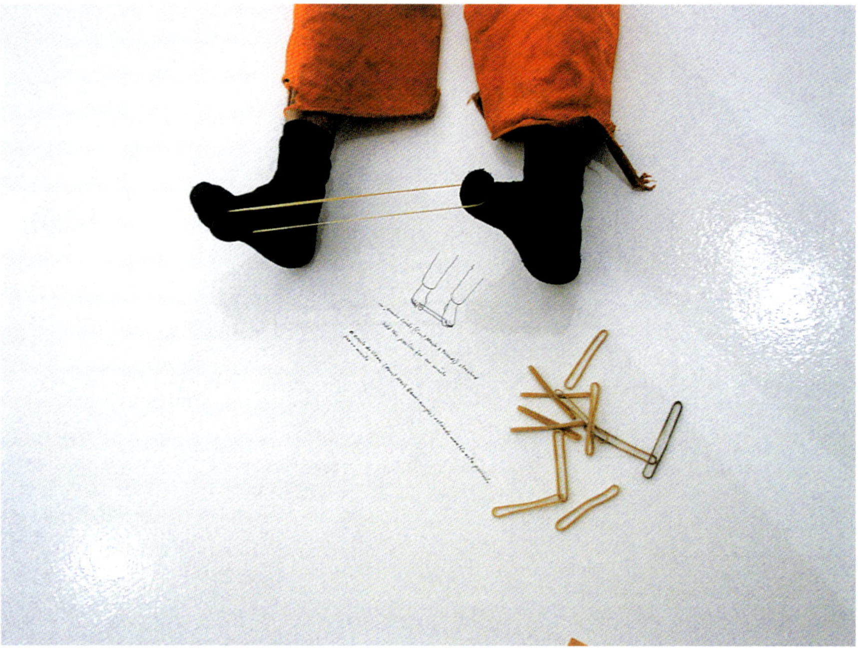

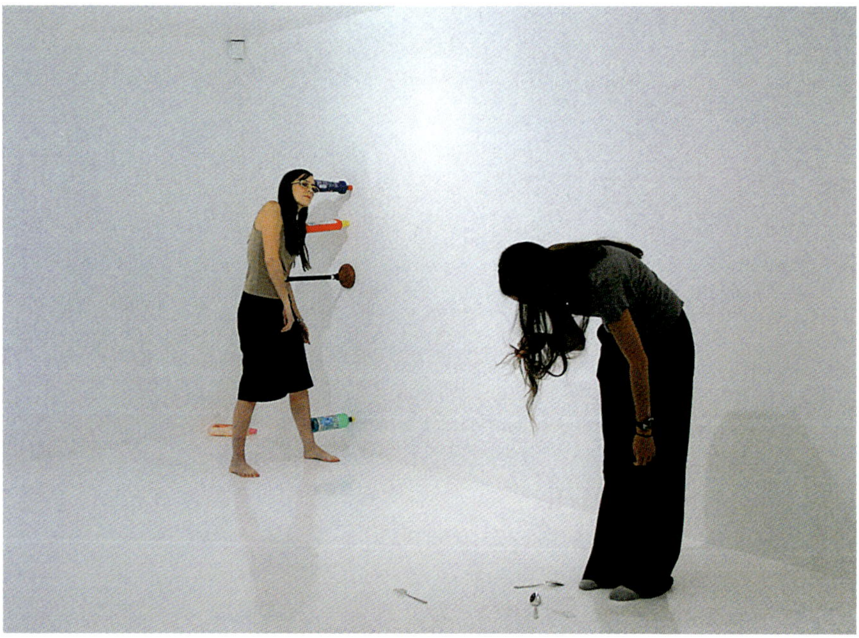

Erwin Wurm
Austrian, b. 1954

In 1913, Marcel Duchamp attached a bicycle wheel to a kitchen stool. He said, "To see that wheel turning was very soothing, very comforting, a sort of opening on other things than the material life of every day. I liked the idea of having a bicycle wheel in my studio. I enjoyed looking at it, just as I enjoy looking at flames dancing in the fireplace."[1] This simple gesture introduced the element of time and duration into the realm of sculpture. From Jean Tinguely's kinetic sculptures and Minimalist artists' concern with a moving viewer to Earth artists' exploration of the natural forces of gravity and entropy, time's convergence with space—indeed, the potential collapse of the two fields upon one another—has been a dominant theme of twentieth-century sculpture.

Erwin Wurm's *One Minute Sculptures* operate within and extend this tradition. The sculptures take a variety of forms. They exist as both drawn and verbal instructions. Sometimes the instructions are framed like a proper drawing; at other times, they simply appear on the wall of the gallery or museum. The wall drawings are accompanied by props and a platform upon which the viewer can enact the *One Minute Sculptures*—hold four bananas (one in mouth, two under arms, and one between legs); balance two felt-tip markers on your shoes while thinking of Descartes; prop two buckets and two plastic balls with your head against the wall—all for the duration of one minute. The sculptures also take the form of photographs, taken either by the artist or by other viewers who can then have them signed by the artist for a $100 fee. *One Minute Sculptures* also tend to draw a bit of a crowd. As Wurm put it, "My basic idea was to make an artwork which can also be realized by the public without my physical presence."[2] He turns the "work" of making art over to the audience, creating highly participatory public sculptures that are infinitely repeatable yet never identical.

One Minute Sculptures can be difficult to perform and hilarious to watch. The sheer ridiculousness of the poses, their gross physical humor combined with the threat of imminent collapse, owes much to the cinematic form of slapstick. In slapstick the laugh comes from something breaking down, from something not working correctly (usually a human being caught in a mechanized or a highly routine set of conditions). By animating the tradition of upright figurative sculpture with slapstick humor, Wurm breathes life into the mausoleum of the museum. He deploys an absurdist aesthetic designed to produce guffaws and simultaneously critiques the fiction of the museum as timeless and neutral and the artist as a privileged purveyor of meaning. HM

1. Anne D'Harnoncourt and Kynaston McShine, *Marcel Duchamp*, exh. cat. (Philadelphia: Philadelphia Museum of Art, 1973), 270.

2. Peter Weibel, ed., *Erwin Wurm: Neue Galerie Graz* (Ostfildern-Ruit, Germany: Cantz Verlag, 2002), 229.

Erwin Wurm, *One Minute Sculpture*, 1997.

Gabriel Orozco

Mexican, b. 1962

Gabriel Orozco's *Mesa de ping-pong con estanque* (*Ping Pond Table* [1998]) is composed of two modified Ping-Pong tables, cut open and intersecting, joined in the center by a lily pond. The tables are curved at each end and have white boundary lines that divide each tabletop into three pie-shaped triangles. The *Ping Pond Table* comes with four paddles and a seemingly inexhaustible supply of Ping-Pong balls. Viewers are invited to play; to do so, however, they have to overcome the (internalized) prohibition against game playing in the public space of the museum. They must generate a set of rules for play, as the *Ping Pond Table* assiduously avoids the normal conventions of Ping-Pong. *Ping Pond Table* operates instead within the Dada tradition of gamesmanship and the assisted readymade, and it can be seen as a consummate realization of Duchamp's famous dictum, "The viewer completes the work." More generally, *Ping Pond Table* also plays with the centuries-old concern of sculpture in its creation of a spatially complicated three-dimensional object that provokes a phenomenological encounter with the spectator.

According to Ernest Mandel, one of the abiding features of late capitalist society is the interpenetration of the realms of work and leisure: "Mechanization, standardization, over-specialization and parcellation of labor, which in the past determined only the realm of commodity production in actual industry, now penetrate into all sectors of social life."[1] This means that even our leisure activities—once considered the antidote to work—now take on the characteristics of highly organized and monitored labor. That is, they often share the routinized and obligatory qualities of work.

Orozco's *Ping Pond Table* interrupts this routinization, however briefly, in important ways. Viewers must participate in the work of art in order for it to have meaning, potentially requiring of them an active rather than a passive engagement with the culture of their time. The creation of a participatory (not simply spectatorial) space mitigates against the shared logic of both organized sports and museum attendance as passive and administered leisure activities. In so doing, Orozco's *Ping Pond Table* offers a means to actualize public space as a site in which persons come together to determine the conditions of their shared existence.[2] This is a classic model of public space, one that has fallen into disuse. That Orozco chooses to stage the public sphere as a space of ludic play is a utopian gesture: through play comes freedom. Yet this vision of the public sphere is also a melancholic one. It is now potentially *only* through play (and not, say, politics) that such a version of the public can even be imagined. HM

1. Ernest Mandel, *Late Capitalism*, trans. Joris De Bres (London: Verso, 1978), 387.

2. On the relationship of Orozco's public sculpture and Habermas's account of the public sphere, see Benjamin H. D. Buchloh, "Gabriel Orozco: The Sculpture of Everyday Life," in *Gabriel Orozco*, exh. cat., organized by Alma Ruiz (Los Angeles: The Museum of Contemporary Art, Los Angeles, 2000).

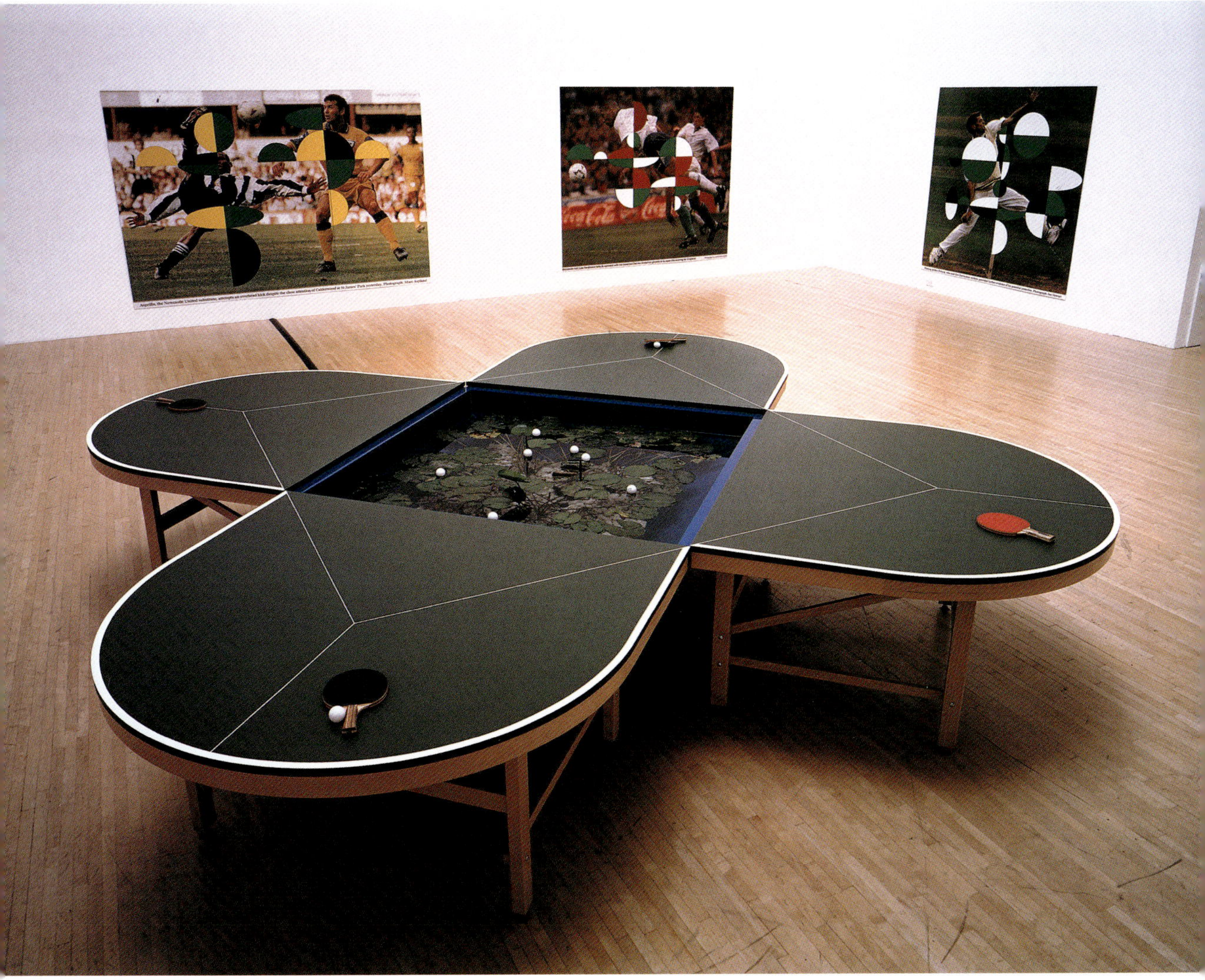

Gabriel Orozco, *Mesa de ping-pong con estanque (Ping Pond Table),* 1998.

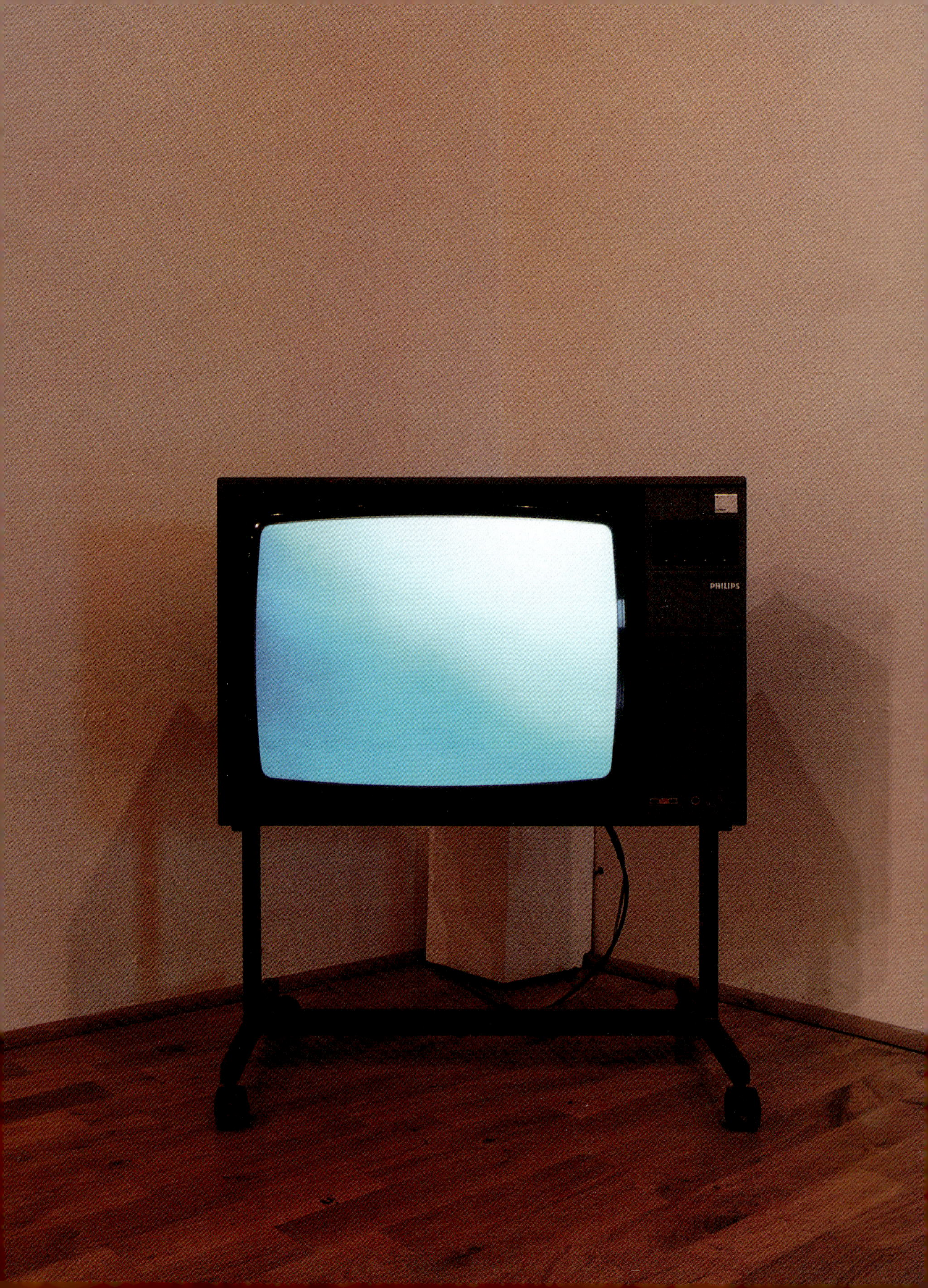
PHILIPS

ONE OF THE MOST scathing attacks that can be made against a person within the highly motivated and work-dominated culture of late capitalism is that he or she is lazy. Indeed, the obligation to work is one of Western capitalism's foremost imperatives. And yet, not working is also considered one of the most supreme luxuries. As the realms of work and leisure have progressively blurred together during the last forty years, however, the luxury of leisure time has also been eroded, and we now routinely regiment our leisure time into productive modes (e.g., exercising) that recall the logic of work.

Throughout the postwar period, artists have explored different ways of not working—or of working as little as possible. Sometimes they have done so in the sharp language of critique, and at other times, in the

QUITTING TIME
The Artist Tries Not to Work

humorous guise of play. But in either mode the result is similar; not working is extremely difficult to do. Experiments in not working have generally taken three forms: mechanization, strikes, and play. In each instance the value of the work of art is made uncertain as the artist explores a fundamental question: How much work does it take to make an artwork?

For some artists, the model of industrial production offers the key to artistic labor and leisure: several artists have built machines to make their art for them (e.g., Jean Tinguely, Roxy Paine). Machine-made sculptures and drawings make both lay viewers and art professionals nervous, though, as art's value has historically come from its unique and handmade attributes. When machines make the work, the distinction between art and mass-produced commodities collapses. But even though machines make the work, they still need to be built and minded. In essence, they create new fields of work for the artist, mirroring the development of managerial labor in the culture at large.

A time-honored method of not working is the strike. When workers strike, they do not do so out of laziness or a desire not to work. They hope instead to promote better working conditions. Traditionally, strikes mean that the labor force organizes itself into a cohesive unit, one capable of bargaining with management. One effect of strikes is to stage the division of management and labor by showing that their needs and desires are different. But artists typically work alone and in a relatively unstructured environment. How could they strike? What would they be striking

Jean Tinguely
Hi Red Center
Piero Manzoni
Peter Fischli and David Weiss
Roxy Paine
Strike
Lee Lozano
Robert Barry
Tom Marioni
Gilbert and George
Elizabeth Sisco, Louis Hock, and David Avalos

Yoko Ono, *Sky TV*, 1966.

against? In the late 1960s, many artists grew wary of the gallery system and its growing demand for sellable commodity goods. Artists such as Lee Lozano and Robert Barry responded by refusing to make such objects. While many others were challenging the gallery system by working in nontraditional materials, Lozano and Barry explicitly refused to participate in business as usual. In "The Function of the Studio," artist Daniel Buren wrote, "The museums and gallery on the one hand and the studio on the other are linked to form the foundation of the same edifice and the same system. To question one while leaving the other intact accomplishes nothing."[1] By refusing to make art objects, Lozano and Barry not only foiled the galleries' demands upon them but also implicated the space of the studio as the site of production in order to challenge the entire studio/gallery/museum "edifice."

The strategy of refusal was a prominent one in the late 1960s. Many artists and critics felt that the very definition of radical art was "anti-art," an art that could not be accepted into the gallery system.[2] Some began to feel, however, that ultimately, no matter how anti-art it was, the art could always, finally, be transformed into a commodity object. In view of the seemingly limitless co-optative power of capitalism, critic Ursula Meyer offered another definition of radical art, one she felt was inspired by John Cage. For Meyer, radical art has a "disruptive function within a given social, political, economic, or psychological framework."[3] Sensing the increasing encroachment of work into all sectors of life, several artists disrupted the professionalized art system's demand for product by converting traditional leisure activities—such as drinking (e.g., Gilbert and George, Tom Marioni)—into artistic labor. This act, while clearly humorous, also offers a provisional stopgap measure against the alienation of labor for money and the regimentation of leisure by forcing the system to pay artists for their leisure as well as for their labor. HM

1. Daniel Buren, "The Function of the Studio," *October* 10 (Fall 1979): 51.

2. This is Gregory Battcock's argument. See "Art in the Service of the Left?" in *Idea Art*, ed. Battcock (New York: E. P. Dutton, 1973), 18–29.

3. Ursula Meyer, "The Eruption of Anti-Art," in *Idea Art*, ed. Battcock, 132.

Jean Tinguely

Swiss, 1925–1991

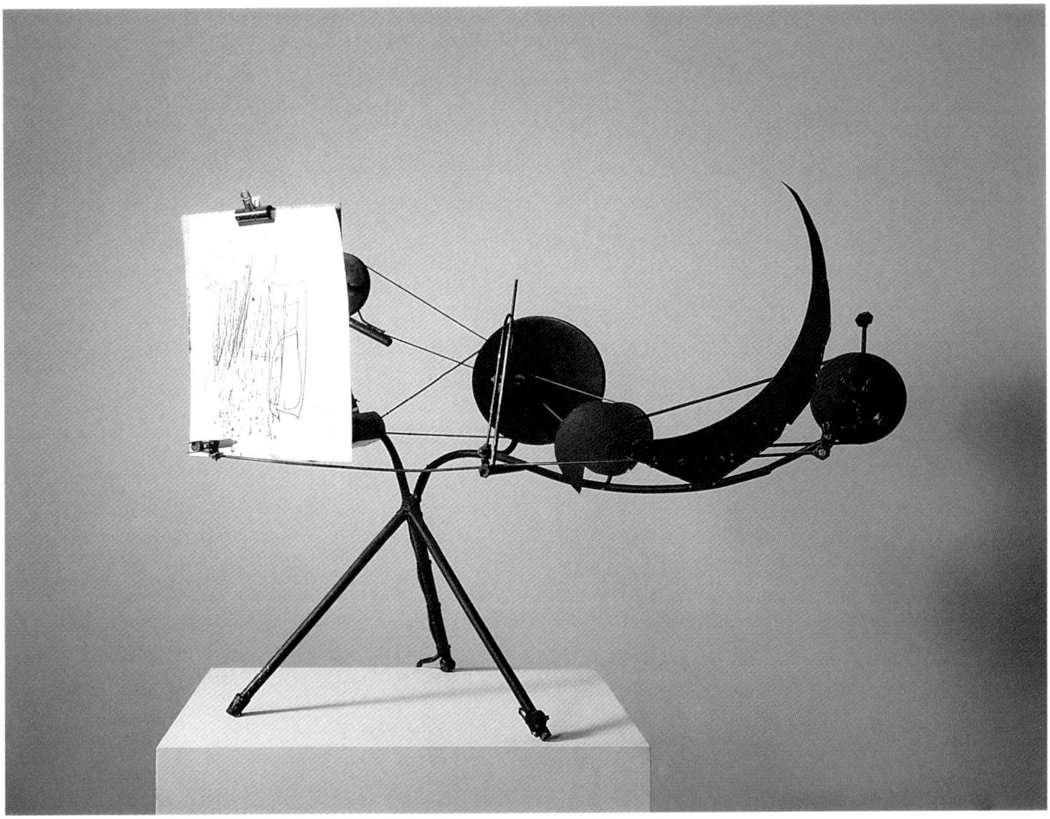

Jean Tinguely, *Meta-Matic No. 10,* 1959.

Jean Tinguely is probably best known for his spectacle-cum-sculpture *Homage to New York*, a large, automated construction that was designed to self-destruct in the sculpture garden of The Museum of Modern Art in the early spring of 1960. Tinguely was a member of the loosely organized Nouveaux Realistes movement in France, which counted among its members Arman, who made constructions of detritus, Yves Klein, who sold identical monochrome canvases at varying prices, and Niki de Sainte Phalle, who encouraged spectators to shoot at her works to release pigment from within. Of this group, Klein was undoubtedly the most influential, particularly through his notorious *Vide* (1959), a piece in which he spent days cleaning Iris Clert's Paris gallery only to then exhibit it empty. According to legend, Tinguely visited the exhibition for three hours and afterward convinced Klein that they should collaborate on an exhibition. All of the Nouveaux Realistes engaged in works that challenged conventional definitions of art and artistic labor—Tinguely most of all.

Tinguely's most fully elaborated works were the *Meta-Matics*—an invented term meaning "more than a machine"—exhibited as a group for the first time in 1959 at the Iris Clert gallery. The *Meta-Matics* were machines for making pictures, and they often looked like a cross between an Alexander Calder mobile and an enormous praying mantis. Each contained a motorized "arm" capable of holding a pen, brush, or pencil. Although a great deal of labor went into fashioning the machine, the result was a device able to produce art without the direct labor of the artist. If one of the promises of mechanized labor was the increased amount of free time for leisure activities, then Tinguely suggests that artists could share in such privileges. The humor of the machines and their products comes from art being subjected to a perverse Taylorization of the artistic process—a grand machine designed to make drawing a more efficient, less troublesome affair.

The critical reception of the *Meta-Matic* drawings varied. William Rubin, curator at The Museum of Modern Art, had no doubt that "these *meta-matics* did not really make art,"[1] whereas Calvin Tomkins, savvy chronicler of the postwar avant-garde, observed (somewhat tongue-in-cheek) that "the results, as often as not, are not only distinctly pleasing but uncomfortably close to certain contemporary paintings produced by the unaided human hand."[2] That discomfort should arise around these works is not surprising. They reveal again the anxious questioning of the skill involved in abstract painting—an anxiety felt perhaps equally by those who championed abstraction and by those who wished to destroy its hegemonic hold over the discourse of high art.

HM

1. William Rubin, *Dada, Surrealism, and Their Heritage* (New York: The Museum of Modern Art, 1968), 23.

2. Calvin Tomkins, *The Bride and the Bachelors: Five Masters of the Avant-Garde* (Middlesex, England: Penguin Books, 1976), 163.

Hi Red Center

Takamatsu Jiro, Japanese, b. 1936
Akasegawa Genpei, Japanese, b. 1937
Nakanishi Natsuyuki, Japanese, b. 1935

The Hi Red Center was a collective composed of three artists: Takamatsu Jiro, Akasegawa Genpei, and Nakanishi Natsuyuki. (The phrase "Hi Red Center" was created by taking the English meaning of the first character of each of the members' names.) The group's work took place against a particularly fraught political and artistic background. As postwar Japan was dealing with its totalitarian past, its defeat in the war, and the large-scale Americanization of its culture, artists began to use art as a dramatic way to confront and rebel against authority. By the early 1960s, Japanese artists were aware of the Neo-Dada movement in America and the Nouveaux Realistes in Paris. Both movements were committed to eliminating the barriers between high art and mass culture—and, in doing so, challenging the status quo of social hierarchies. These ideas were championed in Japan by the influential art critic Okamoto Taro, whose best-selling *Art of Today* (*Konnichi no geijutsu* [1954]) argued that "postwar Japan must peel off the heavy shell of the past and forge a new young culture as if being reborn."[1] In order to make this break from the past, he "encouraged art that was not aesthetically pleasing, not technically skillful, and not complacent in any way."[2]

The Hi Red Center enacted its performances within this milieu. In 1964 they performed two now legendary events: *Ochanomizu Drop* and *Be Clean*. In *Ochanomizu Drop*, the artists dropped old clothes and objects off a roof, and they subsequently gathered them and placed them in a suitcase. The suitcase was stowed in a public locker, and the key to the locker was sent to a person whose name had been chosen at random from the phone book. The event is documented by a series of black-and-white photographs—some banal, some dramatic, but all fundamentally cinematic in nature, given the almost balletic gestures of bodily movement and sheer human glee conveyed through the images. In *Be Clean*, the artists cordoned off a section of a Tokyo street, and dressed in white lab coats, their faces covered in medical or hygienic masks, they proceeded to scrub the sidewalk on their hands and knees. This performance was later re-created in New York's Times Square by members of the Fluxus group led by George Maciunas.

Both performances partake of an extremely high degree of "nonsense and absurdity," strategies designed to flummox spectators and undermine their traditional expectations of art.[3] *Be Clean* shares an affinity with task-based performances, inasmuch as the artists set themselves a task and then follow it through. Here labor has an ostensible function yet is nonetheless absurd, as the spectacle of cleaning public streets by hand is a flagrant mockery of various regimes of authority. *Ochanomizu Drop* functions slightly

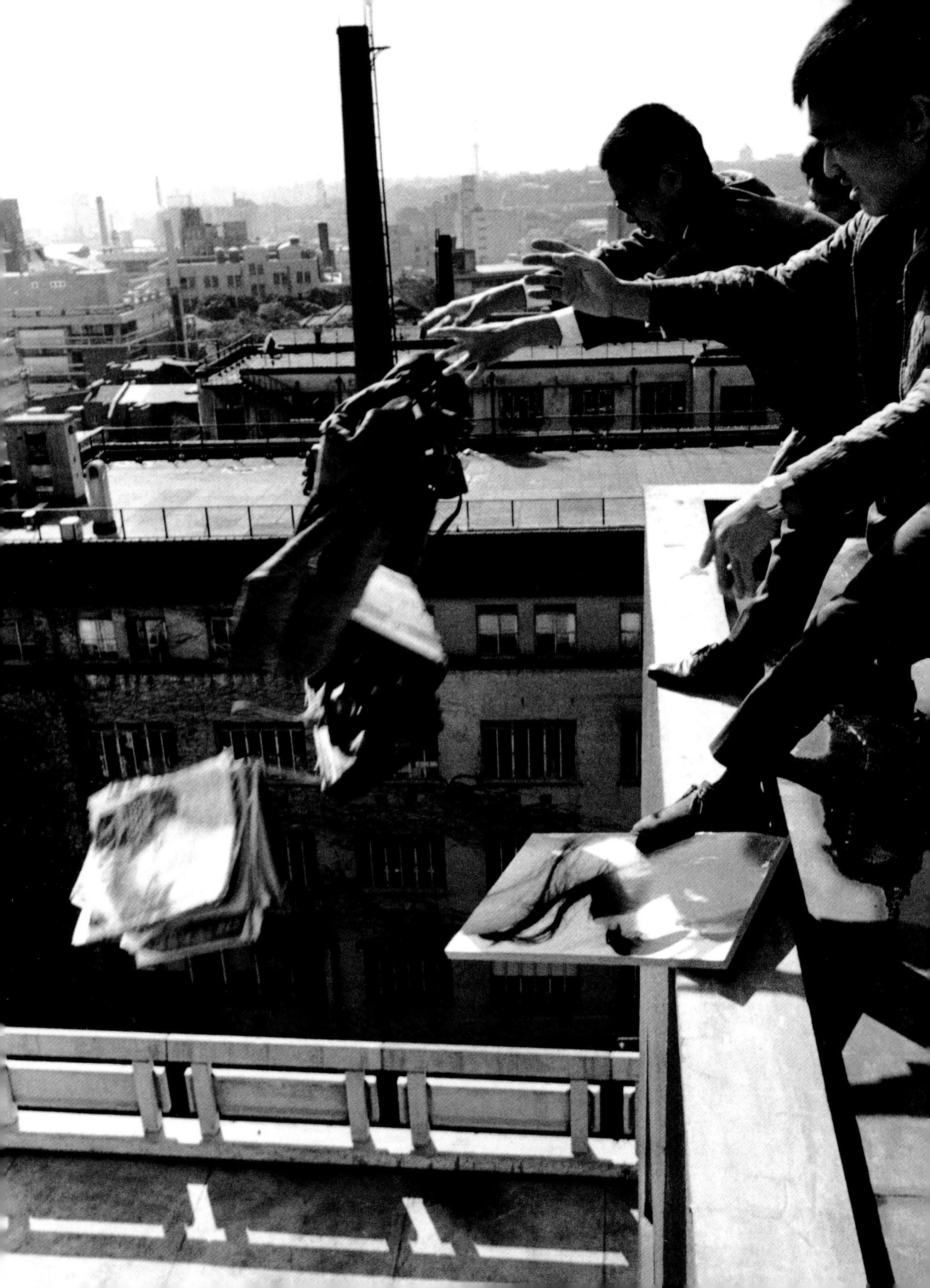

differently. Here the artists have done almost no "work" at all. By allowing gravity to dispense with the suitcase's contents, the artists have abdicated any and all forms of traditional artistic work. The outrageous nonproductivity of the event not only skewers the desire for a commodifiable art object but also revels in a schoolyard sense of humor, in which the nonfunctional is the realm of the truly hilarious. HM

1. As quoted in *Japanese Art After 1945: Scream Against the Sky*, exh. cat., ed. Alexandra Munroe (New York: Harry N. Abrams, 1994), 154.

2. Ibid., 156.

3. Ibid., 395.

Hi Red Center, *Ochanomizu Drop (Dropping Event)*, 1964. Photograph: Minoru Hirata.

Piero Manzoni

Italian, 1933–1963

During Piero Manzoni's brief career—he died in 1963 at the age of 29—he made a number of controversial artworks that were indebted to Marcel Duchamp's legacy of the readymade. These included *Artist's Shit* (1961), one of the most infamous artworks of the twentieth century. *Artist's Shit* consists of ninety tins of the artist's feces, produced as a "limited edition" artwork, hand-signed and numbered. The label on the tins reads, "contents 30 grams net weight, naturally preserved, made in Italy." Canned according to industrial standards, the shit was then sold, by weight, for the equivalent of the price of gold, an amount that fluctuates daily. A commercial transaction becomes an alchemical transmutation as Manzoni turns shit into gold. By pegging the value of the shit to the whims of the market, Manzoni exposed how arbitrary, and often inflated, assessments of art's worth can be. Declaring human waste to be "art" raises questions about the ways an artistic creation—in this case, one literally excreted from his body—is commodified, bought, and sold.

Artist's Shit critiques the marketing of the artist's identity by a system obsessed with authentic signatures and traces. It is also a crude gesture meant to shock. How can shit, the most worthless of "found objects," function in a sphere known for refined consumption? Indeed, by treating the residue of a necessary bodily act as an artistic work, Manzoni's shit takes the conservative complaint about much modern art—"anyone can do that"—to its logical conclusion. On another level, *Artist's Shit* proposes that the human desire to make art comes from base, corporeal urges that should be embraced and celebrated.

Manzoni's act of canning shit demonstrates that in our industrial world, all impulses and actions, however messy or obscene, are subject to packaging, processing, and sanitizing. Manzoni planned a series of artworks containing bodily by-products that, like the shit, would be sold by volume, including *Artist's Breath* (attaching balloons to wooden plaques) and the never-executed *Artist's Blood* (consisting of vials of blood). These works parody mass production and its drive for regulating all aspects of life, as organic matter is made to conform to highly standardized units.

Artist's Shit continues to incite a furor of curiosity. Hidden from view, the shit is open to speculation, and this valuation of a virtually invisible object is part of its ongoing controversy. Ever since the cans appeared, their exact contents have aroused suspicion. The anxiety about what cannot be seen has been heightened in recent years as the cans have begun to degrade. There is a photo of Manzoni next to a toilet, proudly holding a can as some kind of evidence. Ultimately, though, it is perhaps a matter of faith. To open a can would not only be potentially unpleasant but would also destroy the work. Does it matter what, exactly, went into these tins? With *Artist's Shit*, Manzoni asserts that the idea may be more important than the object itself.

JBW

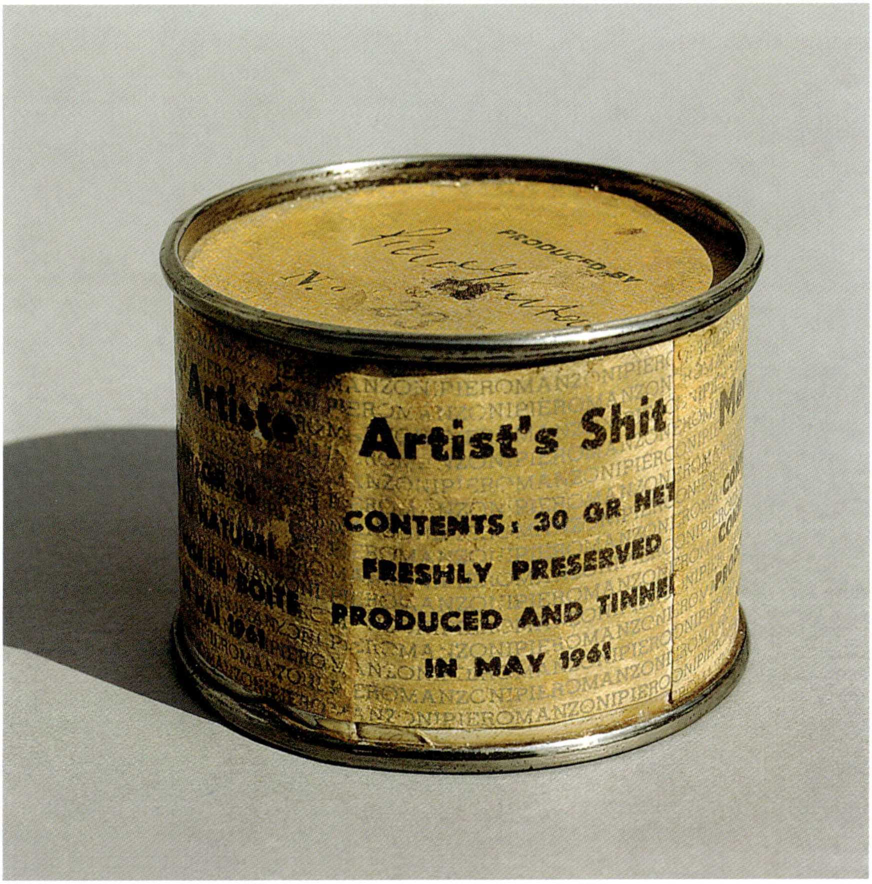

Piero Manzoni, *Merda d'artista,* 1961.

Peter Fischli and David Weiss

Fischli, Swiss, b. 1952
Weiss, Swiss, b. 1946

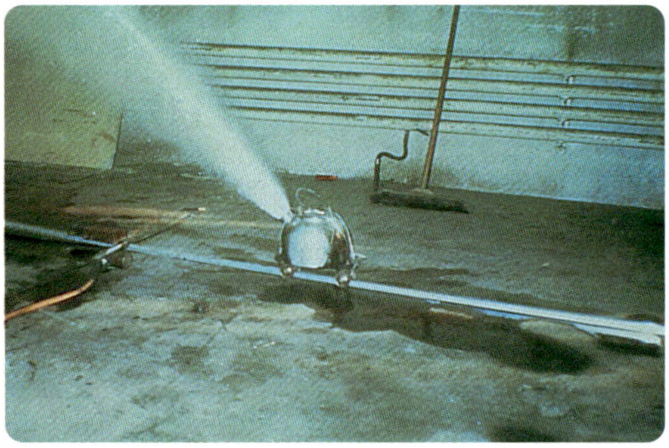

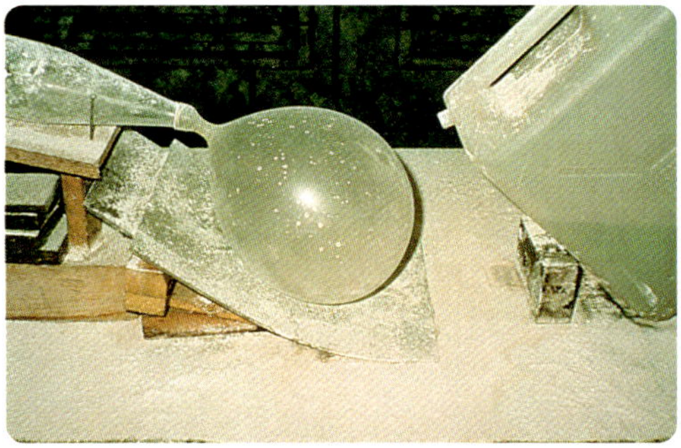

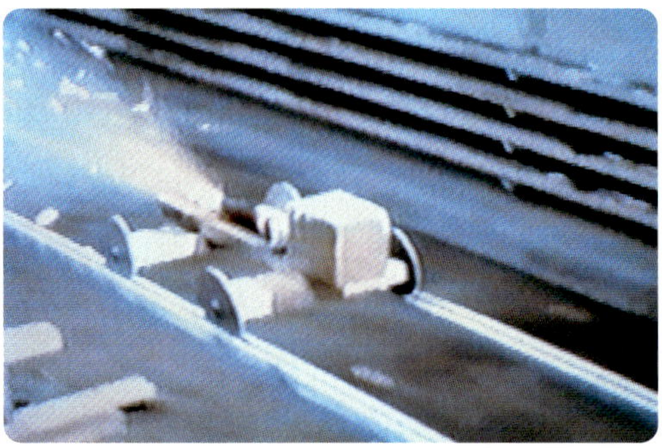

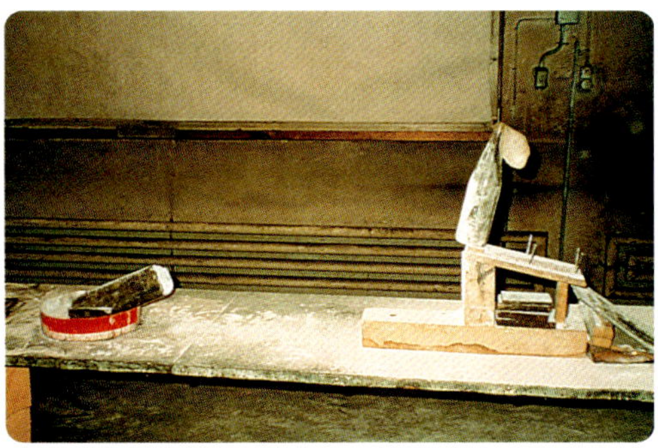

Fischli and Weiss are Swiss artists who have worked together since 1980 in a wide range of media. They have made sculptures of everyday objects found in their studio, taken snapshot photographs of their travels, set up slide projections of luscious garden landscapes, and filmed a cat licking milk out of a bowl. Singular among their achievements is the film *Der Lauf der Dinge* (*The Way Things Go* [1987]). The film documents a half-hour chain of Rube Goldbergesque events, conceivably located in the artists' studio, where "a series of cause and effect relationships is played out using among other things old tires, water-filled balloons, candles, and steam propelled kettles on wheel tracks—all of which are designed for the purpose of setting the next object in motion."[1]

Moving steadily from left to right, objects interact with one another to hilarious effect. This "machine" never produces a successful object, and breakdown and failure is its *modus operandi.* In a brilliant sleight of hand, we never see a single moment of human intervention, nor can we even imagine the human agent who initially set off the bizarre chain of events, so successful is the *mise-en-scène* at creating a complete and utter state of filmic suspension of disbelief. What emerges is a fantasy of a work/studio space that functions without assistants, workers, or, most important, without artists. Yet lest *Der Lauf der Dinge* be read as an apocalyptic vision of a future without workers—a Taylorist's dream-world—Fischli and Weiss create a machine that refuses to make an object, or generate energy, or facilitate communication, or do anything that machines are supposed to do. Rather, their contraption catches fire, sputters, and spills without ever once producing anything—not even meaning.

If Process artists placed the activity of making above and beyond the final product, then Fischli and Weiss take this attack on commodification one step further, for as intensive as their labor surely was to create this chain of mechanical mishaps, they allow the results to be destroyed. Enamored of Gustave Flaubert's classic comic novel, *Bouvard and Pécuchet,* Fischli and Weiss "claim to have particularly enjoyed the spectacle of two grown men spending a great deal of time making useless things. The idea of 'misusing time' (Fischli and Weiss's term)—especially in a culture that puts a premium on the work ethic and the constructive use of time—gives the artists great satisfaction."[2] HM

1. Gary Kibbins, "Laughter and Forgetting," *Afterimage* 16 (November 1988): 16.

2. Elizabeth Armstrong, "Everyday Sublime," in *Peter Fischli and David Weiss: In a Restless World,* exh. cat., ed. Janet Jenkins and Kathleen McLean (Minneapolis: Walker Art Center, 1996), 93.

Fischli and Weiss, *Der Lauf der Dinge (The Way Things Go),* 1987.

Roxy Paine

American, b. 1966

Roxy Paine has made several machines that produce unique works of art. *Paint Dipper* (1997) makes exquisite monochromatic abstract paintings by repeatedly dipping a blank canvas into a pool of paint. Similarly, *Drawing Machine* (2001) is a computer-driven machine with a moving arm that squirts and drips colored inks onto a large sheet of paper. The SCUMAK (*Auto Sculpture Maker* [1998]) comprises two seemingly antithetical forms of technology: a sleek state-of-the-art laptop computer runs an old-fashioned-looking contraption that extrudes polyethylene into amorphous blob-like sculptures reminiscent of Lynda Benglis's early pour pieces. The SCUMAK, like all of Paine's machines, operates within the tradition of Jean Tinguely's *Meta-Matic* machines designed to produce abstract drawings and Allan McCollum's *Plaster Surrogates*, a series of unique paintings that look remarkably similar. Each of the SCUMAKS, as the sculptures are called, is unique; upon being produced, it is subject to the same registrarial cataloging as all other works of art. And, like all works of art, the SCUMAKS are available for sale. Paine programs the computer to produce the sculpture at a varying rate and in a variety of colors, but "no matter how perfect his engineering or strict his instructions, the resulting object is always inflected by random uncontrollable factors."[1] In this regard, the SCUMAK embodies one of Modernism's great dialectics—the tension between artistic choice and reliance upon chance to lessen artistic intention.

If Tinguely's machines sputtered, broke down, and ultimately failed, Paine's SCUMAKS and *Paint Dipper* are extraordinarily competent, producing as many, or as few, sculptures and paintings as the artist desires. Perhaps this is why the SCUMAKS have been described as "portents of a future in which machines will be able to mass-produce 'unique' artworks, conveniently replacing artists, whose messy lives and attendant creative blocks can be inimical to productivity."[2] Substituting the human agent with a machine is a familiar twentieth-century fantasy, sometimes dystopic and sometimes utopic. In its utopian guise, the machine frees humans to exercise their creative energies. Paine plays with this fantasy ironically: his machines ostensibly free artists from the demand to "be creative" and produce art objects, thus allowing them to do other things. As they explore ideas of productivity, creativity, and efficiency, Paine's art machines humorously bring to mind a Taylorist maxim: "The laziest man is always the most efficient." HM

1. Scott Rothkopf, *Roxy Paine*, exh. cat. (New York: James Cohan Gallery, 2001), 25.

2. Adrian Gagnon, *010101: Art in Technological Times* (San Francisco: San Francisco Museum of Modern Art, 2001), 16.

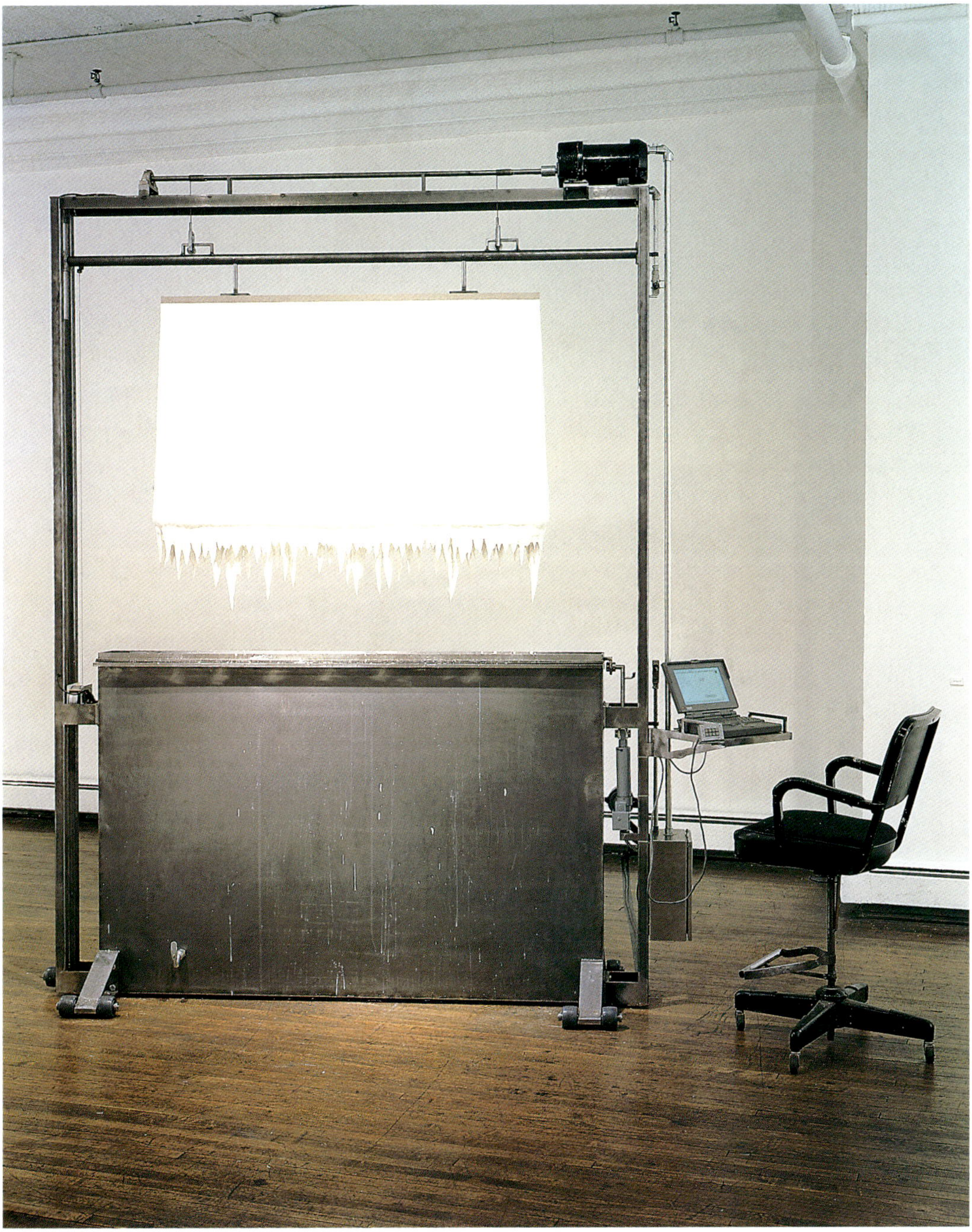

Roxy Paine, *Paint Dipper,* 1997.

STRIKE

A strike is a work stoppage called to halt production, usually in order to protest wages or working conditions. More fundamentally, a strike is a refusal, a powerful way of saying, quite simply, "no." By ceasing to work, strikers seek to make their labor—often so functional and efficient that it goes unrecognized—visible. In artists' metaphoric strikes, art making is not necessarily suspended, but it is withheld from the art market's system of commodification and display. By refusing to participate in the usual channels of art distribution, artists are able to relate their labor to other economic and ideological systems. At times, artists have interrupted their work in order to make evident the material conditions of art production—from personally withdrawing from the art world, as in Lee Lozano's 1969 *General Strike Piece,* to holding a show that consists of nothing more than closing the gallery doors, as in Robert Barry's *Closed Gallery* (also from 1969).

1969 was an especially fertile year for strikes in the art world. While politically oriented art collectives such as the Situationist International advocated the cessation of art making during the post-1968 social crisis, the most literal notion of the art strike was taken up, briefly, by U.S. artists in the late 1960s. What does it mean for artists to go on strike when there is no consolidated workplace? If art is, by nature, individual, how do artists organize for a broadly based mass action? These questions had serious implications as artists struggled with the most effective means to enact reforms within their work sites—museums and galleries. A group called the Art Workers' Coalition (AWC) organized in 1969 to protest museums' unauthorized display of artists' works, but the agenda of the AWC quickly expanded to include an ambitious slate of New Left concerns, such as the antiwar movement and racial diversity in the art world. The AWC, which was active from 1969 to 1971, mobilized around ethical and economic issues that affected artists both locally and globally: increasing artists' representation on museum boards of trustees, agitating for giving art broader access to diverse publics (including free days at museums), and protesting the ongoing Vietnam War.

Although the AWC was not a union, it had certain aspirations toward that identity. By labeling themselves "art workers," these artists and writers—among them Carl Andre and Lucy Lippard—were guided by the utopian ideal that artists might have bargaining power in the face of the gallery and museum system if they came together and resisted the atomized structure of modern art making. The most powerful manifestation of union leverage has historically been the strike, with its aim of the complete halting of production. On May 22, 1970, the Art Strike—an offshoot of the AWC—demanded that New York museums shut down as a part of a nationwide Vietnam War moratorium, which sought to stop "business as usual" for one day as a gesture of protest against U.S. military involvement in Vietnam. Many museums and galleries agreed to participate in the moratorium and closed their doors. The Metropolitan Museum of Art, which failed to do so, was picketed in an action known as the Art Strike Against Racism, War and Oppression, headed up by Robert Morris and Poppy Johnson. Members of the Art Strike later successfully lobbied many artists to withdraw from the American Pavilion at the 1970 Venice Biennale to protest U.S. military policies. These were, of course, symbolic strikes and boycotts—there were no factory lines to halt—but it is precisely on the level of the symbolic that these stoppages sought to make their intervention.

Artists of the late 1960s and early 1970s were interested in what Herbert Marcuse termed "the Great Refusal," which was, as he put it, "the negation of the entire Establishment."[1] In the late 1960s, Marcuse saw hopeful indications that this refusal was undermining mainstream society, especially in the widespread "collapse of work discipline, slowdown, spread of disobedience to rules and regulations, wildcat strikes, boycotts, sabotage, and gratuitous acts of noncompliance."[2] Marcuse's vision of an ideal society in which people worked a great deal *less* also influenced the concept of the art strike.[3] This has its purest enactment in Barry's *Closed Gallery,* in which the artist announced that his one-person show consisted of closing the gallery. His "work" thus existed only in the viewer's mind. By reducing his labor to almost nothing, Barry questioned the gallery's "possession" of the artist's work. In another piece by Barry that intentionally required little actual effort, he wrote a quotation from Marcuse's *An Essay on Liberation* (1969) by hand onto the gallery wall: "Some places to which we can come, and for a while, 'be free to think about what we are going to do'" (*Marcuse Piece* [1970]).

Barry takes a public event (gallery going) and makes it personal. Likewise, Lee Lozano individualizes the notion of the strike, which is inherently about collective action. First announced at a meeting of the Art Workers' Coalition, Lozano's *General Strike Piece* involved her complete avoidance of art events. These two eccentric examples must be seen alongside the Art Strike and its boycotts. By withholding their aesthetic labor, these artists enact strikes in order to question the value of artistic work. They reroute or derail the making and selling of artworks in order to find new ways of thinking about the cult of the artist, the sanctity of the object, the materiality of the gallery space, and the economics of making art. JBW

1. Herbert Marcuse, *An Essay on Liberation* (Boston: Beacon Press, 1969), 25.

2. Ibid., 83.

3. See his *Eros and Civilization: A Philosophical Inquiry into Freud* (Boston: Beacon Press, 1966).

Lee Lozano

American, 1930–1998

Although Lee Lozano died in relative obscurity in 1998, the trajectory of her career reflects the profound shifts in art during the postwar period. Lozano started her career as a painter, but she quickly became an important early practitioner of Conceptual art. Her *Wave Series* (1967–70) was a highly regimented, task-based painting project in which the number of undulating lines, or waves, placed on the canvas was generated through a mathematical system. Furthermore, she completed each painting in one session, such that an element of temporality and physical endurance lent a performance-like quality to the works. Lozano also developed Conceptual works (concurrent with the *Wave Series*) that took the form of journal entries she referred to as "word pieces." Usually handwritten in block letters on graph paper, her word pieces can be divided into two general categories: those that dealt with monitoring some aspect of Lozano's personal life—be it her sex life, her drug consumption, or her interactions with others—and those that dealt in some way with the professionalized art world. The latter grew increasingly critical of the commodification of art and culminated in Lozano's complete rejection of a commodity-based art practice.

In one of Lozano's most important word pieces, *Dialogue Piece* (1969), she invited people to her studio for the exclusive activity of discussion. While Lozano's journal keeps a log of those who visited and when (the list of 1960s art-world luminaries is remarkable), she never divulged the content of the discussions, drawing a line between the public and private dimensions of her work. What is important about *Dialogue Piece* is not its potentially voyeuristic appeal but the idea that art's communicative function could be performed as a dialogue between two people. *Dialogue Piece* typifies artists' desire for increasingly porous boundaries between art and life as well their hope to dispense entirely with the idea that art needs to be realized in object form.

The utopian dimension of *Dialogue Piece* is extended in her *General Strike Piece* (1969). In this work, Lozano resolved to remove herself, slowly but surely, from all "official or public 'uptown' functions or gatherings related to the 'art world' in order to pursue investigation of *total personal and public revolution.*"[1] Her withdrawal began that year. While she continued to have engaging and spirited dialogues with art-world friends, she stopped exhibiting her work and attending art-world functions. By 1971–72, Lozano had left New York for Dallas, Texas, completing her withdrawal from the professional art world of New York.

HM

1. Lee Lozano, *An Open Hearing on the Subject: What Should Be the Program of the Art Workers Regarding Museum Reform and to Establish the Program of an Open Art Worker's Coalition* (New York: Art Workers Coalition, 1969), unpaginated.

("QUOTE"): SOUND OF "DAISY" FADING IN BACKGROUND FOLLOWED BY SOUND OF "ALSO SPRACH ZARATHUSTRA" (R. STRAUSS) FOLLOWED BY SOUND OF "THE BLUE DANUBE" (J. STRAUSS) – SOUNDTRACK, 2001 (S. KUBRICK)

GENERAL STRIKE PIECE (STARTED FEB. 8, '69)*

GRADUALLY BUT DETERMINEDLY AVOID BEING PRESENT AT OFFICIAL OR PUBLIC "UPTOWN" FUNCTIONS OR GATHERINGS† RELATED TO THE "ART WORLD" IN ORDER TO PURSUE INVESTIGATION OF TOTAL PERSONAL & PUBLIC REVOLUTION.° EXHIBIT IN PUBLIC ONLY PIECES WHICH FURTHER SHARING OF IDEAS & INFORMATION RELATED TO TOTAL PERSONAL & PUBLIC REVOLUTION.☌

IN PROCESS AT LEAST THROUGH SUMMER, '69.

* WITHDRAWAL FROM 3-MAN SHOW COMPILED BY RICHARD BELLAMY, GOLDOWSKY GALLERY, 1078 MADISON AVE.

† DATE OF LAST VISIT TO UPTOWN GALLERIES FOR PERUSAL OF ART – FEB. 13 OR 14, 69
" " " " " A MUSEUM – MARCH 24, 69
" " " " " UPTOWN GALLERY OPENING – MARCH 15, 69
" " " " " A BAR – APRIL 5, 69
" " " ATTENDANCE AT A CONCERT – APRIL 18, 69
" " " " " " FILM SHOWING – APRIL 4, 69
" " " " " AN "EVENT" – APRIL 18, 69
" " " " " A BIG PARTY – MARCH 15, 69

° TERMS OF TOTAL PERSONAL & PUBLIC REVOLUTION SET FORTH IN BRIEF STATEMENT READ AT OPEN PUBLIC HEARING, ART WORKERS COALITION, SCHOOL OF VISUAL ARTS, APRIL 10, 69. FURTHER PARTICIPATION IN ART WORKERS COALITION OR ANY OTHER GROUP DECLINED AS PART OF GENERAL STRIKE PIECE. THIS INCLUDES ARTISTS AGAINST THE EXPRESSWAY GROUP & OTHERS.

☌ FIRST PIECE EXHIBITED AT ART/PEACE EVENT, N.Y. SHAKESPEARE FESTIVAL, PUBLIC THEATER, MARCH 5, 69. GRASS PIECE & NO-GRASS PIECE EXHIBITED IN NUMBER 7 SHOW COMPILED BY LUCY LIPPARD, PAULA COOPER, MAY 18, 69. INVESTMENT PIECE & CASH PIECE EXHIBITED IN LANGUAGE III SHOW, DWAN GALLERY, MAY 24, 69.

LEE LOZANO, JUNE 12, 69.

Lee Lozano, *Untitled (General Strike Piece, Feb. 8, 1969)*, 1969, Wadsworth Atheneum Museum of Art, Hartford, Connecticut, Alexander A. Goldfarb Contemporary Art Acquisition Fund.

Robert Barry

American, b. 1936

Robert Barry, *Closed Gallery,* 1969.

In December 1969, Robert Barry held a one-person show at the Art and Project Gallery. The announcement for the show stated: "For the duration of the exhibit, the gallery will be closed." In effect, the plainly worded invitation cards marked the show's opening as well as its closing. The gallery's usual hours were printed neatly onto the announcements, implying that there was art to be seen even if the visitor had no access to it. What would a curious viewer see if she ventured to the gallery? The outside of the darkened and locked space? Or the shadows of employees still duly at their desks? Was the staff sent home for the span of the exhibit, or did workers continue to come in and perform the labor involved in running a gallery? By cutting off the exhibition space from the viewing public, Barry questions what, exactly, the function of the gallery is—if it can "work" without art in it.

Closed Gallery reveals the site of art's display as material and economic, but for Barry, the gallery is also a place of generous participation where viewers are invited to explore their own imaginations. The collective aspect of art's reception—the amassing of an audience in a specific space—is rendered impossible in *Closed Gallery.* Instead, spectators must picture the art solely within the spaces of their own heads. Although *Closed Gallery* relies primarily upon a gesture of refusal and could be seen as a cynical act of negation, for Barry, it also productively turns art into a private and internal (rather than public) experience. Repeated at the Galleria Sperone in Turin and the Eugenia Butler Gallery in Los Angeles, *Closed Gallery* was one of the clearest examples of "dematerialized," or object-less, Conceptual artworks of its time.

Barry stopped making tangible objects in 1969, choosing instead to explore art making as a process that might be freed from the limitations of language and vision. Originally a painter, he has consistently investigated the structure of mental and physical spaces. His Conceptual work of the late 1960s focused upon an almost metaphysical encounter with things unseen and the realm of intuitive experience. He executed a series of "invisible" artworks: bombarding a gallery with electromagnetic waves, embedding radioactive materials into walls, or, in the *Inert Gas Series* (1969), releasing vials of odorless, colorless gases back into the environment from which they were distilled. In these and other instances, his works were detectable only through his written statements, and the audience had to trust that the pieces were what Barry said they were. His leap into an irrational practice reached its apex with works such as *Telepathic Piece* (1969), in which he stated: "During the exhibition I will try to communicate telepathically a work of art, the nature of which is a series of thoughts that are not applicable to language or image." As in *Closed Gallery*, the telepathic pieces sought to forge a bond between artist and audience outside the sphere of the art market. In these pieces, Barry aims for a psychic experience of art based on energies that defy rational explanation. This art requires the viewer to do as much (or as little) work as the artist. Barry utilizes the concept of nothingness—a shut-down gallery, an empty room—in order to test the viewer's imaginative capacities. As he put it, "there is something about void and emptiness which I am personally very concerned with. . . . *Nothing* seems to me the most potent thing in the world."[1] JBW

1. Robert Barry, in a symposium organized by Seth Siegelaub (1968); transcript published in *Six Years: The Dematerialization of the Art Object from 1966 to 1972*, ed. Lucy Lippard (Berkeley and Los Angeles: University of California Press, 1997), 40.

Tom Marioni

American, b. 1937

Tom Marioni began his professional career by functioning as both an artist and a curator, confounding standard divisions of labor such that "he began to view his work as a curator as a sculptural activity in itself by realizing his sculptural concerns through the organization of thematic exhibitions."[1] In 1970, he also founded the Museum of Conceptual Art in San Francisco, and in that same year he began *The Act of Drinking Beer with Friends Is the Highest Form of Art.* Not surprisingly, this ongoing project has had numerous permutations for more than thirty years. Influenced by Marcel Duchamp's abandonment of art as an object and Joseph Beuys's notion of "social sculpture"—the idea that all human activities could be considered art—Marioni investigated the possibility of dialogue and conviviality as art.

The Act of Drinking Beer first took place in the Oakland Art Museum, where Marioni invited friends to join him to drink beer. Afterward, the residue of the activity—empty beer bottles—was exhibited to document the event. From 1973 to 1974, free beer was available on Wednesday nights at MOCA, and artists would come together to drink, talk, and show videos. Eventually this activity became a permanent installation entitled *Free Beer* (*The Act of Drinking Beer with Friends Is the Highest Form of Art* [1970–79]), which comprised an old Coldspot refrigerator, a suspended yellow lightbulb, a print, and a shelving unit stocked with Anchor Steam beer. The work's resolution into a formal object did not stop the gatherings, however. Under the auspices of the Café Society, the meetings continued at San Francisco bars.

Currently, the group is called The Society of Independent Artists (SIA) and meets every Wednesday evening in Marioni's studio from 5:00 to 8:00 P.M. (BYOB). A recent newsletter of the SIA explains that the Society is open to "professional art people" (and notes that art collectors must come in disguise). If Conceptual art permitted and encouraged the dematerialization of the art object and Process art privileged process over product, then Marioni's communal leisure activity can clearly be regarded as art. His drinking pieces point to the infinite possibilities of the category of art; in so doing, however, they too participate in the sometimes pleasurable and sometimes ambivalent blurring of the realms of work and leisure under late capitalism. HM

1. Ann Goldstein and Anne Rorimer, *Reconsidering the Object of Art: 1965–1975* (Los Angeles: The Museum of Contemporary Art, Los Angeles; Cambridge, The MIT Press, 1995), 172.

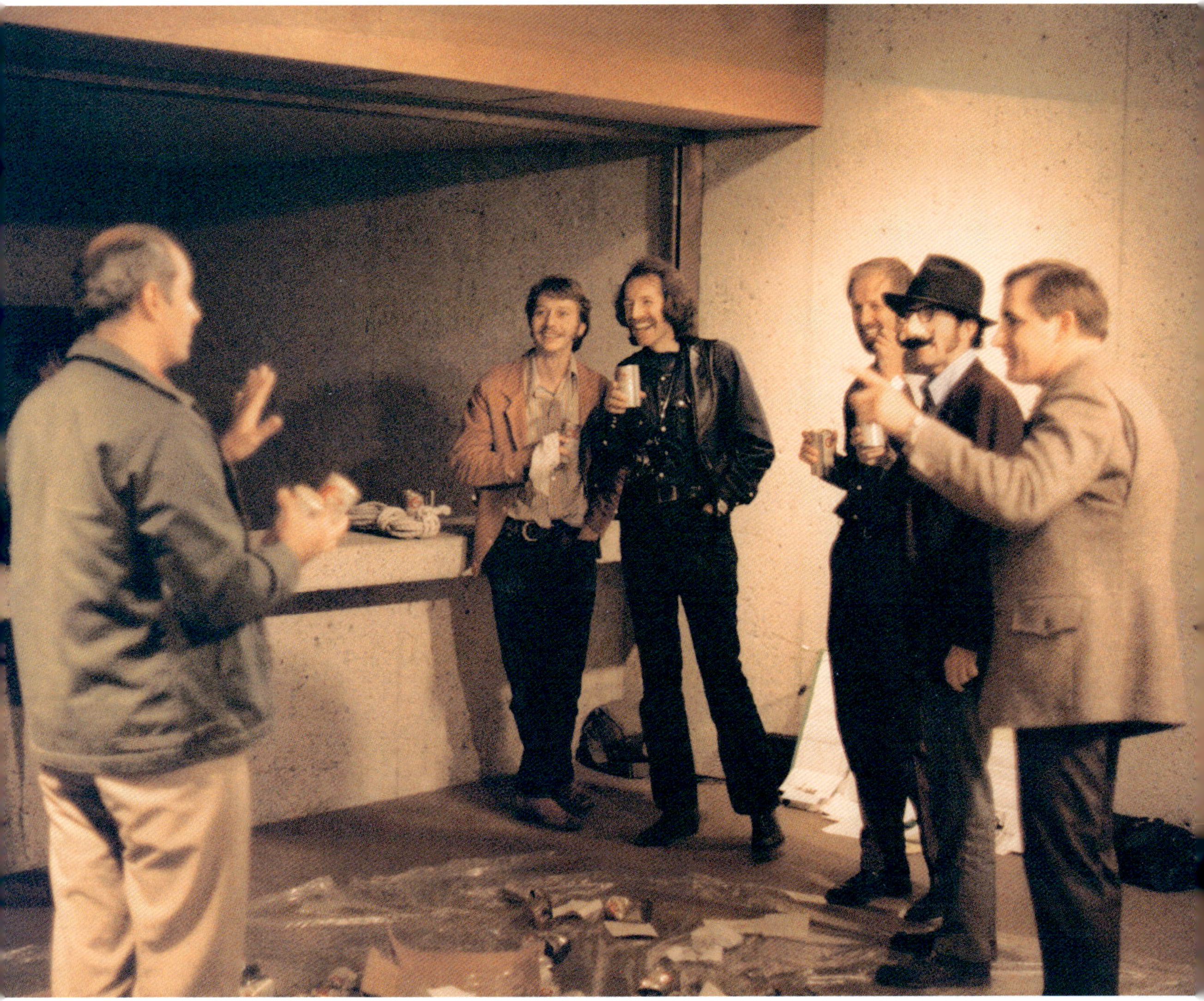

Tom Marioni, *The Act of Drinking Beer with Friends Is the Highest Form of Art,* 1970. Oakland Museum.

Gilbert and George

Gilbert, English, born Italy, 1943
George, English, b. 1942

In an interview late in his life, Marcel Duchamp said, "Deep down I'm enormously lazy. I like living, breathing, better than working."[1] More than any other contemporary artists, Gilbert and George took up this Duchampian way of both living and making work. They did so, however, by transforming it into a paradox: by declaring their lives to be art, they bestowed a value upon a lived life that is usually reserved for made objects. In 1969, in their arguably most important gesture, Gilbert and George declared themselves to be "living sculptures." Rather than submit themselves to the rigors of producing figurative sculpture, they simply declared themselves and everything they subsequently made—including their large-scale photographs—to be "sculpture."

Their first living sculpture took the form of a performance in which they painted their hands and faces with bronze metallic paint, donned traditional upper-class British suits (which would become their hallmark form of dress), and, standing atop a pedestal, lip-synched the lyrics to a recorded rendition of "Underneath the Arches." While the performance was clearly "work," Gilbert and George borrowed the lyrics and music, all the while not actually making anything.

This casual stance was to inflect their next several series of photographic works, particularly the *Drinking Sculptures*, black-and-white photographs of themselves drinking (and drunk) in pubs. Often blurry and dimly lit, these images represent an ordinary leisure activity as legitimate artistic work. The photographs are particularly witty because drinking is usually thought of as a decidedly nonproductive form of leisure, yet in the art world, the blurred spaces between work and pleasure—bars and restaurants—are often places where an enormous amount of work gets done.

By collapsing the category of artist into the category of artwork, Gilbert and George demonstrate how the cult of the artist and the fetishism of the art object are inextricably linked. In *Smashed* (1972), we see several framed black-and-white photographs of the artists standing together at a bar in formal but convivial poses. Gilbert and George arranged the photographs in a tumbled and radically askew manner that looks like an enormous sight gag on Minimalism and Conceptual art's use of the grid as an intellectual and compositional device. Instead of the mathematical rationality of such systems, *Smashed* offers drunken pleasure instead. HM

1. Pierre Cabanne, *Dialogues with Marcel Duchamp*, trans. Ron Padgett (New York: Da Capo Press, 1979), 72.

Gilbert and George, *Smashed*, 1972.

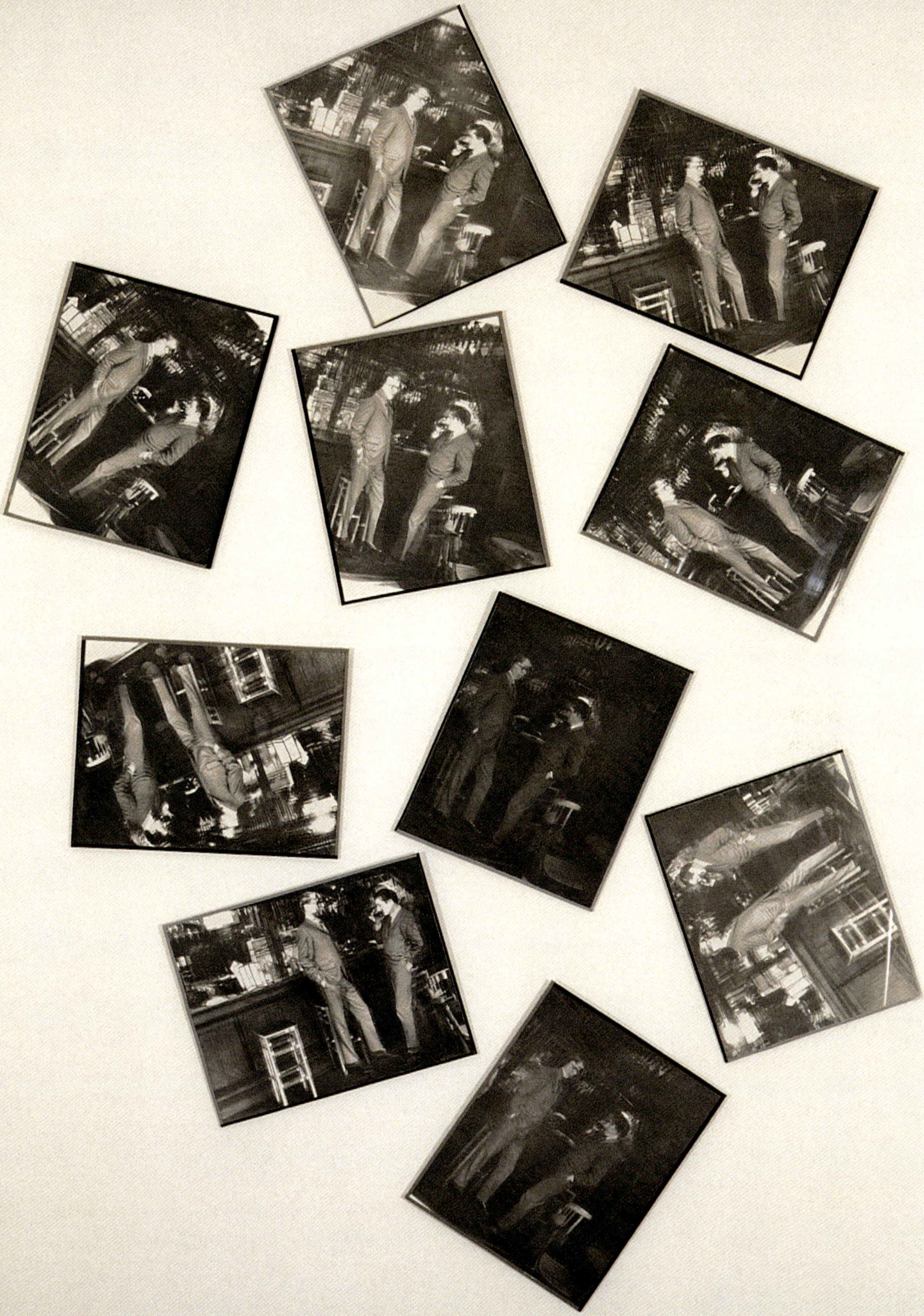

Elizabeth Sisco, Louis Hock, and David Avalos

Sisco, American, b. 1954

Hock, American, b. 1948

Avalos, American, b. 1947

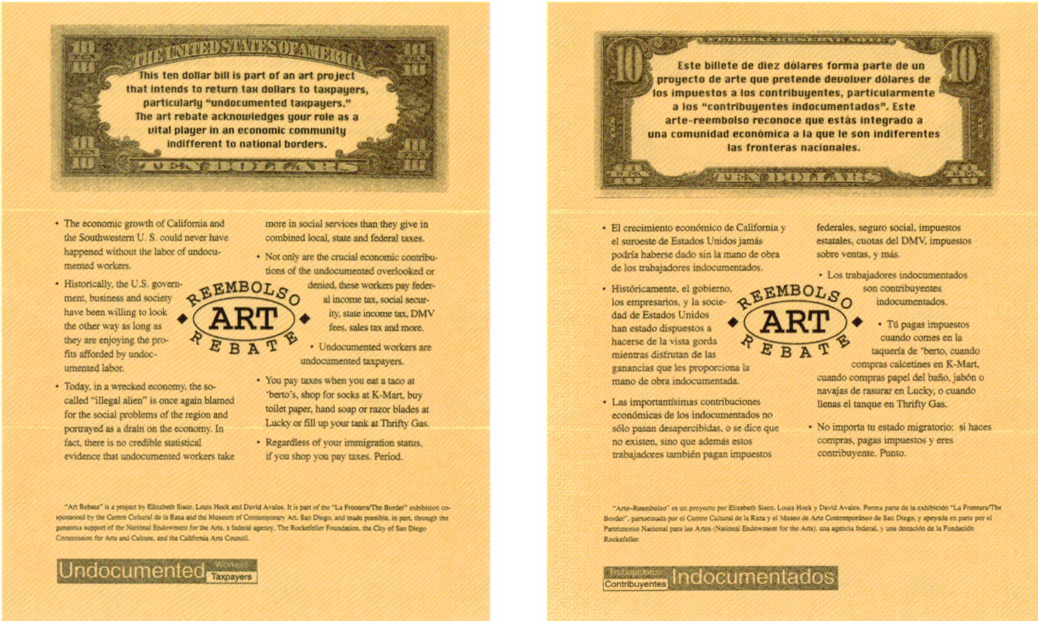

Elizabeth Sisco, Louis Hock, and David Avalos, *Arte-Reembolso/Art Rebate,* 1993.

In 1993, the collaborative team of artists Elizabeth Sisco, Louis Hock, and David Avalos performed *Arte-Reembolso/Art Rebate* in neighborhoods in the San Diego/Tijuana area along the border between the United States and Mexico, where illegal immigrants were known to congregate while looking for work. The piece consisted of the three artists distributing ten-dollar bills, which they had signed, to non-naturalized migrant workers. Translators sometimes facilitated this activity. The artists had been awarded a $5,000 commission, given jointly by the Centro Cultural de la Raza and The Museum of Contemporary Art, San Diego, as part of a larger exhibition entitled *La Frontera/The Border: Art About the Mexico/United States Border Experience.* The exhibition had been awarded a National Endowment for the Arts grant, with the mandate that it be matched three to one. *Arte-Reembolso/Art Rebate* became the subject of extraordinary media attention—most of it in the language of outraged scandal, as editorial pundits and elected officials alike proclaimed the project a waste of taxpayers' money.

The media outcry, far from being unwanted, was the intended result of the work. In their press release, the artists stated their aim: "This art operates at the intersection of public space (the streets and side-

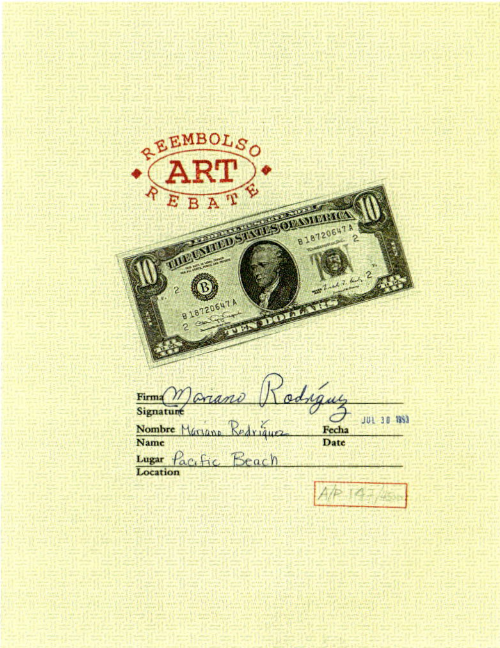

walks), informational space (radio, television, and print media) and the civic space between the public and government officials. It activates a discourse that reveals the shape of contemporary social thinking about immigrant labor." They added, "*Arte-Reembolso/Art Rebate* is an art process that envisions public art as an engagement of the social imagination rather than the presentation of monumental objects."[1] The artists explicitly intended to act as a catalyst for public discourse rather than as producers of objects. *Arte-Reembolso/Art Rebate* initiated a public discussion about whether people who live and work in the United States illegally are entitled to government benefits. When interviewed by the press, the artists consistently argued that migrant workers pay sales tax and ensure and provide cheap goods and services, yet they receive no government benefits in return. The success of the project can be measured in its provocation of others, who then (in large measure) do the "work" of the piece by engaging in a sustained and often heated public debate.

The spectacle of artists not working and instead giving away money donated to support their labor is both astutely political and deeply funny, riffing as it does on the Duchampian tradition of jokes and the refusal to produce art. As the artists went on a metaphoric strike—by refusing to produce commodities—they also, ironically, ended up "working" for free (they received no remuneration for the project and gave all of the grant money away). Their refusal to produce culture on demand also points to the luxury afforded to artists. Illegal immigrants and migrant workers can't strike because they have no legal recourse. They must always produce on demand. *Arte-Reembolso/Art Rebate* uses the public's anxieties about nonproductive artists as a cover for engaging other real and pressing labor problems. HM

1. Found in press materials accompanying the opening of *La Frontera/The Border: Art About the Mexico/United States Border Experience*, held at Centro Cultural de la Raza and The Museum of Contemporary Art, San Diego, March–May 1993.

CHECKLIST OF THE EXHIBITION

The Artist as Manager and Worker

Vito Acconci
American, b. 1940
Step Piece, 1970
6 black-and-white photographs
Dimensions variable
6 Xeroxes
8½ × 11 inches
Courtesy the artist

Trademarks, 1970/2001
7 gelatin silver prints
1 text panel
13 × 10 inches
The Baltimore Museum of Art, Frederick R. Weisman Contemporary Art Fund, 2001.21a–h

Francis Alÿs
Belgian, b. 1959
Turista, 1997
Performance documentation
Dimensions variable
Courtesy the artist

William Anastasi
American, b. 1933
Blind Drawing, 1988
Graphite on paper
14½ × 15 inches
The Baltimore Museum of Art, Purchased as the gift of Mrs. Fenwick Keyser, Reisterstown, Maryland, 2000.364

Without Title (60 Minute Drawing), 1999
Graphite on paper
59½ × 67 inches
The Baltimore Museum of Art, Purchased as the gift of Mrs. Fenwick Keyser, Reisterstown, Maryland, 2000.363

Eleanor Antin
American, b. 1935
Carving: A Traditional Sculpture, 1972
148 black-and-white photographs and text panel
Each photograph: 7 × 5 inches
Text panel: 15½ × 10¼ inches
The Art Institute of Chicago Twentieth-Century Discretionary Fund
Exhibition print provided by Ronald Feldman Fine Arts, Inc., New York

4 Transactions, 1972
Typewritten text and government document
4 pages, 11 × 8½ inches
Collection the artist
Courtesy Ronald Feldman Fine Arts, Inc., New York

Chris Burden
American, b. 1946
Honest Labor, 1979
2 black-and-white photographs and text
20¼ × 23¾ inches overall
Collection the artist

Peter Fischli and David Weiss
Fischli, Swiss, b. 1952
Weiss, Swiss, b. 1946
How to Work Better, 1991
Offset lithography on paper
24 × 17¼ inches
Courtesy Matthew Marks Gallery, New York

Tom Friedman
American, b. 1965
Everything, 1992–95
Pen on paper
36 × 36 inches
Collection of Rena Conti and Dr. Ivan Moskowitz, Brookline, Massachusetts

1000 Hours of Staring, 1992–97
Paper
36 × 36 inches
Collection Dean Valentine and Amy Adelson, Los Angeles

Hope Ginsburg
American, b. 1974
Bearded Lady, 1998–2000
Video, metroshelving, jars of honey
Dimensions variable
Courtesy the artist

David Hammons
American, b. 1943
Bliz-aard Ball Sale, 1983
Performance documentation
20 × 24 inches
Collection the artist
Courtesy Artemis Greenberg Van Doren Gallery, New York

Hi Red Center
Cleaning Event, 1964
Performance documentation
Black-and-white photographs
Dimensions variable
Photograph: Minoru Hirata
Collection Akasegawa Genpei
Courtesy Nagoya City Art Museum

Tehching Hsieh
Taiwanese, b. 1950
One Year Performance, 11 April 1980–11 April 1981, 1981
Performance documentation
2 posters: 18¾ × 13½ and 17 × 11 inches, statement: 11 × 8½ inches, explanation: 11 × 8½ inches, record: 11 × 8½ inches, 2 witness documents: 11 × 8½ inches
Collection the artist
Courtesy Jack Tilton/Anna Kustera Gallery, New York

Edward Kienholz
American, 1927–1994
Concept Tableaux, 1963–67
Plaque of engraved brass on walnut and typed description in walnut frame with glass
Plaque: 9¼ × 11¾ inches
Frame: 13⅜ × 9¼ inches
10 tableaux in series

Collection Nancy Reddin Kienholz, Oregon

Robert Morris
American, b. 1931
Box with the Sound of Its Own Making, 1961
Walnut box, speaker, 3.5-hour recorded tape
9¾ × 9¾ × 9¾ inches
Seattle Art Museum

Bruce Nauman
American, b. 1941
Bouncing Two Balls Between the Floor and Ceiling with Changing Rhythms, 1967–68
16 mm film, black-and-white, sound
Approx. 10 minutes
Courtesy Electronic Arts Intermix, New York

Playing a Note on the Violin While I Walk Around the Studio, 1967–68
16 mm film, black-and-white, sound
Approx. 10 minutes
Courtesy Electronic Arts Intermix, New York

Hugh Pocock
American, born New Zealand, 1963
Drilling a Well for Water, 2003
Site-specific sculpture with well water
Dimensions variable
Courtesy the artist
(Baltimore only)

Volume, 2003
Well water, HVAC system, air, museum interior
Dimensions variable
Courtesy the artist
(Baltimore only)

Martha Rosler
American
Backyard Economy I, 1974
Super 8 film, color
3 minutes, 30 seconds
Courtesy Electronic Arts Intermix, New York

Backyard Economy II, 1974
Super 8 film, color
6 minutes, 36 seconds
Courtesy Electronic Arts Intermix, New York

Richard Serra
American, b. 1939
Verb List, 1967–68
Graphite on paper
2 sheets
8½ × 11 inches each
Collection the artist

Hand Catching Lead, 1968
16 mm film, black-and-white
3 minutes
Collection the artist
Courtesy The Museum of Modern Art, New York

Hands Scraping, 1968
16 mm film, black-and-white
3 minutes
Collection the artist
Courtesy The Museum of Modern Art, New York

Frank Stella
American, b. 1936
Club Onyx, 1959
Oil on canvas
84⅞ × 60⅞ inches
The Baltimore Museum of Art, The Dexter M. Ferry, Jr. Trustee Corporation Fund, 1975.47

Mierle Laderman Ukeles
American, b. 1939
Private Performances of Personal Maintenance as Art, 1970–73
1 black-and-white photograph
8 × 10 inches
4 black-and-white photographs
10 × 8 inches
Photograph: Jack Ukeles
Collection the artist
Courtesy Ronald Feldman Fine Arts, Inc., New York

Transfer: The Maintenance of the Art Object, 1973
11 gelatin silver prints
16 × 20 inches
3 gelatin silver prints
20 × 16 inches
3 text pages
Collection the artist
Courtesy Ronald Feldman Fine Arts, Inc., New York

The Artist as Manager

John Baldessari
American, b. 1931
Commissioned Painting: A Painting by Pat Nelson, 1969
Acrylic and oil on canvas
59¼ × 45½ inches
Courtesy Marian Goodman Gallery, New York

I Will Not Make Any More Boring Art, 1971
Videotape, black-and-white
13 minutes, 6 seconds
Courtesy Electronic Arts Intermix, New York

Mel Bochner
American, b. 1940
Working Drawings and Other Visible Things on Paper Not Necessarily Meant to Be Viewed as Art, 1966
Four identical loose-leaf notebooks, each with one hundred Xerox copies of studio notes, working drawings, and diagrams, displayed on four sculpture stands
Courtesy Sonnabend Gallery, New York

Donald Judd
American, 1928–1994
Untitled, 1976
Plywood
36 × 70 × 69 15/16 inches
The Baltimore Museum of Art, Museum Purchase, with funds provided by her Friends in Honor of Edith Ferry Hooper, Trustee of The Baltimore Museum of Art, 1957–1995, and President of the Board of Trustees, 1973–1975
(Baltimore only)

Working drawings for *Untitled Cube*
4 Xeroxes
8½ × 11 inches each

Courtesy The LeWitt Collection, Chester, Connecticut

Arthur Koepcke
German, 1928–1972
Music While You Work, 1962
Mimeo, ink, rubber stamp on paper
8½ × 11 inches
The Gilbert and Lila Silverman Fluxus Collection, Detroit

Sol LeWitt
American, b. 1928
Wall Drawing #280, 1976
Red, blue, and white crayon, black pencil grid, yellow wall
Dimensions to scale of wall
Private collection, San Francisco

Robert Rauschenberg
American, b. 1923
White Painting (one panel), 1951
Oil on canvas
48 × 48 inches
Collection the artist

White Paintings, 1965
Ink, lined paper, and staples on board
8 × 14½ inches
A letter from Billy Klüver to Pontus Hulten regarding the work's fabrication, 1965
Ink on paper, pigment
13 × 8½ inches
The Gilbert and Lila Silverman Collection, Detroit

Andy Warhol
American, 1928–1987
Campbell's Soup Can (Turkey Noodle), 1962
Synthetic polymer paint on canvas
20$^{1}/_{16}$ × 16$^{1}/_{16}$ inches
Sonnabend Collection, on extended loan to The Baltimore Museum of Art

The Artist as Experience Maker

George Brecht
American, b. 1926
Water Yam, 1963
Fluxus edition (Fluxus C)
Wood, masonite, offset black ink on white card stock
8¾ × 8¾ × 1¾ inches
The Gilbert and Lila Silverman Fluxus Collection, Detroit

John Cage
American, 1912–1992
Score for *4′33″*
C. F. Peters Corporation

Valie Export (with Peter Weibel)
Austrian, b. 1940
Tapp und Tastkino (Touch Cinema), expanded cinema, 1968
Mini (handheld) theater, cinema reconstruction
12 × 11 × 27 inches
Documentation material: photographs, magazines, and Xeroxes
Photograph: Werner Schulz
Archive Valie Export, Generali Foundation, Vienna
(Baltimore and Des Moines)

Hope Ginsburg
American, b. 1974
The Novelty Project, 2002–2003
Little Black Moustache and Rosy Red Cheeks custom temporary tattoos, costumes (designed by Kim Kauffman), mannequins, signage, point of purchase display
Dimensions variable
Courtesy the artist

Felix Gonzalez-Torres
Cuban-born American, 1957–1996
"Untitled" (Rossmore II), 1991
Green candies, individually wrapped in cellophane (endless supply)
Dimensions vary with installation
Ideal weight: 75 lbs.
Private Collection
(Baltimore and Columbus only)

Allan Kaprow
American, b. 1927
How to Make a Happening, 1966
Long-playing record with jacket and vinyl slipcase
12 × 12 inches
Collection Benjamin H. D. Buchloh, New York

Alison Knowles
American, b. 1933
Make a Salad, 1962
Courtesy the artist

Lee Lozano
American, 1930–1998
Untitled (Dialogue Piece April 21–Dec. 18, 1969), 1969
Graphite, ink on paper
8 sheets: 11 × 8½ inches each
Wadsworth Atheneum Museum of Art, Hartford, Connecticut, The Alexander A. Goldfarb Contemporary Art Acquisition Fund

George Maciunas
American, 1931–1978
Can of Water Racket, ca. 1970
Concave Racket, ca. 1970
Convex Racket, ca. 1970
Hole in Center Racket, ca. 1970
Commercial Ping-Pong rackets with mixed media
The Gilbert and Lila Silverman Fluxus Collection, Detroit

Bruce Nauman
American, b. 1941
Live-Taped Video Corridor, 1970
Wallboard, video camera, two video monitors, videotape player, and videotape
Dimensions variable
Approx. 144 × 384 × 20 inches
Solomon R. Guggenheim Museum, New York, Panza Collection, Gift, 1992 (92.4165)

Yoko Ono
Japanese, b. 1933
Painting to Hammer a Nail, 1961–2003
Board, hammer, nails, instruction
Dimensions variable
Collection the artist

Cut Piece, 1964
Film by Albert and David Maysles (Carnegie Recital

Hall, New York), March 21, 1965, transferred to video
Collection the artist

Selections from *Grapefruit*, 1964
Stomach Piece, 1962 summer
Painting to Be Constructed in Your Head, 1962 spring
Map Piece, 1964 spring
Typeset on paper
Dimensions variable
Collection the artist

Gabriel Orozco
Mexican, b. 1962
Mesa de ping-pong con estanque (Ping Pond Table), 1998
Modified Ping-Pong tables, water lilies, water
30 × 167¾ × 167¾ inches
The Museum of Contemporary Art, Los Angeles, purchased with funds provided by The Acquisition and Collection Committee, 2000
(Des Moines and Columbus only)

James Riddle
American, b. 1933
E.S.P. Fluxkit (DOP), 1966
Fluxus edition
Plastic box, colored paper, black ink on paper
4¾ × 3½ × ½ inches
The Gilbert and Lila Silverman Fluxus Collection, Detroit

Tomas Schmit
German, b. 1943
Typewriter Poem, 1963
Ink on paper
8¼ × 11¾ inches
The Gilbert and Lila Silverman Fluxus Collection, Detroit

Mieko (Chieko) Shiomi
Japanese, b. 1938
Spatial Poem No. 1, 1963
Fluxus edition
Ink on fiberboard, masking tape, pins, offset cards
11¾ × 18 × 1 inches
The Gilbert and Lila Silverman Fluxus Collection, Detroit

Star Piece, 1963
Ink on paper
7 × 8 inches
The Gilbert and Lila Silverman Fluxus Collection, Detroit

Events and Games, 1964–65
Fluxus edition, component of *Flux-Kit B*
Plastic box, offset printing on card stock
4¾ × 3½ × ½ inches
The Gilbert and Lila Silverman Fluxus Collection, Detroit

Erwin Wurm
Austrian, b. 1954
One Minute Sculptures, 2000
Instruction drawings and performative objects
Dimensions variable
Courtesy the artist

Quitting Time

Robert Barry
American, b. 1936
Closed Gallery, 1969
4 sheets of printed paper mounted on paperboard
13¾ × 33¼ inches
Dorothy and Herbert Vogel

Peter Fischli and David Weiss
Fischli, Swiss, b. 1952
Weiss, Swiss, b. 1946
Der Lauf der Dinge (The Way Things Go), 1987
16 mm color film transferred to video
30 minutes
Courtesy Matthew Marks Gallery, New York

Gilbert and George
Gilbert, English, born Italy, 1943
George, English, b. 1942
Smashed, 1972
Gelatin silver prints
75 × 52 inches
Private collection

Hi Red Center
Ochanomizu Drop (Dropping Event), 1964
Performance documentation of event held at Ikenobo Kaikan Hall, Tokyo
Black-and-white photographs
Dimensions variable
Photograph: Minoru Hirata
Collection Akasegawa Genpei
Courtesy Nagoya City Art Museum

Lee Lozano
American, 1930–1998
Untitled (General Strike Piece Feb. 8, 1969), 1969
Graphite, ink on paper
11 × 8½ inches
Wadsworth Atheneum Museum of Art, Hartford, Connecticut, The Alexander A. Goldfarb Contemporary Art Acquisition Fund

Piero Manzoni
Italian, 1933–1963
Merda d'artista, 1961
Tin, label, contents
1⅞ × 2½ × 2½ inches
The Gilbert and Lila Silverman Collection, Detroit

Tom Marioni
American, b. 1937
The Act of Drinking Beer with Friends Is the Highest Form of Art, 1970–2003
Wood, glass bottles, yellow lights
76 × 46 × 3½ inches
Courtesy the artist and Margarete Roeder Gallery, New York

Yoko Ono
Japanese, b. 1933
Sky TV, 1966
Video camera, television
Dimensions variable
Collection the artist

Gabriel Orozco
Mexican, b. 1962
La Oficina, 1992
C-Print
22 × 24 inches
Courtesy Marian Goodman Gallery, New York

Roxy Paine
American, b. 1966
Paint Dipper, 1997
Steel frame, dipping tank, acrylic paint, computer, interface, relays, chair
124 × 99 × 24 inches
Courtesy the artist and James Cohan Gallery, New York

Elizabeth Sisco, Louis Hock, and David Avalos
Sisco, American, b. 1954
Hock, American, b. 1948
Avalos, American, b. 1947
Arte-Reembolso/Art Rebate, 1993
Public media project
Performance documentation
Courtesy the artists, San Diego

Jean Tinguely
Swiss, 1925–1991
Meta-Matic No. 10, 1959
Iron with wooden wheels
39 × 52¼ × 27 inches
Museum Jean Tinguely Basel

CONTRIBUTORS' NOTES

Darsie Alexander is Curator of Prints, Drawings, and Photographs at The Baltimore Museum of Art. From 1995 to 2000, she was Assistant Curator in the Department of Photography at The Museum of Modern Art, New York, where she organized *Sets and Situations* (2000) and *Anatomically Incorrect* (1999), among numerous other exhibitions. A specialist in contemporary photography, she has written on the subjects of posing, fictional photography, and the grotesque. She is currently at work on an exhibition on the subject of slide projections.

Julia Bryan-Wilson is a Ph.D. candidate in the Department of History of Art at the University of California, Berkeley. She is a frequent curator and critic of contemporary queer and feminist art and has taught at UC Berkeley and the California College of Arts and Crafts. She is currently completing a dissertation entitled "Art/work: Minimalism, Conceptualism, and Artistic Labor in the Age of Vietnam, 1965–75."

Chris Gilbert is Curator of Contemporary Art at The Baltimore Museum of Art. He was Associate Curator at the Des Moines Art Center from 2001 to 2003. His research interests include conceptual art practices and their influence on the art of the present day, as well as new models for exhibition spaces. Gilbert is organizing the exhibition *Contested Fields: Identity in Sports and Spectacle* (2004) at the Des Moines Art Center. His writings on conceptual art have appeared in *Oxford Art Journal*, *Mute*, and *Conceptual Art: Theory, Myth, and Practice*, ed. Michael Corris (forthcoming from Cambridge University Press).

Janet Kraynak is a New York–based art historian. She is currently working on a book that develops an interdisciplinary theory of performance in relation to Bruce Nauman's art in the art of the sixties and seventies. Her book *Please Pay Attention Please: Bruce Nauman's Words: Writings and Interviews* is forthcoming from The MIT Press.

Miwon Kwon is Associate Professor in the Department of Art History at the University of California, Los Angeles. Her research and writings engage several disciplines, including contemporary art and architecture, public art, and urban studies. She is a founding editor of *Documents*, a journal of art, culture, and criticism, and she serves on the advisory board of *October*. Her book *One Place After Another: Site-Specific Art and Locational Identity* was published by The MIT Press.

Helen Molesworth is Chief Curator of Exhibitions at the Wexner Center for the Arts. She was Curator of Contemporary Art at The Baltimore Museum of Art from 2000 to 2002. Prior to *Work Ethic*, she organized *BodySpace* for the BMA, an exhibition that examined the legacy of Minimalism on an emerging generation of artists. Her writings have appeared in publications such as *Art Journal*, *Documents*, and *October*.

Judith Rodenbeck is Assistant Professor of modern and contemporary art history at Sarah Lawrence College in Bronxville, New York. An art historian whose research concentrates on advanced art practices since 1945, she is coauthor (with Benjamin H. D. Buchloh) of *Experiments in the Everyday: Allan Kaprow and Robert Watts—Events, Objects, Documents*. She was a contributor to *Inside the Visible: An Elliptical Traverse of Twentieth-Century Art in, of, and from the Feminine*, and she is currently completing a book on American Happenings and their relations to avant-garde theater, photography, and music of the 1950s.

SELECTED BIBLIOGRAPHY

Books

Alberro, Alexander, and Blake Stimson, eds. *Conceptual Art: A Critical Anthology.* Cambridge: The MIT Press, 1999.

Barrett, William, ed. *Zen Buddhism: Selected Writings of D. T. Suzuki.* New York: Anchor Books, 1956. Reprint, New York: Doubleday, 1995.

Barthes, Roland. *Image Music Text.* Translated by Stephen Heath. New York: Hill and Wang, 1977.

Battcock, Gregory, ed. *Minimal Art: A Critical Anthology.* With an introduction by Anne M. Wagner. Berkeley and Los Angeles: University of California Press, 1995.

Blum, Linda M. *Between Feminism and Labor: The Significance of the Comparable Worth Movement.* Berkeley and Los Angeles: University of California Press, 1991.

Burn, Ian. *Dialogue: Writings in Art History.* North Sydney, Australia: Allen and Unwin, 1991.

Cabanne, Pierre. *Dialogues with Marcel Duchamp.* Translated by Ron Padgett. New York: Da Capo Press, 1979.

Cage, John. *Silence.* Middletown, Conn.: Wesleyan University Press, 1961.

Crow, Thomas. *The Rise of the Sixties: American and European Art in the Era of Dissent.* New York: Harry N. Abrams, 1996.

Elger, Dietmar. *Felix Gonzalez-Torres: Catalogue Raisonné.* Ostfildern-Ruit, Germany: Cantz Verlag, 1997.

Foster, Hal, and Gordon Hughes, eds. *Richard Serra.* Cambridge: The MIT Press, 2000.

Friedman, Ken, ed. *The Fluxus Reader.* Chichester, England: Academy Editions, 1998.

Gilbert and George: The Complete Pictures, 1971–1985. New York: Rizzoli International Publications, Inc., 1986.

Godfrey, Tony. *Conceptual Art.* London: Phaidon Press, 1998.

Hardt, Michael, and Antonio Negri. *Empire.* Cambridge: Harvard University Press, 2000.

Hendricks, Jon. *Fluxus Codex.* Detroit: The Gilbert and Lila Silverman Fluxus Collection in association with Harry N. Abrams, New York, 1988.

Jones, Caroline. *Machine in the Studio: Constructing the Postwar American Artist.* Chicago: University of Chicago Press, 1996.

Judd, Donald. *Donald Judd: Complete Writings, 1959–1975.* Halifax: Nova Scotia College of Art and Design/New York University Press, 1975.

Kaprow, Allan. *Assemblage, Environments, and Happenings.* New York: Harry N. Abrams, 1996.

———. *Essays on the Blurring of Art and Life.* Berkeley and Los Angeles: University of California Press, 1996.

———. *7 Environments.* Naples and Milan: Studio Morra and Mudima, 1992.

Kellein, Thomas. *Fluxus.* London: Thames and Hudson, 1995.

Kessler-Harris, Alice. *A Woman's Wage: Historical Meanings and Social Consequences.* Lexington: The University Press of Kentucky, 1990.

Knight, Christopher, and Giuseppe Panza. *Art of the Fifties, Sixties, and Seventies: The Panza Collection.* Milan: Jaca Book, 1999.

Lefebvre, Henri. *Critique of Everyday Life*. Vol. 1. London: Verso, 1991.

Leonard, George J. *Into the Light of Things: The Art of the Commonplace from Wordsworth to John Cage*. Chicago: University of Chicago Press, 1994.

Lippard, Lucy, ed. *Six Years: The Dematerialization of the Art Object from 1966 to 1972*. Berkeley and Los Angeles: University of California Press, 1997.

Lukács, Georg. *History and Class Consciousness: Studies in Marxist Dialectics*. Translated by R. Livingston. Cambridge: The MIT Press, 1968.

Mandel, Ernest. *Late Capitalism*. Translated by Joris De Bres. London: Verso, 1978.

Marcuse, Herbert. *Eros and Civilization: A Philosophical Inquiry into Freud*. Boston: Beacon Press, 1966.

———. *An Essay on Liberation*. Boston: Beacon Press, 1969.

Martin, Henry. *An Introduction to George Brecht's Book of the Tumbler on Fire*. Milan: Multhipla Edizioni, 1978.

Meyer, James. *Minimalism*. London: Phaidon Press, 2000.

Meyer, Ursula, ed. *Conceptual Art*. New York: E. P. Dutton, 1972.

Morgan, Robin, ed. *Sisterhood Is Powerful*. New York: Vintage/Random House, 1970.

Ono, Yoko. *Grapefruit: A Book of Instructions*. New York: Simon and Schuster, 1970.

Osterman, Paul, et al. *Working in America: A Blueprint for the New Labor Market*. Cambridge: The MIT Press, 2001.

Pine, Joseph, and James Gilmore. *The Experience Economy*. Boston: Harvard Business School Press, 1999.

Ratcliff, Carter. *Out of the Box: The Reinvention of Art, 1965–1975*. New York: Allworth Press, 2000.

Rorimer, Anne. *New Art in the 60s and 70s: Redefining Reality*. London: Thames and Hudson, 2001.

Rosenberg, Harold. *The Tradition of the New*. New York: Horizon Press, 1959.

Sanouillet, Michel, and Elmer Peterson, eds. *The Writings of Marcel Duchamp*. New York: Da Capo Press, 1973.

Serota, Sir Nicholas. *Experience or Interpretation: The Dilemma of Museums of Modern Art*. New York: Thames and Hudson, 1997.

Serra, Richard. *Writings, Interviews*. Chicago: University of Chicago Press, 1994.

Singerman, Howard. *Art Subjects: Making Artists in the American University*. Berkeley and Los Angeles: University of California Press, 1999.

Sontag, Susan. *Against Interpretation and Other Essays*. New York: Farrar, Straus and Giroux, 1966.

Steinberg, Leo. *Other Criteria: Confrontations with Twentieth-Century Art*. London: Oxford University Press, 1972.

Stiles, Kristine, and Peter Selz, eds. *Theories and Documents of Contemporary Art: A Sourcebook of Artists' Writings*. Berkeley and Los Angeles: University of California Press, 1996.

Tomkins, Calvin. *The Bride and the Bachelors: Five Masters of the Avant-Garde*. Middlesex, England: Penguin Books, 1976.

Tucker, Robert C., ed. *The Marx-Engels Reader*. New York: W. W. Norton, 1978.

van Bruggen, Coosje. *Bruce Nauman*. New York: Rizzoli International Publications, Inc., 1988.

Veblen, Thorstein. *The Theory of the Leisure Class*. New York: Dover Publications, 1994.

Ward, Frazer David. "False Intimacies, Open Secrets: Public and Private in the Performance Art of Vito Acconci and Chris Burden." Ph.D. diss., Cornell University, 2000.

Weber, Max. *The Protestant Ethic and the Spirit of Capitalism.* London: Routledge, 1992.

Weibel, Peter, ed. *Erwin Wurm: Neue Galerie Graz.* Ostfildern-Ruit, Germany: Cantz Verlag, 2002.

Young, La Monte. *An Anthology of Chance Operations.* Bronx, N.Y.: L. Young and J. MacLow, 1963.

Zukin, Sharon. *Loft Living: Culture and Capital in Urban Change.* Baltimore: The Johns Hopkins University Press, 1982.

Exhibition Catalogues

Afterimage: Drawing Through Process. Organized by Cornelia H. Butler. Cambridge: The MIT Press, 1999.

Anti-Illusion: Procedures/Materials. Organized by Marcia Tucker and James Monte. New York: Whitney Museum of American Art, 1969.

Armstrong, Richard, and Richard Marshall, eds. *The New Sculpture, 1965–75: Between Geometry and Gesture.* New York: Whitney Museum of American Art, 1990.

L'Art conceptual: Une perspective. Essays by Claude Gintz et al. Paris: Musée d'Art Moderne de la Ville de Paris, 1989.

Camnitzer, Luis, et al. *Global Conceptualism: Points of Origin, 1950s–1980s.* New York: Queens Museum of Art, 1999.

Celant, Germano. *Piero Manzoni.* London: Serpentine Gallery, 1998.

Chris Burden: A Twenty-Year Survey. Newport Beach, Calif.: Newport Harbor Art Museum, 1988.

David Hammons: Rousing the Rubble. Texts by Kellie Jones, Tom Finkelpearl, and Steve Cannon. New York: The Institute for Contemporary Art, P.S. 1 Museum, 1991.

Davies, Hugh M., and Andrea Hales, eds. *John Baldessari: National City.* San Diego, Calif.: Museum of Contemporary Art, 1996.

D'Harnoncourt, Anne, and Kynaston McShine. *Marcel Duchamp.* Philadelphia: Philadelphia Museum of Art, 1973.

Dreyfus, Charles. *Happenings and Fluxus.* Paris: Galerie 1900–2000, 1989.

Field, Richard S., ed. *Mel Bochner: Thought Made Visible, 1966–1973.* New Haven: Yale University Art Gallery, 1996.

Fox, Howard N. *Eleanor Antin.* Los Angeles: Los Angeles County Museum of Art, 1999.

Francis Alÿs. Antibes, France: Musée Picasso, 2001.

Gabriel Orozco. Organized by Alma Ruiz. Los Angeles: The Museum of Contemporary Art, Los Angeles, 2000.

Garrels, Gary, ed. *Sol LeWitt: A Retrospective.* New Haven: Yale University Press, 2000.

Goldstein, Ann, and Anne Rorimer. *Reconsidering the Object of Art: 1965–1975.* Los Angeles: The Museum of Contemporary Art, Los Angeles; Cambridge: The MIT Press, 1995.

Hopps, Walter. *Robert Rauschenberg: The Early 1950s.* Houston: The Menil Collection/Houston Fine Art Press, 1991.

Jenkins, Janet, ed. *In the Spirit of Fluxus.* Minneapolis: Walker Art Center, 1993.

Jenkins, Janet, and Kathleen McLean, eds. *Peter Fischli and David Weiss: In a Restless World.* Minneapolis: Walker Art Center, 1996.

John Baldessari. Texts by Marcia Tucker and Robert Pincus-Witten. New York: The New Museum, 1981.

Kienholz: A Retrospective. New York: Whitney Museum of American Art, 1996.

McShine, Kynaston, ed. *Andy Warhol: A Retrospective.* New York: The Museum of Modern Art, 1989.

———. *Information.* New York: The Museum of Modern Art, 1970.

Munroe, Alexandra, ed. *Japanese Art After 1945: Scream Against the Sky.* New York: Harry N. Abrams, 1994.

Rothkopf, Scott. *Roxy Paine.* New York: James Cohan Gallery, 2001.

Schimmel, Paul. *Out of Actions.* Los Angeles: The Museum of Contemporary Art, Los Angeles, 2000.

Sol LeWitt. Pasadena, Calif.: Pasadena Art Museum, 1970.

Szeemann, Harald, ed. *When Attitudes Become Form: Works, Concepts, Processes, Situations, Information: Live in Your Head.* Berne: Kunsthalle, 1969.

Articles

Arango, Douglas. "Underground Films: Art or Naughty Movie." *Movie TV Secrets* (June 1967): unpaginated.

Armstrong, Elizabeth. "First Impressions." *The Print Collector's Newsletter* 20 (May/June 1989): 41–46.

Basualdo, Carlos. "Head to Toe: Francis Alÿs's Paths of Resistance." *Artforum International* 37, no. 8 (1999): 104–7.

Bourdieu, Pierre. "Selections from *The Logic of Practice.*" In *The Logic of the Gift: Toward an Ethics of Generosity,* ed. Alan D. Schrift (New York: Routledge, 1997).

Brecht, George, and Allan Kaprow. "Happenings and Events Broadcast by WBAI Sometime During May." *V TRE* 4 (June 1964): 1.

Bryan-Wilson, Julia. "Remembering Yoko Ono's *Cut Piece.*" *Oxford Art Journal* 26 (Spring 2003): 99–123.

Buchloh, Benjamin H. D. "Conceptual Art, 1962–1969: From the Aesthetic of Administration to the Critique of Institutions." *October* 55 (Winter 1990): 105–43.

———. "Readymade, Objet Trouvé, Idée Reçue." In *Dissent: The Issue of Modern Art in Boston,* 106–22. Boston: I.C.A., 1985.

Buren, Daniel. "The Function of the Studio." *October* 10 (Fall 1979): 51–58.

Cameron, Dan. "Through the Looking Glass, Darkly: Fischli/Weiss." *Artforum International* 31, no. 1 (1992): 67–69.

Cohn, Terri. "Conceptualizing Conceptual Art—A Post-Object Perspective." *Art Papers* 24, no. 4 (2000): 14–19.

Dimitrakaki, Angela. "Yoko Ono: Have You Seen the Horizon Lately?" *Third Text,* no. 42 (Spring 1998): 99–104.

Foster, Hal. "What's Neo About the Neo-Avant-Garde?" *October* 70 (Fall 1994): 5–32.

Groys, Boris. "Simulated Readymades by Peter Fischli/David Weiss." *Parkett,* no. 40/41 (1994): 24–39.

Jones, Amelia. "Clothes Make the Man: The Male Artist as a Performative Function." *Oxford Art Journal* 18, no. 2 (1995): 18–32.

Joseph, Branden. "Robert Morris and John Cage: Reconstructing a Dialogue." *October* 81 (Summer 1997): 59–69.

Kaprow, Allan. "La Sfida del Sistema." *Metro* (Venice) 14 (June 1966): 41.

———. "The Shape of the Environment: How Anti-Form is 'Anti-Form'?" *Artforum International* 6, no. 10 (1968): 32–33.

Kibbins, Gary. "Laughter and Forgetting." *Afterimage* 16 (November 1988): 16–17.

Krauss, Rosalind. "The Cultural Logic of the Late Capitalist Museum." *October* 54 (Fall 1990): 3–17.

LeWitt, Sol. "Paragraphs on Conceptual Art." *Artforum International* 5, no. 5 (1967): 79–83.

———. "Serial Project # 1, 1966." *Aspen* 5/6 (Fall/Winter 1967).

Lippard, Lucy, and John Chandler. "The Dematerialization of Art." *Artforum International* 6, no. 6 (1968): 31–36.

Lozano, Lee. *An Open Hearing on the Subject: What Should Be the Program of the Art Workers Regarding Museum Reform and to Establish the Program of an Open Art Worker's Coalition.* New York: Art Workers Coalition, 1969.

Millet, Catherine. "Modern Art's Excrement Adventure." *Art Press,* no. 242 (January 1999): 27–35.

Milman, Estera. "Road Shows, Street Events, and Fluxus People: A Conversation with Alison Knowles." *Visible Language* 26, no. 1/2 (1992): 97–107.

Molesworth, Helen. "From Dada to Neo-Dada and Back Again." *October* 105 (Summer 2003): 177–81.

———. "Housework and Artwork." *October* 92 (Winter 2000): 71–97.

Morris, Robert. "Anti-Form." *Artforum International* 6, no. 8 (1968): 33–35.

———. "Letters to John Cage." *October* 81 (Summer 1997): 70–79.

Rose, Barbara, and Irving Sandler. "Sensibility of the Sixties." *Art in America* (January/February 1967): 44–57.

Santacatterina, Stella. "Piero Manzoni: Art as Reflection on Art." *Third Text,* no. 45 (Winter 1998–99): 23–28.

Sharp, Willoughby. "Nauman Interview." *Arts Magazine* 44, no. 5 (1970): 24.

Silk, Gerald. "Myths and Meanings in Manzoni's *Merda d'artista.*" *Art Journal* 52 (Fall 1993): 65–75.

Tiravanija, Rirkrit. "Real Time Travel: Rirkrit Tiravanija Talks with Fischli and Weiss." *Artforum International* 34 (Summer 1996): 78–86.

Welchman, John C. "Bait or Tackle?: An Assisted Commentary on *Art Rebate/Arte Reembolso.*" *Art and Text,* no. 48 (May 1994): 31–33, 86–87.

Weschler, Lawrence. "The Subversive Art of Ed Kienholz." *Art News* 83 (September 1984): 100–106.

Wilson, Andrew. "Sol LeWitt Interviewed." *Art Monthly* (March 1993): 6.

INDEX

PHOTO CREDITS

In addition to the individuals and institutions credited in the captions and in the preceding Checklist of the Exhibition, we gratefully acknowledge the contributions of the following photographers and collections whose works are reproduced herein.

Vito Acconci, Jose A. Sanchez, Jr., pages 40 and 41; Courtesy the artist, page 63. William Anastasi, Jose A. Sanchez, Jr., pages 109 and 110. Eleanor Antin, Courtesy Ronald Feldman Fine Arts, Inc., New York, pages 125, 132, and 133. John Baldessari, Courtesy Marian Goodman Gallery, New York, page 164; Courtesy Electronic Arts Intermix (EAI), New York, page 152. Robert Barry, Courtesy the artist, page 56; © 2002 Board of Trustees, National Gallery of Art, Washington, Ricardo Blanc, page 218. Star Black, © The Solomon R. Guggenheim Foundation, New York, pages 94 and 95. George Brecht, Aurora Hendricks, page 189. John Cage, © 1960 by C. F. Peters Corporation, used by permission, all rights reserved, pages 169 and 170. Jan Dibbets, Courtesy the artist and Barbara Gladstone Gallery, page 61. Valie Export, © Generali Foundation Collection, Vienna, and Werner Schulz, Photograph by Werner Schulz, pages 86 and 176. Peter Fischli & David Weiss, Courtesy Matthew Marks Gallery, New York, pages 6 and 210. Hollis Frampton, Courtesy Hollis Frampton Estate, © 1984, Reproduction print Lauren Tent, page 35; page 77. Tom Friedman, Courtesy Feature, Inc., New York, Photograph by Oren Slor, pages 116, 117, and 118. Alexander Gardner, Courtesy the Boston Public Library, Print Department, page 57. Hope Ginsburg, Peter Meretsky, pages 146 and 147. Felix Gonzalez-Torres, © The Felix Gonzalez-Torres Foundation, Courtesy Andrea Rosen Gallery, New York, Photograph by David Heald, page 195. Gianfranco Gorgoni, Courtesy Serra Studio, New York, page 52. Hi Red Center, © Minoru Hirata, Courtesy Nagoya City Art Museum, Endpapers and pages 102, 124, and 206. Donald Judd, © Donald Judd Foundation/Licensed by VAGA, New York, pages 162 and 163. Allan Kaprow, Philipp Scholz Rittermann Photography, page 171. Sol LeWitt, Courtesy Sol LeWitt Studio, © 2003 Sol LeWitt/Artists Rights Society (ARS), New York, page 159. Piero Manzoni, Archivio Opera Piero Manzoni, Milan, page 82. Herbert Marcuse, © 2002 AP/Wide World Photos, page 68. Robert Morris, © Seattle Art Museum, Photography by Paul Macapia, © 2003 Robert Morris/Artists Rights Society (ARS), New York, page 112. Ugo Mulas, © Ugo Mulas Estate, all rights reserved, page 36. Hans Namuth, © 1991 Hans Namuth Estate, Courtesy Center for Creative Photography, The University of Arizona, page 55. Bruce Nauman, Courtesy Electronic Arts Intermix (EAI), New York, pages 123 and 126; Solomon R. Guggenheim Museum, Photograph by Paul Rocheleau, Courtesy Whitney Museum of American Art, New York, page 166, © 2003 Bruce Nauman/Artists Rights Society (ARS), New York. Yoko Ono, © Yoko Ono, Courtesy of Lenono Photo Archive, Iain Macmillan, page 88; Minoru Niizuma, page 174; Norman McBeath, page 200. Gabriel Orozco, Courtesy Marian Goodman Gallery, New York, page 16; © The Museum of Contemporary Art, Los Angeles, Brian Forrest, pages 49 and 199. Hugh Pocock, Howard Korn, page 121. Robert Rauschenberg, © Robert Rauschenberg/Licensed by VAGA, New York, pages 24 and 155. Martha Rosler, Courtesy Electronic Arts Intermix (EAI), New York, page 136. Richard Serra, Courtesy Serra Studio, © 2003 Richard Serra/Artists Rights Society (ARS), New York, pages 73, 74, 128, and 129. Frank Stella, Jose A. Sanchez, Jr., pages 26 and 104. Jean Tinguely, Courtesy Museum Jean Tinguely Basel, Photograph by Christian Baur, © 2003 Artists Rights Society (ARS), New York/ADAGP, Paris, page 203. Mierle Laderman Ukeles, Courtesy Ronald Feldman Fine Arts, Inc., New York, pages 78 and 134. Andy Warhol, Courtesy Sonnabend Gallery; © 2003 Andy Warhol Foundation for the Visual Arts/Artists Rights Society (ARS), New York, page 156. Erwin Wurm, Courtesy Galleria d'Arte Moderna, Bologna, page 91.

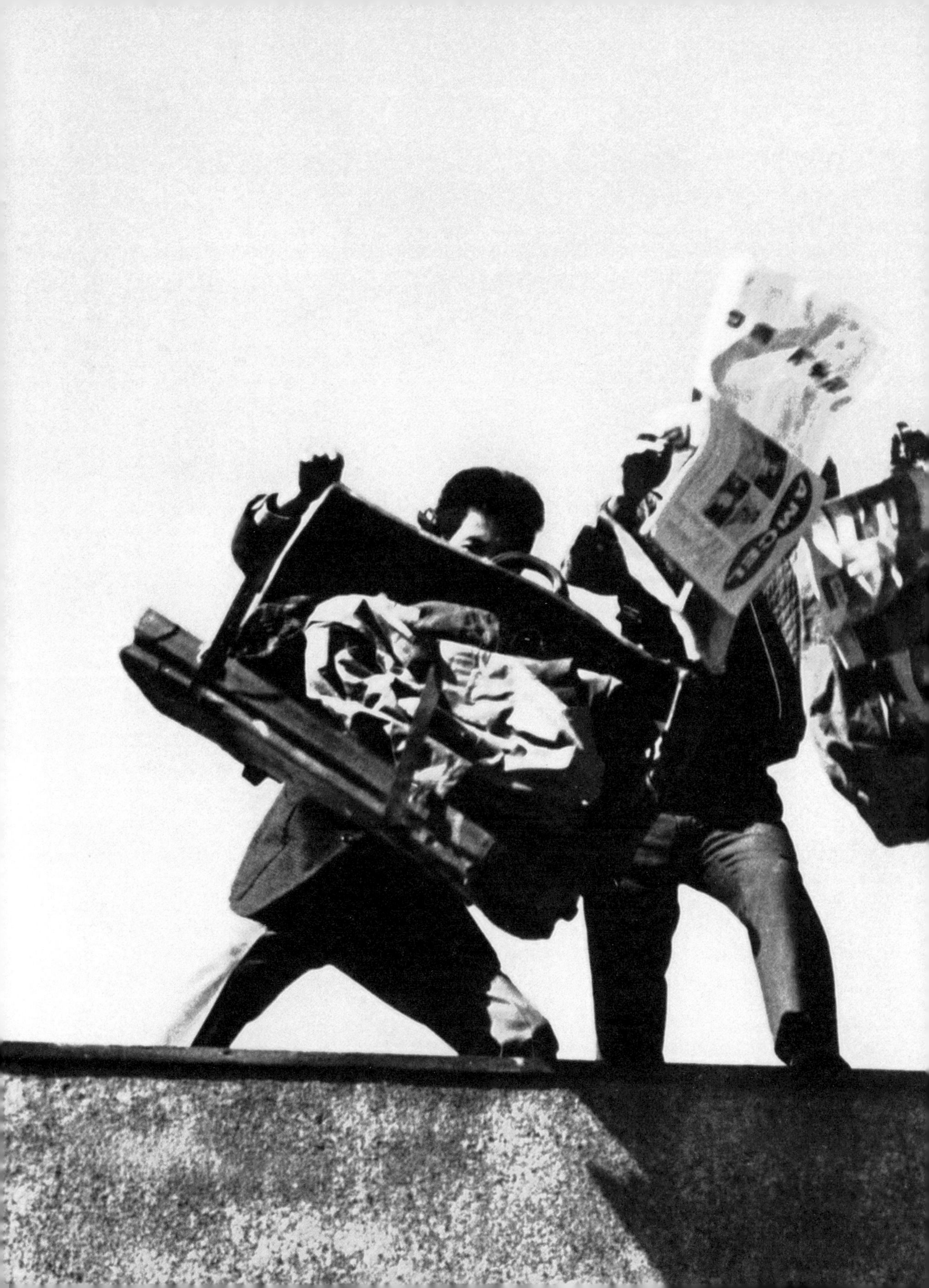
AMCEL